D0828279

KF
37...
.K45
R36
2015

DISCARD

author.

Florynce "Flo"
Kennedy

JUN 14 2017

Florynce "Flo" Kennedy

GENDER AND AMERICAN CULTURE

Coeditors

Thadious M. Davis   Mary Kelley

Editorial Advisory Board

Nancy Cott   Jane Sherron De Hart
John D'Emilio   Linda K. Kerber
Annelise Orleck   Nell Irvin Painter
Janice Radway   Robert Reid-Pharr
Noliwe Rooks   Barbara Sicherman
Cheryl Wall

Emerita Board Members

Cathy N. Davidson   Sara Evans
Annette Kolodny   Wendy Martin

Guided by feminist and antiracist perspectives, this series examines the construction and influence of gender and sexuality within the full range of America's cultures. Investigating in deep context the ways in which gender works with and against such markers as race, class, and region, the series presents outstanding interdisciplinary scholarship, including works in history, literary studies, religion, folklore, and the visual arts. In so doing, Gender and American Culture seeks to reveal how identity and community are shaped by gender and sexuality.

A complete list of books published in Gender and American Culture is available at www.uncpress.unc.edu.

Florynce "Flo" Kennedy

THE LIFE OF A BLACK FEMINIST RADICAL

Sherie M. Randolph

The University of North Carolina Press CHAPEL HILL

*This book was published with the assistance of the
John Hope Franklin Fund
of the University of North Carolina Press.*

© 2015 Sherie M. Randolph
All rights reserved
Manufactured in the United States of America
Set in Utopia by Tseng Information Systems, Inc.
The paper in this book meets the guidelines for permanence and durability
of the Committee on Production Guidelines for Book Longevity of the Council on
Library Resources. The University of North Carolina Press has been a member
of the Green Press Initiative since 2003.

Jacket illustration:
Florynce Kennedy, civil rights lawyer, New York,
August 1, 1969
Photograph by Richard Avedon
© The Richard Avedon Foundation

Library of Congress Cataloging-in-Publication Data
Randolph, Sherie M., author.
Florynce "Flo" Kennedy : the life of a black feminist radical / Sherie M. Randolph.
pages cm
Includes bibliographical references and index.
ISBN 978-1-4696-2391-7 (cloth : alk. paper) — ISBN 978-1-4696-2392-4 (ebook)
1. Kennedy, Florynce, 1916–2000. 2. African American women lawyers—
United States—Biography. 3. African American radicals—United States—Biography.
4. African American feminists—United States—Biography. I. Title.
KF373.K45R36 2015
340.092—dc23
[B]
2015010515

For my black feminist mother and father,
Linda D. Randolph and Kenneth R. Randolph,
and
in memory of my grandmother,
Muriel Randolph

Florynce Kennedy with feminist playwright Myrna Lamb at a demonstration in October 1974. (Photograph © Bettye Lane)

Contents

Acknowledgments

One of the pleasures of completing this book is that I now have an opportunity to express my deep gratitude to all those who helped make it possible.

I first must thank the feminists whose vision and dedication inspired the history the book recounts. I am especially grateful to Dorothy Pitman Hughes, Florence Rice, Ti-Grace Atkinson, Cynthia Epstein, Gloria Steinem, Sandra Hochman, Peg Brennan, Anselma Dell'Olio, Jacqueline Ceballos, Jane Galvin-Lewis, Diane Schulder Abrams, Carol Hanisch, Nancy Stearns, and Assata Shakur for sharing their memories of Kennedy and postwar political movements with me. Atkinson, Rice, and Schulder Abrams shared documents from their own archives, some of which have made their way into this book. David Heeley gave me rare access to his extensive collection of *The Flo Kennedy Show* videotapes. Flo Kennedy's sisters, Joyce Kennedy-Banks and Faye Kennedy-Daly, opened their homes to me, granted interviews, and allowed access to Florynce Kennedy's papers. I am most thankful to Flo Kennedy for our brief interview almost two decades ago and for leaving behind a rich history of black feminist political thought and activism.

Research and writing for this project was generously supported by grants and fellowships from the Schlesinger Library on the History of Women in America; from the University of Michigan, including the Institute for Research on Women and Gender, the Horace H. Rackham School of Graduate Studies, and the Department of Afroamerican and African Studies; from Emory University's James Weldon Johnson Institute; and by a scholar-in-residence fellowship funded by the National Endowment for the Humanities at the Schomburg Center for Research in Black Culture.

The chairs and administrative staff in the Departments of Afroamerican and African Studies and History, especially Tiya Miles, Geoff Eley, Kathleen Canning, and Frieda Ekotto, deserve my deepest appreciation. Ben Twagira, Hannah Noel, Marc Johnson, Rita Bacote and Bernard Bacote provided exceptional research assistance early in this process. I was greatly aided by Garrett Felber's rare ability to track down uncommon documents and hard-to-find information.

I have benefited immeasurably from the insights and generosity of many scholars in my field. Robin D. G. Kelley, Beverly Guy-Sheftall, Adam Green, Lisa Duggan, Martha Hodes, and Barbara Krauthamer provided crucial direction during the initial stages of this project. Kelley and Guy-Sheftall deserve my deepest gratitude for their continued guidance and friendship. From the first moment I met Robin, he encouraged me to write the book I wanted to write; he read the manuscript at various stages and offered sage advice and unwavering support. Guy-Sheftall has been an equally steady source of support, making sure I always had a home at Spelman's Women's Research and Resource Center.

I have been fortunate to be a part of the Black Women's Intellectual History (BWICH) writing group. Farah Jasmine Griffin, Barbara Savage, Martha Jones, Mia Bay, and the entire BWICH writing group have my sincerest appreciation for their meticulous advice and deep insights on an early chapter.

This book has been greatly improved by those who generously read portions or all of the manuscript and offered valuable comments: Stephen Ward, Timothy Tyson, Mary Kelley, Kevin Gaines, Emily Thuma, Ferentz Lafargue, Tanisha Ford, Angela Dillard, Jeanne Theoharis, Komozi Woodard, Dayo Gore, John Carson, Stephen Berrey, Martha Jones, Erica Edwards, Penny Von Eschen, Gina Morantz-Sanchez, Megan Sweeney, Howard Brick, Daniel Ramirez, Anthony Mora, Omolade Adunbi, Nesha Haniff, Julius Scott, Jesse Huffnog-Garskof, Geoff Eley, and especially Kate Babbitt.

My thinking has benefited enormously from a community of friends and colleagues who gave advice, debated ideas, and offered their support in ways both small and large: Emily Thuma, Catina Bacote, Akiba Solomon, Akinyele Umoja, Erica Edwards, Deb Vargas, Mirelle Miller-Young, Natasha Lightfoot, Jennifer Morgan, Dena Goodman, Larry Rowley, Maria Cotera, Erik McDuffie, Michael Gomez, Mary Kelley, Andrea Smith, Donna Murch, Meera Bowman Johnson, Robyn Spencer, Eric Pritchard, Carolyn Brown, Venus Greene, Tyrone Forman, Danielle McGuire, Steve Lefkovitz, Brandi A. Lawrence, Nina Eidshiem, Kimberly Springer, Ina Solomon, Stephanie Solomon, Tanya Huellet, Sala Cyril, Azali Cyril, Austin Greene, Lumumba Bandele, Anu Kemet, Sophia Lafargue, Ferentz Lafargue, Hayarpi Papikyan, Jennifer Freeman Marshall, Marlon Bailey, Jonathan Metzel, Saida Grundy, Minkah Makalani, Erin Miller, Brandi Brimmer, Scot Brown, Hannah Rosen, Chantal Francois, Donna Brindle, Abby Primack, Kiini Salaam, and Obinna Onyeagoro. My many conversations with Mariama Richards, a trusted friend since we were history majors at Spelman College, have helped me to see the broader significance of this project. A very special thanks goes to Sekia, Stephen, and Chaney Ward for being the best-chosen family.

Barbara Ransby, Tiya Miles, Rhonda Williams, and the anonymous readers for UNC Press deserve my personal gratitude for reading the manuscript in its entirety and for offering very detailed comments. Grey Osterud helped me develop my ideas from their formative to final stages and has been an incredible source of encouragement and one of my most highly cherished friends.

Many thanks go to Mark Simpson-Vos at UNC Press for being such an encouraging and insightful editor. The Gender and American Culture series editor, Thadious Davis, provided important suggestions on how to make the book stronger.

Finally, but most important, I extend my utmost appreciation to my parents, Linda Randolph and Kenneth Randolph; my brother Kenneth Randolph II; my nephew Kenneth "Trey" Randolph; my aunts Gloria Williams, Paulette Turner, Patricia Saunders, Barbara Williams, Hattie Randolph, and Sandra Randolph; and my uncles Raymond Randolph II and Arthur Williams II for their unwavering support, continuous prayers, and immense love. My mother read the entire book with a keen eye and provided crucial support when I most needed it; my father offered detailed advice on the book's cover and interior photographs. Their collective support and love has been invaluable.

Above all, I thank God.

Florynce "Flo" Kennedy

Introduction

In 1976, at the age of sixty, black feminist radical Florynce "Flo" Kennedy stood at a podium in front of college students wearing her signature uniform—a cowboy hat and a T-shirt that read "Year of the Woman!," her fingernails painted bright red—bellowing numerous curse words to punctuate her point that for all oppressed people, power rested in their ability to protest individually, collectively, and in inclusive coalitions.[1] "My main message is that we have a pathologically, institutionally racist, sexist, classist society. And that niggerizing techniques that are used don't only damage black people, but they also damage women, gay people, ex-prison inmates, prostitutes, children, old people, handicapped people, Native Americans. And that if we can begin to analyze the pathology of oppression . . . we would learn a lot about how to deal with it."[2] Kennedy understood that, despite the various institutionalized forms of "racist, sexist, classist," and imperialist oppression they suffered, they were ultimately more powerful than the forces aligned against them. If larger and larger numbers of people realized that their exploitation was inextricably linked, she reasoned, they would eventually engage in the radical process of revolutionary change by creating broad-based political alliances. Through an activist career spanning more than fifty years, Kennedy targeted the interconnections among racism, sexism, homophobia, ableism, and various other forms of oppression.

Florynce "Flo" Kennedy: The Life of a Black Feminist Radical demonstrates the central role of black feminists in post–World War II social and political movements. Many scholars, students, and people concerned with political issues assume black women did not engage in postwar feminist actions until after the development of the predominantly white second wave women's movement.[3] While scholars have begun challenging

1

this historical inaccuracy,[4] most works on postwar feminist radicalism still view black feminism as emerging largely in protest against exclusion by white feminists or in opposition to Black Power.[5] Some major contributions of black feminism are acknowledged, particularly the theory of intersectionality, which emphasizes interlocking systems of oppression by gender and race, but black women's postwar activism has been recognized primarily in the scholarship of the civil rights movement.[6] This book, however, demonstrates that black women were present at the creation of postwar feminist movements and articulated a black feminist agenda based on their position as African American women who experienced sexist and racist discrimination in forms that could not be pulled apart and fought separately.

The black feminist organizing and political theorizing of activist-intellectual Flo Kennedy provides a critical window onto postwar radicalism. Kennedy worked in the civil rights, New Left, Black Power, and women's movements. She was among the small circle of northern women who supported grassroots organizers in Mississippi's voter registration campaign, was an early member of the National Organization for Women, and helped to organize the first National Black Power Conference and numerous black feminist organizations. Moving fluidly between these movements and organizations, she extended what she deemed the most comprehensive theories and effective strategies of each movement to the others. Respected—and sometimes disliked—for her intellect, coarse rhetoric, and compelling charisma, she allied with, debated, and influenced many more well-known radicals: singer Billie Holiday, recognized for the antilynching ballad "Strange Fruit"; New York City's longtime congressional representatives Adam Clayton Powell Jr. and Shirley Chisholm; Student Nonviolent Coordinating Committee leader H. Rap Brown; civil liberties lawyer William Kunstler; and Betty Friedan of the National Organization for Women (NOW). Kennedy was at the epicenter of raging debates during this tumultuous period, and her activism demonstrates that the boundaries around movements were far more porous than scholars have previously conceived.

I first came upon Kennedy when I was sitting on my sofa, flipping through TV channels, and old footage flashed across the screen of her arguing that we will know that sexism is worse than racism when we find feminists shot in bed like Black Panthers Mark Clark and Fred Hampton. As a black feminist, she was committed to Black Power. That Kennedy's central references were to Black Panthers who had been killed by the Chicago police illustrated that the women's movement had not yet posed such a threat to the establishment. A friend watching with me who had worked at *Ms.* magazine was familiar with Kennedy's name and knew that she had been active as a black feminist in the 1960s and 1970s, but she knew little else. So there started my fascination with collecting information on Flo Kennedy. Who was this radical black woman?

Color Me Flo: My Hard Life and Good Times was the only published book about her life. It was not a typical memoir but a collection of her speeches and interviews with pictures and leaflets interspersed throughout. The Schlesinger Library had two boxes of her unorganized papers at the time, but I soon discovered that they contained mostly leaflets and *Jet* magazines with Flo's notes scribbled on the edges of a few pages. Still, it was a start. The more I learned, the more I was drawn to the example of Kennedy as a black feminist who fought against multiple forms of discrimination. I was also fascinated by the broad range of her actions, stretching from the legal defense of Black Power organizers H. Rap Brown and Assata Shakur to the struggle to legalize abortion. Kennedy stood at the center of so many battles, yet I had never heard of her, and there was not a single book or even a scholarly article about her life. What started as a hobby of collecting information about this enigmatic black woman developed into a project at New York University and, now, a full-scale biography.

Over fifteen years ago, when I began researching Kennedy, accessible sources on her life were limited. Moreover, the two boxes of papers she donated to the Schlesinger Library in 1986 omitted large portions of her life and political activities. Uncovering Kennedy's story and the history of black feminist radicalism had to begin outside of traditional archives. With few resources open to the public, I conducted most of my research in the private collections of her family, friends, media producers, and allies. I spent several years tracking down every bit of surviving material on Kennedy's long life and conducted dozens of interviews with a range of political activists, lawyers, and family members. Fortunately, family and friends had their own archives and were excited to share their crates of material with me. Sadly, a great deal of the material had not been well preserved and was in total disarray. For more than a year, I sat on the living room floor in the home of Kennedy's sister Joyce Kennedy-Banks in East Orange, New Jersey, sifting through, organizing, and cataloging seventeen boxes of Flo's belongings. I started by placing disjointed pieces of paper together and reconstructing the labyrinth of Kennedy's life from her pamphlets; posters; notes scribbled on cigarette pack liners; meeting minutes scrawled on aged, long yellow sheets; telephone bills; and legal briefs placed next to white fur coats, "Run Jesse Run!" T-shirts, and an array of silver whistles and political buttons. Being the first researcher to read Kennedy's letters to her husband, to identify her hurried notes on the problems and rewards of defending the brother of the man accused of murdering Martin Luther King, and to weave together the disjointed fragments of her unpublished books and early drafts of *Color Me Flo* gave me unique access to the political evolution of her black feminist praxis.

By the time Joyce Kennedy-Bank's private collection of Flo Kennedy's surviving papers finally reached me, much was missing. Since Kennedy had run her own private practice for over twenty years, I expected to find countless boxes of legal documents, but most were gone. Eventually her activist friends told me that they had purposely destroyed some material when Kennedy became seriously ill for fear that the files would be used against already vulnerable organizers. More unsettling was the fact that those who thought they could profit from Kennedy's work removed certain documents around the time of her death. Debates and legal proceedings between Kennedy's family and friends over segments of her papers continued for years after Flo passed away.

Despite everything that Kennedy's papers had undergone, the considerable archive contained valuable evidence of a vast array of interlocking movements and organizations that had engaged black feminist ideas in the 1960s and 1970s. This material transformed the ways I thought and wrote about the history of black feminism and its centrality to postwar struggles. The significant role of Black Power in shaping feminism among white as well as black women became evident through Kennedy's essays, placards, speeches, fliers, and books. Once the pages of Kennedy's unpublished book manuscript "The Politics of Oppression" were placed in the correct order and the chapters were organized in the way she had outlined, the direct line of influence between feminisms and Black Power became clear.

Taken together, Kennedy's song booklets, TV show proposals, videotaped talk shows, political buttons, press releases, speeches, and other ephemera are much more than the sum of their parts. For years, Kennedy has been dismissed by some white feminist critics as an "entertainer" and "not a real feminist" because of her reliance on street theater protests.[7] Kennedy's street theater demonstrates that her savvy performances were strategically deployed to attract media attention to often-ignored issues and were also a way to make fighting for justice irresistibly pleasurable for would-be activists and those already hooked. Kennedy expected "politics to be fun," so she sang loudly, laughed frequently, and recruited and sustained others with her excitement for challenging one's own fears by confronting one's enemies.[8]

As a result of my work in finding and organizing Florynce Kennedy's papers, her significant body of work is now housed at the Arthur and Elizabeth Schlesinger Library on the History of Women in America at the Radcliffe Institute for Advanced Study at Harvard University in Cambridge, Massachusetts.

Drawing on those papers and videos, to which I was the first scholar to gain unlimited access, I stake out the place of Kennedy's black feminism within the narrative of postwar radicalism. Kennedy's story challenges the conventional history of the predominantly white liberal and radical feminist struggles during the 1960s and 1970s through the particular contributions of black feminist politics. Contrary to historical representations and popular belief, black feminists, as members and founders of mostly white feminist organizations and as founders of an independent black feminist movement, attempted to shift the mainstream women's movement away from a single focus on gender-based oppression toward an agenda more cognizant of the intersections of race and gender. They did not voluntarily subordinate their concerns as women to support black men in the struggle, nor did they choose to work only with other people of color in antiracist campaigns. Instead, they critiqued the multiple and simultaneous forms that oppression took in their lives and fought against it in a wide range of groups and movements throughout the postwar period.

Studies of independent black feminist and predominantly white feminist movements accurately cite the increased masculinity that kept feminism and Black Power divided. They are not wrong to do so, but positioning Black Power as primarily an antagonist influence misses what the movement tells us about how black and white feminists understood revolution and liberation.[9] Totally ignoring or underanalyzing the influence of the black feminists within mostly white feminist organizations leaves feminist literature with the misconception that second-wave feminism was initiated and led only by white women.[10] Indeed, Kennedy's story forces us to recognize the Black Power movement's central role in shaping radical feminism. Strategies and theories understood to have originated in Black Power struggles were absorbed, if at times unevenly, by both black and white feminists. The connections that Kennedy forged between Black Power advocates and emerging white feminists provided feminists with a vocabulary for describing gender and racial oppression and fueled the creation of broad-based antiracist alliances.

While Kennedy is best known for being one of the few black feminists who worked in the predominantly white feminist movement, her theorizing and activism has been neglected in histories of the movement.[11] This limited understanding of her activism and theory reduces her to a token and distorts the history of 1960s radicalism and feminism more generally. Radicals and the media knew many of Kennedy's accomplishments during her own time, but until now these actions have been largely lost to history.

■ This book is the first examination of her work that bridges the more mature antiracist movement with the nascent struggle against sexism. Kimberly Springer, Benita Roth, and Stephen Ward, among other scholars, have rescued black feminist organizing in the 1960s and 1970s from historical obscurity to highlight autonomous black feminist organizations.[12] But those groups were not alone; they came from a rich vein of black feminist activism, and they existed alongside a variety of coalitions in which black feminists participated. By drawing on Kennedy's unorganized archive, *Color Me Flo* (as well as early unpublished drafts), federal surveillance reports, interviews, organizational records, the radical press, and audio and visual recordings, along with public and private manuscript collections, this book expands our view of race and gender politics by exploring black feminist theorizing and organizing that remained connected to the Black Power, New Left, and predominantly white women's movements, as well as to autonomous black feminist groups. This biography traces Florynce Kennedy's political career in order to explain the political and intellectual contributions she made to postwar struggles. Flo's story begins with her family in Kansas City, Missouri, where I investigate how her parents contributed to the formation of her black feminist radicalism, which involved claiming ownership of her body as well as defiance of white supremacy. The twenty-six-year-old Kennedy headed to New York City during World War II, where she took full advantage of the opportunities that the wartime city offered African American women to escape the drudgery of unskilled work and to gain a higher education. During her first decade in New York, Kennedy graduated from Columbia University's School of General Studies and its Law School. In this political and social milieu, she expanded and sharpened her radical philosophical perspective and first articulated a black feminist politics.

Kennedy struggled to make a place for herself in the legal profession. As a black woman, Flo did not fit neatly within a system in which the most visible architects of the courts' civil and criminal process, doctrines, and unspoken codes were white men. With very little guidance concerning how to survive in a profession unaccustomed to black women in any role other than defendants, she had to make her own way. Kennedy created a roadmap for becoming a lawyer, surviving as a working attorney, and gaining financial stability.[13] Among her notable achievements was her contribution to intellectual property law, as she defended the rights of writers and musicians against the record labels that exploited their talents and profited from their creativity. Her work as a lawyer left her profoundly disappointed with the legal system, however. Despite the victories secured in the courts by civil rights organizations such as the National Association for the Advancement of Colored People, Kennedy was frustrated with the judicial system as an avenue for securing simple justice, let alone social change. As her disillusionment deepened, she drew closer to radicalism, finding journalism and political organizing more satisfying strategies for change. Kennedy strongly advocated the consumer boycott, which had previously been used by the Urban League, as a tactic that women and other oppressed groups could readily utilize. When Kennedy introduced guerrilla street theater into a protest, she revived and extended one of her favorite weapons.

The emergence of the Black Power, anti–Vietnam War, New Left, and feminist movements in the mid-1960s formed the apex of Kennedy's political journey. Flo managed to be engaged in all of these movements simultaneously, even though their key organizations and approaches were frequently at odds. By focusing on her organizing in the Black Power Conference, the National Conference for New Politics, and NOW in 1967, I establish her significance as a leader who bridged movements and translated ideas and strategies from one struggle to another. She brought the ideas of the Black Power movement to the emerging women's movement and made Black Power into a pivotal ideological influence on the radical feminist politics that was developing among predominantly white women.

Kennedy played a crucial leadership role within the nascent feminist movement. The New York City chapter of NOW, which was the largest and most active in the organization, included black feminists Shirley Chisholm as well as white feminists Kate Millet, Betty Friedan, and Catharine Stimpson. As the women's movement burgeoned, Kennedy's connections with NOW deepened. She rapidly became a leader, although she never held an official position on the executive committee; instead, she influenced the group primarily through her continual and deliberate mentorship of younger white feminists, such as Ti-Grace Atkinson, and through her ability to imagine actions that would capture media attention.

Her activities as a lawyer, fund-raiser, and organizer in the Black Power movement enhanced her contribution. Kennedy's work not only drew on the parallels she saw between Black Power and feminism but was aimed at creating an expansive radical coalition to challenge the intersections of oppression. Flo's inspiration and organizing skills were central to the important early demonstrations, such as the Miss America protest in Atlantic City, which drew new participants to the women's movement. Kennedy was a media savant who critiqued both sexism and racism in the press and on TV, particularly concerning how media outlets inculcated sexism and political passivity. She understood how press coverage might broaden a movement's reach and attract more members. As Kennedy later told an interviewer, she was "the force of them."[14] The force that was Flo galvanized protest actions and inspired participation. She expanded the movement's base, found supportive allies, and carried out actions that gained traction in the media.

At the same time, Kennedy brought her legal expertise and political knowledge to the campaign to repeal New York State's restrictive abortion laws. She served as counsel for *Abramowicz v. Lefkowitz*, the first class action suit in which women themselves insisted on their right to be heard. Coupling speak-outs and demonstrations with constitutional arguments, the case helped to convince the legislature to amend the law before it was settled in court. Although by the late 1960s she was one of the country's best-known black feminists, her role in helping to legalize abortion has long since been forgotten.

Kennedy made a political career of emphasizing the critical linkages between all forms of oppression, especially racism and sexism. By 1972, while she was excited about the growth of the predominantly white feminist movement and its successful push to legalize abortion, she was also profoundly disappointed that the struggle still did not fully embrace a black feminist position and make challenging racism as well as sexism central to its political agenda. Thus, Kennedy worked to create interracial feminist organizations that emphasized a black feminist praxis. Her activism during this period was central to building a women's movement that included women of all races as well as an independent black feminist movement. In keeping with her analysis of interlocking systems of oppression, Kennedy saw no contradiction in carrying out both of these undertakings at once.

To Kennedy's thinking, Shirley Chisholm's quest for the presidential nomination was the perfect opportunity for white feminists to build a broad alliance and support a black feminist politics. In 1971 she created the Feminist Party in hopes of bringing together an inclusive group of feminists to support not simply the candidacy of the black congresswoman from New York but black feminism more generally. Equally interested in advancing black feminist praxis, she worked to create the National Black Feminist Organization in 1973 and pushed black women to form their own autonomous black feminist movement that focused centrally on ending racism and sexism.

This political and intellectual biography of Florynce "Flo" Kennedy not only restores her to the history of U.S. radicalism but also illuminates the interconnections among movements against racial and gender oppression. Rediscovering her life and work reminds us of the possibilities for alliances that remain implicit in resistance to all forms of domination and of the centrality of black feminism's intersectional praxis to radical social and political transformation.

1

Political in the Sense That We Never Took Any Shit

FAMILY AND THE ROOTS OF BLACK FEMINIST

RADICALISM, 1916–1942

Florynce Kennedy was a small child when a group of armed white men paid a visit to her family's home in Kansas City, Missouri, around 1919. The American Neighbors Delegation, as Flo later dubbed it mockingly, told her mother, Zella, that "we weren't wanted and that we'd better leave." They "indicated that they didn't want to have to hurt anybody," but if the Kennedy family did not move from the home they owned, the group of men would have no other choice but to force them out. The neighborhood was for whites only, and black families were not welcome.[1]

Although Flo was too young to remember her mother's exact words to the fifteen or so men on their front steps, she concluded that "whatever she said, or did, and however she acted must have been just right because they went away." Years later, when Flo was a grown woman in her thirties, she asked her father about the legendary confrontation between the Kennedys and the armed white mob. For the first time, Flo heard of her mother's heroism in talking the white men off their property. Flo tried to imagine how the woman she knew as even-tempered could have convinced the men to leave. Finally, she decided that her mother must have displayed just the right amount of strength.[2]

In Flo's adult memory, her father, Wiley Kennedy, was more combative and more likely to challenge whites. He confirmed Flo's impression of him when he said that if he had been the one to confront the white men that Sunday, he would not have kept his temper in check, and the exchange would have ended gravely for them. Wiley told his daughter that he was pretty "tough in them days" and was prone to smack someone when provoked.[3] Indeed, he was furious when he heard about the threats against his wife, mother-in-law, and small children.[4] Wiley had purchased the house on Walrond Avenue around 1913 and was very proud of that accomplishment.[5] The Kennedys had lived there for a few years before the mob attempted to force them out.

The senior Kennedy explained to his daughter that they were not prepared to leave the home they owned, so Wiley and Zella "set about to see what could be done to protect their right to stay in their house." First Flo's father visited the local police station on Twenty-Second and Flora. The officer listened to his account and then told him that his white neighbors could not legally evict them. "It was his home and he could do whatever was necessary to protect it," the officer advised. Wiley took note of the fact that the police offered the family no protection beyond these words. Moreover, he doubted that the officers or the court would side with him against his white neighbors should the thugs return. Flo also surmised that the policeman's words must have "been pretty cold comfort to Zella who was home at night alone so much of the time with only grandma and us."[6]

Undaunted, the Kennedys sought legal counsel, but the attorney gave them similar advice. He cautioned that "there wasn't much they could do to the neighbors" to stop their threats or to punish them for harassment but added "that there wasn't much the neighbors could do to them, Legally, that is."[7] The lawyer and the police had no advice on how to prevent the men from delivering on their promise. In the spring and summer of 1919, black residents of Kansas City, like their counterparts in cities across the country, faced continuous abuse from whites intent on hardening the racial divide after World War I. Anxiety that his home would be the white terrorists' next target no doubt gnawed at Wiley.

These worries were confirmed when a group of young white men continued the campaign of intimidation that the older men had started. They began "making a habit . . . of congregating next door in a little shack" behind the Kennedys' home. One youth would openly have sexual relations with his lady friend there at all hours of the day and night. These young men were brazenly claiming the outside edge of the Kennedy property as their own and showing complete disregard for the family. Perhaps Wiley feared that the men would continue to encroach on his land and eventually lay claim not only to the family's home but also to his wife, mother-in-law, and daughters. He repeatedly asked the white men to leave, but they ignored him and returned to the shed whenever they pleased. Finally, fed up with his family being disregarded and disrespected, Wiley waited until he saw one of the men bringing a woman around back. He walked over and asked the couple to take their business elsewhere. Irritated, the male trespasser puffed up his chest and flatly told Flo's father that he was "lucky he was still there and he wasn't taking any orders from any niggers." As far as he was concerned, the land belonged to the whites and "they didn't want any niggers in the neighborhood." He warned the senior Kennedy that he "better get the hell over in his own yard while he still had one." It would not be long "before somebody [would] come and chase him out of the neighborhood altogether." The girl "giggled" at her boyfriend's swift dismissal of Flo's father.[8]

As the story goes, Wiley then pulled out a piece of broken scaffolding he had hidden close by and "whacked him across the head good a couple of times." All hell broke loose. The white man "started hollerin' and this girl was yelling" as Wiley continued to clobber him, holding him tightly so he could not escape. Finally, "I let him go and he ran like a turkey," Flo's father said triumphantly.[9] The border of the Kennedy property would not be used as a white man's latrine or bordello, and the family refused to be evicted from the home they owned. After that day, the white thugs stopped using the shed as their own and no one ever tried to evict them again. Wiley and Zella raised their five daughters in that house.

That white men were engaging in illicit sex so close to his home no doubt added to Wiley's fear for the safety of his family. Black women and girls were especially vulnerable to sexual violence from white men who used rape and other forms of assault to hinder African Americans from exercising their citizenship rights and to debase and deny their humanity.[10] These brutal acts were routinely ignored by law enforcement and went unpunished. As historian Hannah Rosen explains, "part of a larger performance of [white] power was resisting and disavowing the transformations brought about by emancipation" through the rape of black women.[11]

In the 1960s, when Kennedy was asked about her political background, she normally told the more dramatic and armed version of the story she had grown up hearing, perhaps from her older sister Evelyn, rather than the account she later obtained directly from her father. In the inflated version her father was armed with a gun when he challenged a group of white vigilantes who attempted to evict their family. The steps her parents took to secure the safety of their home and children by contacting the police and an attorney were omitted, and the story centered on her father's unrelenting bravery.[12] "Daddy was ready to shoot somebody and kill him to keep our house," Flo explained to interviewers who were interested in her political roots.[13]

The story of her father's armed defiance in the face of white terrorism was the narrative Flo frequently recounted to reporters, scholars, and audiences who wanted to know how she became a black feminist radical. "Did you grow up political?" they would ask. Most assumed that the Kennedy family was involved in the National Association for the Advancement of Colored People (NAACP) and belonged to a black church. But Kennedy's response was always the same: "We were political in the sense that we never took any shit."[14] Kennedy wanted to make clear that her family's political pedigree was not tied to any organization but to guts and gumption. Flo described her own personality as an extension of her father's confrontational and rebellious persona.[15] In her retelling of the family fable, Wiley was unrelenting, armed, and fearless when faced with injustice.

For Kennedy, her politics developed from her father's defiance of oppression. This was the radical tradition from which she sprang and that she continued to pursue. Her father's strong belief in personal autonomy and freedom contributed to her formation as a black feminist radical. The numerous family stories she heard and the confrontations she witnessed secured Wiley's image in Flo's memory. When Kennedy was active in the radical political movements of the 1960s and 1970s, she strengthened the image of herself as rebellious, fearless, and even outrageous. The Black Power movement's provocative militancy, while often derided and attacked by government officials, the mainstream media, and some civil rights organizations, was celebrated by those who advocated assertive self-defense as the most effective means of securing respect and liberation. The story Flo offered at that time was deployed to inspire her audience of radical activists, especially white feminists, to attempt to mimic her daring.

Flo's mother, Zella, exerted an equally important influence, even though she was absent from the version of the story Flo generally told. As an adult Flo spoke and wrote of her mother's courage, resilience, and unconventional parenting.[16] Zella showed Flo how to challenge the gendered limitations frequently placed on black girls and women in the 1920s and 1930s. She rejected middle-class moralizing and notions of female respectability that limited black women's mobility, pleasure, and sexual expression. Flo's experiences as the daughter of Zella and Wiley Kennedy contributed to her evolving politics and set the stage for the activism that would follow her move to New York City.

"That's Why I Don't Have the Right Attitude toward Authority": Power, Family, and Wiley Kennedy

In 1909, Wiley Choice Kennedy moved to Kansas City to find a better job and to escape the racial bigotry of the Deep South. A decade earlier he had left Elm Bluff, Alabama, where his mother was once enslaved. Far less is known about Wiley's father, other than he too was once enslaved. At the age of twenty, Wiley packed his belongings, left the Dallas County plantation, and traveled more than two hundred miles north to Huntsville.[17] He departed for the city just as Alabama was attempting to reclaim its financial status as Cotton King.[18] Before the Civil War, Alabama had been the country's leading supplier of cotton, and politicians and business elites sought to regain that position by keeping newly freed black families tied to the land as sharecroppers. The most powerful weapon they used to punish those who attempted to leave and to intimidate the rest into staying was the lynch mob. In the 1890s Alabama led the country in the highest number of lynchings per year, while Dallas County had the highest number in the state.[19] When Wiley moved from Elm Bluff, he was fleeing not only the economic limitations of sharecropping but also the threat of death faced by any and every black person who pushed back against the status quo.

Wiley quickly discovered that Huntsville was no promised land. Although he could read and write, he found few opportunities to earn a decent wage.[20] African Americans in the South were routinely barred from the higher-paying jobs in cotton mills and other industries.[21] Most black men picked up work as day laborers or farmhands when it was available.[22] In Huntsville, Wiley toiled as a "lot boy," tending horses and mules for a livestock dealer, until he saved enough money to move over six hundred miles farther north and west with his brother Wilson. He was part of the steady trickle of blacks who made their way to Kansas City, Missouri, and Kansas City, Kansas, during the two decades prior to the Great Migration.[23]

When Wiley arrived in Kansas City in 1909, he found a well-established community of more than 23,000 African Americans.[24] Some of these families had been enslaved in rural Missouri and moved to St. Louis or Kansas City after emancipation, but most were "exodusters" who migrated from the former Confederacy to Kansas after the end of Reconstruction. Many Kansas City residents moved back and forth across the Missouri River, depending on opportunities for work and housing.[25] A few years after he arrived, Wiley garnered a highly coveted job as a waiter and worked his way to headwaiter in the "biggest and brassiest" restaurant in Kansas City: the

Blue Goose Café in the White Hotel.[26] Because northern blacks were frequently relegated to the service sector, they "did their best to obtain the most desirable occupations within this sphere. The most sought after positions were those of waiters, porters, and caterers."[27] Competition for these jobs was intense because workers could make as much in tips as they did in wages. The racially exclusive White Hotel catered to businessmen and travelers interested in Kansas City's burgeoning cabaret and vaudeville nightlife. Besides the financial benefits, the black men who held these positions gained a level of prestige and distinction within Kansas City's African American community.

In Kennedy's recollections, she wrote that her father belonged to the "most exclusive class of the black community" and was respected because of his position. In her published memoir, *Color Me Flo*, however, she attributed his prestige not to his position as a waiter at the White Hotel but to his work as a "Pullman porter on the trains." She explained, "At the time I was born, porters belonged to the most exclusive class—they were the 'pooristocrats' of the Black community."[28] An earlier, unpublished draft of *Color Me Flo* and the Pullman porter registry reveal no evidence that Wiley Kennedy ever worked as a Pullman porter.[29] Through the mid-twentieth century, many African Americans regarded Pullman porters as an elite group of black men. They often espoused radical politics, and in 1925 they formed the Brotherhood of Sleeping Car Porters, a labor union headed by the socialist A. Philip Randolph.[30] In the original draft of her memoir, Kennedy speculated about the various jobs her father may have held as a young man. "My daddy was a waiter at first," she explained. Then, uncertain that this information was correct, she added, "Now I think before I was born he may have been a Pullman porter."[31] In the published memoir, her speculations were treated as fact.[32] It is impossible to disentangle Flo's attribution of this distinguished occupation to her father from her understanding of his political stance and social standing. Nonetheless, her description of her father's status when she was young was an apt portrait of his position within Kansas City's African American community during the 1910s and early 1920s.

Not long after he arrived, Wiley met Zella Jackman, a strong-willed, caramel-colored woman with thick, curly hair from a well-established, middle-class Kansas City family. Although Wiley was ten years older than Zella, he was no doubt impressed with her intelligence and sophistication. Flo described her mother as "awfully smart" because "she had gone to normal school at a time when very few black people did."[33] Like other African Americans who had lived through slavery, Flo's maternal grandparents,

Lucy Simpson Jackman and William H. Jackman, valued education as a way to safeguard their freedom. Both had been enslaved in Kentucky, and William had fought for the Union during the Civil War. After Reconstruction Lucy and William made their separate ways to Kansas, where they met. In Kansas City, William opened a store that sold secondhand goods while Lucy divided her time between caring for her children and being active in the local African Methodist Episcopal church.[34] Lucy, like many other blacks of her generation, placed a high social value on skin color. Proud of her own fair skin and mulatto heritage, she expected her daughter to marry a man with a complexion similar to her own.[35] Flo and her sister explained that although Wiley had ascended to Kansas City's middle class, her grandmother was "snobbish" and never cared for him because of his dark skin.[36]

Defying her mother's wishes, Zella married Wiley Kennedy on October 7, 1912.[37] Lucy's blatant disdain for Wiley made it hard for her to acknowledge the various ways that her daughter's husband helped to rescue her from near poverty. By 1910, after twenty years of marriage, her husband, William, had abandoned her.[38] Anxious to preserve her respectability, she told people that she was a widow.[39] His departure forced mother and daughter to work as a laundress and domestic, respectively, while they struggled to maintain their home and their standing within the community. Not long after Zella married Wiley, both mother and daughter stopped working for pay and Lucy moved into his new home.[40]

At a time when black homeownership was slowly but steadily rising in Missouri, Wiley purchased a house in a predominantly white neighborhood.[41] Many white residents railed against newly arrived black homeowners and tried to dissuade others from following suit. Flo remembered that when "a few more Negroes moved in . . . panic set in" because residents "wanted the neighborhood to be white."[42] Threats of violence were constant and seldom empty. In 1910 and 1911 at least six explosions occurred within a few blocks of the Kennedy home. Indeed, bombings of black-owned houses were so prevalent that members of the black community called the area "the dynamite neighborhood."[43] One witness reported that "thanks to a handful of bombings, the receipt of letters signed 'dynamite' was usually sufficient" to dissuade black families from moving into the area.[44] Despite these threats, Wiley bought a home right in the middle of the dynamite neighborhood, joining the dozens of black families who had long been scattered among whites and were determined to resist the terrorists who aimed to evict them.

When African American soldiers returned home from World War I in

1919, veterans and other black men and women were met with intensified white hostility and violence across the country, including in Chicago, New York City, and Columbia, South Carolina. Spurred by whites' resentment of blacks who competed with them for jobs and housing, as well as by their anger at the assertion of citizenship by black veterans in uniform, numerous lynchings and close to three dozen race riots occurred that spring, summer, and fall. Acts of white vigilante violence against black people were so widespread and ruthless that the NAACP leader, James Weldon Johnson, labeled these volatile months the Red Summer.[45]

Racial hostility in Kansas City was particularly intense for black families who lived near whites. While never escalating to full-scale riots, continued violence marred the city. Stories told by black women and men underscored the uncertainty that residents of these disputed neighborhoods faced. Lucile Bluford, a black neighbor of the Kennedys, reflected on a childhood of seeming contradictions: by day she played with white children in the streets, and at night she witnessed black homes being bombed.[46] The wave of bombings continued for a decade, and the local branch of the NAACP continually sought assistance from the national organization.[47] Between 1921 and 1928, Kansas City suffered as many as seven bombings a year.[48] Initially, neighborhood associations capitalized on the fear of violence to threaten black families and white sellers that "Ku Klux Klan plans might be employed" if blacks continued to purchase homes in white-only neighborhoods.[49] In response to these and other battles over housing, *Kansas City Call* editor C. A. Franklin commented, "There was not an occupied foot of ground where Negroes could go and live without having to fight to do so."[50]

As Jim Crow was imposed in Kansas City at the turn of the twentieth century, neighborhoods became more rigidly segregated, black customers were forbidden from trying on clothing in downtown stores, seating in most major theatres was segregated, black children were educated in separate schools, and black families were treated only at the "colored hospital."[51] After World War I, the Ku Klux Klan experienced a resurgence. Increased Klan activity occurred in both Kansas City, Kansas, and Kansas City, Missouri, with Klan members openly running for office in Kansas and in small Missouri towns. The Knights of the Klan recruitment advertisements published in the Missouri press asked, "Are you native born?" "Do you believe in white supremacy?" If the answers were yes, then both men and women were offered immediate membership. Recent immigrants, African Americans, Catholics, and Jews were all deemed unfit and unsuitable for U.S. citizenship. From its downtown office, the Klan enlisted heavily throughout cities and towns in Missouri, Kansas, and Arkansas. In 1924 the KKK even held its national Klonvocation only a few miles from the Kennedy home, where more than two thousand Klan members plotted the organization's strategies and future actions.[52] As a result of the Klan's heavy recruiting, Kansas City, Missouri, became a central site for Klan organizing and fund-raising during the 1920s.[53]

By the 1920s Kansas City was becoming racially segregated, but Jim Crow was not imposed uniformly. For example, seating on public transportation remained integrated. Black people were not routinely disfranchised, although several accounts demonstrated that at times they were denied the right to vote.[54] As historian Robin D. G. Kelley argues, although African Americans were dissatisfied with the inferior facilities that were available to them, they nonetheless made the most of segregated parks, theaters, and nightclubs.[55] Moreover, they built their own institutions. Kansas City had a black newspaper, the *Kansas City Call*; a baseball team, the Kansas City Monarchs; and a vibrant jazz scene. Blacks used these segregated spaces to find their cultural bearings, build racial solidarity, and mold their own urban setting. For most African Americans, "Kansas City represented two worlds, in which opportunities for advancement coexisted with sometimes strict limitations."[56]

The black community pushed back against the hardening of the color line. The Kansas City branch of the NAACP brought suit against the city for failing to investigate the bombings of the 1910s and 1920s and arrest the perpetrators. Black leaders even hired a private detective to collect evidence to bring before a grand jury. The NAACP and the *Kansas City Call* criticized the police for leaving black houses unprotected and refusing to arrest well-known white suspects.[57] In May 1919, prominent black men in the community met with the Kansas City mayor to demand official protection as citizens with the right to hold property in neighborhoods of their choosing.[58] In this period, the Kennedy family called on the state by going to the police to report the violent threats made against them and seeking the help of an attorney.[59] Without state protection, however, black families stood guard at their homes and at the homes of their neighbors when white mobs illegally attempted to evict them.[60]

Black children who lived in these contested neighborhoods were not shielded from harassment and frequently had to engage in confrontations of their own. As the Kennedy girls—Grayce, Flo, and Evelyn—grew up, the mile-long walk to the black elementary school was a terrifying experience, but their father's lessons helped them deal with white bullying. They tried to avoid clashes with white children by taking side roads or by staying off the "white side" of the street. Flo said that they "tended to go the way that didn't bring us into unnecessary contact with white kids," but confrontations were unavoidable.[61] During their walk to school the Kennedy girls would pass all-white schools and numerous white bullies.[62] Flo explained: "We were taught very early on never to take any shit from anyone. I remember a time when some white kids were chasing us. They had been chasing us on a regular basis, quite a few of them, and we would walk really slowly because we were so scared, and they would call us 'niggers.' So one day we got evil and we said, 'Let's go get 'em,' and Grayce, Lynn [Evelyn] and I turned around and started running after them and calling them 'pecker-wood.' They were so scared they just ran as fast as they could, and after that we had no more trouble, because whenever they started anything we would turn on them, and they would just fly."[63]

Flo described how this experience shaped their understanding of how black girls were to respond to racist violence. "Never take any shit" was the mantra Wiley taught his daughters when they interacted with white girls and boys. "That established very early that although they were the enemy they were scared of us, and anybody calling us 'nigger' had to be a rare thing, and we'd just start after them, throwing rocks, and not taking any shit at all off anybody."[64] She remembered, "From then on, I was never afraid of white people again."[65] No longer fearing white bullies, Kennedy began to enjoy her own and her sisters' power over their adversaries. "[As] soon as we started" fighting back, Flo recalled, "it got to be fun to go home from school."[66] Wiley was adamant that his daughters never be abused or mistreated by either whites or blacks. His central message was valuing oneself and resisting oppression. He would preach to them, "If you sit back and let people scream at you or talk to you like you ain't nothing . . . soon you gonna figure that you ain't."[67]

This rule extended from white neighborhood children to black school officials. Flo recalled that her mother reminded them that she would not allow the teachers to touch her girls.[68] Their grandmother Lucy Jackman echoed this advice and was quick to march down to the school when Flo's older sister Evelyn found herself in trouble with a teacher.[69] Mrs. Jackman reprimanded the teacher and told her never to touch Evelyn. After Flo's grandmother gave the teacher a swift tongue-lashing, Flo said that "we knew that the whole family was on our side! . . . We were so proud!"[70]

Incidents in which her father and grandmother protected the family and their insistence that their girls do the same for themselves forever shifted Flo's understanding of the balance of power between the powerful and those who were perceived as powerless. By the time Flo reached middle school, she no longer blindly respected authority figures; deference had to be earned. She explained, "That's why I don't have the right attitude toward authority today, because we were taught very early in the game that we didn't have to respect the teachers . . . and if they threatened to hit us we could just act as if they weren't there."[71]

Wiley and Zella never physically punished their children, believing that children should not be hit.[72] This progressive thinking was out of step with both black and white modes of child rearing in the early 1900s.[73] Her parents pushed back against the acceptance of violence as a routine part of black life, and Zella often felt it necessary to apologize to onlookers for treating her daughters with such delicate care, which most saw as excessive spoiling.[74] The Kennedys also insisted that the girls treat one another with kindness and respect, instructing them to never hit one another and to maintain a degree of politeness and formality that was uncommon in the everyday interactions of schoolchildren. These instructions for behavior within the family did not mean that her parents frowned at fighting as a response to threats or assault from outsiders; on the contrary, they maintained that their daughters should be prepared to defend themselves.

In retrospect, Flo may have exaggerated her father's ability to protect his family. The fact that he was also vulnerable to racism was all too apparent. Her recollections rarely mentioned him losing against insurmountable odds. The stories told by Zella Kennedy's cousin and close friend Myra Wilson, however, demonstrated that Wiley was sometimes on the losing end of confrontations and was punished for challenging white authority. After spending more than a decade as a hotel waiter, Wiley set up his own taxi business and often served white customers. Following a scuffle with a white passenger who refused to pay, he was arrested and spent Christmas in the jail hospital.[75] For most black men and women who talked or fought back against whites, resistance was often met with equal, or even greater, force.

Flo recalled feeling protected by her father, and she reminisced about her early childhood as "the really good part of our lives."[76] Because Wiley was the sole provider for his family, Zella escaped the fate of most black women of this period, who routinely performed low-paid domestic work in white households.[77] His income allowed his wife and at times his mother-in-law the opportunity to stay home and care for Flo and her sisters. The Kennedy girls' early life included a home filled with furniture carefully chosen by their mother, expensive crepe de chine dresses, and a cross-country train trip during their summer vacations.

"Alive and Happy in Los Angeles": California, Freedom, and the Revolt of Zella Kennedy

At one point around 1925, Zella packed up her three girls—eleven-year-old Evelyn, nine-year-old Flo, and seven-year-old Grayce—and traveled to Los Angeles without Wiley to visit her brother and mother, who were already in LA.[78] Once in California, Zella decided to stay.[79] Even before they had boarded the train, she filled her daughters' ears with visions of a better life in such exciting cities as New York and Los Angeles. The girls almost "died with excitement" over their new adventure.[80] Zella was eager to make a new life for herself and her daughters in California. Flo said that her mother "always wanted to get out of Kansas City and move to California, some place."[81] Another sister characterized Zella as very ambitious and declared that their mother held one principle over others: the "belief that you better make something of yourself."[82] Staying in Los Angeles was Zella's opportunity to make something of herself and her girls on her own terms.

Flo and her family became a part of the wave of blacks migrating to Los Angeles in the 1920s in search of jobs and freedom from Jim Crow. The vast majority came from the South, while some came from the Midwest. During this period the city's black population doubled from 15,579 to 38,894, although blacks never constituted more than 3.14 percent of the total population during the 1920s.[83] While cities like Detroit, Cleveland, and Chicago had developed solid black enclaves by World War I, the neighborhoods where blacks lived in LA did not develop into all-black communities at that time. Scholar Josh Sides argues that the use of restrictive covenants to protect and maintain white neighborhoods produced some racial diversity in the communities where African Americans lived, especially Boyle Heights and East Los Angeles. On one side of the racial dividing line were whites, most of them Protestant, and on the other a "patchwork of races and ethnicities. A large number of Mexicans and Italians lived along Central Avenue, the heart of the African American community."[84]

Zella and her daughters settled only a block from Central Avenue in the home of her brother, Oliver Jackman, and his wife. Flo attended school with Italian, Mexican, and African American children. She remembered that "the whole education scene was different there and we went to an integrated school."[85] Since the schools in Los Angeles were also better funded and better equipped than the black schools in Kansas City, she experienced a higher standard of education.[86] She recalled that she "really loved California" and "felt alive and happy in Los Angeles" but went on to dismiss her thoughts as the memories of a child who simply enjoyed streetcar rides, fresh apricots, and the ocean.[87]

Los Angeles offered a reprieve not only from the harsh Missouri winters but also from Jim Crow. Flo's most vivid memory of the city was the "integrated school," where she learned "to do acting bars and back bends and all these gymnastics and all sorts of stuff."[88] The young black girl relished these physical freedoms. Flo reminisced fondly about the playground in California. Significantly, she had never played in most of the public parks in Kansas City, which were reserved for whites. Instead, her memories included riding past the parks and being unable to enjoy them. Later she recalled black protests against Kansas City's segregated parks and golf course.[89]

Perhaps Flo felt especially "alive and happy in Los Angeles" because her mother was enjoying life without a husband. The record does not explain what marital difficulties might have led Zella to leave Wiley and move to California with their children. Kennedy speculated that Zella was more ambitious and adventurous than Wiley and that her decision to stay in California was motivated more by her desire for excitement than by troubles in her married life.[90] While the complications of their parents' relationship remained hidden from their children and historians, it is clear that once Zella set foot in California she felt liberated from the strictures of wedlock. She took on boyfriends and did not hide these relationships from her daughters.[91] Although Flo's sister Evelyn was hurt by her parents' separation, Flo remembers being impressed with her mother's audacious decision to "get away from Kansas City" and to take lovers while she was still legally married and being partially supported by her husband. "I was proud of her," Flo recalled.[92]

Flo describes both her mother and father as rebels who "never took shit."[93] In Flo's memories, however, Zella's triumphs were primarily against the limits imposed by marriage and a husband and, more broadly, against the pervasive politics of domesticity and respectability. Flo described Zella as the antithesis of the ideal middle-class housewife. Not only did she leave her husband and have open extramarital relationships, but she "did not take house keeping seriously" and "was a total failure when it came to cooking."[94]

It might seem odd that Flo later looked back at her mother's separation from Wiley, whom she described as a good father, as one of the best moments of her young life. Why did Flo not show a greater sense of pain or betrayal as she recalled her parents' split, her mother's affairs, and the move to California? Instead, she appreciated Los Angeles as a place where her mother lived boldly, ventured out without a husband, and reinvented herself. Zella became an unattached and free young black woman in the city, enjoying pleasures usually unavailable to married women with children. Seeing her mother through this new lens provided Flo with an unconventional example of black womanhood in the 1920s. She recalled this image of her unorthodox mother fondly and expressed great admiration for her provocative boldness.

After nearly two years, their stay in California was cut short. Zella apparently suffered from some physical affliction; she told her children that she contracted severe food poisoning and might have said this to her husband as well.[95] Wiley arrived to pack up Zella and the girls and take them back to Kansas City.[96] Flo was deeply disappointed. So, no doubt, was her mother. But Zella recovered quickly from whatever might have ailed her, and in 1927, not long after their return, Joyce Kennedy, Flo's fourth sister, was born.

Kansas City and the Great Depression

With the birth of a fourth daughter in 1927 and a fifth, Faye, in 1931, the Kennedy family struggled to stay afloat amid the Great Depression.[97] The prosperity and relative comfort that had marked Flo's early upbringing ended during the 1930s. By 1933, the gross domestic product had fallen by half and at least a quarter of the labor force was unemployed. The recovery from this economic recession was slow and prolonged, as the Depression lasted close to a decade.[98] African Americans were routinely "the last hired and the first fired," so they were twice as likely to be jobless as their white counterparts.[99] Indeed, in most parts of the United States, the rate of black unemployment averaged almost double the national rate, and for African American women the rate was even higher.[100] Blacks in Kansas City struggled to find jobs in the stockyards and packinghouses that had been open to them a decade earlier.[101] Like most children, Flo saw the Depression "as an incident or condition within" her own family; only later did she realize "it was a national phenomenon."[102]

When Wiley's taxi business declined, Zella had to begin working as a maid for white families. For nearly twenty years she had escaped the double burden of labor that many black women carried and avoided the risk of harassment and abuse that working in white households entailed. In Los Angeles, she had worked briefly as a cook.[103] Now, however, she joined the majority of black women in Kansas City and throughout the nation who worked in the main occupation that was open to them.

Zella was ambivalent about cleaning homes, but she did it when she could. Her temperament, however, was not well suited for the day-to-day injustices that accompanied serving in white homes. Flo described her mother's rebelliousness: "She went to work for a lady who apparently wasn't the most reasonable person in the world. . . . [White women were] constantly running their fingers over things to see if they were dusty, but the lady went beyond the pale one day and accused Zella of stealing. Zella had a fit and started ranting and raving. . . . She wound up taking off every stitch of clothes, and on that day she happened to have the "curse," so she tore off the sanitary napkin too and shook it in the lady's face and said, 'There you see, I don't have to steal from you,' and stormed out of the house."[104] This story of Zella challenging her white employer and quitting her job became legendary in the Kennedy home. "We were so proud of her," Flo explained, and of "the outrageousness of Zella slapping her unmentionables at the lady."[105] Flo drew lessons from her mother's insubordinate and nonconformist behavior and later melded these examples into her own pronounced rebellion against oppression.

While Flo told this story of her mother fighting back against being a domestic, she downplayed her own work in the same position. She described her regular employment as a maid only vaguely in *Color Me Flo* and rarely if ever in her later lectures or interviews.[106] When she did, it was to provide insights into the relationships she witnessed between white women and their families.[107] Her own experiences working as a domestic are left unanalyzed. In fact, to help her family make ends meet during the Depression, Flo began working at the age of sixteen and spent most of her adolescence and young adulthood cleaning white homes and businesses.[108] The Kennedy family had to accept public assistance during the Great Depression; although many other families were in the same predicament, that fact greatly embarrassed Flo's mother.[109] In her memoir Flo focused more on her mother's defiance, along with her own brief stints as an elevator operator and in the hat shop she opened with her sisters when she was twenty-six.[110] Perhaps her reluctance to acknowledge that she worked in positions that were regarded as subservient to whites evinces a degree of dissociation from the full truth of her upbringing. As her family struggled during the 1930s, her economic choices were limited. While Flo said little about her experiences as a domestic, her relative silence signals the stimulating effect it had on her ambitions. Her desire to escape the drudgery of domestic work, coupled with her mother's urging that she "become something," intensified her determination to escape poverty and the vulnerabilities it entailed. Only in passing did she mention that she and her sisters tried all types of jobs after high school "to get away from the house-work scene."[111]

Even when she had to work as a maid after school, Flo found moments of pleasure and joy in her adolescence. Flo said that her mother "never accepted poverty and yet didn't really resent it," and they "laughed a lot" despite being poor.[112] Like other black families, the Kennedys enjoyed socializing. "In the depths of the Depression," Flo wrote, the family "would give parties." Sixty or more young people crammed into their house to sip sweet, syrupy, carbonated soda water, dance to jazz records, and relax on an old sofa that was propped up with bricks.[113]

In the way she parented her daughters, Zella was unlike most other African American mothers of her era and class background.[114] Zella allowed the girls a great deal of freedom during their adolescence. Insisting that they not sneak off to drink or smoke with their friends, she allowed them to experiment at home. "You smoke right here. . . . This is your house, and anything you do you can do right here," she declared.[115] When the Kennedy girls entertained their friends at home, they did so with her approval. Eventually, when they left home to test the possibilities of the wider world, they departed with their mother's permission. Flo remembered Zella as a "very cool" and permissive parent who would "accept any version of what we did, of why we were out late," without judgment or punishment.[116]

Young Adulthood, Sexual Freedom, and Power

Zella's nonconformist views with regard to the upbringing of black girls extended to issues of sex and sexuality. She began these lessons long before Flo reached puberty. When Flo was very small, Zella respected and encouraged her sexual curiosity. One incident at church underscored her mother's unconventional approach to parenting. Never very religious herself, Zella did not force her daughters to go to church, but at times Flo chose to attend the African Methodist Episcopal church where her grandmother was a deaconess.[117] During one service, Flo became aware of women's bodies and their sexual potential. As she and her sisters moved around the pews, they would "smell the different seats to see what the women smelled like. . . . We thought that was funny as hell."[118] Zella was neither outraged nor embarrassed by her daughters' behavior; she laughed about their inquisitiveness and may well have created stories to help explain why women sometimes smelled of sweat or perfume. Flo remembered this light and entertaining discussion as one of the first conversations she had with her mother about sexuality. Zella was "never out-raged in a moral sense at anything I did," Flo affirmed. Indeed, as a child she told her mother "dirty jokes" and enjoyed making her giggle at her bawdy humor.[119]

Childhood jokes turned into adolescent explorations. As her daughters matured, Zella remained supportive of their sexual experimentation, allowing them to drive their father's taxi unsupervised to downtown dance parties and to carnivals sixty miles away in Topeka. The Kennedy daughters enjoyed dressing up, and Flo remembered how she and her sister Grayce were "show offs" and loved to have their hair neatly pressed and curled and their lips painted during these outings. Flo's mother's only rule was that the girls had to be honest and not hide their actions. Kennedy maintained that this trust allowed her to feel special and free as she developed into adolescence.[120] She never associated any stigma with her body, sexual curiosity, or expressions of desire. "I never remember punishment over sexuality,"[121] she said, and "since neither doing wrong nor admitting it ever brought punishment, it was not difficult for me to tend to try (a) not to do something wrong, and (b) not to deny it if I did."[122]

At a very early age Flo allowed boys to feel her breasts under her sweater, kept lists of the boys she kissed on her summer vacations, and compared information with her sisters about sex and, no doubt, about how to avoid pregnancy.[123] She recalled, "Hell, we'd be doing it with fellows on the front porch, but my mother completely absented herself."[124] Kennedy admitted that at the time she and her sisters "were regarded as pretty fast—we would go in the car with almost anybody."[125] Looking back, she joked that even her mother might have been surprised by the sheer number of boys she entertained and appreciated on the front porch. Without curfews or any rebuke from her mother, Flo tested the limits of black society's boundaries for women and rebuffed standards of respectability that dictated that black women appear chaste, virginal, or committed to one man. Black women were especially vulnerable to the assaults of white men. Hence, the standard of sexual morality expected of them was not just about repression of their sexuality but was also about protecting them from bodily harm. This concern affected black women of all classes.

Flo rejected societal dictates and savored her freedom. She remembered that she rarely had sexual intercourse with the young men; the point was to "kiss as much as you wanted but never put out." In short, she was on a "power trip"; after playing games with men, she denied her male suitors the prize they had been led to expect.[126] For Flo, the ultimate goal was to stay in control of the experience and not to let men take advantage of her sexually or emotionally. She recalled deciding that she was not "going to take shit from nobody."[127] By driving her father's car with two of her sisters in tow and conducting much of her sexual exploration in her own home, she exercised control over the terms of her initial sexual experiences. Flo enjoyed the feeling of sexual power she possessed through her own body. She looked back on a youth that was empowered by her ability not only to reject men but also to say yes to the men of her own choosing. This was not a power that most young women who lived at home were able to exercise.[128] Indeed, Kennedy's father did not approve of her conduct with young men. Once, when he found her on the front porch sitting on a young man's lap, he chastised her. Flo explained that although she was embarrassed to be reprimanded in front of her guest, she ignored her father and cared more about what her mother thought of her.[129]

Sexual freedom for women seldom went unpunished in the 1930s. Flo came of age during a time when birth control information and devices were becoming more available (though mostly to married women), but when those methods of protection failed, unmarried women were often left with the responsibility for the child.[130] While Flo was completely silent about any problems her family's sexual openness may have caused, the record suggests that her sister Evelyn became pregnant at the age of sixteen; Evelyn is listed in the 1930 census as a wet nurse.[131] To be designated as a wet nurse by the census taker, a woman had to have given birth and nursed another woman's child for pay. The record contains no information about what happened to the child Evelyn bore. Did the child die, or was he or she informally adopted within or outside the family? Interviews and archival research have revealed disconnected clues about the baby. We can only speculate about why a mother who seemed open to nonmarital sex kept Evelyn's child a secret. Perhaps a grandchild born outside of marriage tested the limits of her defiance.

"My First Real Political Action": The Missouri Protest

As Kennedy matured, she became involved in protests against racial segregation in Kansas City. In *Color Me Flo*, she provided very few details of this early activism and downplayed her activities in the NAACP. In the late 1930s, she participated in a boycott of the Coca-Cola Bottling Company for refusing to hire black truck drivers.[132] The historical record provides very few details about this campaign.[133] During this time she became friendly with the NAACP chapter president, Carl Johnson, a lawyer and longtime activist who impressed Flo with his intelligence and the respect he enjoyed within the African American community. She later admitted that she had a huge crush on him and "came close to having an affair with him."[134]

As Kennedy reflected on her early political life in her memoir, she paid attention to her youthful desires. Rather than rewrite her early twenties in order to demonstrate a nascent radical politics, she downplayed her early activism. She attempted to describe a youth like that of other young men and women her age whose ideas were still in flux and whose youthful desires for fun and adventure were central.[135] In her youth she was often more interested in what affected her personally, including chasing boys and having a good time, than she was in political protests.

We can, however, draw insight from her short time in the NAACP. The Kansas City branch was more than a site for her flirtation with a powerful man. Not only did it conduct what she described as "my first real political action,"[136] but it taught her how to participate in organizational meetings and handle publicity. She learned how useful boycotts could be in forcing businesses to concede to a group's demands and heard new ideas about how to conduct an organized protest. She also witnessed the influence and authority of attorneys for the first time. During this period she avidly read black newspapers, especially periodicals describing successful black social justice movements across the country.[137] By 1942 Kennedy was ready to put these lessons into practice in her own demonstration.

Flo and her sister Grayce staged a nonviolent protest against racial discrimination while traveling on a Santa Fe Company bus from Kansas City to Chicago.[138] They were likely emboldened by the formation of the Congress of Racial Equality (CORE), an interracial, nonviolent student group that had begun to hold sit-ins to protest racial discrimination in public accommodations in 1942.[139] That same year, when Flo and Grayce were at a rest stop in Monroe City, Missouri, they were informed that the bus stop café did not serve "coloreds." Amid a jeering and taunting crowd, the two young black women stood their ground and refused to leave their seats. The crowd pulled them from their stools and threw them out of the restaurant. Kennedy was yanked with such force that her spine was severely dislocated. Grayce struggled to move her sister out of the crowd's wrath, and eventually the two made it back to Kansas City. For weeks Flo remained in bed, "immobilized in a cast that [ran] underneath [her] arms down to [her] tail, with [her] . . . head twisted."[140] Unable to afford proper medical care, Kennedy suffered throughout her life from back pain that left her powerless to move her head quickly or fluidly in either direction. The young women's act of protest, unlike those conducted by CORE, was staged without the backing of an organization or any support.

By the age of twenty-six, Flo was not only committed to "never taking shit" but also was beginning to combine her family's lessons with her expanding knowledge of political organizing. Her action resembled that of the black feminist journalist Ida B. Wells, who had, decades earlier, refused to leave her seat in the ladies' car of a segregated train and join other black men and women in the baggage car.[141] By waging the sit-in in Monroe City, Flo joined with other African Americans who were fighting to desegregate public facilities in the South and the Midwest. The fight for equal access to public accommodations was always a fight for resources, because segregation itself was a tool of economic control and unjust resource distribution. The lunch counter protests were never just about sitting in a restaurant but also about gaining full citizenship and economic equity.[142] While Flo was severely injured during the demonstration, she was not discouraged from engaging in public protest. In fact, in less than a year she would continue her struggle against the bus company and coffee shop. But this time her battle would take place in the courts.

The seeds of Kennedy's political activism were planted in the home of Zella and Wiley Kennedy. The sexual freedom that Flo was allowed and her observations of her parents' battles with both white and black authorities later helped her to embrace a black feminist politics. She rejected the politics of respectability and other social constraints that inhibited black women's freedom, mobility, and political activism. Kennedy learned from both her parents that oppression came from many directions and could—indeed, must—be openly opposed. Since family is a central institution in which political ideologies are formed and reproduced,[143] it holds the key to explaining African American women's resistance. Flo Kennedy's radicalization began with her parents' examples and teachings, and the core of her story is a black woman's effort to shape her family's lessons into coherent political weapons.

2

Similarities of the Societal Position of Women and Negroes

EDUCATION AND PROTEST IN NEW YORK CITY, 1943–1948

By the summer of 1943, Florynce Kennedy had recovered enough from her back injury to take a vacation in New York City. Her sister Grayce had recently married and moved to Harlem to be closer to her husband, a soldier stationed in Virginia. As Zella had done on her trip to California almost two decades earlier, Flo originally planned only a brief stay. Once she began to explore the city, however, she did not want to leave. She was no doubt smitten with the bustle of Harlem, alive with newly arrived black women and men attracted by job opportunities that opened during the war.

New York's advantages over Kansas City quickly became visible to a young black woman seeking to escape the drudgery of low-paying domestic labor in Missouri and always ready for a new adventure. The demands of war production coupled with the military mobilization of men created a labor shortage that black women used to improve their position.[1] Kennedy remembered that New York had "good government jobs," and she soon discovered that the "schools were here" too.[2] The move to New York also offered her a chance to live out her mother's unfulfilled dreams to be fully free and single and to make something of herself in a big city. This connection was not lost on Zella's second-oldest daughter: Flo recalled that "Zella had one dream back in Kansas City, it was to come to New York." She lamented that "now we're all here, and she" had died having never escaped Missouri.[3]

Kennedy's determination to challenge discrimination deepened after she arrived in New York. During her first decade in the city, she attended the Columbia University Program of Undergraduate Studies and Columbia Law School. In this stimulating and diverse political and social milieu, she began to expand and sharpen her family's "take no shit" position. The combination of her formal education and her individual protests outside the classroom encouraged her development as a black feminist. Already concerned with challenging both racism and patriarchal expectations about her freedom of movement and sexual expression, she began in her late twenties and early thirties to critique capitalism, make direct connections between racism and sexism, and confront these interlocking systems of oppression.

Confronting a Harlem Landlord

World War II was a turning point for the civil rights movement in the North. Tens of thousands of blacks migrated to northern industrial cities. Most came from the lower and upper South, while a smaller number hailed from the Caribbean.[4] African Americans flooded these cities in search not only of jobs but also of greater opportunities to live lives less encumbered by racism. New York City's black population more than doubled between 1940 and 1950. While many of those who relocated to New York found wider opportunities in employment, electoral politics, and education, most soon realized that they were still subject to discrimination. In war-related industries, employers remained reluctant to hire black workers despite the acute labor shortage. But black men and women were steadfast in struggling for their rights, not only in the labor market but also in housing and law enforcement. The Great Migration that accelerated in the 1940s generated new opportunities and leverage for activism as African Americans went from being a mostly rural and agricultural population to a predominantly urban and industrial one.[5]

At this transformative moment, Flo followed her sister, a wartime bride, to the city, just as countless other black migrants moved with or joined loved ones. The choice to leave Kansas City was made easier because Kennedy was frustrated by the lack of employment opportunities in Missouri. Moving to New York enabled her to escape domestic and other service work and offered her the possibility of going to college.

In their first months in Harlem, Flo and Grayce rented a room in the Sugar Hill section of Harlem.[6] Black families populated Sugar Hill in the

1920s, years after the rest of Harlem had become solidly black. It flour-
ished during the 1930s and early 1940s and was the home of such prominent and accomplished African Americans as Langston Hughes, Adam
Clayton Powell Jr., and Walter White.[7] Grayce and Flo planned to find their
own apartment and continue living in the exclusive, middle-class black
enclave. Their new friends warned them that they would "not get an apartment because of the war" and encouraged the sisters to move out of Manhattan, perhaps to the Bronx. Flo ignored their counsel: "I am going to
look for an apartment where I want to live!" In the end, she exulted, "we
wound up in . . . Sugar Hill . . . the so-called better part of Harlem."[8]

Flo convinced a white landlord to rent her and Grayce a rundown apartment on St. Nicholas Place. He probably believed that he had outsmarted
these young, newly arrived black women by agreeing to rent to them but
with the catch that black tenants often faced: they would have to pay the
normal rent, but he would not have to fix any of the problems. Flo never
intended to live in inferior conditions, however. As soon as they moved in,
she threatened him with a lawsuit, claiming that the apartment violated
health standards. He was then forced to paint and restore the apartment
to a livable condition. Kennedy reveled in her victory over the landlord:
"Of course . . . he hated us and we got great glee out of that."[9]

Despite being a newcomer to Harlem with few connections, Kennedy
did not avoid conflict when it was necessary to accomplish what she
wanted. Indeed, she relished opportunities to outsmart anyone who attempted to swindle her or assign her to a lower position. In reflecting on
her protest, she reasoned that slumlords and whites generally expected
blacks and other oppressed people to set their standards extremely low
and settle for whatever was handed them. By threatening to sue the apartment owner, she joined scores of black tenants in rejecting discrimination in the housing market.[10] Black residents in Harlem and other areas
of New York typically occupied the worst apartments but paid the highest
rents. Over a decade before Kennedy moved to New York, a government
study found that, on average, blacks in Harlem paid $9.50 per room per
month while the typical white working-class family paid almost one-third
less.[11] Kennedy's confrontation with her landlord resembled the battles
her mother and father had waged against white employers and neighbors
two decades earlier. From Zella and Wiley she learned the importance of
challenging the power of authority. Her move to New York City opened up
the possibility of using the courts as an arena of protest.

Suing the Bus Company and Coffee Shop

Growing up in Kansas City, Kennedy had read about black activism in New York through the *Saturday Evening Post*.[12] She learned of Adam Clayton Powell Jr. and perhaps about his successful protests on behalf of black doctors who were banned from practicing medicine at Harlem Hospital because of their race. The year Kennedy moved to Harlem, he was the senior pastor of Abyssinian Baptist Church in Harlem and a newly elected member of the New York City Council. Kennedy was impressed by Powell's leadership and later recalled that he was "right down my protest alley."[13] She was especially interested in his talent for provoking and even enraging the white establishment.[14]

Like other blacks in New York and throughout the nation, Kennedy soon turned to him for advice and assistance.[15] The previous year's assault in Monroe City, Missouri—after she and Grayce had refused to leave a segregated coffee shop during a bus trip—had left her frustrated that the bus company and coffee shop got the best of her, and she wondered how to get back at them and gain justice. Kennedy resented the fact that white businesses could exclude and abuse people with impunity because they were "colored." The attack had left her debilitated, unable to work, without proper medical care—and angry.[16]

Once Kennedy moved out of Missouri, still sore and sour from her injured spine, she had resolved to seek justice. She brought the brutal racial assault to the attention of Powell's office, and with the help of the Abyssinian Church's main lawyer, Harrison Jackson, she sued the two businesses for damages. No doubt to her delight, the case was settled in her favor. Later, however, she lamented the fact that the final settlement of a few hundred dollars did not cover all her medical expenses or compensate for her lifelong pain and suffering from an injured back and "a neck that doesn't turn."[17] Nonetheless, she was beginning to see how the courts could be useful in helping to oppose discrimination. In her first three years in New York she had twice challenged racist discrimination through the legal system and won.

In waging the sit-in and suing the businesses that forcibly evicted her, Kennedy was similar to other African Americans who were fighting to desegregate public facilities in both the South and the Midwest. That campaign was always a struggle for resources, because segregation itself was a tool of economic control. Lunch counter demonstrations were never just about a seat but also about gaining full citizenship and economic equity.[18]

Moreover, these personal victories in court showed Kennedy the value of the legal system in helping to rectify injustice.

Schools and Jobs in New York City

In her first years in New York, Kennedy continued to learn about the courts as a tool for justice, retribution, and protest—but first she had to find a consistent way to support herself. She and Grayce were intent on finding "good government jobs."[19] Only a few months after she arrived she began working at the Veterans Benefits Administration as a researcher. By 1944, however, she was eager to spend more time behind a desk so that she could rest her injured back. After receiving good marks on the civil service exam, she was hired as a grade 2 clerk in the U.S. Treasury Division of Disbursements.[20] Had she arrived in New York a few years earlier, she would have found it difficult to secure a position in a government office. Before the war, black women were mostly confined to the lowest level of federal employment, often working as charwomen or laborers.[21] But government agencies reluctantly lowered some of the barriers against black people when wartime imperatives and black political pressure left them no choice.[22] In June 1941, threatened by plans for a massive march on Washington, President Franklin D. Roosevelt signed Executive Order 8802 banning racial discrimination in workplaces with government contracts. The federal government then took steps to desegregate the civil service. The biggest growth area for black employment was the federal government: the number of African Americans quintupled, rising from 60,000 to 300,000. The year Kennedy began working for the Treasury, approximately one-fifth of federal employees were black.[23]

As one African American woman recalled, "The war and defense work gave black people opportunities to work on jobs they never had before. . . . Their expectations changed."[24] The number of employed black women rose from 1.5 million to 2.1 million during the war. In that same time frame, the proportion of African Americans working in domestic service declined while the proportion in skilled and semiskilled occupations doubled. The manufacturing and clerical jobs that black women obtained were often those that remained unfilled after white women had taken the better-paid posts left vacant by men who were drafted into the military. By leaving the service sector, black women could earn much higher wages.[25] Kennedy took full advantage of these wartime opportunities and never again worked as a domestic.

The influx of men into the military also opened opportunities for women in higher education. As white men left colleges and universities for military service or war production jobs, women were recruited to take their place. The vast majority of those admitted were middle-class white women, but Kennedy, who had always aspired to go to college, found a way to squeeze through the door. In Kansas City, that ambition had seemed impossible: "There was only" Kansas University, "which at the time was completely white. . . . I always thought I might ultimately get to college somehow, but it was really kind of unheard of."[26] Both segregation and cost deterred her, but only temporarily. "I knew I hadn't the money to go to college, but I always said . . . to myself that if I ever had the money I would go."[27]

Since public education in Missouri was segregated and institutions designated for blacks were grossly underfunded, blacks from Kansas City had to attend Lincoln University, over two hours away in Jefferson, Missouri. In the 1930s, Missouri became a battleground in the NAACP's legal campaign against segregation in public higher education. The University of Missouri refused to accept blacks into its law school and other professional schools, which meant they were excluded rather than merely segregated. In 1938, the U.S. Supreme Court ruled that under *Plessy v. Ferguson* (1896), the public educational system had to provide equal curriculum and facilities to black students. Establishing separate institutions for them might have been legally acceptable, but Missouri's flat denial of professional education to its black citizens was a violation of the equal protection clause of the Fourteenth Amendment. The landmark case of *Missouri ex rel. Gaines v. Canada* (1938) forced the law school to accept blacks. In the NAACP lawyers' long-term perspective, the failure and, indeed, inability of segregated public educational systems to provide equal opportunities to blacks became the grounds for overturning *Plessy* by showing that separate schooling was by definition unequal, which they finally accomplished in *Brown v. Board of Education* in 1954.[28]

The University of Missouri refused to open its doors to black undergraduates until the 1950s, when the U.S. Supreme Court ordered them to admit blacks because Lincoln University did not offer the same curricular opportunities.[29] This legal victory came too late to benefit Kennedy and others of her generation, but she held on to her aspirations even though they seemed unattainable in her home state.

Once she arrived in New York, Kennedy made a plan to use the salary from her government job to pay for college.[30] During her first year in the city, while she prepared for the civil service exam, she applied to Columbia. Some of her friends warned her that she would not be accepted and should not even bother to apply but instead should set her sights on City College of New York, the public institution that was just a few blocks from her Harlem home. At the time CCNY was dubbed "Harvard-on-the-Hudson" because of its high academic standards, even though tuition was free.[31] In applying to Columbia, Kennedy was not just trying to make sure she received a good education; she was seeking entry into the most elite private institution in the city, the bastion of white male privilege. She recalled that her friends' low expectations stimulated rather than deterred her desire to apply, and she "had no trouble getting into Columbia." At age twenty-nine, Kennedy entered its freshman class.[32]

Columbia University Undergraduate

Kennedy enrolled in the Columbia University Program of Undergraduate Studies (later the School of General Studies) in June 1945, when the university had lost thousands of male students to World War II and in many of its schools women outnumbered or equaled men.[33] Colleges and universities like Columbia turned to women to fill the seats in their classrooms and pay the tuition they needed to survive.[34] The University Undergraduate Program (also called University Extension) was established in 1891, but before the war it had attracted fewer than 180 students, who ranged in age from eighteen to eighty and often held full-time jobs. These students desired Columbia University–caliber courses during their evening hours. Both non-matriculating and matriculating students attended the program designed for the "grown-up" student: some already held a bachelor's degree and were taking supplementary courses to hone their professional skills, others were interested in working toward a Columbia degree, and still others were simply taking courses for their own edification.[35] The program became coeducational in 1904 and graduated its first women in 1921.[36]

In the 1940s, women took full advantage of the wartime necessity that widened their access to the university. Columbia recruited and accepted thousands of tuition-paying women, many into its University Undergraduate Program.[37] Almost all of them were white; Kennedy remembered being the only black person in her courses.[38]

Columbia was notorious for discriminating against women, Jews, and African Americans, and the university was financially beyond the reach of working-class students. Indeed, Columbia College did not become coeducational until 1983. Until then undergraduate women were admitted to Barnard, a separate but coordinate institution. They could also attend other schools at the university, such as Teachers College, the School of Nursing, the School of Library Science, and the University Undergraduate Program.[39] Although Columbia never had an official policy of excluding black men, the university admitted its first black male student in 1906, decades later than most other Ivy League institutions, and black students remained few and far between.[40] Hence, the campus Kennedy entered in the summer of 1945 was in the midst of a potent, although not necessarily permanent, process of change.

During the war years, women educators sought to facilitate women's entry into professional and technical fields formerly held primarily by men and to promote their access to positions of power. Virginia Gildersleeve, the dean of Barnard, pushed for women to enter engineering, and Columbia's School of Engineering opened its doors to women. The historian Rosalind Rosenberg argues that Barnard had a stimulating effect on the environment at Columbia during the war, helping to increase the presence of women on campus and in positions previously closed to them.[41] The college newspaper paid close attention to discussions concerning women and women's roles in institutions of higher education and in society at large.[42] Although the small flood of women into Columbia did not generate a feminist campus environment, the position of white professional women was strengthened. In her first year, Kennedy had an opportunity to discuss gendered concerns in classes with white women.

American women were encouraged to see themselves as making a crucial contribution to the war effort as they took on jobs previously reserved for men. Married and older women joined or returned to the labor force. Women of all races found better work, and women of color moved up a rung on the job ladder. Professional women were especially astute about taking advantage of opportunities made possible by the war. For example, college-educated white women took the place of white men in banks, insurance agencies, civil service, education, and health care. Organizations such as the Association of American University Women and the National Federation of Business and Professional Women lobbied government agencies to open positions of authority to women.[43]

Making the most of this moment of opportunity, Kennedy registered as a pre-law student.[44] She later commented, "I guess it was unusual for a black woman at that time, but I didn't feel particularly black, and I'd always wanted to be a lawyer—not only to right wrongs, but because most of the people I knew who were lawyers were better off than others."[45] After successfully challenging racial discrimination through the courts, Kennedy could see that becoming a lawyer was a way to seek justice. The legal profession also represented a path to financial stability and success. In the 1940s, black professional women worked largely in nursing and education.[46] Kennedy knew that her occupational choices were limited, even with a college degree. She explained later that by becoming a lawyer she was not simply avoiding the careers conventionally pursued by educated women but also determinedly sidestepping what she saw as the vocation society promoted for all women: wife and mother.[47]

Two years before Kennedy moved to New York and one month before the United States entered World War II, her mother passed away at the age of fifty-three. During her final years, Zella struggled to care for her two youngest daughters, Joyce and Faye, while holding a job and battling breast cancer. Nearly fifteen years earlier, in 1925, Flo had watched Zella attempt to break away from her marriage in California only to have to return to Kansas City, raise two more children, and toil as a domestic. While Flo described Zella as a loving mother who adored her girls, she did not seek to emulate her mother's life. Flo was proudest of her mother when she got "away from Kansas City" and from the demands of marriage and enjoyed personal freedom as well as the attention of various boyfriends in Los Angeles.[48] Flo noted with irony that although Zella wanted to make something of herself in the big city, she never made it there.

Seeing her own mother briefly separated and living as a single woman no doubt affected Flo's ideas about marriage and motherhood. Zella provided Flo with an unconventional standard of black womanhood that Flo idealized as free, as well as a sad example of what happened if a woman relinquished her independence. In 1946, her sophomore year, Flo wrote her first public critique of the institution of marriage and romantic love.[49] She went on to describe a satirical piece she hoped to write and publish on the dangers of marriage. In the brief sketch, the bride-to-be "decides that she won't like doing dishes and ironing." On her wedding day she surprises everyone by saying, "But, mother[,] I changed my mind."[50] In Flo's happy ending, the young woman escapes the burdensome familial obligations and confinement being a wife entailed, which Flo viewed as a life of perpetual domestic servitude.

In reflecting on her childhood and young adulthood, Flo described how, as a young girl, she knew that she did not "want to be anyone's mother."[51] She saw becoming a lawyer as an escape from marriage and motherhood.

> All I had to do was to look at lawyers and then look at mothers to know which I would rather be. . . . And very early in the game I said if I did get married, I would have a cooky jar I wouldn't tell my husband about,

where I would save money, and I would have that money set aside very handy, close by, where I could get a divorce right away. I wasn't going to get caught in that trap. I never bought the okeydoke, and when you don't buy the okeydoke, then you are free to look around to see what you should do, because you've established what you don't want to do, understanding that that's a crock of shit. And from there on its [sic] very simple to realize that [if] you don't get caught in the trap you may not do al[l] that well, but at least you are free to make a change.[52]

Most of the women and men in Kennedy's classes laughed at her "crazy ideas" about marriage.[53] Unlike many of her fellow students, Kennedy viewed marriage as a trap that prevented women from being "free to look around" and discover their other aspirations. She was intent on not being carried away by the wartime propaganda that touted heterosexual romance, marriage, and motherhood as every woman's primary ambition. The postponement of marriage that had been necessitated by the Depression was abandoned as military mobilization encouraged couples to marry quickly, often shortly after meeting.[54] The rate of marriages dramatically increased at the outset of the war and skyrocketed in 1946 to 118.1 marriages per 1,000 unmarried females (over the age of fourteen), one of the highest rates of marriage in U.S. history.[55] Some college administrators feared that women students "might be swept off their feet by a uniform or the thought that their men may go overseas" and would drop out of college.[56] Barnard's Dean Gildersleeve encouraged women students who were married to soldiers not to leave college to join their husbands but rather to continue their education and prepare for careers. Another dean argued that the Columbia woman graduate was "strong enough to marry, and to work and have a baby all at once."[57] Promoting the wartime marriage boom was one of the ways the state attempted to reconcile support of conventional family norms with the necessity of women's employment.

Marriages between black men and black women also rose dramatically during the war.[58] Black newspapers and organizations encouraged black women to marry and stand beside their men, as well as hold jobs in war production.[59] Kennedy pushed back against the wartime pressure to marry and freely shared her philosophy with other students that marriage was a trap and motherhood was a burden.[60] Her nonnormative ideas went beyond university-sponsored discussions about delaying marriage until after graduation or staying in school while one's husband was away at war. Rather then shy away from their incredulous amusement, Flo seemed to revel in the attention she received and expressed her radical ideas whenever possible. "I think the folks in my writing class love me, but they (especially my friends) can't help laughing at my long, tumbling, 'wordy' sentences [and] . . . my crazy ideas. I don't believe in marriage, horizontal romance or religion, church, and/or the Bible; I love the hiccups, words and fighting," she mused to an attentive classroom audience.[61] Having fashioned herself as a bit of a comedian in all-black circles in Kansas City, through interactions with family and especially her mother, it seems that her classes in an all-white environment now gave her a new audience: white women. Kennedy used humor to convey radical ideas that would normally be rejected out of hand if they were presented solemnly. She was adept at making extreme statements that were humorous because they were exaggerated but cast a new light on social patterns and interactions that had been taken for granted.

At Columbia, Kennedy sharpened her humor into a weapon for challenging social conventions and oppressive relationships, in particular gender inequality. As she addressed her white female peers, humor became a fundamental part of her political arsenal, a skill that later distinguished her from other activists. It is possible that her wry wit was brought out even more severely because it was a useful tool for a black woman to wield in an all-white setting. Under the cover of comedy she could share her controversial opinions and avoid being seen as too black or too angry. She preferred to be seen as witty, sharp, and even outrageous.

Throughout college Kennedy celebrated the fact that her opinions had not changed: "I'm still contemptuous of marriage, the religions, the gods, and the churches, but am not surprised to find that some of the nicest people I know are up to their necks in the first and carefully sidestepping the others. Most of them seem quite happy in what I loftily regard [as] their abysmal ignorance."[62] Although Kennedy felt alone in her complete rejection of marriage and motherhood, she continued to criticize gender relations in a way that did not fit neatly with the ideas held by even her most career-oriented white counterparts.

Kennedy's critique of the institution of marriage was part of a long history of feminist objections to the subordination it entailed. At the turn of the century the "New Woman" ideal expressed a rejection of Victorian ideals of domesticity and respectability. Suffragists, bohemians, educators, and journalists, many of them living and working in New York City, advocated independent womanhood. The period around World War I ushered in what historian Christine Stansell has called sexual modernism, a period when women and men were far more open to conversations and experiences animated by not only love but also sexual curiosity.[63] In a society that condemned African American women as sexually available and failed to convict men who raped them,[64] black women who openly espoused beliefs and curiosities about sexual freedom faced special risks.

Despite the existence of milieus in which women and men questioned marriage and monogamy, most social institutions promoted the idea that women, including college-educated women, should marry.[65] It is important to note, however, that the first generations of college-educated white women who entered professions often remained single or lived in partnerships with other women (for example, as Jane Addams did, first with Ellen Gates Starr and then with Mary Rozet Smith). What shifted in the 1920s was the idea that educated women had to choose between marriage and career. Increasingly, educated women sought to combine child-care responsibilities with professional demands.[66] Many middle-class black women embraced a similar standard, seeing that marriage conferred respectability and helped in the racial uplift project.[67] But Kennedy found this standard limiting and saw most women as "abysmally ignorant" about the constraints they faced within marriage.

Kennedy's view that marriage and motherhood limited a woman's independence and ability to control her own life was perhaps colored by her experiences during the 1940s. As Zella slowly succumbed to breast cancer, her three older daughters had to take care of her, along with their father and their two younger sisters. After Zella died, Grayce and Flo moved to New York City, and the rest of the family soon followed. While Evelyn was mainly responsible for the day-to-day care of Joyce and Faye and their aging father, Flo and Grayce also served as surrogate mothers to their younger sisters and caregivers to their father. Flo recollected that after her mother's death, "we raised" Joyce and Faye while she paid the household bills and took charge of selling their Kansas City home.[68] Faye and Joyce both said, "Flo was both a mother and a sister."[69] Flo's critique of motherhood and marriage could have reflected the difficulties she experienced in trying to raise two children, manage a household, hold a job, and attend school full-time—all while attempting to live the life of a young, single black woman in New York. She learned with deafening clarity the limitations that motherhood placed on a woman's personal freedom. Although Flo was in the city living her own mother's unfulfilled dream, this dream was burdened by the full weight of her mother's children and aging husband.

During Kennedy's sophomore year, she expanded her ideas about gender and the possibilities for women outside of marriage and began to articulate clear connections between racism and sexism. Her mind was fixed on understanding the origins of racism and how racism was fomented by wealthy whites to prevent class-based alliances between white and black workers in both the North and the South, as well as on recognizing the ways in which racism and sexism similarly shaped the lives of African Americans and white women.

In an essay titled "Poisoned Soup," completed for Kennedy's professional writing course, she examined the origins of white supremacy and argued that theories of race were "poisoned by contemporary bigots, exploiters, and troublemakers." Flo demonstrated that slaveholders with the help of science "spread baseless rumors about the difference between white men and dark men" and justified enslaving Africans by classifying them as inferior mammies and buffoons. The "fantastic tales" and "thrilling myth of white superiority" worked to place and keep black people at the bottom of the social and political hierarchy. Moreover, she argued that these lies masterfully colluded to thwart any possibility of alliances "between migrant whites and migrant Negroes from the South." Like such black thinkers as W. E. B. Du Bois and Zora Neale Hurston, Kennedy poked holes in the fallacy of white superiority and pointed out that these falsehoods helped to undergird laws and practices that narrowed opportunities for black people.[70]

In her sociology class, Kennedy elaborated on the myths and the oppression shared by black people and white women and on the ways in which white male hegemony worked to consolidate its power around their mutual subjugation. As the war ended, women workers were quickly fired or demoted from their jobs to make room for returning soldiers.[71] Despite the gains they had made in the clerical and sales sectors, black women were routinely the first to be fired, and many had to return to domestic service and other low-paying, menial forms of employment.[72] At the same time that they saw their hard-won economic and political advances reversed, they increasingly encountered police violence. Black men and women did not sit still in the face of white attacks, and civil rights protests increased in New York and throughout the country.[73] Kennedy saw the radicalism of African Americans as a potentially valuable model that white women, who were also facing job losses and demotions, could emulate in challenging white male supremacy.

The GI Bill made it possible for veterans to go to college with government subsidies, and Columbia opened its doors to thousands of veterans returning from fighting or working for the government. In 1947, responding to the influx of students after the war, the University Undergraduate Program became the School of General Studies. As one faculty member acknowledged, a "college for adults . . . with classes at hours convenient to students otherwise employed . . . has existed in the university for the last quarter century. This year numbers over a 1000 students, many of them veterans."[74] The creation of the School of General Studies recognized and supported what was already in existence and helped to accommodate the scores of returning soldiers. As a result, by Kennedy's sophomore year and the war's end, veterans dominated the small program; the enrollment jumped to 1,179 students with male veterans representing close to 70 percent of the student body.[75] The entire university was experiencing a similar influx of veterans and the accompanying celebration of their presence on campus.

Kennedy wrote her paper "A Comparative Study: Accentuating the Similarities of the Societal Position of Women and Negroes" at a moment when classes once small in size and filled with white women were bursting with white men. Amid this dramatic change she reflected on the common social position of white women and black people vis-à-vis white male hegemony and privilege.[76] The essay displays a rising dissatisfaction with peacetime society's failure to deliver on what the wartime economy promised. Writing the essay allowed Kennedy to continue conversations she had had in class with white women peers about the similarities in their positions. Perhaps she hoped to garner support for fighting against oppression by linking two seemingly discrete groups, African Americans and white women.

Kennedy opened her essay by attempting to silence those critics who argued that there were no parallels between the oppression experienced by white women and that suffered by African American men and women. She agreed that African Americans were treated far worse than white women by the dominant white society, but she contended that similar strategies were used to keep both groups from gaining economic independence from white men. In particular, "women and Negroes are less apt to be hired and more apt to be fired." Although the government and businesses were willing to make exceptions during the wartime emergency, white women and African Americans generally "command lower wages and are usually confined to lower bracket positions." Both groups were continually barred from highly skilled occupations. Moreover, she maintained, even when the exceptional few were allowed into these specialized fields, they were banned from the key sites where the important decisions were made.[77]

This resentment was palpable at Columbia when male soldiers returned and filled the seats next to Kennedy and other women. The school newspapers reported male students' frustration with women occupying space once off limits to them in the cafeteria and the student lounges. One letter to the editor stated, "There is a persistent penetration of ladies. . . . I have always found it difficult to eat with ladies. . . . Furthermore, women have an annoying habit. Actually more than one. They are always putting on lipstick first on coffee cups and then on their lips. Not to mention the powder which gets into my soup. . . .We demand that the administration look into the matter. The Board of Trustees has no women—why must we students suffer?"[78]

As Kennedy reflected on the resentment expressed by white men who returned home and found their jobs and universities filled by women of different races and black men, she observed that powerful white men unfairly manipulated this moment to heighten hostility against black people and white women. In doing so, white employers and officials deflected attention and hostility from themselves onto less powerful groups. She also countered the myth that "women are getting all the best jobs" and that "Negroes are 'taking over' the theatre" when black people and white women made a few small advances. These "fatalistic" statements, she contended, failed to acknowledge the disparity of power between oppressed groups and white men and exaggerated the few "hard won" gains made by black people and white women in spite of severe repression. Kennedy asserted that the media, schools, churches, and courts all deserved part of the blame for treating black people and white women as children in need of the paternalistic help of white men and their institutions, thereby disempowering them.[79]

In conclusion, Kennedy maintained, "there has never been a question . . . whether the subordinate groups are capable of self rule and equal rights, but the real question is 'whether or not any group is worthy of the right to dominance and autocracy.'"[80] She called upon white women and African Americans to join together to disrupt "societal peace" and "revolutionize" the U.S. so that no group could exercise power over any other. Indeed, her call for a society free of both sexism *and* racism reflected the black feminist assertion that ending sexism and racism made society better not just for black women but for all people. Her paper revealed a nascent black feminist consciousness and her attempt to construct a politics that addressed the multiple dimensions of oppression.

"Got Fired from That Job": The U.S. Treasury Department

Through the Missouri sit-in, her early legal cases, and her papers and conversations in class, Kennedy was becoming adept at speaking out against injustice. Her protests and writings demonstrated her emerging critiques of the links between racism and sexism. By her junior year at Columbia, she had become aware of the class biases in U.S. government policies and practices. While working in the U.S. Treasury Department, Flo became increasingly vocal about the government's role in oppressing poor people.

During her second year at the Treasury Department, Kennedy wrote a letter to editors of several different periodicals who she hoped would consider publishing her writing on political topics. She boldly declared that "folks in Washington would rather kill people than feed them" and said that government programs privileged the wealthy while asking the poor and working class to tighten their belts. She suggested that, since working people produced all the wealth, they deserved higher wages and had a powerful weapon in the strike: "if the workers can paralyze the country, they ought to be pretty valuable."[81] Her ideas may have been influenced by the postwar strike wave that challenged businesses for not ensuring that wages kept pace with inflation. She worried that "any day now I'll probably be thrown out of [the] Treasury Department" for "my outburst to Washington." Indeed, she feared that her rebellious disagreements "will probably get me . . . indicted by the un-American activities committee."[82] Although she did not detail the specifics of her protests, her reference to the House Un-American Activities Committee (HUAC) suggests that she had discussed with other government employees her belief that the working class could bring the country to a halt by staging a general strike and her hope that African Americans and white women could join forces to revolutionize society.

HUAC was established in 1938 as a special investigating committee to research alleged disloyalty and subversive activities on the part of private citizens, public employees, and organizations suspected of having communist or fascist ties.[83] In the spring of 1947, President Harry Truman created the Federal Employees Loyalty Program, which set up review boards to investigate alleged disloyalty among government employees and recommend termination for those who were suspected of being "un-American."

In the second Red Scare, which began as World War II ended, disloyalty was rapidly becoming synonymous with free speech.[84] While there is no evidence that the review board investigated Kennedy, she came under increasing pressure to keep silent about her criticisms of the government if she hoped to keep her job. By the spring of 1947, Kennedy had concluded that she was a "rebellious government employee" and "not quite the civil service type" and that her days at the Treasury were numbered.[85] It seems that the government agreed with her, and by September 1947 she "got fired from that job."[86]

Released from the constraints of her federal employment, she began writing more directly about her criticisms of the government. As the Cold War between the United States and Eastern European countries and their former ally, the USSR, gathered force, she expressed support for the Soviet Union. In an autobiographical essay written in 1947, she pointed out that a "different form of government and economy, of which most of us know pitifully little, has become identified with witches, goblins, two-headed monsters, abstract evil and ghosties." Kennedy described being "ashamed and embarrassed by chortling headlines that gloat over Russia's defeat in four major showdowns."[87] In place of hostility toward the communist countries of Eastern Europe, she advocated peaceful negotiations between the United States and the Soviet Union in hopes of averting World War III. She was sure that that it would "be a lot easier for our government to get along with that of the Soviet Socialist Republics than for some nameless veteran to get along with an artificial leg."[88] She was critical of how much easier the U.S. government found it to foment hostility toward the USSR than to heal the wounds of the previous war.

During her senior year at Columbia, Kennedy found an opportunity to sharpen her critiques of the U.S. government and refine her thinking on communism in a sociology class with Bernhard Stern. Stern was the editor of the Marxist journal *Science and Society* and had edited numerous books decrying the oppression of African Americans and expressing sympathy with the Soviet Union.[89] Having been denied tenure at the City College of New York because of a lecture he had sponsored celebrating the social and economic achievements of the Soviet Union, he taught briefly at a few other colleges before becoming an instructor at Columbia in the early 1930s. The FBI, which began following his activities as early as 1930, noted that he edited many communist publications and participated in protests with communist and liberal human rights groups.[90] Kennedy described Stern as a "first-rate" teacher whose class was a "real turning point" in her thinking. She considered the possibility that a communist society, in which no one was exploited for the sake of profits, offered a viable alternative to a capitalist society that was based on racial oppression.[91] For Kennedy, the Communist Party offered the potential for blacks and other oppressed people to challenge American hegemony and racism in the Cold War era.

In her memoir, Kennedy recalled that she was not impressed by most of her instructors. "Dividing teachers into finks and good people," she tried to take classes with those she saw as interested in challenging oppression, particularly racial oppression.[92] Stern was that kind of professor. Scholar David Price describes how activist intellectuals such as Stern and Columbia anthropology professor Franz Boas were persecuted during the Red Scares of the late 1940s and early 1950s. According to Price, what attracted the most intense scrutiny from the FBI and congressional committees was not their Communist Party membership or their Marxist theories but their social activism, particularly their efforts to secure racial justice.[93] Kennedy never said whether she joined any communist groups or attended their meetings in the 1940s. Many leftists did not readily answer questions about whether they were or had ever been members of the Communist Party. Even Stern, who was openly communist, took the Fifth when interrogated by HUAC in order to avoid being asked to give the names of others who were in the party and was cited for contempt for not complying.[94] The only evidence we have that Kennedy may have joined a group affiliated with the Communist Party is from the FBI's investigation of her activities. In 1945, the FBI listed her as a member of the Freedom Road Club of the Manhattan New York City District of the Communist Party, and it is highly likely that she attended meetings or activities it held.[95]

She had little time, however, to participate consistently in any political group. In 1947 she lamented, "I am not active in any organized effort to modify the various institutions of which I disapprove," a situation that was due "in part . . . to the fact that I work eight hours a day and take twelve points of work in school." She mused that she was also temperamentally unsuited to joining a group: "I suspect . . . that I am too erratic to lead and too undisciplined to follow."[96]

By 1948, Kennedy was working at the Columbia Library, although she also received New York State rehabilitation benefits for her injured back. Still aspiring to become a lawyer, she applied to a Columbia program that allowed pre-law students to attend Columbia Law School during their senior year.[97]

3

All Men and Flo

STRUGGLING TO SURVIVE AS
AN ATTORNEY, 1948–1960

Florynce Kennedy received a letter from Columbia Law School in the spring of 1948, describing how her application had been rejected. Having earned excellent grades as an undergraduate, she was surprised by the law school's refusal to offer her admission. Determined to find out the reason for this decision, she requested a meeting with the dean; the assistant dean, Professor Willis Reese, agreed to meet with her.[1] Strategizing carefully, Kennedy planned the appropriate uniform, suitable comportment, and effective arguments she would use to gain the law school's attention. She decided against subtlety and humility; instead, she entered the room boldly, "cocky," and brazenly, wearing a "Henry Wallace for President" button on her lapel. She understood that announcing her support for Wallace was tantamount "to saying I am communist" at a moment of anticommunist hostility.[2] She described her exaggerated self-confidence and the proclamation of her radical political views as a tactic to make the dean feel nervous, as if she had a legion of other radicals behind her. In 1947, Henry Wallace, who had been Franklin Delano Roosevelt's vice president, had run for president as the candidate of the newly formed Progressive Party. Wallace was highly respected by many in the black community because he advocated equal voting rights, supported African American candidates on the Progressive Party ticket, and defied segregation laws while campaigning in the South, in spite of harassment by white supremacists. He also consistently spoke out against fighting fascism abroad while segregation loomed large at home. The media and the state represented the Progressive Party as pro-communist and therefore un-American.[3] Flo hoped that her association with Wallace and the Progressive Party would prove to be an effective weapon against Columbia's discriminatory policies.

During their meeting, Kennedy accused the university of discriminating against qualified black women and men in favor of white male applicants. She described the merits of her application, asked how a Columbia College student with an excellent GPA could be overlooked, and contended that it must be because "I was a negro."[4] Kennedy remembered Reese's attempt to reassure her by explaining that "they had rejected me because of my sex and not because of my race."[5] This did nothing to pacify her. As soon as Kennedy left his office she wrote him a letter declaring that the university's rationale did not matter and asserting, "If you have admitted any white man with lower grades than mine then I want to get in too."[6] Reminding the assistant dean that other radicals stood behind her, she claimed, "Some of my cynical friends believe I'm being discriminated against because of my race. You say I can't go to Columbia because I am a woman. Either way it feels the same"; it was *all* discrimination.[7]

The administration no doubt understood her as making a specifically legal threat. Shortly after this meeting and letter, Kennedy received notice that the law school had reevaluated its decision and accepted her into the first-year class. Flo was no doubt thrilled. Once again, her legal threats against racism—and, now racism and sexism—were successful. Kennedy's victory became another example of how "not taking shit," her parents' mantra, yielded rewards.

As a black woman, Kennedy did not fit neatly within a legal system in which the most visible architects of the courts' civil and criminal process, doctrines, and unspoken codes were white men. With very little guidance on how to survive in a profession unaccustomed to black women in any role other than defendants,[8] she had to make her own way. Now in her thirties, Kennedy created her own road map for becoming a lawyer, surviving as a working attorney, and gaining financial stability.

"Justice Was Really a Crock of Shit": Law School and a Legal Education

Kennedy, like many other black women and men of her generation who became lawyers, hoped to use the tools of the profession to challenge racial inequality.[9] "I went to law school thinking I would go to the courts and I would defend [black] people," she explained; "I would get justice for them."[10] She also hoped that becoming an attorney would enable her to become someone. Neither leap could be made in a single bound.

The absence of men during World War II forced Columbia and other universities to undertake a pivotal, albeit temporary, change in admission policies for many of their professional schools and some of their under-graduate colleges. Although, after much debate and protest, Columbia Law School had finally opened its doors to women in 1927, very few women had entered or graduated from the law school in the years before the war.[11] During the war, however, the law school began to recruit women in hopes that they would help keep the institution afloat at a time when many law schools were forced to close their doors or offer only night courses.[12]

Other black women took advantage of the wartime opening for women at Columbia. Constance Baker (later Motley) entered the law school in 1944, two years before Kennedy joined the undergraduate college.[13] Even though they were in different schools at the university, Baker and Kennedy had similar experiences at Columbia, finding themselves the only black women in small classes with a sizable number of mostly white women stu-dents.[14] While men had made up more than 90 percent of law students in the years before the war, women were more than 40 percent of the much smaller student body during the war.[15]

This temporary but significant transformation in the law school came to a complete standstill at the war's end. The GI Bill gave veterans an op-portunity to gain higher degrees by offering them tuition subsidies and living allowances for themselves and their dependents. In the spring of 1947, the *Columbia News* celebrated the fact that the university was filled past capacity and "the student body is now veteran-dominated, 92.83 per-cent of the 795 male students."[16] The entire country was going through a similar reconversion; women were being compelled to leave their govern-ment and defense-related jobs to make room for returning male veterans.[17]

By 1948, Columbia Law School was flooded with male applicants. While several women were accepted into the law school after the war, their numbers decreased dramatically.[18] Kennedy was attempting to be-come an attorney at the very moment when the school was filling past capacity with white men. She hoped to participate in the wartime Option Plan that allowed Columbia pre-law juniors to accelerate their education during the war by using their senior year as their first year in law school.[19] The law school also had an admissions policy that privileged Columbia undergraduates.[20] With this knowledge in mind, Kennedy reasoned that her rejection was not a reflection of her aptitude and certainly was not in keeping with Columbia's prior record. Years later she would argue that her rejection was clear "evidence of racism and sexism."[21] A review of the surviving registrar's information in regard to students entering during the immediate postwar years demonstrates that several Columbia white male students with considerably lower grade averages than Kennedy's were accepted.[22] She was correct to assume that being a woman impeded her admission, even though she refused to accept the assistant dean's explanation that her sex was the sole cause of her rejection and that racial discrimination was not involved.

Kennedy recalled that as a college student, she had heard that "black people were beginning to sue the graduate and professional schools for their racist admission policies," and she realized that "Columbia didn't want to be mixed up in *that kind* of publicity."[23] She attempted to exploit the postwar upsurge in civil rights activism by arguing that the law school was racially prejudiced in denying her admission.

The NAACP, one of several organizations active in the battle to end racial segregation, continued to challenge segregated state law schools in the postwar period. In 1948, the winter of Kennedy's sophomore year, the national and local press detailed the NAACP's Supreme Court victory in the case of *Ada Lois Sipuel v. Board of Regents of the University of Oklahoma*. Sipuel, an honor student, was denied admission to her home state's law school "because of her race."[24] While Kennedy's recollections never directly mention Sipuel, the landmark decision was no doubt a prominent example when she threatened to sue Columbia for racial discrimination. Although Kennedy was not affiliated with the NAACP or its Legal and Education Defense Fund, she built on its victories in challenging Columbia's postwar practice of privileging underqualified white men and excluding well-qualified black women. By the mid-1940s she was becoming adept at utilizing the tactics of civil rights groups in her own battles against discrimination. Here, as in her sit-in to protest segregated lunch counters a few years earlier, she showed her willingness to employ movement strategies without organizational support—although in this instance she attempted to project the idea that she had many supporters.

Kennedy had demonstrated her understanding of discrimination against women of all races and African Americans in the essay she had written the previous year, "A Comparative Study: Accentuating the Similarities of the Societal Position of Women and Negroes," in which she showed that "both groups are barred from many specialized fields" and criticized the ways in which "the withholding of training and education preclude[s] development of potentialities."[25] She also argued that "exclusion from intimate situations where powerful combines are made places a definite barrier in their path" to success.[26] White women and black women and men were not invited to informal occasions at which their white male colleagues socialized, exchanged vital information, and forged alliances. By challenging her rejection, she defied the university's unwritten postwar policy that denied black women entry and sought access to the training ground of the legal elite. By underscoring the parallels between the university's sexism *and* its racism, Kennedy contended that her race could not be separated from her gender and pushed back against postwar discourses and policies that championed a return to an idealized construction of the woman as homemaker who did not occupy male-defined public spaces.[27]

Many women who attended law school during this period experienced a discouraging mixture of hostility and indifference from administrators, professors, and male students.[28] Kennedy was one of ten women who entered Columbia Law School in 1948; the other 195 first-year students were men.[29] The university had not made many allowances for women students, and as a result their bathrooms were located across the campus at Barnard, the women's college, and many of the legal fraternities remained closed to women during Kennedy's law school years.[30] Flo and other women remembered how most professors continued to equate litigators with men and addressed all students as "gentlemen" when calling the class roll. At times, Kennedy recalled, "women were openly ridiculed" and "jokes were directed at them."[31]

Kennedy quickly discovered that presenting her ideas forcefully was not tolerated at the law school, as it had been at the college. Once, in a conversation with other students, Kennedy "accused a professor of being . . . prejudiced,"[32] arguing that he "made a point of not being able to pronounce the plaintiffs['] names if they were foreigners."[33] "He refused to pronounce an Eastern European name," saying that enunciating such surnames was impossible. "I knew that was bullshit. . . . A law professor to[o] dumb and chauvinist to pronounce a long but fairly simple Russian . . . name had no damn business on the faculty. . . . I said as much to a bunch of fellow students and damn near got lynched."[34] No longer in small classes with women students and teachers who prized her wit and strong opinions, Kennedy struggled to succeed academically while continuing to voice her views.[35] Her dismal law school record confirms that she found it difficult to make sense of the new curriculum and rules and that her ideas were not readily embraced. The onetime A student "sank to the bottom of her class," often receiving mediocre or poor grades.[36]

Kennedy's frustration with law school was amplified when she came to the painful conclusion that the law as an institution was culpable for creating and maintaining oppression: "As I went through law school I even saw that the Supreme Court had a doctrine of separate but equal. And I saw that the Supreme Court had really justified slavery. It had justified all the wrong things."[37] Until then, Kennedy had not fully realized just how much the courts supported state-sanctioned racism. Her experience at Columbia laid the groundwork for her growing disillusionment with the legal system.[38]

Kennedy's surviving papers and exams demonstrate a skeptical attitude toward the law's self-proclaimed commitment to objectivity and fairness.[39] Very few of her professors engaged her mind or took an interest in her; the sole exception was Walter Gellhorn, a longtime defender of civil rights.[40] Most of her surviving exams suggest a student who was alternately bored and trying very hard to succeed. With a less receptive audience for her unconventional ideas, Kennedy no longer critiqued the limits of marriage or the failures of the state. Instead, her exams display her attempts to learn the vocabulary of the profession while seeking recognition from her professors. In essay examinations, she repeatedly apologized to her instructors for her "naiveté" and the "enormity of [her] ignorance" and praised their writings and the readings they assigned as "unpretentiously magnificent" and "brash brilliant."[41] However, Kennedy's growing cynicism about the law is evident in a paper titled "On the Good, the True, the Beautiful, in Law, i.e. Cardozo," for her third-year law and society course, taught by the renowned Karl Llewellyn. Llewellyn, author of the popular *Bramble Bush*, a collection of his lectures given to first-year Columbia law students, was known for his energetic and engaging classroom discussions that mixed sociology and anthropology. An early theorist of "realistic jurisprudence" or "legal realism," he anticipated the move toward interdisciplinary courses and the breaking down of rigid boundaries between fields.[42] His new course was designed to help the advanced law student to understand the law in its everyday application. The course was especially focused on debating "the function of a lawyer in handling current problems" in society.[43] The class also devoted a good deal of time to open discussion and debate. This organization and content allowed Kennedy to share more of her opinions, which revealed her deep frustration with the legal philosophy she was imbibing at Columbia.

In her paper critiquing the collection of Justice Benjamin Cardozo's lectures delivered at Yale Law School titled *The Nature of the Judicial Process*, Kennedy affirmed that she had always wanted to be a lawyer but acknowledged that her life experiences had not prepared her for Cardozo's,

Llewellyn's, and other jurists' understanding of legal impartiality.[44] With her sarcasm held barely in check, she wrote, "My legal education began (of course) many, many years before I had the foggiest notion what a law school was. . . . My prelaw school legal education perhaps accounts for my appalling lack of success in accepting, embracing, utilizing or even recognizing such valuable legal techniques as how to walk past a pool of blood and say, 'what a beautiful shade of red.'"[45] Kennedy used the metaphor of a pool of blood to exemplify the ways lawyers ignored the violence that accompanied and, indeed, constituted oppression and coercion in the name of legal reasoning and then celebrated their stance as objectivity. Years later, she described herself as not having the type of "legal mind" that did well in law school: "They want an almost mathematical mind, the kind of person who can walk past a pool of blood and think, 'what a beautiful shade of red'—they call it 'objectivity.' They want to divorce you from your nigger state, to de-niggerize you, but they think being de-niggerized means living in your head and not in your heart or your soul or your body."[46] Flo remembered having a difficult time in law school because she could not separate herself from the visceral knowledge and emotions associated with people's experience of trauma and violence. As a result, she said, "law school made me see clearly for the first time how the law was used to maintain the bullshit rather than to change things, that justice was really a crock of shit."[47]

Having entered law school after succeeding with her prior legal threats and actions and effectively threatening legal action against Columbia, Kennedy had learned that the law could be used as a tool to confront injustice, especially racist and sexist discrimination. Kennedy had hoped to study civil rights law, but the newly emerging field was primarily developing at Howard University and through the NAACP's Legal and Education Defense Fund. The NAACP's cases were not a part of Columbia's curriculum in the late 1940s and early 1950s.[48] Like Constance Baker Motley, Kennedy had to look outside Columbia, which did not offer courses on challenging racial segregation.[49]

Despite her frustration with Columbia's approach to law, Kennedy attempted to make inroads into the places "where powerful combines" were formed.[50] Once Kennedy received New York State rehabilitation benefits for her injured back, she did not have to work full time while attending school. These benefits, along with her earnings from intermittent, part-time sales clerk jobs and student employment at the law school library, allowed her to pay her rent and tuition and to keep her family afloat.[51] At the age of thirty-four, with a few free hours in her packed schedule, Flo joined campus student groups for the first time. She attended meetings of the mostly white male Young Democrats and the Legal Survey group.

In her third year, Kennedy joined the Women's Law Society, which was formed in 1950 to serve the approximately thirty women who attended the law school. Their main objective was to "integrate themselves in a predominantly masculine school and profession, while avoiding any differentiation of women students from other students."[52] They hoped to secure a promise from the dean to hire a woman who would work in the placement office and help "toward attaining one of the Society's important goals, that of securing good jobs for qualified women lawyers."[53] At that time, the placement office did not send women on interviews and women lawyers suffered from a lack of practical experience. Kennedy was soon elected treasurer and helped plan weekly luncheons with prominent judges and lawyers to discuss "opportunities open in various fields of law to women graduates."[54]

There is no record of Kennedy joining civil rights organizations in her Harlem neighborhood during this time. Two factors may have inhibited her activism. First, the Left in New York City was being aggressively attacked after the war and black radicals were especially vulnerable to postwar repression.[55] Second, Flo's determination to achieve a degree of success and security always drove her choices. Despite her heated disputes with other students and her alienation from the curriculum, she was deeply attuned to the necessity of making connections if she hoped to eventually work and survive as an attorney. Like other women left out of the "fraternities of lawyers," she made professional relationships where and when she could. Kennedy spent much of her free time in the student lounge talking with other students and catching up on legal debates in a social setting and was most alive in arguments with interlocutors who, whether they agreed with her or not, also cared about the issues under consideration.[56] Toward the end of her time at Columbia Law School she also hosted parties at her Harlem home for her classmates. Settings with fewer rules and less formality played to Kennedy's strength in entertaining as she educated and made personal and intellectual connections while discussing issues. As one classmate of Kennedy's later explained, "Your career was determined by who you knew."[57] Flo was attempting to chart a career path as a black woman in a white male–dominated profession whose customs and rules she was just learning. As she wrote in one of her exams, in the legal world, "these people seem to know each other so well!"[58]

In the 1950s, rising to the top of her class would not win Kennedy an associate's position at a prominent New York City law firm. Women of any race and black men were not typically hired at the top firms, nor did they receive the prized state and local clerkships. As a result, they were ineligible for membership in the major bar associations, which reinforced their exclusion from privileged legal networks.[59] Although Kennedy's graduation from law school was a necessary step toward the fulfillment of her childhood dream of becoming an attorney, she was mindful that a law degree and passing the bar did not guarantee a black woman work as a lawyer. Her June 7, 1951, commencement ceremony and passing the New York State bar a year later were bittersweet accomplishments.[60]

Working in the Law

In 1951, Columbia Law School's placement office boasted that its graduates received jobs at prestigious law firms and clerked for prominent judges.[61] Kennedy's experiences at Columbia, however, made her well aware that those firms and judges "did not even bother to interview women."[62] Consequently, she "didn't even try for the big law firms."[63] Her attempts to gain employment at New York's Legal Aid Society, which regularly hired recent graduates who had passed the bar exam, were thwarted as well. "I begged to work for them but was repeatedly turned" down, she recalled.[64] Major New York firms hired few women of any race or African Americans, and when they did, these attorneys were restricted to specific areas of practice.[65] Scholar Karen Berger Morello demonstrates that "since the nineteenth century, women have been trying to break down the barriers at these large corporate law firms, but except in the limited areas of trust and estates . . . they have met with little success."[66] Trust and estate work involved little interaction inside the courtroom, so some firms felt comfortable allowing women access to these narrow areas of the law. By 1940 there were only 57 black women lawyers in the entire United States, and the picture for black women wanting to enter the profession was bleak. The situation had not changed much by 1950, when of the 6,271 women lawyers in the country, only 83 were African American.[67] A few worked with their husbands or fathers, while others had to take jobs as clerical workers in larger firms. The rare exceptions in New York were Jane Bolin, who rose to the rank of judge, and Constance Baker Motley, who was practicing on behalf of the NAACP during the 1950s.[68]

Kennedy's aspirations to become somebody and to attain financial security were still far out of reach. Years later she detailed the racism and sexism she faced upon graduation: "I mean, those guys discriminate against just about everyone—everyone but white Anglo-Saxon Protestants, that is. They don't want to know . . . Jews, Puerto Ricans, black people and females. I couldn't see what they wanted with me since I was two of those."[69] Many of these firms rationalized excluding black lawyers by placing the blame on clients, who, they contended, refused to deal with anyone who was not white. Left out of the training that was acquired primarily on the job, black lawyers had limited opportunities for professional development. Black women lawyers had even fewer options.[70]

Consequently, Kennedy accepted a job as a clerical worker at a small law firm, assisting the bookkeeper at Hartman, Sheridan and Tekulsky in midtown Manhattan. "I did shit work," she recalled. "I ran errands. I got people sandwiches, researched their dumb little cases."[71] For three years she worked at chores usually assigned to a bookkeeper or a law student. In between her assigned tasks, Kennedy gained legal knowledge and experience whenever she could by performing routine legal services for the firm's attorneys. Some associates, Kennedy stated, "encouraged me to see myself as a potential lawyer."[72] Nonetheless, her job offered her little opportunity to gain knowledge and experience in the field.

The firm Hartman, Sheridan and Tekulsky was open to hiring women lawyers, and around the time of Kennedy's employment a few white women were associates there.[73] Their personal accounts demonstrate, however, that in practice white women were also relegated to running errands and making coffee. A decade earlier, Blanche Goldman Etra, a Columbia Law School alumna, left Hartman, Sheridan and Tekulsky and joined her husband and brother-in-law's firm after she became "tired of being sent out for coffee."[74] Both black and white women were frequently reduced to gendered domestic roles that discounted their legal training and intellect, but having black women deliver coffee and serve lunches reinscribed their raced and gendered roles as servants. Moreover, Kennedy was formally assigned to a subordinate position and remained there, no doubt receiving a much lower salary than the white female associates. Etra came from a wealthy family and eventually married a lawyer and left Hartman to practice with her husband. Without the familial connections and financial security that Etra enjoyed, Kennedy had to plan her next move very carefully.

With a Columbia law degree and her "take no shit" ingenuity, Kennedy fashioned an "old white boy" network of her own. Law firms and law schools frequently hosted parties and smokers for clients. Kennedy was generally excluded from, or on the margins of, those held by Columbia and by Hartman, Sheridan and Tekulsky, but she quickly recognized the importance of creating networks of association and influence. During law school and her years as a clerical worker, her two-bedroom Harlem apartment became the site for her alternative path to professional development. Columbia Law School student Bernard Stollman, who frequented her smokers, said that Kennedy's events attracted "literally a hundred law students" and described the apartment as filled with "all men and Flo."[75] Her younger sisters were often the only other women present; most guests were white male aspiring lawyers from Columbia who would catch cabs or take the train uptown to her soirees.[76] During these gatherings she met future attorneys, debated the law, and, more important, ensured that her name was not far from their minds when they arrived at their prestigious firms or clerkships. "It was really brilliant," Stollman recalled; "it was how I met her and knew who she was." Some of her guests assumed that she was an associate at Hartman; they did not know that Kennedy was merely a clerical worker.[77] Undaunted by her marginality in the profession, Kennedy positioned herself as an attorney and Ivy League alum in anticipation of founding her own firm.

In the winter of 1954, Kennedy opened a private practice with an office on Madison Avenue only a few blocks from her old firm. She was one of only nineteen black women lawyers in the state of New York and the only black woman with her own law office in midtown Manhattan.[78] As was often the case for new law firms, business was sluggish, and Kennedy frequently had to work part-time as a sales clerk to help pay the rent.[79] To make up for her lack of legal experience, Flo, like other new attorneys, accepted a few pro bono criminal cases and eventually carved out a practice handling civil matters, especially matrimonial and estate cases. Unable to afford any clerical assistance, she wrote her own briefs, typed her own letters, and answered her own phone. Kennedy's clients came from all five boroughs, and she traveled throughout the city to represent them in court. The work of building a firm was tedious, and often her clients did not pay her on time—or at all.

Kennedy's demanding schedule was only compounded by an ongoing illness. Flo first experienced severe abdominal pain growing up in Kansas City. While in law school, she sought out financial assistance and time off from Columbia to see a doctor but was rebuffed. Her inability to obtain proper medical care meant that her illness went undiagnosed and untreated for years. Whenever the pain subsided, she would convince herself that she was getting better and blithely labeled her vomiting, nausea, and diarrhea "the mollygrabbles"—a pretend name a parent might jokingly call a child's illness to coax her out of a complaining mood.[80] But Kennedy's illness was far more serious than this name suggests. When

Flo was finally hospitalized in 1956, she was terribly ill with diverticulitis, an acute bacterial infection of the digestive tract in which pockets of the colon and intestine become infected. Her sister Joyce recalled that "the doctors were preparing us" for the end as Kennedy's colon and intestines had gangrened and "Flo was dying."[81]

After surgery that removed the damaged portions of her intestines, Kennedy's recovery was slow. Dozens of her friends, including former Columbia classmate Leonard Cohen, raised money to pay her firm's rent and her hospital bills, while her sisters provided her daily care and slowly nursed her back to health. Joyce and Faye recalled that the doctors "had pretty much given up" and were convinced "that she would not make it," although Kennedy claimed that she did not know about her poor prognosis at the time.[82] Not long after this severe illness and gradual recovery, Flo was described by family as joking about her impending death and humorously labeling herself as a "cripple" with "three feet of intestines" missing and a fused spine.[83] Now forty years old, Flo was nearing the age at which her mother had died of cancer, and this no doubt made her especially conscious of her own mortality. Kennedy's illness and spine injury became a fixture in her conversations and her humor as she continued to use comedy as a shield to distract others from her differences and ongoing health struggles.

Wilkes, Kennedy and Fields: Law Partners

Over the next year, Kennedy acquired a slow but steady flow of clients and returned to the onerous process of building her firm, one case at a time.[84] By 1957 she had expanded her firm to include Donald E. Wilkes, a white lawyer from Florida five years her junior who had previously worked as an associate for the major New York firm of Phillips, Nizer, Benjamin and Krim and had clerked for a judge on the U.S. Court of Appeals.[85] Phillips specialized in entertainment law during this period and represented high-profile clients such as the surrealist painter Salvador Dali and the stage and screen performer Mae West.[86] Wilkes probably joined Kennedy because he had not been promoted to partner after several years at his firm and because her prime location offered him an opportunity he could not find elsewhere.

They renamed the firm Wilkes and Kennedy. It was customary, then and now, for a firm to be named after its founders. Listing Wilkes's name first, reversing alphabetical order, was probably intended to attract a broader clientele. Kennedy was aware of the business side of being an attorney. Her choice of a white male partner and her agreement to list his name first demonstrated her desire to enlarge her power and influence in the profession.

By the late 1950s Kennedy's friends were mostly lawyers but also included a growing circle of entertainers, artists, and writers. Theodore Kupferman, Maely Dufty, and Dufty's husband, William Dufty, were frequent guests at her midtown parties. Kennedy's soirees were her route into an interracial world of progressives and creative thinkers. Maely Dufty, a Jewish émigré from Germany, was known in Harlem as a fighter for justice, a lover of jazz, and a writer for the *New York Citizen-Call*. She often supported musicians, in part by finding them legal assistance to fight narcotics charges.[87] After work, Kennedy spent some evenings listening to music at Birdland with Don Wilkes, Wilkes's wife, and the Duftys.[88] When they were in high school, Flo and her sisters could not afford tickets to the popular nightclubs at Eighteenth and Vine in Kansas City, so they would peer through the windows while listening to the bebop bands.[89] Her love of music and amusement led her to New York City's nightclub scene, but now she could afford the cost of entry. Kennedy may well have become more closely affiliated with the entertainment industry through Wilkes's legal connections. Typically, Kennedy was the only black woman in both her professional and social circles; as her sister Faye later recalled, at that time "Flo's friends were all white."[90] She continued to throw parties and smokers for her friends and colleagues, but now they were held at her midtown office.[91]

The firm continued to expand and attracted additional attorneys. David Fields, a graduate of New York University Law School who had spent a few years in private practice in Union Square, joined as a partner, and the firm was renamed Wilkes, Kennedy and Fields.[92] Bernard Stollman, who attended Kennedy's parties as a student, spent several months at the firm as an unpaid assistant. Upon returning from two years in the military, "I found that she was practicing law in midtown Manhattan, [so] I approached her directly and offered my services."[93] The firm's "professional office space" and "diverse clients attracted" him immediately. For several months he worked under Kennedy's direction, mostly on cases involving jazz musicians.[94]

Kennedy's Unconventional Marriage

During this period, Kennedy gained not only two partners but also a husband. Charles Dye, or Charlie, as he liked to be called, was a white science fiction writer from California nine years Flo's junior.[95] He had published *The Man Who Stalked the Stars* in 1952, which received some acclaim, and was a member of the Hydra Club, a small clique of science fiction writers that included Isaac Asimov and Fredric Brown.[96] Flo and Charlie met at one of her many parties. Charlie thoroughly enjoyed anyplace where he could drink, joke, and entertain an audience with his long, rambling stories. By all accounts he was at his best when he was winding details of his day into a witty tale. By some accounts, several women found his humor and intelligence appealing.[97] Charlie had been married to Rita Dragonette-Dye, a poet and writer, and had dated other young artists. His cadre of friends included New York judge George Stark, the graphic artist Ronald Clyne, and the science fiction writer David Kyle.[98] Through Charlie, Flo gained broader entrée into intellectual and artistic circles, as well as companionship, pleasure, and love.

After a quick courtship, Flo and Charlie were married on November 30, 1957; the ceremony was held in the Upper West Side apartment of her friend Leonard Cohen and presided over by Charlie's friend Judge Stark, while Kennedy's law partner, Don Wilkes, served as their witness.[99] The most exciting days during their courtship and marriage were spent an hour outside the city on Fire Island, where they rented a house with Leonard and his wife, or when they walked through car and boat shows in the city. While they were courting, Charlie would gently hold her hand as they strolled. Flo laughed at the sight of them walking with intertwined fingers, "seeing I was [nearly] ten years older than him."[100] She thought that their age difference—in addition to their racial difference, which she did not mention—must have struck onlookers as strange, and she was tickled by Charlie's public display of their union.

Beyond his brashness, Charlie could really make Flo laugh. She fondly recalled that at one outing Charlie poked fun at her shuffling walk. In those days Flo's spinal injury forced her to step gently, with her back slightly bowed. She recounted that he "used to make fun of the way I walked because I had this bad spine and always had when he knew me. He would say 'You bicycle when you walk' and he would bend slightly from the hips as I do and then bring his knees up toward his chest . . . he would show me how I walk." She often laughed at his impressions of her and his amusing stories. She found him charming and diverting. "He was really very, very amusing and funny," she recalled.[101]

Their union was not a typical marriage of the 1950s. In addition to their age and racial differences, Flo was not interested in being a conventional wife and mother.[102] Charlie did all of the cooking, and she thoroughly enjoyed the small dinner parties they hosted where he prepared "wonderful spaghetti with clam sauce" or "thick pork chops very well cooked"; on special occasions Charlie would make a "fruit salad . . . of pears and pineapple spears and apricots with peaches on lettuce with mayo."[103] After they wed, Flo moved some of her things into his Lower East Side apartment but she never officially changed her address to his. Nor did she ever change her name legally or professionally. She was still Florynce Kennedy to all who knew her. Characteristically, these choices were both nonconformist and deliberate.[104]

In Kennedy's undergraduate writings, she declared that she did not believe in marriage because it robbed women of freedom and tied them to a man and children as domestic servants. As a young girl she imagined that if she had to marry she would secretly hide money in a jar so she could escape whenever she wished.[105] For Kennedy, marriage and motherhood signified confinement. It might seem surprising that a woman who dreaded dependency on a husband would commit herself to marriage. Kennedy's marriage, however, was to a man who made considerably less money than she did and came at a moment when she was financially autonomous.[106] Moreover, Kennedy was forty-one, when she was far less likely to become pregnant than she had been earlier. As a woman without children and with her own profession, income, and a car in her firm's name, she was not subject to a husband's totalizing control. Kennedy strategically evaded most of the dictates that hemmed women into wedlock. In their marriage, in fact, Kennedy was the breadwinner and Charlie relied on Flo to pay half the rent at his apartment.[107]

Though Flo's marriage to Charlie allowed her an unusual degree of independence and she appreciated many aspects of his personality, by most accounts he was an abusive alcoholic who regularly flew into hysterical shouting rages.[108] She knew this when they first met but fell in love with him anyway.[109] Although much later Flo claimed that she never loved Charlie, what she wrote during this period displays her love for him.[110] Flo had dreaded the loss of freedom that a conventional marriage entailed, but she treasured the tenderness that came with romantic relationships, the doting and handholding. She perhaps feared not only that a husband would gain too much power by being the sole or main breadwinner but also that men were often unreliable providers, whether as a result of their own folly or because of their problems on the job. Her own father's history and the harsh reality of their lives during the Depression no doubt underscored this point for her.

Flo often playfully called Charlie a "ragamuffin" because his habitual dress was quite unkempt. Although he claimed that writers did not care about their appearance, she ignored his excuses and carefully washed and folded his clothes and enjoyed buying him fresh pajamas, a crisp trench coat, and new socks. She prized style and cleanliness and relished caring for him. For example, before their first anniversary, Flo searched for "a wonderful olive beige corduroy suit exactly like the one he loves that is worn out." For days she left her office early or returned late after combing Brooks Brothers and Saks for the perfect gift. Once she found a jacket she thought Charlie would love, she paid extra to have it delivered. The night of their anniversary she proudly gave him the jacket. But, in an example of his abusive outbursts, as soon as he opened the package he exploded into a "shouting fury. He screamed, 'only low classed fools cared about clothes.'" Charlie's rage continued until a stunned and wounded Flo began "crying and threatening to leave him." Only after Flo's threat did his tirade stop. Charlie's abusive episodes continued, however, and Flo repeatedly left him, telling her family and friends that they had separated. She was never silent in the face of his abuse.[111] She wrote him letters threatening to "divorce him once she could afford it," stating that she would "call the police" and detailing her embarrassment, anger, and frustration with his behavior.[112] Like most abusers, he would feel remorseful and then appear at her door bearing gifts, professing his love, and begging for her forgiveness.[113]

His drunken outbursts were so frequent that on one occasion Kennedy spoke with her partner Don Wilkes, who agreed to intercede on her behalf. In a letter, she told Charlie that Don "agrees with me that you should not come to our office for the party or for any other purpose. . . . If you come, you will be asked to leave, if you don't leave you will be put out."[114] Kennedy was probably warning Charlie that she would not hesitate to call the police; she had previously contacted the authorities when his actions were especially threatening. While Flo never provided details about it, we know from her own writings that Charlie had physically abused one of his previous intimate partners. In her memoir, she says that, not long before she met him, he had "pushed [the woman] down the subway stairs."[115] *Color Me Flo* remains silent about any physical abuse she may have experienced during their relationship. While it is possible that Charlie never laid a hand on Flo, it is hard to imagine that a known abuser would limit his battering to verbal insults in his conflicts with his wife. Flo would have wanted others to believe otherwise, at least in part to defend her own dignity. Often women do not admit to having been the victim of rape for the same reason.[116]

While Flo saw in Charlie a man who would not usurp her economic independence, she did not bargain for the toll his alcoholism and abuse would take. It was a gamble women made every day. Flo was attempting to have it all and not sacrifice career, pleasure, marriage, or independence. Where was the roadmap for this type of life for a black woman in the 1950s? How could a black woman successfully have all that she wanted in a world of white male privilege, state-sanctioned male violence, and the continued denial of black women's subjectivity?

The Billie Holiday Case

While Kennedy's marriage was collapsing, her firm attracted a new high-profile client who raised her visibility as an attorney. The firm's representation of the jazz musician Billie Holiday in the winter of 1959 was covered in the local and national black press.[117] Holiday was arguably one of the most well known female jazz vocalists of her generation and had several popular recordings, including "God Bless the Child" and "Lady Sings the Blues." Bill Dufty, Kennedy's friend and the coauthor of Holiday's autobiography, *Lady Sings the Blues: The Searing Autobiography of an American Legend*, contacted Flo in January 1959 when the U.S. attorney's office threatened to indict Holiday for failing to register with the Customs Bureau before departing on a European tour.[118] The Narcotic Control Act of 1956 mandated that all convicted narcotics users obtain prior permission to travel outside the country. Since Holiday had been convicted for use and possession of narcotics in the late 1940s, this new law applied to her. Two years earlier, Dufty's wife, Maely, had sought help from the NAACP to defend musicians against drug charges but was quickly rebuffed. The NAACP did not touch cases involving narcotics violations, but Kennedy did.[119] Flo was appalled that Holiday's management company, Associated Booking Corporation, had failed to advise Holiday of the federal statute. After some debate, Wilkes and Kennedy convinced the U.S. attorney's office not to indict Holiday.

Kennedy and Wilkes were contacted again six months later, when the singer was charged with possession of narcotics while she lay dying in her hospital bed. Their major objective was to allow her to spend her last days in a hospital rather than in jail.[120] After some negotiation they blocked her removal, and on July 22, 1959, Billie Holiday passed away at the Metropolitan Hospital in New York City at the age of forty-four. Kennedy's firm's work on behalf of Holiday in the last year of her life comes into sharp relief when juxtaposed with the counsel Holiday received during the majority of her career. Agreeing with Kennedy's assessment, scholars Farah Jasmine Griffin and Stuart Nicholson have concluded that Holiday's previous legal representation was inadequate and the business advice she was given was "criminally ignorant."[121] As a black woman, Holiday was also vulnerable to exploitation by the white men who controlled the music business.

The *United States v. Billie Holiday* case of May 27, 1947, underscores this point. After Holiday performed at the Earle Theatre in Philadelphia, police arrested her, claiming to have found drugs and needles in her hotel room. Following the counsel of her manager, Joe Glaser, Holiday waived her right to a lawyer and pleaded guilty to the charges of use and possession of narcotics. She then asked that the court grant her treatment instead of jail time.[122] While the judge acknowledged that drug addiction was an illness, he nevertheless sentenced her to one year and a day in federal prison, where she had to quit heroin abruptly and without proper medical care and preparation. In addition, New York cabaret laws prohibited musicians and singers who had been convicted of drug offenses from performing in licensed premises. The unequal enforcement of these laws coupled with the unfair targeting of black performers by narcotics agents affected black musicians disproportionately.[123]

In general, law enforcement and the courts treated addicts as criminals who should be quarantined or policed rather than as men and women in need of medical help.[124] Kennedy later argued that the imprisonment of black people because of their use of drugs was "part of the CON [Control of Niggers] game" that was designed to contain black people.[125] In her view, Holiday was entitled to a team of capable legal advisors to defend her.

Holiday's position as a self-described "race woman" who often spoke out against racist terrorism made her especially vulnerable to surveillance and repression by the police, FBI, and narcotics officials.[126] In 1939, Holiday's recording of "Strange Fruit" helped to cement her role as an artist critical of lynching and American racism. Kennedy emphasized Holiday's political importance in her memoir, which describes the first time she heard Holiday sing "Strange Fruit," at a benefit concert in Harlem in honor of Emmett Till in 1955. The singer was one of many black people outraged over the murder of a fourteen-year-old boy for allegedly whistling at a white woman. Kennedy characterized Holiday as an outspoken activist on behalf of black people who, despite her genius, was often exploited.[127]

Black musicians have historically been unfairly persecuted for the political content of their lyrics and for their nonconformist positions. Musicians such as Holiday and Paul Robeson who insisted on creating and performing antiracist music faced the brunt of police and FBI surveillance and repression. Those who, like Robeson, had been affiliated with the Communist Party were treated as enemies of the United States by the federal government.[128] Throughout Holiday's career she was adamant about performing "Strange Fruit," despite objections from club and theater owners and harassment from the FBI.[129] She maintained that it was no coincidence that her 1947 arrest came the day after she defied an order not to sing the song during her concert.[130] Holiday's insistence that she was hunted like an animal for most of her career is supported by her FBI file, which documents that she was continually tracked and monitored.[131]

Kennedy recognized that Holiday was being unfairly exploited by her management and her record label. She argued that the publishing and record companies were complicit in supporting black performers' drug habits; it enabled them to take advantage of Holiday and musicians such as Charlie Parker who "were highly exploitable by the publishing and record companies because of their addictions." Had the companies "not benefited by their being on drugs, and therefore highly dependent and vulnerable, they would have [been supported in] kick[ing] the habit long before."[132]

Kennedy's work defending Holiday against narcotics charges should be understood as an attempt to provide effective legal counsel to a political artist who had long been denied competent representation both inside and outside the courtroom. Griffin points out that legal experts who have recently evaluated Holiday's 1947 conviction concluded that, had Holiday been properly represented, "it is highly unlikely she would have done one day behind bars."[133] In 1959 Holiday was in financial straits and was unable to fully compensate Kennedy for her services. Kennedy recounted that "because of her desperate financial situation a bill of $250 was sent to Miss Holiday . . . [even though] the value of services rendered in the hearing . . . was $1000 to $1500."[134] Kennedy's acceptance of a nominal fee for her work on the case demonstrated her conviction that Holiday deserved legal counsel regardless of her ability to pay for it.

William Dufty wrote an article in the *New York Post* detailing Kennedy's success in defending Holiday, and word of her firm traveled quickly.[135] Black artists and their families as well as everyday folks began to contact the firm for assistance with music contracts, the estates of deceased spouses, and criminal charges. Kennedy's success with Holiday, she later acknowledged, served as her "true initiation into the black community."[136] Flo admitted that before the Holiday case, she "hardly knew any black people," and most black people did not know that they could go to her for legal assistance.[137] In the midst of this new attention, however, the firm of Wilkes, Kennedy and Fields was unraveling.

A Law Partner's Betrayal

While Wilkes helped Kennedy with the Holiday cases, he failed to win many of the firm's everyday suits in civil court. Wilkes experienced several big losses, and Kennedy recalled an especially significant defeat in a case involving Joseph Vallelunga, an engineer at Columbia Records, who was attempting to recover compensation for personal injuries his wife, Catherine, sustained after she slipped on the wet floor of the basement laundry room of their apartment building and fractured her skull.[138] According to court records, tenants had previously complained about this problem to the property owners, but the "floor remained wet and slippery."[139] Mistakenly believing that the case could be easily won, and in an attempt to "hasten a recovery on some of the most serious cases we had in the office," Wilkes "brought the cases to trial in front of a judge, waiving a jury."[140] Kennedy recalled warning him that judges do not typically favor the plaintiffs in cases involving insurance companies. Wilkes ignored her advice and insisted on going "into these accident courts without realizing for a second that they were owned lock, stock and barrel by the insurance companies . . . without a jury trial! Can you imagine anything quite so stupid! You need a jury. It's the only chance you've got."[141] Kennedy pointed out that "any half brained lawyer from a mail-order law school . . . knows that you try to avoid going on a judge's decision alone."[142]

As Kennedy had warned, Judge A. David Benjamin ruled that "the evidence established that the tenant was guilty of contributory negligence."[143] As a result, the landlord and the insurance company were only partially responsible and had to pay less in damages than Wilkes or the family expected. Kennedy was not surprised but was nonetheless infuriated by the ruling. She thought it was absurd that the court believed that a woman with a small child should forgo washing her family's clothes "on the only day her husband was home" (and could watch their child) just because the laundry room floor was wet, as it usually was. The judge "called it contributory negligence as though she could have walked four inches above the floor and not slipped in the water," Kennedy asserted.[144] She was appalled by the decision and even more disgusted by Wilkes's stupidity in handling this case. Wilkes probably did know that this was a bad strategy, but by the summer of 1959 he was desperate. Unbeknownst to

Kennedy and Fields, Wilkes had been stealing clients' funds and bringing cases in front of a judge instead of a jury in hopes of making the money back quickly.[145]

Kennedy believed that Wilkes's failures in court were taking a toll on him and he was starting to go crazy.[146] Both Kennedy and Fields were frustrated with the outcome of several cases he handled, and tensions in the office escalated to the point where Fields and Wilkes were barely on speaking terms.[147] By that fall, as court records later demonstrated, Wilkes was repeatedly breaching the ethical and legal guidelines governing attorneys. He "violated canon 9 of the Canons of Professional Ethics by directly communicating with a party represented by counsel in an attempt to influence a favorable settlement of a personal injury action." In another instance, he misadvised and helped a client obtain an invalid Mexican divorce; in a third, he counseled a client to hide over $20,000 in his own Swiss bank account.[148]

Around the Thanksgiving holiday, Kennedy returned to the office to find that Wilkes had cleaned out his desk and disappeared. He "ran away with $57,000 of the firm's money,"[149] abandoning not only his partners and clients but also his two sons from a previous marriage.[150] Kennedy's firm was collapsing at the very moment her name as an attorney was gaining more recognition in New York City. Though she was furious with his duplicity, in the end "it seemed easier to just resign myself to sit down and do the work to repay the money. I was just kind of glad he was gone."[151] Fields was equally outraged over the disaster Wilkes left in his wake, and in hopes of having him disbarred, Fields filed a complaint with the Bar Association detailing Wilkes's impropriety. Within months of Wilkes's disappearance, he was "disbarred from the practice of law."[152] Both Fields and Kennedy claimed to have no knowledge of Wilkes's defrauding of the firm's clients and were not charged in connection with his misconduct. Nonetheless, Kennedy felt personally responsible for repaying the clients Wilkes had swindled. There is no evidence that Fields assisted her in making these reparations. "I had to spend the next eight years working like a dog to pay people back," she recalled. "I sent them checks of twenty and forty dollars every month."[153] Kennedy did not have the luxury of assuming that Wilkes's crimes would not be counted against her. Already on the margins of the legal profession because she was a black woman, she quite reasonably feared that her partner's misconduct might reflect badly on her. In repaying the money her partner had stolen, she was saving her career.

After years of struggling to be independent and to make something of herself, Kennedy was now obligated to her debtors. Desperate for money, she even considered selling her typewriter but decided against it after she realized she would be unable to continue to practice without it.[154] She worked at Gimbels department store at night and took on any and every case she could during the day.

At this moment of acute need, Flo returned to Charlie Dye. She had to handle Wilkes's cases and her own, reassure clients, and figure out how to pay the bills Wilkes left behind. Charlie helped her in what she describes as one of her most debilitating and trying moments of her life. He typed legal documents and answered the phone, and Flo remembered that he drank less during those months and was far less abusive toward her. She appreciated his help in the office and his attempt to stay sober.[155]

Charlie's support did not last long; within months he was back to drinking, and Flo left him again. This time, however, Charlie insisted that she pay him for the more than one thousand hours he had worked, which, he claimed, could have been spent writing novels or advancing his own career. He had not helped her for free; he was another creditor, and she owed him. Flo could have certainly dismissed him and argued that they did not have a verbal or written contract to that effect or that his help was a gift to his wife, which he was now using to manipulate her into staying with him. But Flo did not. Instead, she wrote him a letter saying that she would pay him back "$20 a month and was exceedingly grateful" for his assistance. At the same time, she informed him that when she could afford it, she would file for a divorce.[156] Flo would not be forced to stay with him, and twenty dollars a month, she may have reasoned, was a small price to pay to be rid of him. Perhaps Flo worried that if she did not pay Charlie before her divorce case was heard, he would seek to gain the assets of her law firm in divorce court. That was a genuine risk. At the time Flo wrote Charlie the letter, in 1959, it was incredibly difficult to gain a divorce by mutual consent in New York State. "Habitual drunkenness" was an acceptable ground for divorce in some states after women's rights advocates won that reform in the late nineteenth century. However, a woman could also be found at fault for refusing to live with her husband or for denying his conjugal rights. New York State divorce laws were particularly strict. It was not until 1968 that the New York Divorce Reform Law went into effect and allowed for divorce if one party could prove that the other had committed adultery, been abusive, or deserted the marriage. So Flo's sense of her vulnerability was well founded.[157] Kennedy's divorce case, however, never made its way to court. Within months of their separation, he drank himself to death and died from cirrhosis of the liver.

In law school and during the first years of her legal career, Kennedy had attempted to carve out a space for herself in a world governed by white men. Her determination to be a practicing lawyer in New York City with her own firm on Madison Avenue; to have a marriage where she lived independently and was financially autonomous; and to enjoy success, pleasure, and freedom was clear, but how a black woman might attain those goals was not. Indeed, these were audacious dreams. What woman, of any race, could she point to who had the sort of life she wanted? Her only available role models for having everything she desired were successful white male alumni from Columbia Law School. Kennedy learned the hard way that black women could not travel the same road as their white male counterparts. The white men she trusted most, professionally and personally, had more power to hinder her independence and success than she calculated. While her law partner and her husband exposed her to larger circles of intellectuals, artists, and attorneys, they also abused and manipulated her and threatened her security and livelihood. After the end of these relationships, Kennedy guarded her independence even more carefully. Kennedy would never marry or have a law partner again.[158]

Kennedy kept her romantic relationships private; from this time on, only her sisters knew about her love life.[159] Her experiences confirmed her beliefs that marriage was an oppressive institution for women and that a black woman could not practice law in the same ways that her white male counterparts did.

4

The Fight Is One That Must Be Continued

IN THE COURTROOM, IN THE PRESS, AND IN POLITICAL ORGANIZATIONS, 1961–1965

A year after Don Wilkes left their law firm, Florynce Kennedy was still gasping for air and trying to keep her practice afloat. His embezzlement and abrupt departure left her stunned, both emotionally and financially, and forced her to take stock of her commitment to practicing law. Kennedy's problems were compounded when David Fields, her remaining partner, left to start his own firm.[1] Back to practicing alone, Flo held tightly to her remaining music industry clients and worked even harder to attract new ones. The estates of Billie Holiday and Charlie Parker were her most prominent cases in the early 1960s. Parker's widow and Holiday's widower both hired Kennedy to represent them against the record and publishing companies that were withholding the artists' full earnings from their estates. Kennedy's work on these two cases cemented her reputation as an entertainment lawyer willing to battle the industry on behalf of artists and their families.

In representing these musicians' estates, Flo discovered the insidious relationships among record and publishing companies, advertisers, and the courts. She became especially interested in cases involving intellectual rights and infringement of copyright, whereby large corporations profited while artists received little or no monetary compensation for their creative work.

Despite Kennedy's success in some entertainment cases and her growing show business clientele, she later complained that the law was a "one-ass-at-a-time-proposition" and was therefore not an efficient use of her energy.[2] Her inability to make substantive change or to garner substantial financial, political, or personal rewards from her profession pushed her even further away from seeing the law as an avenue for justice "or even simple resistance to oppression."[3] In this period, she came to understand the power of the media as a way of challenging injustice and began to devote some of her time and energy to journalism. The press, she was learning, was a powerful avenue for public influence because it reached and immediately affected a wide swath of people. Once Wilkes's debts were almost paid off and her practice and reputation were saved, Kennedy began to explore political organizing outside the courtroom. Kennedy's intellectual and political journey both inside and outside the courts during the early 1960s formed a key foundation for her later politics.

The Billie Holiday and Charlie Parker Estates: Fighting in the Courtroom

A year after Billie Holiday's death, Kennedy became the attorney for her estate. Holiday's widower, Louis McKay, was frustrated by the original lawyer's lack of diligence in collecting all that he believed the estate was owed and in selling the movie rights to Holiday's life story.[4] No doubt impressed with Kennedy's earlier legal work on Holiday's behalf, McKay contacted her for help.

As the estate's lawyer, Kennedy moved forward vigorously with the customary legal tasks involved. She began by contacting Holiday's previous counsel, the performing rights associations, the insurance companies, and the artists' unions. Much to her surprise, she found that Holiday's management company, headed by Joe Glaser of the Associated Booking Corporation, had not affiliated her with Broadcast Music Inc. (BMI) or the American Society of Composers, Authors and Publishers (ASCAP). "Even worse," she said, "they had never collected from her last European tour."[5] For Kennedy, the management company's "stupidity and cupidity" was only surpassed by its failure to collect her benefits from the American Guild of Variety Artists (AGVA),[6] despite the fact that Holiday had been a union member since April 1940.[7] Reflecting later on the mismanagement of Holiday's business affairs, Kennedy wrote, "I have no way of knowing whether the agency was too stupid, too corrupt, or just didn't give a damn, but if they didn't know, they were criminally ignorant, and if they did they were exploitative and racist."[8]

During the same winter of 1960, she also became the lawyer for the estate of Charlie "Yardbird" Parker through his widow, Doris Parker, and briefly for Leon Parker, Charlie's adult son from a previous marriage.[9] Parker's management company, like Holiday's, had failed to affiliate him with BMI and ASCAP. Instead, Kennedy discovered, the companies affiliated themselves with these organizations only to "collect performing rights royalties as publishers without alerting the composer or artist."[10] She explained that this "was virtually criminal ... and of course [after their deaths] the record companies brought out memorial albums, on which they made good chunks of money."[11] Kennedy immediately affiliated both artists with BMI and ASCAP to prevent future records from being released without compensating the estates.

Still struggling to make ends meet, and with legal assistance only from an unpaid intern, Kennedy was not in a financial position to sue all of the companies that owed Holiday and Parker royalties. The record and publishing companies had an army of attorneys and were "ready to pit from 10 to 12 lawyers against any one lawyer representing an artist."[12] Aware that she would be vastly outnumbered and outspent by the defense, she devoted countless hours to researching effective legal strategies. Finally, Kennedy decided to utilize the law in a way that she stated had not been done before and was cost-efficient for her office and for the artists' families. She filed an "order of discovery," which at that time was not typically used for estate cases. Kennedy argued that she could not understand why this law could not be applied to a situation "where 10 or 15 or 20 publishing and record companies owed money to the estate of a jazz artist."[13] While the two cases were handled separately, Kennedy utilized the same legal strategies for both.

As was customary, Kennedy placed a "Notice to the Trade" in popular music periodicals warning "publishers and record companies that all money due . . . is hereby demanded payable immediately."[14] The estates belonged to the artists' families, and anyone who profited from Parker's or Holiday's intellectual products had to remit payment to Kennedy's office or be subject to "an immediate audit."[15] At the same time, Kennedy issued press releases and held press conferences in which she announced the two estates' battles with the record and publishing companies and warned black artists that they "stand to lose thousands of dollars if they are not careful with contracts they enter with American Guild and Variety Artists."[16] During one interview she described AGVA's maneuvers to deny the estates full restitution as a "breach in workers and union rights[,] seeing AGVA is a branch of the AFL-CIO."[17] These labor violations were so serious, Kennedy declared, that she had no choice but to contact New York's

Democratic congressman and chairman of the House Committee on Education and Labor, Adam Clayton Powell Jr., for assistance.[18] Powell was a prominent civil rights leader and had served as pastor of Abyssinian Baptist Church in Harlem before his election to Congress. When Kennedy arrived in New York during World War II, she had contacted Powell's office for assistance in filing a lawsuit against the Missouri bus and café company that had abusively evicted her from her seat. Powell was the most powerful African American in Congress and was respected by his constituents—and feared by his antagonists—for his willingness to take controversial positions and for his media savvy.[19] Moreover, he was probably the best headline-grabber of any black activist at that time. By contacting Powell, Kennedy was setting these cases within a political context and making them a matter of public debate. She understood that winning these cases would require a multifaceted approach that utilized the media and political pressure as well as the courts.

In the end, Kennedy's tactics were successful, and she gained both clients royalties once denied them as well as funds from BMI and ASCAP. She was particularly successful in supporting McKay's position as the Holiday estate's executor and in preventing numerous publishers, record companies, and writers from releasing records and films without his permission or without giving the estate its full share of the profits.[20] Although the exact amount of the legal settlements paid to the artists' families remain undisclosed, it is clear that Kennedy gained both Louis McKay and Doris Parker a "fair amount" from the record companies.[21] Kennedy later remarked that while looking after the estates of her clients, "I was also using my profession to strike a blow against the Establishment."[22]

Despite Kennedy's victory on behalf of the Holiday and Parker families, she lamented that the justice system did not offer many opportunities to alter relationships of power.[23] "Handling the Holiday and Parker estates taught me more than I was really ready for about government and business delinquency," she explained.[24] Kennedy understood that she would have had a far more difficult time fighting for the very same artists when they were alive because "the record companies would just have cut off their livelihood."[25] Furthermore, she maintained that the courts were utterly ineffective "in rectifying the imbalance between the talented performers and the millionaire parasites who suck their blood."[26] In the end, although Kennedy was using her profession to "strike a blow" against the record and publishing companies and learning a great deal about the ways in which power circulated in the industry, her commitment to the practice of law was continually being tested. Kennedy said that "these experiences . . . marked the beginning of a serious disenchantment, if indeed I ever was enchanted with the practice of law. . . . Not only was I not earning a decent living, there began to be serious questions in my mind whether practicing law could ever be an effective means of changing society, or even [of] simple resistance to oppression."[27]

Some of Kennedy's close friends were highly critical of her choice to work for Louis McKay and Doris Parker. Many believed that Doris was not Charlie's legitimate widow. At the time of his death, Charlie and Doris were estranged, and for several years before his death, Charlie had lived with and had children by Chan Richardson Parker.[28] Bernard Stollman, Kennedy's white male intern, was convinced that Doris was a fraud after "Maely Dufty came to me and urged me to leave Kennedy," warning him that "'something was about to blow up.'"[29] Chan had hired a prominent New York entertainment lawyer, and Mealy convinced Bernard that this lawyer would quickly defeat Doris's claim to the estate. Maely also persuaded Bernard that Flo would be brought up on fraud charges because "Doris was not Charlie's wife."[30] In court, Chan Parker's lawyer claimed that Doris Parker was never legally married to Charlie Parker and that Chan was Charlie's true heir.[31]

Even more seriously, during a press conference about the Parker estate, Kennedy had named Bernard Stollman as her associate working on the suit. Stollman was surprised and upset by this announcement because he had only conducted legal research on the case and was not privy to the overall legal strategy. At Maely's urging he quickly resigned from Kennedy's firm for fear that he too might face charges. Before Stollman began working with Kennedy he had been ignorant of the entertainment industry; as he later admitted, "I didn't know anything about jazz."[32] Kennedy's practice exposed him to a completely new legal and social world, and after he left her firm he began working as an entertainment attorney and opened ESP-Disk' in 1963. This record label gave musicians complete control of their recordings without any commercial expectations, eventually becoming a major label for what was called free jazz. Stollman admitted to building on the connections he garnered while working for Kennedy.[33]

At the time of Stollman's abrupt departure, he did not realize that Maely was either embellishing the facts or entirely misinformed. Despite what most people in the industry had come to believe, Chan and Charlie were not legally married, and Charlie had never divorced Doris.[34] More important, Stollman was quick to devalue the ways in which Kennedy had elevated his status from an intern to an associate.[35] In the press conference and in legal documents, Kennedy made it appear as if she were not just a lone black woman lawyer but had a full legal team behind her.[36] Already outnumbered and outspent by the defense, Kennedy identified Stollman as an attorney in this and in other cases in order to give the impression that she was part of a well-resourced firm with a white male associate. In this instance, however, seeking to avoid the risks she had incurred in her partnership with Wilkes, Kennedy controlled and limited her exposure in her relationship with Stollman. She deployed his name and utilized his work as a researcher but tightly guarded the inner workings and finances of her practice.[37]

Kennedy was well aware that many clients, the courts, and the public viewed a black woman attorney as powerless and disregarded her ability and acumen. Indeed, the press repeatedly listed Stollman first when reporting on the Parker case. It is unknown whether Kennedy gave the reporters her own name second or if the journalists inverted the names despite the fact that Kennedy was the only lawyer being interviewed at the press conference for the Charlie Parker estate case.[38]

While Stollman believed that Kennedy's description of him as an associate was simply "puffery . . . and self-serving," it was puffery that also served him well.[39] The elevated impression Kennedy created of his place in the firm allowed him to present himself to musicians as an entertainment lawyer with experience beyond that of an unpaid intern. After Stollman's unexpected departure at Dufty's behest, Kennedy soldiered on without him.

Maely Dufty had her own reasons for seeking to undercut Flo. By 1961, Kennedy had taken legal action against the Duftys. Although Bill Dufty had recommended Kennedy to Billie Holiday, Kennedy's work on behalf of Holiday's estate had strained their friendship. Maely was no doubt offended when she received a letter from Kennedy's office with Louis McKay's signature "announcing that he will take action against anyone who published unauthorized writings" about Holiday.[40] In addition, as the coauthor of *Lady Sings the Blues*, Bill was listed alongside Holiday's record and publishing companies in various legal complaints, and he was sent instructions to inform Kennedy's office about publications related to Holiday's memoir.[41] Both Maely and Bill must have been bruised by Flo's legal actions. Being treated like intruders into Billie's business affairs surely seemed all the more galling because Holiday was estranged from McKay at the time of her death while the Duftys were with her during her final days in the hospital.[42] Moreover, Lou's reputation as a womanizer "who used to play around" on Billie and as her sporadic drug supplier—rumors that circulated in her inner circle—damned him in the eyes of these friends.[43] Stollman remembered that although Maely and Flo had "a certain relationship, a certain bond . . . it was being tested . . . and Maely was angry" with Flo.[44]

For Kennedy, neither her friendship with the Duftys nor the low opinion that many people held of her clients mattered to her legal defense of the Holiday and Parker estates. Both Louis McKay and Doris Parker had a legal claim to their spouses' estates. More important, Kennedy argued that the record and publishing companies were withholding much of the artists' earnings. Ultimately, for Kennedy the real fight was against the record companies and publishers that repeatedly profited from the intellectual property of their artists and then paid them very little or nothing in return. The Parker and Holiday cases demonstrated to Kennedy just how vulnerable black musicians were to the industry's hustle.

"Piracy of Ideas": Fighting for Intellectual Property Rights

Kennedy's work on behalf of these estates was part of her broader entertainment work involving infringement of copyright and intellectual rights by corporations. One of the lingering clients from the Wilkes, Kennedy and Fields days was a writer who sued the popular sitcom *The Ann Sothern Show* for stealing one of his ideas. In preparation for trial, Kennedy read up on the rules of copyright and the Federal Communications Commission's many hearings on the issues it involved.[45] Kennedy discovered "the financial structure of the media"[46] and learned "how much a half-hour of TV time was worth, how much the advertisers pay, [and] how the advertisers and networks co-produce" shows.[47] She began to realize that advertisers and TV networks had very close, mutually advantageous relationships and that the courts failed to regulate both the connections and the new media technologies that were emerging at this time. Advertisers played a crucial, even decisive role in programing; now, Kennedy said, she understood the reasons "why we had such terrible programs."[48] This knowledge, along with the lessons from the Parker and Holiday cases, deepened Kennedy's awareness of the problem of intellectual property rights.

By the early 1960s, Kennedy's reputation as an attorney who worked for struggling artists was spreading, and clients from New York City to small towns in North Carolina contacted her for help. One potential client wrote to Kennedy for assistance with a "lawsuit against CBS Television

Network for airing a television program" without compensating him; another wanted to sue NBC and MCA for misappropriating a title for a television series.[49]

As in her fight on behalf of musicians against the music industry, Kennedy hoped that she could help protect the rights of writers whose works were presented on the small screen. But protecting living writers and artists was very difficult. In inviting a potential client to meet with her, Kennedy warned him not to be overly hopeful: "I am sorry that I cannot report stunning success in the handling of the piracy of ideas suits with which I have been connected. I doubt that clearcut victories are in the cards. Nevertheless, I think the fight is one that must be continued relentlessly. . . . Meantime, good luck and keep swinging—and writing."[50]

In order to find more effective approaches to these cases, Kennedy contacted other lawyers for help and advice and sketched out possible legal arguments, conceivable outcomes, and settlements previously achieved by other firms.[51] Despite her preparation, the cases against *The Ann Sothern Show* and CBS were unsuccessful. Frustrated by the courts' refusal to recognize her clients' demands for protection of their ideas, she also reached out to the federal bar associations for help.[52]

Kennedy knew that the battle for artists' rights would be prolonged, and if she was going to get the courts to move even an inch she would need to build a wide coalition of support. She hoped the Federal Bar Association would be just such an ally. As a member of the New York, New Jersey, and Connecticut branch of the association and also the secretary of the association's Committee on Children and the Courts, she pushed the president, Peter Megargee Brown, to form a committee on "law of idea protection; copyright, unfair competition, trade regulation, etc." Kennedy argued that "idea protection should begin where the ideas begin," with the artist, and suggested that the Federal Bar Association, as a representative of the lawyers, could help to place this issue on the courts' agenda.[53] "Call it what you will, show business law, entertainment law, theatrical law, amusement or copyright law, this is a field which in my opinion, needs greater scrutiny by the bar, the courts and governmental agencies," she wrote. "Government agencies such as the F.C.C. which theoretically could set up machinery to guard the interests of the creative members of our society have seemed . . . consistently to encourage a 'laissez faire' atmosphere. From the Internal Revenue Service and the Federal Trade Commission to the Department of Labour and the Copyright Office."[54] Kennedy maintained that the government was ineffective in safeguarding the interests of the "creative segment of the public," while the "interests of film companies, network theatre producers, literary and music publishers, record companies and talent agents, radio stations and television producers are well protected" by the courts and governmental agencies. "These companies are purveyors and communicators of ideas," not the originators of these ideas, and therefore they should not be compensated and protected as if they were.[55]

Part of the difficulty, she recognized, lay in "the rapid growth of technological progress in fields of reproduction," which had accelerated during the past decade.[56] In the 1940s and 1950s, a variety of technological advances in radio, television, and record production transformed the entertainment industry. The creation of new high-fidelity equipment improved the sound quality on radio and encouraged the growth of FM stations.[57] At the same time, the music industry was undergoing rapid development, since long-playing (LP) vinyl records held twenty minutes of music on each side.[58] The television industry experienced a profound and far-reaching expansion during the 1950s. In the late 1940s, AT&T built a network that tied together TV stations throughout the United States. By 1956, most cities were linked to network programming. The growth was startlingly rapid: in 1950 only 5.9 million houses had TV, compared with over 42 million with radio, but "by the next decade the market penetration of television had almost equaled that of radio with 45.2 million homes compared to radio's 49.5 million."[59]

Kennedy complained that performing artists were not benefiting from these new advances and innovations. "Electronics has given rise to problems which are the public responsibility of no one," she argued. Both the law and government regulation had failed to keep pace with change, leaving the field open to predatory behavior by large media companies.[60] She believed that the Federal Bar Association in New York City in particular, where the entertainment industry was most prominent, could be a leader in spearheading this legal battle and setting the tone for the courts.

In Kennedy's letters to clients she referred to the frequent theft they experienced at the hands of corporations and the lack of government regulation as the "piracy of ideas."[61] She argued that large television networks and music labels, "due to their size in the industry and the scope of their operations," exercised unfettered power over a lone artist and could "effectively foreclose [a] single entrepreneur from a means of presenting his product to the public."[62] She likened the imbalance of power between artist and employer to "that of a mouse to a mountain,"[63] enabling these corporations to take the artist's ideas without adequate, or even any, compensation. Moreover, she critiqued the courts and government agencies for turning a blind eye to this theft and allowing it to continue.

While Kennedy's letters to the Bar Association president and to her clients do not mention the racism that exacerbated the exploitation of black artists, her experiences with Holiday and Parker made her acutely aware of the ways in which the work of black entertainers was repeatedly stolen and their assets mismanaged. Later Kennedy maintained that, in addition to stealing ideas from black artists, the "crummiest types" tended to attach themselves to black musicians and "pick what little flesh is left on their bones."[64]

Kennedy was not satisfied with what she saw as Peter Megargee Brown's lukewarm response to her letter. Brown responded that the Federal Bar Association was overwhelmed by other projects and responsibilities and did not have time to take up copyright theft.[65] The issue of revising copyright laws came up repeatedly, not only in the FBA but also in Congress, throughout the 1940s. Yet nothing went past the point of committee hearings and debate. Scholar Albin Zak writes that "squaring both the practical and conceptual ramifications of sound recording with existing legal principles and statutes proved a thorny and persistent problem."[66] In 1955, reviewing the situation, Harvard law professor Benjamin Kaplan wrote that "copyright law, precisely because it has taken shape around the model of a book communicated to the public by multiplication of copies, has experienced difficulty, not to say frustration, with cases where communication is by performance or representation." In his view, the problem was larger in scope than could be handled by individual court cases. "Better than any solution to the courts (or to the state legislatures acting severally)," he concluded, "would be a proper rewriting of the Copyright Code to take care of the question of phonograph records." Unfortunately for Kennedy, this rewriting would not occur until the early 1970s.[67]

Although the courts and professional legal associations were slow to take up the task of challenging the piracy of artists' ideas, Kennedy continued to push for recognition of the rights of musicians and other creative artists. In 1964, seeking a wider audience, Kennedy began writing a weekly column for a local black newspaper, the *Queens Voice*. The newspaper had a readership of close to four thousand people by the mid-1960s and focused much of its attention on political and social issues.[68] Her mounting frustrations with the failings of the legal system, the government, and the media made them her most frequent targets.

"We Have to Make Our Own News": Fighting in the Press

Kennedy's ire was aroused by repeatedly witnessing the duplicity and hypocrisy of the U.S. government, the mainstream media, and those self-satisfied members of the body politic whom she sarcastically termed "the good people." Ever since starting law school, Kennedy had been disappointed to discover that the American ideals of fairness were meaningless in practice. Her work as a lawyer demonstrated that neutrality and objectivity were subject to the interpretation of those with the deepest pockets and were applied unevenly at their command and for their benefit. Through her weekly "Once Upon a Week" column, Kennedy indicted local, state, and federal governments for their failure to address systemic injustices ranging from police brutality to corporate embezzlement. These miscarriages of justice dovetailed with the mainstream media's racist and biased journalism and those "good people" who tended to blame and criticize oppressed people for the offenses committed by government and the media.

Black feminist investigative journalist Ida B. Wells wrote numerous activist-oriented exposés during the nineteenth and early twentieth centuries that stirred public debate and pushed for changes in law and policy. Her articles on lynching challenged the mainstream media's depictions of black men as rapists of white women.[69] Kennedy's columns presented a similar accounting of the social and political problems she found most glaring and a searing criticism of those she found were to blame. Like Wells, Kennedy understood that black people could not rely solely on the mainstream media's coverage of them or of the issues they found most important. Instead, she argued, "we have to make our own news."[70]

Kennedy's column regularly critiqued the government, especially "government sponsored violence paid for by tax payers." She wondered out loud why oppressed people were continually asked to be their "brother's keeper" and to be nonviolent by a government that employed excessive and repeated violence on the shores of Cuba and in Vietnamese villages. For the U.S. government to resort so readily to violence but to arrest, condemn, and jail people of color when they fought back against their violent oppression was hypocritical. Kennedy was appalled by the CIA-sponsored attempt to overthrow Cuba's anti-imperialist government, which had seized and nationalized American-owned companies and property in Cuba, and the government's political and military intervention in Vietnam that almost thwarted the anticolonial movement against the French.[71]

Moreover, Kennedy questioned why local, state, and federal governments expected black people and other oppressed groups to do nothing in response to church bombings and police brutality while their tax dollars financed the wars and counterintelligence programs waged by the military and the CIA. Kennedy's column expressed outrage about the numerous bombings of black churches that occurred across the South, particularly that of the 16th Street Baptist Church in Birmingham, Alabama, where four little girls were killed while in Sunday school.[72] Bombings of black churches and homes associated with civil rights activism frequently went unpunished or ignored by local and state authorities, who claimed they could not find the culprits.

At social functions in and around New York City in the early and mid-1960s, Kennedy's conversations with whites repeatedly turned to the "Negroes." Often, she explained, "I go to cocktail parties or a dinner party where I am the only Negro" in a room filled with whites.[73] Inevitably, Kennedy recalled, some white man would turn to her and question her about the civil rights movement, asking why blacks were so angry and engaging in civil disobedience. "What do you think of Milton Galamison, Malcolm X, Brooklyn CORE, James Baldwin?" whites would always ask.[74] Kennedy had been educating these folks for over a decade, so she understood their expectation that the lone black person at an otherwise all-white party would speak for their race. But those who did not know her often received an unexpected earful. Not only did she refuse to deplore black civil disobedience or regard black activists as criminals, but she also criticized the government and the media for fomenting racial hostility.

Kennedy's columns for her black readership often detailed her sharp retorts to the white people she encountered. She redirected questions about black people's civil disobedience and retaliatory violence toward public policy and media practices, arguing in one of her editorials that the actions—and inaction—of politicians, coupled with biased media coverage of the civil rights movement, triggered forceful dissent. "You add the sparks of smart aleck cracks from high placed government officials, and more sparks from a weakling helpless Congress, stymied by anti-social 'filibusteros,' and more sparks from 'fizzling' fruitless peaceful demonstrations and more sparks [from] radio and T.V. announcers, who characterized non-violent behavior as 'failures' and soon you have the making of anything from a grass-fire to a forest fire," she wrote.[75] Kennedy's remarks turned the tables on media coverage that attributed all violence to blacks by demonstrating that government policies and statements aroused blacks' anger.

In her writings, Kennedy derided the mainstream media for their yellow journalism and blatant hypocrisy just as loudly as she criticized the government for its unethical and biased dealings. She repeatedly asked, "Whatever happened to responsible reporting? Not to mention journalism?" The media's branding of peaceful demonstrations as ineffective because white officials did not immediately grant their demands was misleading and encouraged violent dissent, Kennedy argued.[76]

The mass media were Kennedy's frequent target because of the numerous demeaning images they propagated, their biased coverage of black people, and their failure to report accurately on institutional racism. Articles in the *Daily News* detailing an alleged robbery of a white male Hofstra student sparked some of her most searing criticism of the press. The student reported to the Long Island police that "two black hoodlums" viciously mugged him. He went on to describe one of the alleged robbers as a "six-footer, weighing 200 pounds, [who] wore a grey straw hat and purple socks." Kennedy reported that the *Daily News* printed a retraction once it was discovered that the student had made up the entire incident. In the follow-up story, the reporter stated forthrightly that the student had reported a false crime to police. But Kennedy was frustrated that the journalists gave "the story itself [a] . . . tender touch. While the NEWS called the attackers 'hoodlums,' the student is now called 'THE YOUNG BOY.'" Kennedy wondered why the student was not portrayed as a liar and a criminal. She was equally critical of the press for not seeking corroboration of the student's account and for not being skeptical of the stereotypical description of the black man. Kennedy found the student's account rather suspicious, perhaps because a black man wearing a straw hat and purple socks would resemble a minstrel caricature more closely than it would an actual person at the time.[77] These racist images had been a staple of films, TV, and radio shows during the 1940s and 1950s.[78]

When Kennedy was at yet another party with white northern liberals and the conversation turned to the "Negroes," Flo expressed her frustration with "all accounts that I have heard" that "contained direct or indirect denial of racial significance" or racism in the *Daily News* reporting. For Kennedy, "the sixty-four thousand dollar question then become[s], why refer to the race [of] the alleged assailants" at all or furnish unsubstantiated details without investigating their accuracy? The news coverage of this alleged robbery seemed especially biased, since journalists frequently "refer to 'alleged discrimination' in housing, 'alleged segregation' and 'de facto' segregation" despite overwhelming evidence that segregation and discrimination in housing were chronic systemic problems. Kennedy's outrage at the *Daily News* specifically and at the media in general for their racism fueled her editorial. In the end, she argued that the mass media made up "one very small aspect of a very large and complicated problem."[79] In this moment, Kennedy was attempting to understand the networks of institutional power and theorize the media's role in the perpetuation of injustice. Like biased courts and inept governmental agencies, the media professed a standard of objectivity and fairness that they repeatedly violated.

Kennedy did not confine her criticism to institutions that wielded power and influence. She also used her column as a vehicle to raise readers' awareness of numerous issues that she regarded as urgent and in need of debate and action. In the process, she argued against commonly held viewpoints that, she believed, promoted the acceptance of inequality among ordinary people, including those who were oppressed. For example, black and white "good people" who clung to holier-than-thou religious attitudes ignored and even implicitly supported injustice by failing to address the reality of people's lives.

Having grown up in a home where religion-based norms of respectability were flouted and sexual curiosity was encouraged, Kennedy was conscious of the ways in which religion helped to crush individuals' choices, especially for women. Kennedy's concern about a woman's control of her body and the availability of legal abortion took center stage in her May 22, 1964, article. The piece responded to the class disparities in the availability of medical abortions. After watching a "frustratingly interesting discussion on abortion" on a WNBC program called *Open Mind*, Kennedy critiqued "the good people" who held onto "old-fashioned religious views" about women's duty to bear children. In contrast, she supported the right of all women, and especially poor women, to have access to abortions performed legally and safely in a hospital.[80]

In the mid-1960s, *Open Mind* was briefly moderated by historian Eric Goldman, who served as a special policy advisor to President Johnson and taught at Princeton University.[81] Kennedy was impressed with Goldman's attempt to "clarify national and international outlines" of the abortion debate, as well as with the guest feminist sociologist Alice Rossi and Alan Guttmacher, gynecologist and president of Planned Parenthood. Kennedy called the other two guests, whom she did not name, "the good people" who "hung on to old-fashioned religious views."[82] She deplored one speaker's insistence that "no matter what the social institution or the physical condition of the mother or child, abortions should be kept at an absolute minimum" as unrealistic, given the realities of impoverished women's lives. Kennedy pointed out the contradiction posed by those who would deny legal abortions to poor women but then "cluck their tongues and shake their heads . . . at the illegitimate children on welfare." She wondered how anyone could ask these women to carry children they could not afford to raise and then judge them when they did so and needed financial support. Kennedy found their statements irrational and illogical. Indeed, she considered the abortion debate a complete "mess" and insisted that "something's got to give."[83]

Kennedy described how Rossi and Guttmacher countered these arguments and "helped bring the discussion down the ladder of abstraction where the anti-abortionists seemed most comfortable." Moreover, Kennedy underlined the point "that the more prosperous person had little difficulty obtaining an abortion" legally and safely. As "with most things 'illegal,'" "rules were bent" for the privileged.[84] Many well-respected hospitals performed abortions for married women who could afford to pay a psychiatrist to say that her unwanted pregnancy represented a threat to her mental health. A psychiatrist's recommendation that a woman needed a therapeutic abortion to protect her physical or mental well-being had become an acceptable justification for the practice in the 1940s and 1950s. An analysis of abortions performed in New York hospitals revealed that a fifth of all the abortions were induced for psychiatric reasons.[85] The panelists on *Open Mind* underscored, however, that the "less privileged, who can't afford a psychiatrist to support a therapeutic abortion in a hospital," were denied access to the procedure. Kennedy emphasized the hypocrisy and double standard of the "good people" in society and the district attorneys who continually policed and chastised poor women for seeking illegal abortions while hospitals that performed therapeutic abortions for wealthier families received little to no rebuke.

"It Seems to Me That What They Need Is a Few Bullet Proof Vests": Fighting in Political Organizations

In the summer of 1964, Kennedy was one of several black and white women from New York who participated in Wednesdays in Mississippi (WIMS), an organization that provided material and moral support to civil rights organizers in the South. WIMS grew out of a phone call that Dorothy Height, president of the National Council of Negro Women (NCNW), received from Student Nonviolent Coordinating Committee (SNCC) member Prathia Hall. Hall told Height about the women and girls who were repeatedly arrested when attempting to register voters and once inside the Dallas County jails faced beatings and sexual assaults by the officers.[86]

Hall hoped that the NCNW would help protect the female protesters from abuse at the hands of Mississippi officers who were violently defending white supremacy.[87]

The NCNW and predominantly white organizations such as the Young Women's Christian Association, the National Council of Catholic Women, the National Council of Jewish Women, and Church Women United met in Selma, Alabama, and Atlanta, Georgia, to brainstorm about ways they could assist SNCC and Council of Federated Organizations (COFO) organizers. In 1962 SNCC began working with COFO, an umbrella group that united several civil rights organizations in an effort to register black voters in the state of Mississippi.[88] White activist Polly Spiegel Cowan of the Citizens Committee for Children of New York was from a wealthy family of German Jews in the Midwest. She had become radicalized in the 1930s and had a radio show in New York City in the 1950s. Cowan became especially concerned about the potential abuse of COFO workers when the organization announced that during the summer of 1964, hundreds of upper- and middle-class white students from the North would travel to Mississippi in hopes of drawing national attention to the racial violence in the South. Cowan's own sons were planning to participate, and she wanted to find ways to help lessen the violent hostility that COFO organizers would encounter.

Cowan suggested that the appearance of a small team of prominent middle- and upper-class northern white and black women, what she termed the "Cadillac crowd," could have a "quieting influence" on white antagonism and could perhaps help to "build bridges between black and white women."[89] WIMS leadership decided that several small groups of women would travel to Mississippi during Freedom Summer as "sensitive interpreters" and serve as a "ministry of presence."[90] Each week throughout the summer of 1964, the interracial group of women would arrive in Jackson on Tuesday evening and then drive to a smaller Mississippi town early Wednesday and finally depart on Thursday. The NCNW and the other organizations agreed to help coordinate and finance the plan.

During the summer of 1964, seven teams of middle-class women from northern cities such as New York, Boston, and Chicago traveled to places such as Ruleville and Jackson, Mississippi.[91] Kennedy's team included four white women: Claudia Heckscher, Trude Lash, Frances Haight, and Marjorie Dammann.[92] Marie Barksdale, the president of the black sorority Delta Sigma Theta, was the other black woman on the team. All of the women fit the profile of middle-class prominence and respectability that the WIMS leadership hoped to establish. Most were professionals whose husbands held notable positions in New York City. With the exception of Kennedy, who was explicit about having no religious affiliation, all of the women were Christians or Jews. The WIMS women, like Kennedy, were in their forties and fifties; all had attended college or preparatory schools; and most held advanced or professional degrees as well. Their activism on various community boards and social welfare programs serving women and children of all races made them ideal candidates for this mission.[93]

The WIMS team left New York on Tuesday, August 4th, in the early afternoon and were greeted by the WIMS staff in Jackson early that evening. Not long after they arrived, they heard that the bodies of three missing COFO workers—James Chaney, Michael (Mickey) Schwerner, and Andrew Goodman—had been found in a ravine a little over an hour outside of Jackson. The young organizers had been missing since June 21 and were last seen when police officers arrested them for allegedly speeding. What was discovered later but was not known at the time was that the officers had waited until nightfall and released them on the side of the road to a mob of Klansmen. The outcry over the missing civil rights workers, which was louder than usual since two of them were white, forced the federal government to take notice.[94] Thus, on their first night in Mississippi, the WIMS women bore witness to local communities' initial responses to the brutal murders.

Marie Barksdale, a member of the WIMS "negro team," noted that on "the night that they found the three bodies," she observed "the reaction and the pathos" firsthand.[95] The WIMS women said that most of the black people they met, especially those from the rural areas, were not surprised that the missing COFO workers had been murdered. "We've known it and we've lived with this knowledge for six weeks," they said. The WIMS women described many in the black community as both resigned and deeply shaken: "The reaction was . . . now everything that . . . we believed and really felt [we] knew had happened." For many blacks in Mississippi, finding the bodies made their everyday reality "common knowledge all over the world."[96]

Some of the white southern women the WIMS "white team" met believed that the murders and other violence against blacks were simply false reports from northerners. One of the white southern women "even agree[d] that there had been killings," but when pressed by the WIMS team to describe who she believed to be responsible, the Jackson woman retorted tersely, "Who does these things in the North?" To her way of thinking, the answer was simple: the murders were the actions of a few "errant hoodlums," not reflective of the law or the way of life in Mississippi.[97]

The WIMS leadership did everything in its power to ensure the safety of the northern women who traveled south. In order to be selected, the women had to agree to obey southern racial protocol to avoid drawing unnecessary attention to themselves and the WIMS mission. As a result, Kennedy walked off the plane with Barksdale by her side and acted as if she did not know the white women on the team. For three days, the black and white women lived separately and often traveled in separate cars. Black women lodged with members of Jackson's black community, while the white women lodged together at a segregated, Klan-owned hotel.[98] Dorothy Height described following southern practices as a strategy designed to protect the women and widen their organizational reach: "We would have to go into tension-filled communities quietly . . . [and] anonymously," and "even when our most deeply cherished principles were violated in the process," the Wednesdays in Mississippi organizers worked "with respect for local custom."[99]

Local customs required that the white women behave like proper "ladies," while black women on the team were supposed to dress in the way self-respecting southern black women did when they attended church, wearing dresses, white gloves, and hats. Kennedy, who by 1964 had already begun to shed her professional skirts and dresses in favor of slacks, was now being asked to assume that attire again. "Wednesdays in Mississippi ladies" were coached to explain to anyone who asked or was within earshot that they were in Mississippi simply as a "ministry of presence."[100] Southern and northern traditions alike encouraged women, especially women of means, to minister to the poor and downtrodden. WIMS women utilized the cover of acceptable female behavior in hopes that their ladylike appearance and their assumption of acceptable racial and gender demeanor would permit them to go unnoticed and unmolested.[101] As scholar Debbie Harwell argues, "Black and white team members employed the intersecting identities of their gender, class, and age to open doors that otherwise would have remained closed to them. In this way, following southern protocol in public served as both their vehicle and their protection."[102]

On their first night in Jackson, all of the women quietly observed a large civil rights meeting at a local church where black preachers and community members debated a boycott of Barq's beverage company for failing to hire blacks in executive positions and asked for volunteers to help integrate the Jackson public school system.[103] The WIMS women later reported that tension was high as residents disagreed with the preachers who held leadership positions about when and if the boycott should end.[104] Predictably, there was also some trepidation among the crowd when the discussion turned to having their six-year-old children become the first students to integrate Mississippi's elementary schools. The WIMS team was aware that their presence at the front of the church affected the proceedings and led some organizers to be more reserved in their words and actions.[105] Despite the disturbance their presence no doubt caused, they recalled witnessing a black Jackson community prepared and eager to negotiate strategies and tactics and keen on pressing their ministers to follow the community's leadership.

The next morning the WIMS women rose early and traveled separately to the rural town of Ruleville to observe a COFO-organized Freedom School. Kennedy and some of the WIMS women met with Fannie Lou Hamer, a SNCC organizer from Ruleville. The forty-seven-year-old Hamer had worked most of her life as a sharecropper in and around Ruleville. She had joined SNCC two years before and since that time had helped to register voters throughout the South. Hamer was no doubt one of the SNCC women Prathia Hall had referred to when she approached Dorothy Height for help in protecting those who had been abused after their arrests. During the summer of 1963, when Hamer was traveling back from a voting workshop with other SNCC activists, they were forced off a Trailways bus and arrested.[106] Hamer greeted the WIMS women and then detailed numerous incidents of widespread discrimination in Mississippi. Kennedy and the other women sat and listened as Hamer described her brutal beating by two black prisoners who had been ordered to do so by a white state patrolman. Perhaps she also told them that the white officer had hoisted up her dress while the men circled around her and continued pounding her body into the jailhouse floor. Ten days after recounting the incident to Kennedy and the WIMS women, Hamer would sit and "report to the credential committee [of the Democratic National Convention] in almost the same words she reported" to the WIMS team the horrific beating she had experienced in Mississippi when attempting to register blacks to vote.[107]

During Kennedy's time in Mississippi she did not operate as a lawyer but rather as an investigative journalist listening to "atrocity stories" and recording narratives of the civil rights movement for her column.[108] While Kennedy and the other women were instructed to protect the names and identities of the women and men they met, WIMS leaders hoped that the northern women would return to their home cities and bear witness to the goings-on in Mississippi. WIMS women were expected to draw attention to the COFO workers' attempts to integrate schools and register voters. Height and Cowan anticipated that the northern women would influence others to become active supporters and donors to civil rights organizations. In September 1964, after Freedom Summer ended and all of the WIMS groups returned to their home cities, Kennedy was free to publish her observations about Mississippi and to encourage support of the movement and organizers.[109]

Kennedy also continued conversations with her team members and WIMS leaders about the ways in which northern women could assist the civil rights movement. Weeks after their return, the WIMS women had vivid and troubling memories of the numerous stories they had heard of violence meted out by white employers and police officers against activists as well as of the poor segregated schools that they had observed. Black Mississippians repeatedly told them of the brutal beatings they received from whites when they attempted to register to vote and threats by the white superintendent to "fire any Negro school teacher who registered his or her own child for a desegregated class."[110] WIMS individual reports detailed at great length the various legal injustices that the women on the teams collectively observed or were told about. Three items represent the dozens of injustices the women encountered:

> Item—A mother and seven children receives $62 per month (either ADC [Aid to Dependent Children] or Public Assistance . . .). But, then when the authorities found that she was getting some food and clothes at the Freedom School, they reduced her allotment $18 [each month]. . . .
>
> Item—The state provides $60 per Negro pupil, $150 for white pupils. . . .
>
> Item—A Negro woman, illegitimately pregnant a second time, may be sterilized without her consent.[111]

Although Kennedy and the other women came to the South with knowledge of its regime of white supremacy and the complicity of the Mississippi state government in refusing to obey federal law and desegregate, they were still shocked by what they witnessed. While Kennedy recorded the "horror stories," her experiences of connecting with black civil rights organizers and working in an interracial group left her with an array of other impressions about the civil rights struggle in Mississippi and the imperative necessity for northern white women to confront racism not only in the South but in the North as well.[112] Kennedy's retelling of her experiences in the South differed substantially from those of the WIMS leadership. Both at that time and in later years, Dorothy Height and Patty Cowan focused on the alliance building between white northerners and white southerners that took place during their trips to Mississippi. They also noted the bridges built between black southerners and both white and black northerners.[113] Yet while Kennedy found women's interracial alliances built on antiracism extremely useful, her own accounts reveal that she was most interested in troubling the falsehood of white northerners' racial tolerance and acceptance. Height had also mentioned the importance of understanding and challenging racism in the North, but this was not WIMS's major focus. Furthermore, Kennedy's description highlighted the various ways in which black southerners coped with and challenged white hostility.

Like Cowan and Height, Kennedy was impressed by COFO workshops that explained nonviolent resistance. During one workshop, she witnessed organizers showing black men and women how to protect themselves from police attacks when attempting to vote. Kennedy described how activists were "supposed to bend or tuck [their] head . . . to keep from getting badly hurt." They were also told not to respond to police goading.[114] Cowan was especially inspired by her experiences of talking with moderate southern white women about the need for black people to gain their rights. Height echoed Cowan's attitude when she described Dorothy Rogers Tilly, a white woman who combated racism in the South.[115]

Yet Kennedy was much more fascinated by stories of armed middle-class black civil rights organizers. She was intrigued by her hostess on the WIMS trip, Thelma Sanders, a civil rights leader in Jackson who had worked with Medgar Evers of the NAACP before he was assassinated.[116] Kennedy described her as the proprietor of a rather large dress shop with a lovely family and a very nice house with "air conditioning throughout." But one feature of Sanders's home quickly caught Kennedy's attention: it "had a big gun leaning against the front door, a big gun." She described seeing guns during several of her visits with other black Mississippians as well.[117]

The presence of nonviolent civil rights organizing alongside armed self-reliance demonstrated the reality of southern black militancy. Some black activists who espoused nonviolent tactics for the mass movement were nonetheless prepared to defend themselves against whites who sought to murder them. Furthermore, Kennedy's descriptions support Timothy Tyson's argument that during the civil rights era, independent black politics, black cultural pride, and armed self-reliance operated in tension and in tandem with legal efforts and nonviolent protests in the quest for African American freedom.[118] Although at the time Kennedy seemed a bit perplexed by the conjuncture of these two realities, her choice to retell her WIMS story both by carefully detailing activists' training in nonviolent resistance and by highlighting the fact that some also had weapons and were prepared to use them helped to portray the conditions in the South through a more complicated and accurate lens. Kennedy's descriptions ran contrary to those of many of her northern white and black counterparts. Height's and Cowan's accounts focused primarily on blacks' nonviolence, interracial alliances, and white northerners' benevolence. The WIMS leaders' accounts often centered on the importance of northern white women talking to southern white women and on finding ways to support blacks engaged in passive resistance in Mississippi. Kennedy's descriptions, in contrast, did not emphasize whites' progressive attitudes, interracial sisterhood, or blacks' nonviolence.

Kennedy's frustration with the limits of this cross-regional interracial coalition led her to voice her concerns to the group: "On the way back on the plane I alienated them all by saying in my opinion racism wasn't that different in the South."[119] She adamantly maintained that the prevalent assumption that the South was an exception to the national racial norm was seriously wrong and that reinforcing it by appealing to white northerners' self-conception that they were racially unbiased and that their society was a model of tolerance was damaging as well as ineffective. WIMS was one of Kennedy's first major experiences in collaborating with both white and black women against racism, and she recognized the potential of these types of coalitions. Nonetheless, she insisted that interracial groups be honest partnerships that addressed the full scope of white supremacy in the United States and not simply scapegoat the South. This truth was not something that the other team members were prepared to hear, but she persisted. Even after they returned, Kennedy continued to tell them that many of the forms of racism they witnessed were endemic to the North as well. She pressed the group to imagine challenging racism at home, not just in the South.

Kennedy's disagreements with the team extended to the type of education she believed that Mississippi blacks and COFO workers needed in order to challenge and overturn racism in the South. Some WIMS women argued that the young organizers needed training in regard to appropriate dress, proper hygiene, and suitable comportment so as not to appear to white southerners like unkempt beatniks. Another WIMS woman proposed that the "best . . . most promising young" black children, particularly a black girl they had met in Ruleville, should be brought to New York to attend college.[120] Kennedy was incensed at the suggestion that a New York education would help the civil rights struggle in Mississippi. "Education has now been shown to be an unsatisfactory answer," she fumed.

"I believe it is more important for people like her to stay on the scene and broaden their power." Kennedy had heard of far too many educated middle-class people in the United States and abroad who were a part of the "hold back crowd." The suggestion that WIMS build an education project that took young black people away from their community was wholly "incomplete and thoroughly unsatisfactory." "It isn't education they need alone," she argued.[121]

Challenging their presumptions, Kennedy asked the other women to tell her what training black Mississippians really needed and to describe how giving some of them a college education in the North would help the movement. When the other women could not come to any agreement on what they meant, Marjorie Dammann explained to Kennedy, "It would be like someone going to the law court unless they knew what the law was."[122] Dammann's comment revealed her presumption that black southerners who were not formally educated did not understand the law, even though they constantly witnessed it being applied to their detriment and knew full well how difficult it was to assert the rights to which they thought they were constitutionally entitled. Perhaps she hoped that, as an attorney, Kennedy would appreciate her argument that stressed formal training. Dammann was entirely unaware that Kennedy had found the practice of law in and of itself to be a useless means of achieving justice. She did not hesitate to tell Dammann as much: "I think [if] the few that went to law court didn't know the rules you might get a little justice. . . . I think lawyers are the best people in the world . . . but they know too much about procedure" and far too little about justice.[123]

Kennedy continued to argue with the team over the suggestion that the COFO workers be taught how to present themselves so as not to offend white southern folks. "As far as I am concerned if these people have no money, if they have no facilities, if they are living with people who are rural, and don't have bathing facilities, it doesn't worry me" if they wore overalls or smelled.[124] She did not see how enforcing middle-class standards of dress and comportment would help the movement, protect COFO workers' lives, or ensure the stability of their relationships in the black community where they worked. Historian Tanisha Ford contends that the longer black women in SNCC "labored among working-class members of the South, the more likely it was that they would abandon their neatly coiffed processed hairstyles, dresses, cardigan sweaters, and modestly heeled pumps for short-cropped natural hairstyles, denim overalls, and blue jeans. In adopting the dress of African American sharecroppers, these women enacted a performance of their own in which they rejected middle-class notions of black female respectability and illustrated how clothing could be used to put on and take off particular ethnic, class, and gender identities."[125]

Although Kennedy wore the appropriate female attire during this trip, as she did for her courtroom performances, she rejected the idea that middle-class costumes would provide real protection for black or white civil rights workers. Like black people as a group, they were targets of violence no matter the uniform. Rather than an armor of neat dresses and white gloves or crisp chinos and white shirts, Kennedy pointedly argued, "it seems to me that what they need is a few bullet proof vests."[126]

Kennedy's disagreements with the black and white women in her group, while impassioned, were neither lasting nor alienating, and some of the WIMS women reconsidered their suggestions in the face of Kennedy's chiding. All accounts agree that the WIMS members shared the goals of supporting the Mississippi movement and ending Jim Crow, but they diverged about what strategies to adopt. WIMS represented Kennedy's first experience in an interracial coalition of women that aimed to fight racism. As a member of WIMS she learned the value of an alliance that was majority white but was spearheaded by black women and had black women in key leadership positions.[127]

Kennedy made valuable connections with black civil rights organizers in Mississippi. Her host in Jackson, Thelma Sanders, benefited from that relationship after her home was firebombed three months later. The summer of 1964 was an especially harsh season for black Mississippians and COFO workers. By late August, "four project volunteers had been killed, four others critically wounded, 80 physically beaten, and 1000 arrested. During the Freedom Summer, 37 black churches were firebombed and burned, and 30 black-owned homes and businesses were destroyed."[128] With the help of Louis McKay, Kennedy sponsored an event at a Manhattan club on Halloween weekend to help Sanders and "other victims of terrorists" rebuild their lives. Speakers from Mississippi were invited to give an account of what had transpired there since Freedom Summer.[129]

Kennedy's organizing efforts within political groups and in the press intensified after her return from Mississippi. She began hosting a thirty-minute WLIB radio program on Sunday nights called *Opinions*, in which she debated issues that were similar to those she raised in her newspaper column. Her writing and radio show challenged police brutality and gave a spotlight to both black nationalist and socialist views. Flo often challenged the notion that men were the primary spokespersons on behalf of these topics; for example, she invited Dorothy Pitman (Hughes) of African Americans against the Vietnam War to debate black leadership and white backlash with Youth Against War and Fascism's Joan Hamilton.[130] As Kennedy's organizing efforts increased, so too did the FBI's surveillance. The FBI made note of the broad scope of her activities, from her radio show and column through her participation in WIMS to her role as an organizer of the Committee of Concerned Mothers, a group founded by black women to help support Malcolm X's family after his assassination, as well as her attendance at meetings of the Workers World Party (WWP) and Youth Against War and Fascism (YAWF).[131]

The presence of a range of left-wing groups on this list shows that Kennedy refused to adhere to the political orthodoxies that fueled sectarian divisions. One informer who was active in YAWF, which was affiliated with the radical WWP, described Kennedy as an "outspoken . . . liberal" who attended the group's meetings but said that "YAWF is cautious" about upsetting her or turning her away "since she is a helpful middle class Negro attorney, who has a wide variety of friends in many circles."[132]

By 1965 Kennedy's political interests were sprawling and her spheres of influence were expanding beyond the circle of predominantly white male lawyers with whom she had associated since law school. Kennedy was becoming known for the extent of her reach into diverse political groups and middle-class circles as well as for her frank opinions. She was actively and deeply engaged in a quest for a comprehensive political theory and strategy. But Kennedy did not find what she was looking for in any of these groups since each espoused a set of ideas that she regarded as incomplete. Instead, she had to work out these political questions for herself. Despite Kennedy's successful practice and growing cachet in political and middle-class circles, however, she was still seen as an interloper in the mostly white New York City neighborhood where she lived and worked.

"Flo Was Different after the Arrest": Fighting Police Brutality

Sometime in 1960 Kennedy leased an apartment on East Forty-Eighth Street. This central Manhattan location served as both her home and the location of her law firm at a time when her relationships with her husband and legal partners were crumbling.[133] On August 9, 1965, after five years of living and working in midtown, while she was walking home from a doctor's appointment she noticed a police barrier on Madison Avenue. Apparently there had been a gas main explosion, and the police and firemen were attempting to secure the area. Kennedy waited behind the barricade until she witnessed three white men being allowed to pass by the same policeman who had blocked her.[134] She proceeded to show the officer her identification with her address and explained that she was "hurrying home to take medicine for an eye infection," but her words did not persuade the officer that she lived in the upper-class neighborhood and should be allowed to pass just like her white neighbors. After seeing "15 other men, all white," being allowed through after they told the policeman that they were going to Grand Central Station, she was furious. She waited until the cop had turned his back and another group of men and a bus were being allowed to pass with the officer's permission, and then she walked right alongside them. Instantly a team of policemen surrounded her and pushed her into the patrol car. Angry and humiliated, Kennedy loudly protested her arrest. She questioned them about the double standard in allowing the white men to pass while forbidding her to do so and reiterated that she was a lawyer and lived in the neighborhood. The officers reported that she became "loud and boisterous" and resisted being taken to the precinct headquarters.[135] At the station she was charged with resisting arrest and obstruction of justice.[136] Kennedy described the brutality and humiliation she endured: "I was stripped naked by a policewoman. My clothing was searched, and I was even made to squat naked to see if there was anything concealed internally."[137]

For Kennedy, the refusal of the police to allow her to go home while others were permitted to do so and then the arrest and strip search happened for only one reason: "It was a situation of old fashioned discrimination," she contended; "in my opinion the real situation was that they didn't think I lived in the area."[138] After all, black women lawyers were rare, and her professional title did not outweigh the fact that she was a black woman in an elite white neighborhood. Kennedy's resistance to the officer's authority no doubt served as confirmation of his impression that she was a criminal and threatening. Her smart summer suit, slightly hobbled walk, and middle-aged appearance (she was forty-nine at the time) did nothing to protect her. Indeed, she argued, "the weaker they think you are, the worse they treat you."[139] Having practiced law for over fourteen years, waged her own battles against discrimination, and joined organizations to combat discrimination, Kennedy was not weak, nor was she weakened by this experience of police brutality.

That night Kennedy left the police department visibly shaken and fuming, her sister Joyce remembered; "she was on a mission."[140] Calling her sisters, Kennedy railed against the police. Then she called every reporter she could think of and described the incident in detail. Three days later Kennedy's story was covered in the *Amsterdam News*, a Harlem-based black newspaper with a national audience.[141] Kennedy no doubt announced her arrest on her radio program as well. Despite her numerous encounters with racism throughout her life, she was taken aback by her arrest. In court, she was charged with obstructing justice and resisting arrest. Despite a vigorous defense led by her lawyer and Kennedy's own media blitz, which continued into the fall, she was convicted of obstructing justice, although the other charge was dismissed. For years she continued to appeal her conviction, but all her appeals were denied.[142] At one point Kennedy even announced that she was suing the police department for $500,000 in damages for brutalizing her.[143]

Kennedy had come to understand that being a lawyer and "becoming somebody" could not shield her from oppression. She had, of course, known that intellectually long before the arrest, but that day in August of 1965—when she was forced into a police car in front of her white neighbors and had to remove her pants and underclothing, spread her legs, and squat in front of a police officer, all because she was determined to walk alongside her white male counterparts—drove home the meaning of racism and gave it new emotional significance. Her sister Joyce recalled, "Flo was different after the arrest."[144]

■ The change in Flo was palpable. To Joyce, Flo appeared even "more impatient" with the coercive power of racism. Over the years, Joyce had witnessed her sister as a fighter in a range of battles. Kennedy's work as a lawyer, her education in various groups, the numerous speakers on her radio program, and her conversations with organizers at meetings all reflected a profound course in radical movements and political philosophy. Kennedy had attempted to "strike a blow" against what was commonly referred to as the establishment through the law, through journalism, and in political organizations, yet no movement or organization had won her full commitment. The burgeoning Black Power movement in the mid-1960s, however, would give her a frame for her various ideas and for her increased impatience with white supremacy. Its frontal attack on the state, relentless critique of racist images of blacks in the media, and commitment to black leadership, self-defense, and self-determination for black communities made the call for Black Power in 1966 uniquely compelling.

5

Black Power May Be
the Only Hope America Has

BLACK POWER, FEMINISM, AND

THE NEW LEFT, 1966–1967

On July 29, 1966, Congressman Adam Clayton Powell Jr. and Student Nonviolent Coordinating Committee chairman Stokely Carmichael held a press conference in Washington, D.C., to announce the first National Black Power Conference. Their main objective was to create a forum in which black men and women from diverse political perspectives could examine the implementation of Black Power. The conference would capitalize on SNCC's recent call for black people to embrace Black Power as a political strategy. A month before the press conference, during the March Against Fear, Carmichael and fellow SNCC organizer Willie Ricks replaced the familiar civil rights chant of "Freedom Now!" with "Black Power!"[1] Activist and law student James Meredith began the March Against Fear on his own. He was committed to walking from Memphis, Tennessee, to Jackson, Mississippi, defying the constant threat of white violence, in order to encourage blacks to register to vote, a right that was newly protected by the Voting Rights Act of 1965. Not long after Meredith left Memphis, a white supremacist gunned him down and left him severely injured in the middle of the street.[2]

Black leaders from the Southern Christian Leadership Conference (SCLC), the NAACP, the Congress of Racial Equality, and SNCC quickly organized to continue the march in his name. An intense debate ensued, however, when SNCC and CORE challenged the NAACP and SCLC's plan to have the march focus national attention on supporting congressional passage of President Lyndon Johnson's new civil rights proposal.[3] SNCC argued that the march should continue to focus on eliminating blacks' fear of white supremacy rather than on legislation. Even more controversially, SNCC openly welcomed the participation of organizations that advocated armed self-defense, such as the Deacons for Defense and Justice.[4] During the march, SNCC announced its deepening commitment to the ideology and practice of Black Power and black self-determination.

Prominent civil rights leaders, including Martin Luther King Jr. and Roy Wilkins, quickly denounced the call for Black Power as shortsighted and a formula for increased white violence against blacks.[5] Theirs and others' criticisms were repeated by the mainstream press in articles that described Black Power as "naked and empty" and "just as vicious and anti-human as white power."[6] In search of a broad base of allies to support Black Power, Carmichael reached out to Congressman Adam Clayton Powell Jr., whose recent public statements had criticized the Black Freedom movement agenda that privileged integration and alliances with white northern liberals over black self-determination and Black Power. Powell was elected to Congress in 1945 and had enough seniority to become chair of the powerful House Committee on Education and Labor in 1961. In May 1966, giving the baccalaureate address at Howard University, he chided civil rights leaders: "Instead of telling us to seek audacious power . . . black power—instead of leading us in the pursuit of excellence, our leaders led us in the sterile chase of integration as an end in itself."[7]

Powell welcomed Carmichael's request to help organize a national Black Power conference to unite black people and clarify the meaning of Black Power.[8] During the press conference, Carmichael explained to reporters that since the March Against Fear, the "white press had taken the slogan 'Black Power' and had distorted its meaning." For Carmichael and Powell, black men and women themselves would define Black Power as an ideology and political practice. "My definition of black power," Carmichael declared, "is power coming from black people. . . . Black people from all over the country coming together forcing economic and political power and forcing their representatives to speak for them."[9]

Interest in the Black Power Conference was immediate and overwhelming—so much so that organizers decided that a large national conference would have to be postponed to allow enough time to properly plan and prepare. Florynce Kennedy was among the hundred black women and men (plus a handful of white organizers) who attended the national Black Power Conference planning session in D.C. that Labor Day weekend.[10] Powell presided over the meeting, held in the very same building where he chaired sessions of the House Committee on Education and Labor. He ordered federal guards to secure the doors, as the meeting was closed to the press and other uninvited guests.[11]

In keeping with their goal of attracting a wide variety of perspectives, organizers had invited a broad range of black organizations and leaders to attend the D.C. planning meeting. Despite SNCC's conflicts with the SCLC and the NAACP during the March Against Fear, invitations were extended to these civil rights organizations, as well as to the other five black congressmen. While Martin Luther King (SCLC), Roy Wilkins (NAACP), and Powell's black congressional colleagues declined the invitation, Kennedy welcomed the opportunity to be a part of the Black Power Conference's early planning stages. She sat alongside Powell; Lincoln Lynch of CORE; Maulana Karenga, founder of the US Organization, a California-based black cultural nationalist organization; and Adelaide Cromwell Hill, a professor of sociology at Boston University, to discuss Black Power "guidelines for action" and planning the national conference.[12]

The Black Power Conference's stress on broad, politically diverse coalitions was in keeping with Kennedy's increasingly antiestablishmentarian politics. In the nascent stages of the movement, Black Power held the promise of a multidimensional confrontation with what many activists during this period termed "the establishment"—that is, the media, big business, and the entire government, from local law enforcement and state courts to Congress, the president and executive branch, and the U.S. Supreme Court—through the creation of broad-based, black-led coalitions. This strategy did not preclude the creation of other groups and movements; indeed, in Kennedy's estimation it necessitated their development.

The women's liberation movement that was burgeoning in the mid-1960s was a welcome addition to the forces for progressive change. Kennedy was an early and enthusiastic participant in the women's movement and rushed from one meeting to another in the course of a week or even a day. She never abandoned one struggle for another; instead, she attempted to tie these movements and their theories together in hopes of building a more powerful, comprehensive alliance. Frequently identifying this political practice and ideology as "antiestablishmentarianism," she quickly made friends with groups and individuals who confronted the establishment in any way. What bonded them, at least in Kennedy's arithmetic, was the act of questioning and challenging "business as usual." Kennedy built her notion of antiestablishment politics by focusing primarily on openings that revealed and contested the interconnections between racism, sexism, and imperialism. Her politics expanded into a pronounced black feminist identification during the mid-1960s as she attempted to make these connections a reality in the everyday practice of the varied movements and organizations that were her political and intellectual homes.

Kennedy's black feminism was profoundly shaped by her relationship with the Black Power movement, and she brought the vision of Black Power to the emerging, predominantly white women's movement. As one of the only black women in the National Organization for Women, she made Black Power into a pivotal ideological influence on the radical feminist politics that was developing in New York City. She was a bridge builder within these movements, demanding that the women's movement partner squarely with Black Power and continue to participate in antiwar struggles. Kennedy welcomed the prospect that women could unite to end sexism. It never occurred to her, however, that a women's movement would not also fight against racism and imperialism. These battles, for Kennedy, were profoundly interconnected; she later declared that for the Black Power and women's movements, "the enemies are the same."[13] To Kennedy's way of thinking, the two movements were logical allies that should work in coalition and avoid what she termed "horizontal hostility." The Communist Party had espoused the strategy of a united popular front against fascism in 1935. Its rhetoric and programs had enabled black activists and intellectuals, who ranged from liberals to socialists and advocated both union organizing and civil rights agitation, to tie the fight against fascism abroad to the fight against Jim Crow racism at home, which became a major rallying cry during World War II. Significantly, black activists had joined with many white leftists and left-liberals to promote a mass-based, democratic movement seeking racial equality, labor unionization, and social welfare policies that would benefit working people.[14] The upsurge of social movements in the 1960s presented another opportunity to form broad-based coalitions.

Kennedy's later assertion that she could "understand feminism [and sexism] better because of the discrimination against Black people"[15] and because of her work in black movements helps us to identify the Black Power movement as a significant force in shaping feminist struggles. Earlier scholarship on the women's movement has ignored or undervalued the connections between Black Power and feminist struggles. Studies of independent black feminists and the predominantly white feminist movements accurately present Black Power's intense focus on recuperating black masculinity as a major factor dividing it from black and white feminists.[16] But positioning Black Power primarily as an antagonistic influence misses what Black Power might reveal about how both black and white feminists understood liberation and revolution. Probing the intellectual and political relationships between black and white feminists and Black Power thinkers and organizations tells us a great deal about how feminists worked toward reconstructing the society in which they lived. While some recent scholarship has helped to expand our understanding of the Black Power movement's relationship with feminist activism,[17] there is still much to be discovered about the ways in which the Black Power movement was connected to feminist radicalism. Kennedy's activism forces us to see how strategies and theories that originated in Black Power struggles were absorbed, though at times unevenly, by both black and white feminists.

The Media Workshop: A Black Power Organization

During the summer of 1966, Kennedy immediately saw ways in which both white and black activists could utilize the call for Black Power. On August 14, Kennedy hosted a special segment on her radio program titled "Black Power and the Growing White Power Backlash" in which she questioned whether the "problems could be solved on the bargaining table . . . or is . . . the future to be a series of battle grounds with ever larger confrontations?" The panelists included black and white women organizers like Dorothy Pitman (Hughes) and Joan Hamilton.[18] During the weeks leading up to the Black Power Conference planning meeting, Kennedy worried aloud that white activists were not paying enough attention to racism. "Nobody seemed to be doing anything about racism at home," she observed; "the major focus was on the war."[19] Although she did not name any particular organization, Flo was questioning the antiwar and student movements' commitment to freedom and justice.

By 1966, the antiwar movement was expanding, and left-wing youth groups including Students for a Democratic Society, which was originally affiliated with the socialist League for Industrial Democracy, and the Youth Against War and Fascism, which was affiliated with the Workers World Party, were at the forefront in critiquing the U.S. escalation of the war in Vietnam. Kennedy attended several organizing meetings and demonstrations opposing the war that spring and summer. She was especially visible at protests that challenged the disproportionate numbers of African American and Latino soldiers being drafted by the U.S. government to fight what many argued was an illegitimate war.[20] Kennedy continually argued "that it is very important to oppose" the Vietnam War, but she expected organizations that fought to end the war to keep the goal of ending racism at home at the forefront of their agenda. In particular, she said, "I thought it was really important to deal with racism in media and advertising," and she became convinced that there should be an organization devoted to this issue.[21]

One afternoon in mid-August 1966, some of Kennedy's friends from YAWF and a few union organizers were walking from an antiwar march to Kennedy's apartment. As the group debriefed during their walk down Forty-Eighth Street, Flo voiced her increasing frustration with the state of antiwar organizing and its lack of attention to fighting racism.[22] Jim Haughton, a black union organizer and the founder and director of the Harlem Unemployment Center, agreed with Kennedy that more could be done to challenge racism at home.[23] Flo suggested that they create an organization that targeted racism in the media, especially advertising. That very afternoon the group sat in her living room hammering out what would become the Media Workshop. Its early members included black women, such as Dorothy Pitman (Hughes) of African Americans against the Vietnam War and Florence Rice of the Harlem Consumer Education Council; white trade unionists, such as Edna Slatkin and Harry Halsey; and left-wing white women activists, such as Joan Hamilton of YAWF.[24] With Kennedy as the director and Haughton as the Harlem coordinator, the group began to define its goals and plan its first protests.

The Media Workshop was formed at the same time that Kennedy was participating in planning the Black Power Conference. Consequently, she immediately connected the Media Workshop's goals with the objectives of the nascent Black Power movement and anticipated that the organization would "harness sufficient Black Power to make a meaningful protest against . . . Jim Crow advertising and the segregated media." One of the Media Workshop's first objectives was to "revolutionize the buying practice of the apathetic consumers and through buying clubs and cooperatives to make Black Power a reality."[25] For Kennedy, Black Power meant mobilizing the collective power that black people, and other poor communities of color, could wield as consumers. Significantly, she saw Black Power not as something to be conferred by the establishment but as something that was within the reach of black people themselves, provided that they exercised it effectively.

Kennedy argued that blacks could utilize their united economic power to reverse the media's racist coverage of their movements and communities. In her *Queens Voice* column, she often critiqued the news for its excessive coverage of blacks' alleged criminality. Studies of the media's coverage of blacks and whites in the 1960s have revealed that during the Kennedy and Johnson administrations, stories about antipoverty initiatives often depicted poor whites sympathetically but portrayed African Americans as fraudulently obtaining welfare benefits.[26] Kennedy argued that big businesses that manufactured consumer goods, TV and radio broadcast networks, publishers of magazines and newspapers, and advertising agencies profited from black patronage. Black consumers watched their "unrealistic programming," paid "for television that does not represent them,"[27] read their "racist news," and then went out and purchased the products they advertised.[28] Kennedy was particularly incensed that black people, who constituted a substantial proportion of the consumer market, nonetheless were subject to discrimination in hiring and in programs and news coverage that trafficked in stereotypes. Their spending financed advertising agencies, media outlets, and large corporations, yet they were entirely ignored, tokenized, or depicted like buffoons and criminals.[29] Moreover, Kennedy pointed out, the media's racist hiring practices meant that qualified black candidates for employment were systematically turned away. Blacks were unrepresented on television and in advertising despite the fact that they, and other people of color, constituted a financially significant market for their programs and products. The Media Workshop estimated that blacks had a purchasing power of $27 billion annually and thus once mobilized could become an economic force to be reckoned with.[30] Indeed, five years earlier the *Wall Street Journal* had come to a similar conclusion when it noted that blacks had an annual purchasing power of $20 billion, "almost equal to that of all Canada."[31]

Large corporations, television stations, and advertising agencies, Kennedy argued, should share their profits with blacks, in keeping with how much money black consumers spent. In addition, the Media Workshop contended that black audiences needed relevant and representative TV and radio programming produced by blacks themselves that more accurately addressed the diversity of black politics, life, and culture. The Media Workshop aspired to produce such programming. Moreover, funding for black media should come from the mainstream media, advertising agencies, and major corporations. Kennedy warned that black communities' buying history required proper compensation or blacks would stop watching the major networks, stop reading major newspapers, and, more important, stop buying advertised products. This statement implied a threat, for urban African Americans had long used the boycott against businesses that failed to serve or hire them.[32]

The Media Workshop was created to unify the black and low-income "unorganized consumer against big, monopolistic national business."[33] Among its far-reaching goals and demands were the following:

Join in negotiations with advertisers and business enterprises for the return of an equitable percentage of the consumer dollar to the black or other low-income community. Such returns should take the form of capital investment in ghetto industrial construction, wages, housing projects, apprentice training, reduced prices, hospital wings or equipment, recreational facilities, neighborhood parks, community centers, ghetto controlled television production training and rehabilitation for welfare recipients—academic, art, music and professional scholarships to adults as well as youths. . . . Launch a long range educational program to acquaint the low income consumer with the high cost of financing the war chest of large national advertisers. . . .

Return of an equitable percentage of between 25% and 35% of the advertising budget to black and Spanish speaking communities in the form of ad and TV training centers and recreation—including special training and rehabilitation for welfare recipients.[34]

With these goals in mind, the Media Workshop confronted Benton and Bowles, a leading advertising agency in New York City representing such businesses as Procter and Gamble, Mattel Toys, and General Foods, and requested that it supply information about its hiring practices and programming policies.[35] Benton and Bowles immediately dismissed the Media Workshop's demands.[36] Undeterred, Kennedy helped plan the group's first major protest that targeted the agency, and by extension the advertising industry, through a two-day picket line in front of its downtown office. Media Workshop protesters demanded that Benton and Bowles hire more black employees and share its profits with low-income communities of color or these consumers would boycott the products it advertised.[37]

Kennedy most likely chose to direct the Media Workshop's initial action against Benton and Bowles because of its prominence among advertising agencies and because many black and low-income consumers utilized products made by its major clients. Using fliers and placards that mentioned everyday food and household products such as Kool-Aid, Maxwell House coffee, and Camay soap, Kennedy sought to focus the public's attention on the larger issue of racist discrimination in the media.[38] Through Kennedy's prior legal case against *The Ann Sothern Show*, she came to understand that ad agencies like Benton and Bowles created not just advertising spots but rather entire radio and TV programs. For example, in 1919 Benton and Bowles invented the "soap opera" for radio, so named because the sponsors were typically detergent companies. Later in 1956, Benton and Bowles created the successful soap opera *As the World Turns* for CBS.[39] Thus, by targeting Benton and Bowles, Kennedy also focused public attention on advertising as a key segment of the media industry that created and maintained racism.

On Thursday and Friday, September 15 and 16, 1966, members of the Media Workshop and activists from CORE picketed Benton and Bowles's office at 666 Fifth Avenue in midtown Manhattan. In order to drum up support for the protest from diverse groups, they prepared letters and fliers to be distributed at CORE and union meetings condemning Benton and Bowles and its major clients for making large profits from black and low-income consumers "while less than 1% of the advertising budget is returned, in any form[,] to the ghetto communities."[40] Kennedy, Jim Haughton, and Florence Rice were among the protesters who marched up and down Fifth Avenue chanting and holding signs that read "Is there a bigot in your market basket?" and "Jim Crow lives on Madison Avenue."[41] Rice's Consumer Education Council had held similar boycotts against the phone company for overcharging African American customers.[42] In an effort to garner support for the picket against Benton and Bowles, union organizer Edna Slatkin argued that the dollar power of the black consumer was not valued; even worse, the black consumer "picks up the tab for the wasteful, racist combination of big business, the media and the advertising costs" and pays for "the discrimination practices of advertising agencies, the tokenism in TV news coverage, with unrealistic programming." Furthermore, the interracial protesters asserted that the Media Workshop aimed to help "make Black Power a reality."[43]

After only two days of picketing, Kennedy celebrated that fact that the Media Workshop was invited from "the streets . . . to the suites" of Benton and Bowles to negotiate an end to the protest.[44] The group won its demand to have the agency hire more black employees; later Benton and Bowles sponsored a charity event for low-income families during the Christmas holiday.[45] As noted by a few observers, the protest hampered the company's operations for two days and caught the attention of the media and other advertising agencies.[46] Other ad agencies were also forced to reconsider their lack of racial diversity in hiring.[47]

Kennedy was not satisfied with these advances; she wanted Benton and Bowles to support a Media Workshop–produced television program called *Roundtable* (originally named *Afterhours*) that would be similar to her WLIB radio program *Opinions*. *Roundtable* would have various celebrity guests and hosts and represent a wide breadth of political and intellectual views. Kennedy's list of hosts and guests included many of those she described as "non-establishmentarian politicos par excellence." The list included Media Workshop members Jim Haughton, Joan Hamilton, Dorothy Pitman (Hughes), and Florence Rice; political writers and artists such as James Baldwin, Beah Richards, and Nina Simone; and emerging Black Power leaders such as Stokely Carmichael and Floyd McKissick. *Roundtable*'s list of program topics reflected the range of Kennedy's interests and organizing issues: "Where Do Whites Fit in the Freedom Fight of the American Black?," "The War against the War on Poverty," "The Consumer Rebellion," "Should Parents Forbid Their Sons to Serve in Vietnam?," "Flo Kennedy Interviews the Deacons [for Defense]: Should Negroes Organize a Military Defense?," and "Adam Clayton Powell on Adam Clayton Powell."[48]

Benton and Bowles refused to sponsor the program that Kennedy and the Media Workshop believed would more fully represent black life and culture than those shows airing on CBS and ABC. Although Kennedy was frustrated by their response, she continued to organize picket lines in front of Benton and Bowles throughout the fall and winter of 1966 and 1967 in hopes of pushing advertisers to provide financial backing for black-produced and politically radical television shows.[49]

"Catch a Nigger by the Toe": The Media Workshop's Defense of Representative Adam Clayton Powell Jr.

By the fall of 1966, Flo Kennedy and the Media Workshop had not slowed down and were deeply involved in defending Representative Adam Clayton Powell Jr. against his white colleagues' attempts to deny him the seat to which he had been reelected. The group argued that the press played a crucial role in supporting the congressional campaign against Powell, which was based on allegations of neglect of legislative business, financial mismanagement, nepotism, and sexual impropriety. The Media Workshop argued that the press published a disproportionate number of articles criticizing him while failing to report with the same diligence on white members of Congress who engaged in identical behavior.

The plan to remove Powell came to a head two weeks after the Black Power planning session ended. On September 15, Representative Sam Gibbons (D-Florida) announced that Powell had missed 75 percent of the roll and quorum calls that year. The next week Gibbons, who since 1963 had served on the Committee on Education and Labor that Powell chaired, joined with some of his colleagues in an attempt to limit Powell's power by persuading the committee to adopt new rules that forced Powell to consult and gain approval from a majority of the committee members on everything from the formation of subcommittees to basic staffing.[50] These rules in effect stripped Powell of his authority and put power in the hands of the six subcommittee chairs.[51] Moreover, Gibbons argued that Powell not only was a thief but was standing in the way of racial progress and that his actions "contributed to worsening race relations."[52]

Over the previous decade, Powell had defended himself against various accusations that he had stolen money from the government's coffers. Indeed, historian Derek Musgrove argues that soon after Powell arrived on Capitol Hill in 1944, he "recognized that kickbacks, bribes, misuse of office and committee funds, personal travel on the public dollar and various other forms of graft were so widespread as to constitute an institutional culture."[53] Like other congressmen, he placed family members on the payroll, vacationed overseas at the government's expense, and accepted financial kickbacks.[54] As Charles Hamilton explains in Powell's biography, Powell was not the worst offender in Congress, and he used his knowledge of others' misdeeds to his advantage when older, white members of Congress threatened him with exposure.[55] As a black politician, however, Powell was especially vulnerable to criticism and censure for committing the unethical and illegal acts that were common in Congress.

Kennedy argued that the campaign to unseat Powell during the summer of 1966 had little to do with charges of impropriety but was a direct result of his support of the nascent Black Power movement. Kennedy saw Powell's involvement in organizing the Black Power Conference as "the beginning of the downfall of Adam Clayton Powell." She did not believe that the House of Representatives' "decision to de-ball him" had anything to do with the stories about his unethical behavior that were rampant in the press. Rather, the attack on Powell, Kennedy contended, was a direct act of political castration by white members of Congress and was designed to strip him of his power as a legislative leader and as a leader in the emerging Black Power movement. "It was because he became peripherally involved with the whole concept of Black Power . . . allowing some of the people to use his office and so forth" that the campaign to unseat him began in earnest, Kennedy insisted.[56] Powell added legitimacy to the Black Power movement when he hosted the Black Power planning meeting in a government building with federal guards manning the doors. As a result of his actions, Flo reasoned, the House sought to limit his power and strip the budding Black Power movement of the legitimacy that his participation had conferred.

Within days of Gibbons's public criticism of Powell, Kennedy sent a telegram to Gibbons and other politicians on behalf of the Media Workshop declaring a boycott of Florida oranges because of "Sam Gibbons' racist attack on Harlem Congressman Adam Clayton Powell."[57] Kennedy saw a clear connection between big business and politics. She understood that if sales of oranges from Gibbons's home state fell, Gibbons would come under pressure from the Florida citrus industry and would therefore be more likely to hear the Media Workshop's demand to leave Powell's seat alone.

In January 1967, a substantial number of new members took their seats in the House of Representatives. The Ninetieth Congress included over forty six newly elected Republican members, most of whom were younger and more conservative than the men whom they replaced. An emerging alliance composed of conservative Republicans and Democrats began to formulate a language that "associated crime with race and over spending with a growing welfare state."[58] Powell's exploits were an easy target for this group to take advantage of. Sam Gibbons protected himself by cultivating an image of a squeaky-clean World War II veteran, while the newly elected representatives were immune to their older colleagues' fear that Powell would expose them as thieves and hypocrites.

Powell had previously frustrated conservative factions not only because of his staunch support for President Johnson's War on Poverty programs but also because he had joined forces with the NAACP and insisted on adding a rider to legislation that stated that federally financed programs that practiced racial discrimination could not receive government funding.[59] This proviso was the source of Title VI of the Civil Rights Act of 1964. Hence, there were major material interests at stake on the Hill in limiting his power.

In January of 1967, once it became clear that Powell would be stripped of his seat when the new Congress was sworn in, Kennedy and the Media Workshop again asked consumers to stop buying Florida citrus products because "racist Florida representative Sam Gibbons contributed to the eeny, meeny, miney, mo" that singled out Powell while white congressmen were not investigated or unseated.[60] This familiar rhyme was used by children to randomly designate who would be "it" during a game. Kennedy invoked the rhyme to point out that the choice to select Powell was deliberate and racist, as the next line of the most familiar version was "catch a nigger by the toe."[61] The Media Workshop's press releases and fliers critiqued the "double standard of the media" in not extensively reporting on "widespread nepotism among congressmen" or on congressional misappropriation of funds. Kennedy called for a boycott of the media, specifically the New York Daily News and "the liberal [New York City mayor John] Lindsey's mouthpiece The New York Times," with its "Brooks Brothers Racism," as well as their advertisers, such as Macy's and the S. Klein department stores.[62] Although Powell did not mention that these challenges in Congress affected his leadership of the Black Power Conference, by the end of 1966 he had stepped down as a convener.[63]

Planning the Black Power Conference: Harnessing the Power of the People

After numerous delays, shifts in location, and changes in leadership, the first Black Power Conference was scheduled to be held in Newark, New Jersey, in July 1967. The planning committee included several notable emerging figures in the Black Power struggle, including Omar Abu Ahmed, who had served as Malcolm X's bodyguard and was chairman of the Harlem–East River chapter of CORE; Amiri Baraka, who had published poetry under his previous name, LeRoi Jones; and Nathan Wright, an Episcopal priest, scholar, and poet who led the National Council of Negro Churchmen. Those figures alone suggest the range of support for Black Power. Kennedy continued to help plan and publicize the conference and agreed to cochair the panel on the media.[64]

As new Black Power groups formed at the same time that Black Power ideas spread among established civil rights groups such as CORE and SNCC, misinformation about the movement's goals and strategies continued to circulate in the press. Kennedy argued that the mainstream media utilized their power to undermine black people and their movements by circulating untruths. The media-driven myth Kennedy was most interested in challenging was the notion that Black Power was a totally new concept without a legitimate history. She understood that the central principles of Black Power had much deeper roots than the white public realized.[65] For Kennedy, Black Power had always existed but "was like the wind that turns no windmill or the waterfall that was not harnessed to run a generator."[66]

In an interview about the Black Power Conference with a journalist from the *New York Times*, Kennedy asserted that it was vitally important to organize blacks' "efforts for the sake of effectiveness."[67] Kennedy hoped that through the Black Power Conference, diverse black voices and discrete organizations could be brought together in alliance to generate Black Power by transforming it from an ideology to a movement. Like other black organizers, she was becoming increasingly frustrated with the failure of the judicial system and the federal and state governments to recognize black women and men as full citizens and to protect their rights. Having worked with Wednesdays in Mississippi, she understood that building relationships between blacks and liberal whites was an important tool, but its potential was limited, especially if black leadership was not predominant. Furthermore, Kennedy was completely dissatisfied with the courts as an avenue for justice and thought that the national NAACP's focus on legal strategies was no longer effective. Though Flo still worked as an attorney during the day, she found the courts an inefficient mechanism for creating change and devoted much more of her time to activism. Kennedy argued later that those in power always manipulated laws. When rich white male institutions "find a law that doesn't work for them, they change the law" to suit their needs.[68] Kennedy was interested in discussions that underscored the ability of oppressed communities to challenge the structure of power relationships.

Strategies black men and women could use to protect themselves from racist violence that was condoned and sponsored by the state dominated Kennedy's comments. Two years earlier she had been brutally arrested while walking to her midtown apartment because, she believed, the police did not imagine that a black woman could live in a largely white neighborhood. The painful memories of her arrest and strip search were not forgotten; she frequently mentioned this outrage in conversation. Being a lawyer, holding degrees from Columbia, and living in one of the North's most diverse cities did not protect her from racial violence. Kennedy continued to question the reliance on a movement strategy of nonviolent direct resistance that was often advocated by civil rights activists. As Kennedy said previously, she had learned through Wednesdays in Mississippi that what black activists and other oppressed people needed most was "a few bullet proof vests."[69] As members of SNCC and CORE were questioning the effectiveness of nonviolent direct action, Kennedy was privy to these debates. She welcomed the fact that young black radicals were rethinking their previous strategies and placing diverse movement tactics on the organizing table. Kennedy was excited that they might harness the revolutionary potential of Black Power's assertion that black people constituted a single community and therefore had a right to determine their own destiny and overturn unequal relationships of power.

At the same time that Kennedy was deeply involved in the Black Power movement, she was invited to attend a meeting of a new feminist organization that was committed to challenging sex discrimination. Flo said that as "soon as I heard about" the new group, "I was excited."[70] The National Organization for Women was founded in the fall of 1966 in Washington, D.C., at the same time that a variety of women's study groups and organizations were emerging across the country.[71] Kennedy had witnessed white organizers support principles of Black Power at meetings and events held by the WWP, YAWF, and the Media Workshop. Thus, she saw Black Power as offering white activists an opportunity to redouble their commitment to ending racism and as a potential model for organizing both in their own interest and as part of broad-based progressive coalitions.

The Women's Movement: The National Organization for Women

On February 6, 1967, Kennedy braved the cold air with a friend she knew from her work on a case involving the rights of the United Scenic Artists Union to arrive just in time for the first meeting of the New York chapter of NOW.[72] Dozens of women and a handful of men filled the Upper East Side townhouse of Muriel Fox, cofounder of NOW and an executive at Carl Byoir and Associates, one of the country's largest publicity firms. Most of the guests had received invitations in the mail, while others, including Flo, came with an invited friend because they were interested in becoming a part of an organization dedicated to challenging sex discrimination. Everyone was asked to introduce themselves to the group. Jean Faust, Cynthia Epstein, Ti-Grace Atkinson, and Muriel Fox's husband, Shepard Aronson, were among those in attendance. Betty Friedan, founder of NOW and the national president, welcomed the group.[73] In 1963 Friedan had written the popular book *The Feminine Mystique*, which described the limits of women's traditional roles in the home. At the meeting, she explained the motivation for starting the new organization and its future goals.

Friedan expressed the hope that NOW would challenge sex discrimination against women just as the NAACP challenged race discrimination against African Americans. In other settings she recounted that NOW was originally conceived of as a type of "NAACP for Women."[74] The group hoped to challenge unequal employment and divorce laws and to be advocates of the civil rights of women.[75] NOW's statement of purpose declared that it would "organize to initiate or support action, nationally or in any part of this nation, by individuals or organizations, to break the silken curtain of prejudice and discrimination against women in government, industry, the professions, the churches, the political parties . . . and every other field of importance in American society."[76]

At some point, those in attendance were asked if they had any questions or comments. Kennedy's hand flew into the air. Cynthia Epstein, then a graduate student at Columbia, immediately recognized Flo as one of the few women attorneys practicing in the city.[77] By then, Kennedy was "making a name . . . in New York City."[78] Flo thoroughly agreed that an organization devoted to fighting sex discrimination was necessary and articulated her ideas about how NOW should initiate that struggle: "Women ought to oppose the war!"[79] "We . . . control so much money . . . and [do] much of the purchasing . . . [so] we [should] bring consumer action against the media and against the war."[80] NOW "should be for Black Power!"[81] Fox and Friedan were stunned by Kennedy's suggestions. Was she not listening to them? Did she not understand that NOW was created to eliminate discrimination against women? Both women looked at Kennedy as if she were crazy or "demented."[82] One after the other, they attempted to silence Flo before her assertions derailed the meeting. "We are not here to talk about the war" or about Black Power, they scolded.[83] In the view of NOW's founders, Black Power and antiwar politics were not central to a feminist movement.

Kennedy was undaunted by her public reprimand. In fact, one onlooker remembered Flo continuing to voice her opinion and not appearing at all flustered or unnerved by their rebuke.[84] When the meeting ended, the founders of NOW no doubt hoped that Kennedy would not attend subsequent meetings. Yet she returned and voiced the very same suggestions. Despite Kennedy's differences with Friedan and Fox, she joined the organization and faithfully attended the monthly meetings.[85] Several NOW members recall Kennedy repeatedly offering proposals even though she was "the only one voting for this or that motion."[86] Her suggestions no doubt involved NOW joining a Media Workshop protest against racism at CBS or participating in a march against the Vietnam War. Surely, after her reception at the first meeting, Kennedy was aware that her motions would be rejected. Yet this did not deter her from proposing new ideas and actions. Obviously, Kennedy's goal was neither to win the argument nor to gain support from NOW's national leadership. On the contrary, she was far more interested in raising the key questions that would insert Black

Power and the antiwar movement into the dialogue surrounding sexism. Kennedy sought to make these feminist activists think.

Later, she suggested that others utilize the strategy of offering ideas even when they knew they would be scorned or dismissed. "The idea is just not to sit still in the boat. But, rock it . . . make your feelings known."[87] For Kennedy, if this new organization wanted to build a movement alongside the struggles that were already under way, feminists would have to join the movements for Black Power and against the Vietnam War. Flo was a steady and persistent agitator in NOW meetings, offering suggestions and comments that tied the nascent struggle against sexism to ongoing efforts to end racism and imperialism.

Although other NOW chapters developed across the country not long after the New York chapter was created, the New York group became the national organization's largest, most active, and most visible chapter.[88] That first year several committees were created, including those on the image of women, employment, and finance. A number of new members, including Ivy Bottini, Joan Hull, E. Betty Barry, Anselma Dell'Olio, Kate Millet, and Catharine Stimpson, joined the chapter in 1967 and 1968.[89] But Kennedy was the only black feminist to consistently attend New York chapter meetings during NOW's first year. While the black state assemblywoman from Brooklyn, Shirley Chisholm, belonged to the New York chapter and served on NOW's national board, she rarely attended chapter meetings.[90] The black feminist lawyer Pauli Murray was a founding member of NOW but lived in South Carolina in 1967 and therefore was not a member of the New York chapter. Kennedy was often the sole black person in the room—a position she had become accustomed to during her legal career but one that did not prevent her from raising the issues that most deeply concerned her. Despite Kennedy's presence and her steady flood of suggestions, she was never elected to chair a committee. Nor was she elected to serve on the national executive committee that was also housed in New York City. It is possible that Kennedy would have declined these positions even if she were nominated.[91]

The fact that Kennedy did not hold an official leadership position in the organization did not stop her from having influence, especially on the younger women in NOW. By this time, it had been almost two decades since she had first theorized in an undergraduate paper a potential alliance of white women and black people to combat racist and sexist oppression. NOW represented a prime opportunity to build just such an alliance to defeat racism, sexism, and imperialism. Despite the fact that Betty Friedan and others in NOW's national leadership did not share her vision, the organization was new, and in Kennedy's view it offered the potential for alliances.[92]

While those in NOW's national leadership tried to ignore Kennedy, they could not stop several of the younger white women from being drawn to her message. Flo carried her briefcase plastered with antiwar stickers to NOW meetings and often opened it up to hand out fliers detailing organizing meetings and protests throughout the city.[93] During a gathering in the summer of 1967, Kennedy announced that the national Black Power Conference was being held less than an hour away in Newark, New Jersey. Describing how blacks were uniting to achieve their own liberation, Flo encouraged feminists to learn from Black Power's lead.

The Black Power Conference and the
Black Revolutionary Struggle

On July 20–24, 1967, more than one thousand black women and men from the United States, the Caribbean, and Africa gathered in Newark.[94] The delegates represented several different organizations from various political perspectives. A riot in Newark that had occurred only days before the conference helped to nearly triple the registration rolls from the initial projection of only four hundred participants.[95] The riots in Newark and Detroit that summer and the masses of blacks who descended upon the convention also forced organizers to engage the concept of Black Power as a tool for revolutionary change at the grassroots. At the workshops, speakers such as Amiri Baraka; SNCC's new chairman, H. Rap Brown; and Maulana Karenga, chairman of US, all stressed self-defense against white terrorism and warned whites of the radical change in black people. Other black leaders in attendance emphasized a more moderate and reformist view of Black Power, stating that "blacks needed to be like other ethnic groups in America who developed their own solidarity as a basic approach toward entry into the American mainstream."[96] Whether left-wing or more traditional in their goals, all espoused the idea that black people should rely primarily on their own power to claim their liberation.

The Black Power Conference was important for Kennedy because it emphasized black people's use of their collective power to challenge American racism and imperialism. Through the five-day conference, Kennedy more fully defined her thinking on power and on oppressed people's ability to make use of their group strength. She advocated a pluralistic view of Black Power represented by leaders as diverse as Adam Clayton Powell, Nathan Wright, and Malcolm X (after his split from the Nation of

Islam). Black Power pluralists argued that in the United States, power was monopolized by whites; in order for blacks to challenge this oppressive monopoly, they needed to move toward a position of community strength. Most pluralists believed that they could translate racial solidarity into decision-making power at the local and national levels. As a result, they maintained, black people, the nation, and the world would be fundamentally transformed for the better.[97]

Kennedy credited no other movement with having as much potential for illuminating the fundamental contradictions of American democracy and thereby rearticulating American democratic principles and ideas, not only for black people but for all oppressed people. Like many other radicals, she saw the emerging women's movement as a logical extension of Black Power's emphasis on liberation and self-determination.[98] Later, reflecting on the inspiring influence that black struggles had on other groups, she remarked that "black people are more politically aware, generally, than other oppressed groups in this country. . . . And most of these people pattern their resistance after blacks."[99]

As a facilitator of the conference's Black Artists, Craftsmen, and Communications Personnel workshop, along with Carol Green and the actor, director, and playwright Ossie Davis, Kennedy used the session to discuss strategies for challenging the media and to stress the importance of sharing tactical information across movement lines.[100] The three stood at the front of the room detailing their thoughts on the media. Kennedy no doubt described her recent efforts in the Media Workshop to force advertising agencies and major TV networks to support black-produced programs that emphasized black politics and culture.

Not long after the session began, Kennedy was interrupted by a commotion in the back of the room. Queen Mother Moore was standing up, demanding that two white intruders seated in the last row be asked to leave. Moore was a forceful voice in black nationalist circles and had been active in black radical politics since the 1920s. Once a member of Marcus Garvey's Universal Negro Improvement Association and the Communist Party (USA), she was now leading the reparations movement through the Reparations Committee she had founded in 1962.[101] Her voice bellowed throughout the room: "These white women have to get out! This meeting is for blacks only!" The activists seated in the front rows turned around to see young white feminists and NOW members Ti-Grace Atkinson and Peg Brennan shrinking into their seats as Moore hovered over them. From the front of the room Kennedy quickly came to their defense: "These are my guests! I don't invite people some place then tell them to leave!" But Moore and the other attendees did not care whose guests the white women were; they just wanted them out.[102]

For Moore and the other organizers, the Black Power movement differed from the civil rights struggle in which white participation was directly encouraged. Black Power promoted independent black politics, and white participation in the conference threatened to disrupt this goal. As the argument between Kennedy and Moore escalated, the atmosphere became tense and bodies began to rise from their seats. Atkinson remembered someone in the crowd threatening to kill Kennedy for bringing white women to the Black Power Conference. "Do what you have to do," Kennedy retorted; "I've lived my life."[103]

There was another unwanted guest in the room as well, although this attendee escaped notice—the FBI agent monitoring Kennedy. The informant recorded that Kennedy became louder and more belligerent as she "directed profanity at Negroes present, and refused to ask whites who were present to leave."[104] Afraid of what might happen next, Peg Brennan "got out of there fast." When Kennedy saw Brennan leave, she ordered Ti-Grace Atkinson to "stay where you are!" Shaking, Atkinson froze, not daring to leave her chair. To her surprise, Moore and her backers eventually gave way. Kennedy and the other facilitators returned to their presentations as Atkinson listened quietly, staring at her feet.[105]

Years later, with the benefit of hindsight, Atkinson said that deciding to attend the conference was "nuts." Yet she profoundly appreciated the opportunity Kennedy had provided her to witness the Black Power movement during its formative years. Hearing black activists plot strategies and formulate resolutions "transformed" her growing feminist politics. Atkinson commented that Kennedy "was always trying to pull it together, and [I] have to say in many ways maybe it was a bad idea or clumsy or difficult, but it's why people like myself became really transformed not only in terms of politics generally, but because of my feminism. It deepened everything."[106]

Even after this incident, Flo continued to invite young white feminists from NOW to Black Power meetings, as well as to antiwar marches. Kennedy sought to educate white feminists, especially those who did not come out of the antiwar or civil rights movements, about imperialism and racism. Atkinson remembered that Kennedy wanted feminists to witness "a group of people in transition and evolving" and to learn from the Black Power movement's mistakes and hard-won victories.[107] The confrontation at the conference workshop reveals the value Kennedy placed on white feminists learning from the Black Power struggle and becoming an additional arm in the battle against the repressive state.[108] Commotions over the presence of white feminists in black spaces did not bother Kennedy. If white feminists were rebuffed or embarrassed, she believed the lesson of black rejection was still a good and humbling experience for them. Flo thought that whites who had had little direct contact with black people needed to understand the depths of the injuries that had been done to black women and men and the power of their anger. "What [white] people don't want to admit," she explained "is that they are receivers of stolen property and being receivers of stolen property they should not be surprised that they are not loved."[109] Moreover she argued that whites should realize that black people could decide whether and where whites were allowed in black-controlled spaces, rather than only vice versa, as was the case under segregation.

Kennedy's ability to quiet the room and to have Atkinson remain at the conference despite other blacks' objections suggests that Kennedy held a degree of authority in Black Power gatherings that was not readily shaken by the confrontation. Kennedy's involvement in the Black Power conferences helped connect her to the larger Black Power movement. Historian Komozi Woodard argues that the Newark conference and the Black Power conferences that followed served as key sites for the development of movement leadership. The Black Power conferences that were held between 1966 and 1969 mark the beginning of what Woodard describes as the Modern Black Convention Movement. He contends that this movement generated leadership at all levels, nurtured local leaders' identification with a national movement, and created an atmosphere for the development of black united fronts.[110] In many ways, Kennedy's organizing work at the conferences substantiates Woodard's conclusions. Through her efforts to develop a black united front, she built relationships with local and national black radicals and became a leader in the larger black convention movement. Equally important, she showed the white New Left, particularly white feminists, ways in which they could continue working with the Black Freedom movement after the rise of Black Power. For Kennedy, Black Power had the potential to end oppression broadly and to create not only a black united front but also a larger interracial front with the Black Power struggle at the helm.

Racism Is "Deadly": The Black Power Movement Should Lead

Kennedy came to NOW believing that racism shaped relationships of power and domination in the United States and was therefore the litmus test for American democracy. Like other black radicals such as Ella Baker and W. E. B. Du Bois, Kennedy reasoned that racism affected every major social problem in the United States, especially the oppression of women.[111] By 1967 Kennedy was using the term "niggerizing" as a synonym for oppression, a rhetorical strategy intended to force others to understand how the racist techniques developed against blacks could be deployed against all oppressed people. Although Kennedy recognized oppressions as interconnected, in the final analysis she believed that racism was the foundational form of inequality in American society and that it shaped other modes of exploitation and oppression. Moreover, like other Black Power leaders and some white leftists, she argued that black people "started this revolution," spent more time on the front lines, and "struggled first, struggled more, [and] struggled harder"; therefore the Black Freedom movement and specifically the Black Power struggle had earned the right to claim vanguard status within the larger struggle.[112]

Kennedy was not the only or the first black feminist lawyer who saw the fight against racism as a catalyst for ending sexism or who analogized these oppressions. Legal scholar Serena Mayeri demonstrates how the black feminist lawyer Pauli Murray deployed the logics of the civil rights movement within feminist legal strategies. Murray fought "Jane Crow"— the laws and practices that discriminated against women—by emulating battles against Jim Crow. For Murray, "the race-sex analogy depicted the struggles for racial justice and sex equality as intertwined." Similar to Kennedy, Murray linked the struggles against racism and sexism because she "hoped to close the divide between the reawakening feminist movement and the black civil rights cause."[113]

Kennedy argued that the Black Power/feminist/antiwar coalitions "were not going to be like the labor movement."[114] Perhaps she was pointing to the heated battles that had taken place on the Left in the 1930s and 1940s, when blacks fought in labor struggles and were utilized in pickets and protests but were often excluded from the high-paying jobs and leadership positions after the protests were over. Although she was too young to have participated in those struggles, the black union organizers she worked with in various organizations must have reminded her of this problem.

While Kennedy privileged black movements and emphasized racial oppression, she stressed that it was still necessary to challenge all forms of oppression because, as she later put it, they all "hurt like crazy." In her opinion the only way to overthrow a particular form of exploitation successfully and permanently was to conquer all forms of exploitation.[115]

Kennedy believed that a steady and consistent attack against oppression from a variety of organizational fronts would help to speed revolutionary change. This approach helps to explain her relationships with white left-wing and feminist organizations. While working in predominantly white spaces, she demanded that white activists focus on ending racism and support the Black Power struggle. During this period she frequently instructed white radicals on the importance of understanding how power and force circulate in the United States: "If you test the fences of this society and dare to influence the direction of this society, they know you mean business by the extent to which you identify with the black revolution. . . . If you want to absolutely communicate the depth of your determination to bring down this society that is committed to racism, then indicate determination to frustrate racism with a coalition with the black revolutionary struggle."[116]

"A Coalition with the Black Revolutionary Struggle": The National Conference for New Politics

Only a few weeks after the Black Power Conference in Newark ended, Kennedy invited NOW feminists to another important organizing conference. The National Conference for New Politics (NCNP) in Chicago promised to bring white leftists together in conversations with Black Power and civil rights advocates about meaningful ways they could collaborate. An outgrowth of several meetings held during the summer and fall of 1965 between anti–Vietnam War radicals, reform Democrats, and civil rights organizers, the NCNP had several broad objectives: to end the Cold War and U.S. military intervention abroad, to establish racial equality, to encourage both world disarmament and constructive relations between people undertaking revolutionary change, and, finally, to address the needs of the decaying cities and depressed rural areas in the United States.[117] The convention's white organizers were especially hopeful that the meeting would unite the differing tendencies within the Black Freedom movement with white liberals and radicals of the peace movement.[118]

Believing that NOW feminists should attend this meeting to learn how to form broader connections with other radicals, Kennedy pushed younger white feminists to register as delegates and arranged for them to travel on a fourteen-hour bus ride sponsored by black Muslims from Harlem. On August 30, 1967, Ti-Grace Atkinson boarded a bus to Chicago, where she met Omar Abu Ahmed, organizer of the Black Power Conference and chairman of the Harlem–East River CORE, as well as other black nationalists. For hours they talked about black self-determination and black nationalists' plans for achieving the goal of black liberation.[119]

As soon as the conference convened, the coalition between civil rights, Black Power, and antiwar organizers began to fall apart. Black Power leaders criticized the New Politics Conference organizers for failing to include black people in the early planning stages. Frustrated by the conference's lack of attention to full black participation and black leadership, some black delegates walked out and announced they would hold their own convention.[120] The majority, who remained, formed the Black Caucus. Some, like Kennedy and James Forman of SNCC, traveled back and forth between the two groups.[121]

Black Caucus members met privately to hammer out an agreement. Their strategy recognized the fundamental connections between black liberation and the antiwar movement. The caucus demanded support for the Newark Black Power Conference resolutions, the organization of "white civilizing" committees in white communities to eliminate racism, support for all wars of national liberation worldwide, and, finally, 50 percent voting power on all convention committees.[122]

While many white organizers supported these demands, much debate arose over the 50 percent provision, given that blacks made up only 15 or 20 percent of the participants. Most mainstream news reporters and some white leftists saw the acceptance of the Black Caucus's demands as giving black people an unfair and undemocratic advantage; some even argued that white leftists were now being forced to "lick [the] boots" of black activists.[123]

For the Black Caucus conferees, it was important that black people who fought on the front lines and faced the brunt of the government's attacks be granted significant power and leadership positions. Black Power leaders framed that summer's riots in Newark and Detroit as urban rebellions similar to the rebellion of the Vietnamese people against the puppet dictatorships imposed by the French colonialists and then by the United States and as evidence that the revolution had come home. For them, the use of military and police forces to suppress these urban rebellions demonstrated that black lives were at the vanguard of this battle.[124]

In an essay published in the *Islamic Press International News Gram* a few months after the New Politics Conference ended, Kennedy challenged those "dissident delegates" and reporters who argued that giving blacks 50 percent of the vote meant white activists had "lick[ed black] boots," asserting that "white people don't lick boots when they make a good alliance, Mr. Racist." The "constructive rise of black power may be the only hope that America has," she maintained. "We guess any recognition of the value of the voting power of blacks is 'craven surrender.'"[125]

Kennedy, James Forman, H. Rap Brown, and the other black organizers wanted white leftists to understand one central message: in order to be effective antiracist allies, white activists had to grasp the importance of black self-determination. The influence of the Black Power movement's ideology and organizing strategies was evident throughout the rest of the convention. In particular, the Black Revolution resolution, created by a majority-white workshop, emphasized black leadership and connected the revolts in Detroit and Newark to the struggles of the Vietnamese. "Black people are demanding change with equal determination. White radicals[,] like everyone else, must decide whether we stand with the majority on this earth who resist the acts of the U.S. power structure, or whether to cling to some pitiful little bribe, real or imaginary."[126]

"We Were Observing and We Copied": Black Power's Influence on the Genesis of the Radical Feminist Movement

The influence of Black Power theories and tactics on white participants at the NCNP was exemplified when the mostly white Women's Workshop demanded 51 percent of the convention votes. The Black Caucus protest provided a framework for feminists to understand how to organize separately, inspiring women to create their own agenda that challenged the hegemony of male leadership, both at the convention and in the New Left more generally.

Unlike the Black Caucus, the Women's Workshop was already planned before the conference, but its primary focus was on the ways that women could challenge the Vietnam War. Feminists Jane Adams, Shulamith Firestone, and Jo Freeman and NOW member Ti-Grace Atkinson attended the Women's Workshop in hopes that it would also address sexism. During the conference some of these women voiced their disagreement with the agenda of the Women's Workshop, arguing that its leaders, many of whom were from Women Strike for Peace, were more concerned with challenging the war than confronting sexist oppression.[127] According to Freeman, she and Firestone stayed up all night after the session drafting alternative resolutions that took a more direct stance against the oppression of women. Following the example of the Black Caucus, the women demanded 51 percent of the convention votes on the grounds that women represented 51 percent of the population.[128] They also insisted that the convention support the total equality of women in education and employment, condemn the mass media for perpetuating stereotypes of women, unite with other liberation struggles, and recognize that black women were doubly oppressed.[129] These women threatened to tie up the conference with procedural motions if their resolutions were not debated on the convention floor. The conference organizers finally conceded and added them to the agenda. Freeman, Firestone, and several other women handed out two thousand copies of their resolutions to the delegates.[130]

But William Pepper, executive director of the NCNP, quickly dismissed the women when it was time to read their resolutions. Frustrated, several women ran to the microphone and attempted to make their resolutions heard. Pepper disregarded the women's concerns in a particularly offensive manner: he patted "Shulie [Firestone] on the head and said 'move on little girl we have more important issues to talk about here than Women's Liberation.'" For Freeman, this was the last straw; in her view, the incident represented the "genesis" of the radical, predominantly white women's movement.[131]

Kennedy supported the women's demands and insisted that women's oppression be addressed on the convention floor. Indeed, at the same time Freeman and Firestone were writing their resolutions, Kennedy was in her hotel room coaching Atkinson as she drafted a statement on the connections between sexism, racism, and imperialism.[132] Each evening Kennedy returned to the room and shared her Black Caucus experiences with Atkinson and two other white feminists from NOW. Atkinson stated that Kennedy had a "profound influence . . . on some of us. . . . We were observing and we copied" the Black Caucus strategy.[133]

Years later, Atkinson and Peg Brennan remembered that Kennedy helped them to understand the importance of supporting other social justice movements as part of their feminist politics.[134] Atkinson described how Kennedy pushed white feminists to support black movements because it "was really fundamental . . . to expand understanding and support."[135] Kennedy may well have viewed the feminist organizing at the conference as the type of practical borrowing of movement tactics that needed to take place between organizers. Both Kennedy and Atkinson hoped that the mostly white Women's Workshop participants would continue fighting to end imperialism, sexism, and racism after they left the conference.

The statement Atkinson drafted with extensive coaching from Kennedy emphasized the struggles black people were waging at the conference and throughout the country, describing racial oppression as the most "justifiably immediately pressing" problem. It then went a step further, arguing that "the discrimination against black people should remind us of the discrimination affecting women." Utilizing statistics from NOW's statement of purpose, Atkinson and Kennedy dismissed the then-popular notion that women were not an oppressed group. Citing information on working-class and professional women, the statement demonstrated that women held "only a token handful" of the professional jobs and that "[two-thirds] of Negro women workers are in the lowest paid service occupations." They insisted that "working women are . . . becoming increasingly—*not less*—concentrated on the bottom of the ladder" and earned on average only 60 percent of what their male counterparts earned. They urged the Women's Workshop participants to follow the lead of the Black Caucus and press for their own liberation.[136]

Through a detailed list of suggestions for "immediate action," Atkinson and Kennedy emphasized the connections between women's specific oppression and the responsibility of women to support social movements more broadly. They called particular attention to the fact that not all women are white, a presumption that the media often reinforced. The statement Kennedy coached Atkinson to create also repeated Kennedy's now commonplace refrain that women should understand their "buying power" as consumers and "enforce their demands on the irresponsible media, business and government"; insisted that women participate in all activities affecting the entire community; and argued that women should "assume leadership in self-determination for women and children."[137] One of the last suggestions underscores Kennedy's understanding of the ways in which white women should engage in feminist organizing. As feminists, Kennedy maintained, they should be antiracist and anti-imperialist and unite firmly with both those struggles: "New Politics women should assume their political responsibility by actively supporting protests such as those against the draft and those in black communities. This support should be actively demonstrated through protest against criminal policing activities and through appearing in court-room proceedings involving draft resistors, black protestors, or accused demonstrators. Women must increase their support of those who bear the real burden of their stated moral commitments."[138]

Atkinson and Kennedy signed the letter and invited New Politics women to join NOW's New York chapter if they were interested in addressing these intersecting oppressions. In so doing, Kennedy and Atkinson reframed NOW as an organization with a black feminist agenda—committed to ending racism, sexism, and imperialism and firmly in coalition with other radical movements. As historian Robin Kelley argues, black feminists have "never confined their vision to just the emancipation of black women or women in general, or black people for that matter. Rather, they are the theorists and proponents of radical humanism committed to liberating humanity and reconstructing social relations across the board."[139] Although the statement insisted that white feminists support black social justice movements, Kennedy believed that Atkinson should have been more forceful in supporting the Black Power movement, and in a private discussion she even characterized the statement as racist. Atkinson was confused as to how the very words that Kennedy had dictated to her could now be considered racist. "I'm doing exactly what she told me to do," she remembered.[140] Perhaps Kennedy believed that the statement did not convincingly represent her insistence that the growing women's movement commit itself fully to ending racism and supporting Black Power. She might have also worried that white feminists were attempting to eclipse the Black Caucus's demands. Setting aside whatever reservations she may have held, Kennedy signed and supported the statement because she believed that the connections between racism, imperialism, and sexism had to be addressed at the conference.

Kennedy was encouraged by the growth of the women's movement, and she wanted to do anything she could to create a feminist movement that would eliminate sexism together with racism and imperialism. The black feminism Kennedy espoused was deeply rooted in the theories and strategies of the Black Power struggle, most notably in its commitment to ending white supremacy and imperialism. Indeed, she grounded her critiques of sexism within the Black Power movement's radical criticism of racism and empire. Like many other radicals, she viewed the Black liberation movement as the vanguard movement of the era.[141] Moreover, Kennedy maneuvered among what most contemporary observers and many scholars perceived as divergent and conflicting struggles. Seeking to make connections where others saw divisions, Flo extended Black Power outside black radical circles into primarily white feminist spaces.[142]

By this time, Kennedy had become extremely politically promiscuous and involved herself in the Black Power, New Left, and women's movements. She managed to engage all of these movements simultaneously, even though their key organizations and approaches were sometimes at odds. Kennedy hoped that the burgeoning feminist movement would embrace a coalition with the Black Power and antiwar movements. This examination of Kennedy as a bridge builder between the Black Power Conference, the NCNP, and NOW helps us to center Black Power as a pivotal ideological influence on the predominantly white feminist politics that emerged in the mid-1960s—leading many younger white feminists to a comprehensive view of feminism. When the NCNP meeting came to a close, Kennedy returned to New York City, where she would continue to link these agendas as a member of NOW.

Florynce Kennedy seated with the Columbia Law School Legal Survey Organization in 1951. (Columbia University Law School Library)

Fannie Lou Hamer, Dorothy Height, and Polly Cowan of Wednesdays in Mississippi at a reception in 1967. (Mary McLeod Bethune Council House National Historical Site, National Archives for Black Women's History)

(above)
Betty Friedan talking in November 1966 to a group in New York about discrimination against women and the new feminist organization the National Organization for Women. (AP Images)

(below)
Rep. Adam Clayton Powell Jr. (standing) and Stokely Carmichael of SNCC at a press conference in July of 1966 announcing the creation of the Black Power Conference. (Bettmann/ Corbis/AP Images)

Gloria Richardson, leader of the Cambridge Movement, speaks to reporters at the Black Power Conference in Newark, New Jersey, July 22, 1967. Seated to her right are Omar Ahmed, chairman of the East River CORE chapter in New York City, and Jim Tayari, vice chairman of the US Organization. (AP Images)

Cocounsel Florynce Kennedy and William Kunstler reading a statement from SNCC chairman H. Rap Brown outside the Federal House of Detention in New York City, August 20, 1967. Brown was jailed on federal charges of transporting a gun across state lines while under indictment. (Bettmann/Corbis/AP Images)

H. Rap Brown being led away in handcuffs after his arrest by FBI agents on charges related to his speech in Cambridge, Maryland, in July 1967. (Bettmann/Corbis/AP Images)

Florynce Kennedy outside St. Patrick's Cathedral during an anti–Vietnam War demonstration, New York City, circa 1967. (Jill Freedman/Getty Images)

Valerie Solanas, author of the *SCUM Manifesto*, being led away without handcuffs by New York City police after her arrest for shooting Andy Warhol in June of 1968. (Bettmann/Corbis/AP Images)

Feminist organizers protesting the Miss America Pageant in front of the convention hall in Atlantic City, New Jersey, on September 7, 1968. (Santi Visalli/Getty Images)

(top) Ti-Grace Atkinson being taken into custody outside President Richard Nixon's campaign headquarters in New York City on October 23, 1972, after police said she and other demonstrators were blocking the sidewalks and traffic. Feminist organizers Flo Kennedy, Atkinson, and Gloria Steinem were among those protesting Nixon's position on child care and abortion. (AP Images)

(bottom) After unofficially announcing her bid for the U.S. presidency, Rep. Shirley Chisholm of New York met with students at the University of Miami in January 1972. (AP Images/Steve Starr)

Feminist activists and speaking partners Gloria Steinem and Florynce Kennedy at Syracuse University in 1971. (Ron Sherman)

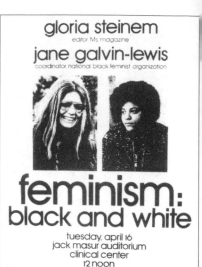

gloria steinem
editor Ms. magazine
jane galvin-lewis
coordinator, national black feminist organization

feminism:
black and white

tuesday, april 16
jack masur auditorium
clinical center
12 noon

a federal women's program presentation

Feminist activists and speaking partners Gloria Steinem and Dorothy Pitman Hughes holding up the Black Power fist in 1971. (© Dan Wynn Archive)

Poster advertising feminist speaking partners Jane Galvin Lewis and Gloria Steinem at the National Institutes of Health's Clinical Center in Bethesda, Maryland, circa 1974.

Florynce Kennedy at a National Organization for Women Conference in 1974.
(Photograph © Bettye Lane)

Harlem consumer rights advocate and black feminist Florence Rice in 2008 at the age of ninety-eight wearing an "I had an abortion" T-shirt publically announcing that she had had an illegal abortion. (Tara Todras-Whitehill)

Florynce Kennedy wearing a large placard and singing songs from the Feminist Party songbook, protesting Channel 13 in New York City, May 10, 1975. (Photograph © Bettye Lane)

(left)
Florynce Kennedy at an Equal Rights Amendment workshop during a NOW conference, September 6, 1974. (Photograph © Bettye Lane)

(below)
Feminists Ti-Grace Atkinson, Flo Kennedy, Gloria Steinem, and Kate Millet in 1977. (Bettye Lane Photographs, David M. Rubenstein Rare Book & Manuscript Library, Duke University)

6

Absorbed Her Wisdom
and Her Wit

CREATING THE WOMEN'S LIBERATION

MOVEMENT, 1967–1968

Inspired by her experience at the New Politics Conference, Ti-Grace Atkinson wanted to connect the National Organization for Women to the Black Power movement and to implement Flo Kennedy's theory of feminist politics. Atkinson wondered how feminists could adapt Black Power strategies to create a liberation movement of their own. How could feminism challenge all forms of oppression—not just the sexism that loomed largest in middle-class white women's consciousness but also racism and imperialism—that intersected with sexism? If the statement she wrote for the New Politics Conference at Kennedy's behest was not strong enough, how could a white feminist make a more powerful statement? Atkinson considered these questions during the months after Kennedy took her to the Black Power and New Politics conferences. To Atkinson's way of thinking, a deeper connection with the Black Power movement was key to discovering the answers.

As members of the New York chapter of NOW Atkinson and Kennedy circulated a statement encouraging women who had participated in the New Politics Conference to join NOW if they wanted to end sexism, racism, and imperialism. In writing from that position, Kennedy and Atkinson reframed NOW as a feminist group with a black feminist politics. Unfortunately, NOW's leadership did not share their excitement about Black Power and resented their using the group's name in connection with the New Politics statement. The executive committee was not pleased that Kennedy and Atkinson wrote the statements on behalf of NOW "without permission" from them.[1]

Despite criticism, Atkinson suggested holding a panel discussion at the organization's November general meeting to discuss Black Power's relationship to the women's movement. Kennedy and Atkinson invited Nathan Wright and Omar Abu Ahmed to speak; both men were organizers of the Black Power Conference and had attended the New Politics Conference. They also invited Betty Shabazz, widow of Malcolm X, and another woman delegate to the New Politics Conference, Black Arts movement actor Vertamae Smart-Grosvenor.[2]

The New York chapter's handwritten and printed minutes from the meeting provide rare insights into what some white feminists took away from the discussion. Next to the name of each speaker, the secretary briefly described the speaker's connection with the Black Power movement and recorded general impressions of each presentation. As if to reveal her own lack of interest in the discussion, she wrote "did she come?" in the margin next to Smart-Grosvenor's name. The minutes describe Wright arriving early and becoming "furious because he wanted to speak" but was asked to wait until NOW's general meeting had finished. The secretary derisively summed up the gist of his talk: "you are O-pressin' me!" This bastardized mimicry of black dialect reveals the dismissive ways some white feminists viewed Black Power and the extent to which they remained unaware of their own racism. The secretary described Ahmed's speech as unintelligible and "insane" and noted his statements that "blacks should have babies until they equal white pop[ulation]" and that "white women envy black women's hairstyles."[3]

These brief, derogatory comments are all that was recorded about the two-hour panel discussion. Although Betty Shabazz did not attend, both Smart-Grosvenor and Kennedy spoke at the meeting, yet the secretary omitted their voices and took notes only on the words of black men. Enacting the stereotype that black men represented the Black Power movement, she ignored the leadership of black women. Moreover, the notes illuminate NOW's repressive organizational culture and point toward the interpersonal and racist power struggles that would plague the organization.[4]

Ti-Grace Atkinson remembered the meeting quite differently than the secretary. Omar Ahmed, she recalled, asked NOW members a series of pointed questions; "he wanted us to educate him about the new women's movement and our goals." The feminists may have told him that they were attempting to challenge discrimination in the labor market and described their recent efforts in Albany to win antidiscrimination legislation.

He listened to their answers and then pressed them about their movement's uniform: "Why do you wear miniskirts? What message are you trying to send?" In contrast, he said, "in the black movement we are concerned about our appearance."[5] Many NOW members were appropriately offended by his inquiries; they felt he was criticizing them as immoral, interested in attracting undue sexual attention from men, and not serious because some of them wore very short skirts.[6]

Despite his interrogation and paternalistic judgment of them, Atkinson recalled thinking, "What *is* our uniform?" What message were feminists trying to send to the world through their appearance?[7] Perhaps she also looked at Kennedy, who by late 1967 was customarily dressed in an eye-catching pantsuit and a short-brimmed felt hat often worn by men and sported her signature long red fingernails. Flo decorated her lapel with numerous political buttons, and the briefcase she carried with her was covered with political stickers.

Kennedy's self-presentation defied conventional dictates for middle-class, middle-aged women, both black and white. Her clothing bore scant resemblance to that of other political leaders in her generation, such as Betty Friedan and Shirley Chisholm. Although by the late 1960s young women in NOW were following fashion trends and wearing slacks, miniskirts, and even blue jeans, the older women typically donned professional-looking dresses and skirt suits and wore subdued makeup and nail polish for public events.[8] Kennedy's distinctive attire became her signature, announcing her presence and signaling her wholesale rejection of prevailing gender norms. By 1968, Flo had cut her straightened hair and wore a short natural. Although black performing artists such as Nina Simone and Abbey Lincoln had been choosing short, natural hairstyles since the early 1960s, Kennedy did not do so until the Black Power movement transformed the look into a celebration of black pride. Flo's work within the Black Power movement influenced her appearance and politics. In choosing to eschew accepted professional women's attire, Kennedy gave younger feminists such as Ti-Grace Atkinson an alternative model for how to style herself as a feminist. To Ti-Grace, Flo looked "elegant" and "militant"—like a revolutionary feminist.[9]

While Atkinson left the meeting disappointed that NOW's leaders had shown so little interest in Black Power, Kennedy was not surprised that only a few were receptive to the speakers. By now she had become accustomed to her proposals being voted down during NOW meetings. Atkinson and Anselma Dell'Olio acknowledged that Kennedy was frequently "putting up her hand and making suggestions that just sounded like she was from Mars" and seeing her motions dismissed.[10] But Flo did not let NOW's lack of interest in Black Power and in forming broad-based coalitions with those struggling against racism deter her from advocating on behalf of Black Power inside as well as outside of NOW.

Defending Black Liberation Leader H. Rap Brown

The trial of H. Rap Brown was one of the Black Power movement's first legal battles, and Kennedy's spirited defense of him became a model for radical lawyers' defense of Black Power leaders both inside and outside the courtroom. She encouraged NOW members and other white radicals to view Brown's arrest as an attack on the Black Power movement and on all radical struggles. Freeing Brown was a cause they all shared.

From the summer of 1967 through the spring of 1968, Kennedy worked as an attorney and organizer for H. Rap Brown, chairman of the Student Nonviolent Coordinating Committee, against charges that he had incited a riot in Cambridge, Maryland, on July 24, 1967. At the invitation of Gloria Richardson and the Black Action Federation, Brown had left the Newark Black Power conference to give a speech in Cambridge.[11] For decades, black activists in Cambridge had battled with city and state authorities over segregated educational facilities, police violence, and inadequate housing. In the days leading up to Brown's arrival, city officials feared that Brown would help to incite a riot; they ordered all municipal police officers to work on the day of Brown's Speech and called in the state police and the local company of the National Guard. They patrolled the border between the black neighborhoods and white neighborhoods and enforced a rule that residents of the predominantly black Twelfth Ward could not go past the neighborhood divide.[12] Arriving in the late afternoon to a crowd of over a hundred people, Brown called on black people to take up arms against state repression and criticized the Cambridge police and state officials for treating black people like criminals. Brown reminded his listeners that black men and women throughout the country were not standing still in the face of these blatant attacks. In so doing, he pointed to parallels between Cambridge and other U.S. cities and asked if "it's time for Cambridge to explode," just as Newark and Detroit had only days earlier.[13]

Reports about what occurred after the speech are conflicting, as black and white participants and observers disagreed about what transpired. The unpublished findings of the National Advisory Commission on Civil Disorders gives the most accurate and in-depth overview of the incident. Basing its analysis on police and state troopers' logs compiled at the time, the report cleared Brown of inciting a riot and even disputed the notion that a riot had occurred: "If we accept widespread mass violence as one of the definitive characteristics of a riot, the term seems inappropriate to the events in Cambridge."[14] The report suggested that Brown's primary role was to "induce in city officials a sense of impending riot, which became the basis of their subsequent actions and interpretations of events."[15] City and state officials, nonetheless, claimed that Brown's speech provoked a riot, and within weeks of his Cambridge speech he was arrested on numerous felony and misdemeanor charges.

One of the charges against Brown was transporting a registered gun to Louisiana while under indictment for inciting a riot. Brown was traveling home to Louisiana and registered his gun with the airline authorities, but while he was on the plane the Maryland grand jury indicted him on riot and arson charges. Once he arrived in New Orleans, authorities arrested him on charges of carrying a gun across state lines. The Maryland court sentenced Brown to five years in jail and fined him $2,000 for illegally transporting the weapon. Bail was set at $25,000 pending his appeal. Kennedy, along with veteran defense attorney William Kunstler, attempted to have Brown's bail reduced and to find a bond company to post such a large sum, but both efforts were rebuffed. Kennedy saw the charges and the entire court proceeding as extremely biased and admonished the bond companies for being a part of this prejudiced process, stating, "I don't know whether they are afraid or whether it's a plot."[16]

While attempting to raise money, Kennedy set up an ad hoc committee to help free Brown. She held fund-raisers and spoke at numerous demonstrations in support of Brown, often inviting NOW members to these events. Kennedy connected the government's attacks on Brown to the repression of *all* oppressed people. As a speaker at the "Vietnam and Black American" rally on August 29, 1967, sponsored by the predominantly white National Mobilization Committee to End War in Vietnam, she linked the repression of blacks in the United States to the repression of people of color in Vietnam and asked participants to help free Brown by donating to his defense. Someone in the audience "asked a question concerning guns." The FBI agent following Kennedy noted that she responded by saying "she was surprised that an attempt to get H. Rap Brown out of jail had not been made. . . . Who needs guns, all you need is a rag, a coca cola bottle and some gasoline."[17] Attorney Gerald Lefcourt remembered being in the audience at a rally during this period on behalf of H. Rap Brown and hearing Kennedy speak: "She was powerful."[18]

Kennedy understood from her own family experience and from the

Wednesdays in Mississippi organization that black people were accustomed to defending themselves against white violence. The Black Power movement, however, placed armed self-defense out in the open. Flo did not believe that a nonviolent approach should be announced as a movement's only or primary defense tactic. "Why give your opponent the upper hand?" she wondered. To her way of thinking, the oppressor would always use violence. "But, the oppressed can't?"[19] Violent resistance or self-defense was a part of the struggle, and she thought it shortsighted for black people and women to announce that they were committed to nonviolence. She saw this as an establishment ploy to scare all oppressed people and limit the weapons available to them, making them more vulnerable to repression.

The FBI intensified its surveillance of Kennedy's activism on behalf of Brown and the Black Power movement after her speech at the "Vietnam and Black American" rally. In December 1967 it first noted that, in addition to being "active in many black militant organizations," she was "active in the National Organization of Women which is an inter-racial group dedicated to gain[ing] equal rights for women."[20] Kennedy claimed that the FBI's surveillance continued on a bus trip she organized that carried feminists along with other black and white activists from New York to Maryland to meet with Maryland governor Spiro Agnew. When the activists arrived at City Hall for the meeting they had been promised, they discovered that Agnew had sent William Yates, the state's attorney general. The group tried to convince Yates to drop the charges against H. Rap Brown or make available all the information implicating him.[21] Those representing the Brooklyn Congress of Racial Equality, SNCC, and NOW argued that the charges should be dropped based on the National Advisory Commission's findings. Yates retorted that the unpublished government report "was made up of lies and didn't constitute evidence." Kennedy warned city officials that more intense repercussions would follow if nothing were done to address the charges against Brown.[22]

Kennedy's threat was matched by increased surveillance on the bus ride home. Police cars pulled in front of the bus, and officers attempted to force their way inside to conduct a search. The officers informed Kennedy that the group from Brooklyn CORE, which was traveling in a separate vehicle, had been stopped in Delaware and charged with speeding and possession of concealed weapons. So, they argued, they had to conduct a search to make sure everyone on the bus was unarmed. Kennedy and the other activists argued, "You can't come on this bus unless you have a search warrant," and warned, "You will have to arrest us all. . . . We would never retreat." Without warrants, the officers did not have the authority to board the bus, so they departed. Kennedy quickly found the nearest pay phone "and made some calls to find out what had happened to those [CORE] fellows."[23]

Within hours of returning to New York, Kennedy went straight to *The Bob Fass Show* on WBAI radio and detailed the arrests of the two Brooklyn CORE members for supporting Brown.[24] She argued that the police had no right to search a car they stopped for speeding.[25] Adept at dealing with the media, she stated her case for Brown and the members of CORE in a way that would elicit support. She often reasoned that repression of Black Power radicals on trumped-up charges should outrage everyone because oppression was "contagious" and no one was safe.[26]

Kennedy invited NOW members to other demonstrations and fundraisers as a way to widen support for Brown and the Black Power movement. Feminists attended these protests, donated money, and signed petitions.[27] All the while they were learning from the Black Power movement and from Kennedy's strategies for utilizing the media in order to generate coalitions. Through these efforts Kennedy helped to challenge the state's attempt to vilify and imprison Brown.

As they observed the Black Power Conference, the New Politics Conference, the Black Power panel, and the defense of H. Rap Brown, NOW women were becoming students of the black liberation movement as a model for their own struggle. By the summer of 1968, as the women's movement was expanding rapidly across the country, many feminists were attempting to mirror the language, theory, and strategies of the Black Power movement. The legal defense of Valerie Solanas provided an opportunity for the growing feminist movement to create broad support for their own women's liberation heroine.

Defending Valerie Solanas:
Creating the First Women's Liberation Heroine

On June 3, 1968, Valerie Solanas arrived at the artist and filmmaker Andy Warhol's loft in Union Square. Recognizing Solanas as a recent acquaintance, Warhol welcomed her inside. Not long after Solanas arrived, she began to fire at Warhol as he quickly ran to protect himself by hiding under a desk. Of the three shots she fired only one hit Warhol; leaving him severely injured but alive.[28]

Before Solanas shot Warhol, she was a relatively unknown actress and writer who had written the *SCUM Manifesto* and sold copies of it on the streets of Greenwich Village. The manifesto argued that because "no aspect of 'society' is relevant to women . . . civic-minded, responsible, thrill-seeking females . . . [should] overthrow the government, eliminate the money system . . . and eliminate the male sex."[29] Kennedy and Atkinson had heard of the manifesto, and after the shooting they quickly became familiar with Solanas as the supposed "leader of a radical and militant feminist group called S.C.U.M. (Society for Cutting Up Men)."[30] Other radical feminists in the New York area were interested in Solanas's analysis of men's biological inferiority, her endorsement of relationships between "independent women," and her dismissal of sex as "the refuge of the mindless."[31]

Within hours of the shooting, media reports began to sensationalize the incident. Reporters portrayed Solanas as a disgruntled, "mannish," "lesbian," "man-hating actress" who shot Warhol for unexplained personal reasons.[32] Frustrated that the media and the courts were dismissing her act as whimsical, apolitical, and rash, Solanas maintained that she shot Warhol because "he had a legal claim on" her work and because he would not let her publish wherever she chose.[33] Warhol insisted that he did not have a legal right to her work and that he was unable to return the manuscript of her play *Up Your Ass* because he had lost it. According to Maurice Girodias, a publisher at Olympia Press, Warhol was not Solanas's only target.[34] Girodias had paid Solanas a nominal fee to produce two novels based on the *SCUM Manifesto*, and she believed that both men were attempting to swindle her out of her publishing rights.[35] Solanas procured a gun and went to Girodias's hotel in hopes of confronting him. Unable to reach Girodias, Solanas then traveled to Warhol's loft to confront him. Solanas reasoned that she had to take justice into her own hands because the legal system was designed to benefit only men.[36]

During her arraignment, Solanas waived her right to counsel and insisted on defending herself against charges of attempted murder.[37] When Solanas asked Kennedy to serve as her legal advisor, Kennedy agreed. During the case Flo stated to a reporter that Valerie was "a damn good fighter. She wants to defend herself. Yes, she doesn't want any legal aid. I took the position that she was very intelligent, and best able to fight for herself."[38] Solanas insisted that she was competent to stand trial and should be released from the psychiatric ward where she was being held for observation. She declared that "it isn't often I shoot somebody. I didn't do it for nothing!"[39]

At Solanas's initial arraignment on June 13, Kennedy attempted to persuade the court that Solanas was competent to defend herself and to stand trial. Kennedy used the courtroom as a political stage to defend Solanas and, by implication, the feminist movement against imputations of insanity. She portrayed Solanas's act as a form of political protest but did not collapse feminism into the *SCUM Manifesto*. In this moment, Kennedy's defense both inside and outside the courtroom was an attempt to cloak Solanas in feminism because it made her seem less crazy. Flo's first order of business was to move "for a writ of habeas corpus on the grounds that [Solanas] is being improperly detained in the psychiatric ward of Elmhurst City Hospital in Queens" and thus was not being allowed to defend herself properly.[40]

Kennedy attempted to build a case that Solanas's actions were not those of an insane person but the tactics of a feminist whose voice was not being heard by the court or the media. Throughout the proceeding, Kennedy argued that Solanas was "one of the most important spokeswomen of the feminist movement" and that she was the "female [Jean] Genet" who "has not been taken seriously."[41] Some even speculated that Kennedy would help Solanas by submitting the *SCUM Manifesto* as part of her legal brief, along with other feminist texts.[42]

In the courtroom proceeding, Kennedy placed the judge and the sexist legal system on trial. From the very beginning, indeed, feminism was at issue. Kennedy arrived at the courthouse dressed in pants and a brown hat with a black and red "Freedom for Women" button pinned to it. Judge Thomas Dickens was astounded by her appearance and chastised Kennedy for not presenting herself appropriately as a woman in a courtroom. Before he could even finish his sentence, Kennedy retorted, "Well, your honor, you are there in a dress. How can you question me?"[43] The judge's face turned purple as he continued to reprimand Kennedy for her unladylike attire and behavior. Unmoved by his disapproval, Kennedy proceeded to argue her case. Atkinson remembered this as one of Kennedy's best moments: "She was incredible in a courtroom."[44] Female attorneys were not supposed to dress like male attorneys, in pants, but rather like "ladies," in a dress or a skirt suit. The problem arose because the categories of "woman" and "lawyer" were seldom combined in one person, which made Kennedy exceptional no matter how she dressed. A few years later, Kennedy stated that by wearing pants to court, she was purposely confronting the status quo of the legal system.[45]

Kennedy reasoned that the courtroom defense was most effective when it was strengthened by outside support, which she mobilized through the media. Kennedy and Atkinson held a press conference at which they portrayed the shooting as an act of feminist resistance. Kennedy understood that a broad base of support was needed to gain Solanas's freedom, or at least a lenient prison sentence. Atkinson, having studied Kennedy's actions within the Black Power movement, was beginning to see these connections as well. "I did know about prisons, because Flo was very involved with Black Panthers [H. Rap Brown later joined the Black Panther Party in 1968] and I shared a place with her and all of the lawyers who were representing the Panthers—so I was very affected by that. I knew you have to have money coming in from the outside; it had to be known that people cared about you on the outside."[46] At first, Atkinson said, Solanas "did not have a big crowd around her," so it was vital to attract supporters.

Only when Kennedy became Solanas's legal advisor and Atkinson became her strongest advocate did the media begin to portray Solanas's actions as politically motivated and connected to a feminist movement. Kennedy worked alongside Atkinson to bring the political import of Solanas's crime to the public's attention. In the Brown case, Kennedy had placed the state on trial for conspiring against Brown and convicting him unfairly for crimes he did not commit. In the Solanas case, she attempted to force the courts to see Solanas's actions as those of a political actor who was defrauded by a male-dominated industry. Thanks to their efforts, the media started to depict Solanas as a "super feminist" and a "revolutionary."[47] Reporters even described Kennedy and Atkinson as part of NOW's "most militant affiliate," the New York chapter.[48] In this way, Kennedy and Atkinson succeeded in building a larger base of support for the growing women's movement and Solanas. Kennedy not only used the women's movement to gain support for Solanas but also used Solanas as an exemplar of many women's grievances.

Despite Kennedy's best efforts to demonstrate the political import of Solanas's crime and to show that she was competent to stand trial, the judge denied her motion to have Solanas moved from the mental hospital. Perhaps in order to defend himself from continued criticism as one of the publishers who swindled Solanas, Maurice Girodias criticized Kennedy for "trying to turn this into something political, which it is not."[49] He argued that the case was not connected to feminism.[50]

For some feminists, Kennedy and Atkinson placed Solanas's crime and grievances within a political context. Within days of the shooting and press conference, Solanas became a cause célèbre for various women in the growing feminist movement. Reflecting on the interest in Solanas then and later, Atkinson said that "we as women, as feminists, yearn for some violence, or somebody to fight back, and she looked like she was fighting back. . . . Is it an expression of somehow the woman not being the victim all the time?"[51] Several other feminists remembered hearing of the shooting through the media and being captivated by depictions of her as a "Super-Woman Power Advocate" who unapologetically shot a man for attempting to defraud her.[52] Roxanne Dunbar, a white feminist from Oklahoma, was living in Cuba when she first heard of the case. She recalled her mind racing as she wondered, "Could it be true that finally women were rising up? . . . It changed everything for me, and gave a focus to my mental chaos."[53] Later Dunbar stated that she did not want to "miss that delicious, exciting, formative time" in the women's movement, so she decided to return immediately to the United States.

Kennedy and Atkinson's strategy was working: the media was beginning to portray Solanas and the women's movement as revolutionary. Valerie "dragged feminism kicking and screaming into the 20th century, in a very dramatic way," Atkinson later commented.[54] Atkinson and Dunbar were not alone in their admiration of Solanas as a radical feminist. A few feminists speculated that perhaps Solanas would be at the forefront of this struggle. Throughout the summer of 1968, women from across the country contacted Kennedy and Atkinson to find out more about this new feminist heroine. With Kennedy's help, some of them visited Solanas in the hospital; later they spent time in Kennedy's apartment learning about the Solanas case and the radical feminist movement.[55]

For several years, Kennedy's cramped two-room apartment in Manhattan had been a gathering place where political organizers held meetings, planned actions, and developed strategies. Now more young feminists were becoming part of this web of activists, meeting their counterparts in other political movements around the country. Atkinson later recalled that Kennedy's apartment was always littered with fliers and bustling with people: "Everybody knew, no matter where in the world you came from, you were supposed to go to 8 East 48th Street, Apartment 3C. . . . You would meet everybody in the world there. She'd make sure you'd have a flyer and they were all in her briefcase. . . . She was a one-woman coalition builder."[56] Many young feminists from across the country "literally and figuratively sat at her feet and absorbed her wisdom and her wit." As these women recollected being at Flo's, they emphasized that she made "no distinction between members of NOW or radical groups, whites, Hispanics, or blacks, lesbians or straights."[57]

It was through these networks of budding feminists that the *SCUM Manifesto* was read by radical feminist groups, including Cell 16, which Dunbar created after she moved to Boston in the summer of 1968. Some feminists considered Cell 16 members to be the "movement heavies" because they lauded many of Solanas's directives and advocated a program of self-defense, celibacy, and women's separatism.[58]

In the summer of 1968 the women's liberation movement was expanding, and groups were forming with goals and structures that often did not fit neatly with NOW's stated positions and official leadership. Scholars have demonstrated that the expansion of the women's movement and the development of its radical wing happened independently of NOW. The women it attracted tended to be younger than NOW's founders, typically in their twenties, and had not yet established professional careers.[59] At the same time, Kennedy led the development of radicalism in NOW that looked to Black Power and called for a comprehensive feminist movement. By that summer feminists both inside and outside of NOW were beginning to challenge the organization's goals and tactics as too moderate or even conservative and overly reliant on litigation and legislation, rather than on direct action, for challenging women's oppression.[60]

In opposition to this model, women from across the country defined themselves as radical and created their own agendas through groups like Cell 16. This radical feminist organization and others engaged in civil disobedience and advocated a revolution in gender relations, not just reforms that would give women more access to the power structure. Borrowing from the black liberation movement, radical and socialist feminists called themselves the women's liberation movement and advocated organizing independently from men.[61] Kennedy was in the center as ideas from the Black Power movement fused with those from the women's movement. She wanted the "women's movement to explode and to be the next thing to confront the establishment."[62] Kennedy welcomed radical movements in almost any form, although she did not always agree with some of the self-styled radical feminists' definition of what radicalism meant.

■ While some radical feminists seized upon Solanas as a symbol of the anger they felt and of the militant, direct action they longed to take, NOW's executive committee was outraged that the press was associating NOW with the Solanas case. Betty Friedan, in particular, was furious with Atkinson and Kennedy for supporting Solanas.[63] She saw Solanas as a crazed criminal and feared that the anti-male position she articulated would be the death of the nascent movement. Several months before the Solanas case, Atkinson had become president of the New York chapter with Friedan's support, but Friedan was beginning to regret her decision. After the Solanas press conference, Friedan and NOW sent Kennedy a telegram demanding that she "desist immediately from linking NOW in any way with

Valerie Solanas." In their view, her actions against Warhol were "entirely irrelevant to NOW's goals of full equality for women in truly equal partnership with men."[64] Friedan later explained that she rejected the media's depiction of Solanas as a "feminist heroine." She declared categorically, "We'd never heard of her and that's not what feminism was all about—cutting up men."[65] Friedan was also highly critical of the new women's liberation movement that was gathering strength during the summer of 1968. She believed that these "hippie" women borrowed too heavily from the Black Power movement. "Because they had cut their political eye-teeth on the doctrines of class warfare applied to the problem of race," she explained, "they tried to adapt too literally the ideology of class and race warfare to the situations of women."[66] Thus, Friedan argued, radical feminists undermined the women's movement by adopting abstract ideas of separatism, "manhatred," and "sex warfare."[67] Friedan worried about women seeing themselves as a class engaged in violent conflict with the class that oppressed them.

Atkinson was stung by this reprimand. She saw Solanas's situation as an example of sex discrimination and therefore in line with NOW's principles; a woman was being mistreated by the male-dominated publishing industry and was not being properly compensated for her work.[68] But Friedan and others quickly made it clear that from NOW's point of view, Solanas's actions were not related to the feminist movement. Following NOW's rebukes, Atkinson continued to support Solanas, but from that point on she told reporters that she worked as a friend on behalf of Solanas and not in association with NOW.[69] In contrast, Kennedy had more political experience than Atkinson and was not easily intimidated by anyone, whether supposed ally or direct enemy. She disregarded Friedan's disapproval and began publicly criticizing NOW for being weak in the face of a strong feminist like Solanas: "Valerie is superior to many of the people in NOW. . . . She already says Simone de Beauvoir, Sartre and Genet are overrated windbags so you can imagine what she thinks of NOW. She's worth all the NOW members put together."[70]

It is important to recognize that Atkinson had her own agenda in defending Solanas that at times differed from Kennedy's. Perhaps Atkinson wanted to prove the legitimacy of the new feminist movement to other organizers, Kennedy, and the country, and Solanas's act of violence, while not the perfect example, allowed her to support and create a feminist heroine. Flo was also interested in the feminist movement being seen as militant and revolutionary, but she did not think the growing movement should fully embrace Solanas's ideas about women's separatism. Kennedy saw the Solanas incident as a criminal case that needed recasting in a political light with a strong defense in the media and courtroom. She also saw it as an avenue to gain publicity for a movement. Kennedy was not interested in Solanas's theory of women's separatism or man-hatred, especially not as a movement philosophy. In this moment, Ti-Grace was Flo's student as she attempted to develop her own ideas and fashion a women's movement from the lessons she had learned from watching Flo and Black Power. She was debating whether Solanas's ideas and actions could be directly applicable to a women's struggle.

Although the two differed in some of their views of the incident, Kennedy and Atkinson won support for Solanas and for the women's movement among many younger feminists.[71] Kennedy was hopeful that the women's movement would "be like the campus thing" and that many more direct actions by women would take place in the coming months. Students across the country and specifically at Columbia University were occupying buildings in opposition to the Vietnam War and entrenched discrimination against black communities.[72] Two months before the Solanas incident Kennedy had participated in a protest at which Columbia's Hamilton Hall was occupied by black students opposed to a gym being built in Morningside Heights.[73] The media described these hundreds of students as a potential revolutionary force, and in the wake of the Solanas incident Kennedy wondered if "women may be the third force to link up with youth and black people" to challenge the oppressive system.[74]

Like other black and white radicals during this period, Kennedy saw the black liberation movement as the vanguard movement of *all* oppressed people and believed that coalitions between blacks and other oppressed groups were necessary to help speed revolutionary change.[75] Kennedy understood that some radical feminists attempted to gain credibility for their cause by underscoring their connection to the Black Power movement. The portrayal of Solanas as a revolutionary demonstrated that feminists were just as interested as Black Power advocates in defending themselves "by any means necessary."[76]

Atkinson said that Solanas began to revel in the newfound attention of her feminist followers. Unaware that Friedan was repulsed by her actions, Solanas hoped to gain more support from feminists and suggested to Atkinson and Kennedy that Friedan might come to her aid. She even accused Kennedy and Atkinson of trying to exploit her to gain fame for themselves. Insulted, Kennedy immediately withdrew from the case. Solanas's plan backfired as both Kennedy and Atkinson distanced themselves from her. Solanas soon regretted her accusations and called Atkinson for help in convincing Kennedy to rejoin the case. After much cajoling, Atkinson persuaded Kennedy to visit Solanas at Mattewan State Hospital in New York.[77] "I remember sitting there with all of the nail[ed] down tables and everything else and of course Valerie wanted Flo to represent her again. And Flo said 'Valerie, you only insult me once. Now, I don't understand crazy so I have to believe that you know what you are doing and when you disrespect me in this way—I'm finished.'"[78]

Kennedy and Atkinson continued to defend Solanas in the media and within feminist circles, but Kennedy never worked closely with her again. Kennedy was interested in depicting Solanas as a feminist heroine in order to attract attention to the case and to the women's movement. But she did not trust Solanas. Over the next several years Solanas was transferred from one mental institution to another. While scholars have been fascinated by the Solanas incident, they have paid little or no attention to the ways in which Kennedy helped to captivate the public imagination by presenting the image of Solanas as a feminist fighter, similar to the black liberation leader H. Rap Brown. The defense of Valeric Solanas became one of the first instances in which feminists used outrageous actions to draw media attention and expand the movement. Kennedy helped feminists interpret Solanas's acts as political and called for increased direct actions like the occupation of Columbia's Hamilton Hall.[79]

7

I Was the Force of Them

LEADING THE WOMEN'S LIBERATION
MOVEMENT, 1968–1969

Florynce Kennedy was instrumental in mentoring young white women in the National Organization for Women and other feminist organizations and played a crucial role in building the feminist movement, especially in organizing the important early protests that drew media attention and new participants. By the fall of 1968, the feminist movement had captured the media's attention. Articles in the *New York Times* and the *Wall Street Journal* began to depict the feminist movement's leaders and goals more consistently. Kennedy was a media savant who understood how the press helped to broaden a movement's reach and attract more members. Later Kennedy told an interviewer that she was "the force of them."[1] The formidable force that was Flo galvanized protest actions and inspired participation. Both inside and outside of NOW, she served as legal counsel, expanded the movement's base, found supportive allies, and gained media attention.

NOW's Picket, Street Theater, and the Politics of Pleasure

Despite Kennedy's strained relationship with Betty Friedan and NOW's national board, she continued to attend meetings of the New York chapter after the Valerie Solanas case. While Anselma Dell'Olio was the main organizer of NOW's next major direct action—a boycott, picket, and "flush-in" of the Colgate-Palmolive Company—Kennedy had a key role in planning it. She was especially pleased that the younger voices in NOW were beginning to shape the direction of the organization and pushing forward despite the leadership's timidity and single focus. The Colgate-Palmolive demonstration at the end of the summer was one of the last protests that included both factions of NOW. The division between them was becoming decidedly more pronounced. Members such as Kennedy, Dell'Olio, Ti-Grace Atkinson, Kate Millet, Carol Goodman, and Jacqui Ceballos were becoming more closely aligned with radical feminist circles in the New York City area. On the other side stood members such as Friedan, Muriel Fox, Jean Faust, and Marguerite Rawalt, who wanted NOW to focus on opposing sex discrimination in employment and were hopeful that NOW's new Legal Defense Fund would increase the organization's capacity to take action on the issue.[2]

NOW's Legal Defense Fund was created, in part, to assist southern blue-collar factory women working for Colgate-Palmolive and Southern Bell who were denied jobs and promotions under the guise of state laws that "protected" women from working more than eight hours a day. These laws, which had their roots in early twentieth-century reformers' efforts to regulate women's working conditions, were invoked by the companies to deny women jobs, promotions, and overtime pay. Several women at Colgate-Palmolive and Southern Bell had challenged the laws and were harassed by employers and union leaders while fighting for their rights under Title VII of the Civil Rights Act of 1964.[3]

To garner public attention for their legal battles, NOW created actions outside the courtroom that highlighted discrimination against women. The women of the New York chapter planned a major boycott and picket of Colgate-Palmolive.[4] Anselma Dell'Olio was the official NOW organizer, but Kennedy directed the New York chapter's organizing meeting on August 23, 1968, and during the strategy session she helped coach the demonstrators about the importance of picketing. Some members feared that the picket and boycott were too extreme and that they might be arrested or even shot. Kennedy helped to assuage their fears by describing how picketing could actually be an "exciting" way to challenge discrimination against women.[5] Later, recalling her participation in protests, she stated, "I can't understand why a person would rather go on a ski slope than a picket line because I think a picket line just happens to be more fun, and the fact that it is politically astute is just a bonus."[6] She also understood that "the best way to recruit is to be having fun. . . . [Other] people like to be dreary. I try to be as undreary as I can be."[7]

Moreover, Kennedy hoped to make fighting for justice irresistibly pleasurable to organizers by emphasizing every moment of joy and humor that could be found in working together and defying an enemy. In this way, her street performances at protests not only were meant to agitate and captivate the media and her adversaries but also were designed to inspire the demonstrators. Kennedy chanted "make it swing" to the NOW picketers, and later feminists recalled that she did not exhibit any signs of fear or fatigue but rather beamed with satisfaction during these demonstrations. Flo's pleasure in movement organizing was contagious and often decreased the anxiety of the feminists at her side.[8] Part of what annoyed her adversaries and attracted some feminist followers was Kennedy's privileging of satirical amusement and unleashed pleasure as part of her political actions. Feminist Gloria Steinem later commented on how Kennedy "energizes people" to be politically engaged: "Some people take life and energy away from others. She gives it."[9] Flo wanted activists to feel the thrill of the picket line and the joy in overcoming their fears.

Kennedy always came dressed for her performances. By 1968, Flo's uniform still included crisp pants, and she had not grown tired of her painted red nails, stylish hats, or long false eyelashes. As far back as her days in Kansas City, Kennedy was a complete "show off" when it came to dressing up in hats, makeup, and other bright and colorful accessories.[10] As a young woman she had applied makeup for both work and play. Sixties radicals would be greeted by her same dedication to style and glamour. Her affinity for all types of men's hats expanded during the decade, and she began wearing men's leather and suede cowboy hats and short-brimmed cloth caps on most occasions. On her jacket lapels and on the side of her hat one would often find a peace symbol or a button that read "Freedom for Women!" Scores of colorful plastic bangles decorated her wrists, while her neck was laced with silver whistles used to gain the attention of a group or to start an impromptu chant.

Kennedy's fashion mixed feminine articles like her red fingernails, false eyelashes, and bright bracelets with more masculine pieces such as her cowboy hat and well-tapered pants. Years later she could even be spotted wearing a green military helmet with the strap fastened loosely at the chin or a multicolored cape draped around her shoulders. Catching the attention of onlookers was her goal, and the press commented on her captivating style that seemed perfect for guerrilla street theater.[11] Later Kennedy confessed, "When I go to do combat, I come dressed for it."[12] Since the 1920s, scholar Rebecca Arnold argues, women have merged both male and female gender signifiers in an attempt to gain greater independence and to "inscribe masculine power upon the female body." In the late 1960s, androgynous styles for some feminists gained even greater prominence because it "denoted freedoms gained and the rejection of a preceding claustrophobic femininity."[13]

Kennedy was one of the most charismatic leaders of the feminist movement, captivating audiences with her energy, colorful style, and improvisational wit. She inspired many activists with the sarcastic bite of her brusque humor and political lucidity. Kennedy's example shows how humor is closely tied to charismatic leadership. It should come as no surprise that some of the most alluring and charismatic leaders of the twentieth century—Malcolm X, Stokely Carmichael, and Adam Clayton Powell Jr.— knew how to deliver a punch line. Kennedy rejected the notion that comedy, especially in the hands of a woman, should be equated with a lack of seriousness. Like black women radicals Toni Cade Bambara and Queen Mother Moore, who were both known for their sarcastic wit, Kennedy made great use of laughter as a weapon and a shield.

To make sure the movement capitalized on the attention it gained from guerrilla theater actions, Kennedy encouraged women at the NOW protest and other actions to invite more than just white women from their own political and social circles. Instead she implored them to "bring men, bring women, bring black people, [bring people] from the Village—the East Village and the West Village, bring people from uptown. Get campus people, get business people. Bring kids—kids love to picket. Let your mother come down—old ladies love to picket."[14] Kennedy argued that broad-based alliances irritated and confused companies because they could not clearly identify the picketers. Moreover, such demonstrations showed that the issue of discrimination against women was a problem everyone was willing to tackle.[15]

On the day of NOW's demonstration against Colgate-Palmolive, the women decided to engage in elaborate forms of street theater and to fully embrace humor as an organizing weapon. Kate Millet set up a toilet on the sidewalk, and Kennedy and the other feminists poured Colgate products into it.[16] Their actions symbolically stated that women would not tolerate being continually denied employment by the very companies that their purchases helped to keep in business. While some of NOW's founders later acknowledged that they had been concerned that this type of street theater would offend some women, they were beginning to see the need for dramatic actions to garner public attention and support. Kennedy was helping to wedge the door open to the acceptance of "zap action" as one of the effective ways to focus public attention on oppression.[17]

Kennedy later pointed out the value of such actions: "You may not win the war . . . but you let them know that you are fighting a battle. I always say, if you spit on someone at a cocktail party you're not trying to drown them; you just want to let them know you don't like them."[18] She maintained that "the purpose of dramatic chants and songs" was "to get the attention of the public." So "every bit of bizarre, attention-getting behavior helps. If you can watch weird behavior on television why not indulge in it yourself?"[19]

Kennedy would sing loudly "Stop the fuckers from fucking over you" at these types of protests while holding a homemade poster.[20] Her constant use of profanity frustrated not only some NOW feminists who worried that her language might alarm the "women in middle America" but also radical feminists like Carol Hanisch of New York Radical Women who thought Flo's cursing "could be a bit much . . . sometimes her outrageousness turned people off."[21] Kennedy, however, did not care what some feminist critics thought of her; she was playing to the audience of potential feminists and other activists who laughed at her jokes and were thrilled by her frank and coarse humor. The media, as always, was Kennedy's other major target, and she hoped that the evening news or the morning paper would catch her message and then broadcast it widely. More than anything, Flo relished opportunities to challenge societal norms that sought to control her voice and the voices of other oppressed people. She argued that if U.S. leaders could use profane language, so could she. "There is not a so called swear word I use that is not White House language," she argued. "These are the words of Lyndon Johnson," whose use of expletives during meetings with Bobby Kennedy were leaked to the press.[22] Kennedy argued that accepted societal norms regulated oppressed people by controlling what they could say and what they were allowed to wear in public. "Fashion, style, language, are the stuff of which societal reins on the oppressed are made. Grow a beard, wear a dashiki, say 'shit' or 'fuck' at the wrong time or place and you can get on the open-season-for-niggerizing list."[23]

Kennedy succeeded in gaining media attention during the days leading up to the Colgate-Palmolive protest, but the media almost completely ignored the actual demonstration. It was eclipsed by the announcement of another protest being waged a few days later by a "wide coalition of women's liberation groups" at the Miss America Pageant in Atlantic City.[24]

The Miss America Pageant Protest

During the weeks in August that Kennedy attended NOW meetings to plan the Colgate-Palmolive demonstration, she was also planning the protests against the Miss America Pageant.[25] On September 7, 1968, hundreds of women's liberation activists from New York, Connecticut, New Jersey, and even Florida gathered in Atlantic City to protest the pageant's exploitation of women. Scholar Alice Echols marks that protest as the first national action of the radical women's movement and as the event that signaled the end of the movement's relative obscurity.[26] The nightly news displayed the feminists crowning a sheep Miss America and chaining themselves to a life-size Miss America cutout. Women from NOW, such as Kennedy and Kate Millet, along with Carol Hanisch, Kathie Sarachild, and Robin Morgan from New York Radical Women, marched along the boardwalk singing songs and carrying posters that read "Can make-up cover the wounds of our oppressor?" and "Welcome to the Miss America Cattle Auction." Originally the women planned to burn "articles of torture," but they were denied a fire permit and decided instead to throw their girdles, bras, hair curlers, and wigs into a large "freedom trash can."[27] The media coverage quickly derided these women as "bra burners." Most feminists scorned the term, arguing that it did not accurately portray their actions that day.[28] While Kennedy also criticized reporters for being "clumsy liars," she rather liked the label "bra burners" because she believed it made the women "seem tougher than we really were."[29] For Kennedy, while the feminists were "very brazen and very brash" during their Atlantic City demonstration, they were still far too "law-abiding" to burn anything without legal permission.[30]

As the women marched along the boardwalk, they gave onlookers pamphlets reading "No More Miss America" that outlined their ten major criticisms of the pageant and its corporate sponsors. High among them was this critique: "*Degrading Mindless-Boob-Girlie Symbol.* The Pageant contestants epitomize the roles we are all forced to play as women. The parade down the runway blares the metaphor of the 4-H Club county fair, where the nervous animals are judged for teeth, fleece, etc., and where the best 'Specimen' gets the blue ribbon. So are women in our society forced daily to compete for male approval, enslaved by ludicrous 'beauty' standards we ourselves are conditioned to take seriously."[31]

As they protested on the boardwalk, some spectators called them names: "You're all a bunch of lesbians!" "Mothers of Mao!" "Man haters!"[32] As Kennedy had done several days earlier at the NOW protest, she encouraged the feminists to have fun and be daring in the face of a hostile crowd. She later argued that one of the few sources of power that oppressed people held was their ability "to be loud and draw a big crowd."[33]

Kennedy not only helped to organize this action but also was charged with the task of recruiting black women to join it. Carol Hanisch recalled that the handful of black feminists who were present at the Miss America Pageant demonstration were there through Kennedy's connections. Indeed, Kennedy's links to the black community extended even further. Always attempting to pull struggles together and expand support, she enlisted black residents of Atlantic City to provide demonstrators with a "place to rest, eat dinner, and change in the black community."[34] Uncertain about how the crowd on the boardwalk would respond to their protest, the organizers wanted to be sure that the women had a safe place to take cover.

In order to meet this need, Kennedy arranged for support from a small local black-owned resort. Throughout the day the women were welcome there. The four women who later slipped inside the convention hall to hold up a women's liberation banner used the restaurant as a place to change from their street clothes into evening dresses so they could blend in with the audience.[35] As agreed, the black owners did not alert the authorities of their plans. Once inside, the women disrupted Miss America's farewell speech when they held up their banner and began yelling "Freedom for Women!" and "No More Miss America!"[36] The resort owners supported the women's demonstration even though doing so could have cost them future business or led to heightened scrutiny from Atlantic City officials. Support of the protest from this local black business complicates the then-familiar generalization that black women and men opposed the women's movement.

The feminists involved in the protest inside the convention hall were quickly kicked out. Another women's liberation activist, Peggy Dobbins, was not only ejected but also arrested after releasing a foul-smelling bomb, which was actually a can of Toni hair spray manufactured by one of the sponsors. Dobbins was a cofounder of New York Radical Women and one of the organizers of the protest.[37] The coalition did not plan or approve of her actions, so some were irritated that she did not follow agreed-upon protocol. Nonetheless, the group quickly collected the thousand dollars needed for her bail. Kennedy then traveled to the jail with Kate Millet to post her bond and serve as her lawyer.[38] Flo was one of the main attorneys on hand to defend all of the women in case they were arrested.[39] Dobbins's charges of disorderly conduct and "emitting a noxious odor" were later dropped. Kennedy was impressed by Dobbins's bravado in orchestrating her own guerrilla theater that challenged the pageant and in defying the rules of the feminist coalition.

Although Kennedy was a lawyer and a leader of the protesters, she also refused to follow all of the rules. The coalition had decided that protesters should speak only to women reporters, fearing that male reporters would not take them seriously. Similarly, Black Power activists at the Black Power Conference and many other Black Power demonstrations spoke only to black reporters.[40] Kennedy agreed with this rule but obviously did not think it applied to her. In Atlantic City, she said, "a male reporter came over and asked me something and I answered." Robin Morgan remembered how Kennedy kept "reporters captive with her sound bites about how racist the pageant was."[41] She was intent on having the racism of the pageant underscored alongside its sexism. Among the coalition's major criticisms of the Miss America Pageant was this statement: "Since 1921, the pageant has not had one Black finalist, and this has not been for a lack of test-case contestants. There has never been a Puerto Rican, Alaskan, Hawaiian, or Mexican American winner, nor has there ever been a true Miss America—an American Indian."[42] Flo recounted that as soon as she opened her mouth to begin answering the male reporter, one of the demonstration organizers came over and told her to stop. "Then I said what the fuck is all this. Get out of here and leave me alone. Whenever I was involved in a feminist or any other movement, if anybody at the flake level came and tried to give me orders, I told them to piss off."[43]

While Kennedy had no problem serving as a leader, she sometimes had a difficult time taking directions and being a follower. She had exhibited this behavior at the Black Power Conference in 1967 when she refused to honor the all-black rule, as well as when she did not follow instructions to speak only to women reporters. As younger and less experienced activists developed their own leadership skills, Kennedy had a hard time conforming to their decisions. On several occasions Kennedy listened to the group, but in a pinch she preferred to operate under her own direction.

Though she was one of the only participants in the demonstration who spoke to reporters that day, the national media completely ignored Kennedy and only a few news outlets made passing mention of the racist beauty standard of the contest.[44] In this key moment, although Kennedy was associated with NOW and the Valerie Solanas case and was quite willing to seek the media spotlight, the national media overlooked her in favor of younger white feminists. As one scholar later noted, the press seemed anxious about conferring leadership of the new women's movement on a black woman.[45] Kennedy was not only black but also middle-aged, and her image seemed not to fit neatly with the media's growing fascination with this new "young," "hip" women's movement.[46] The media were developing a bias toward stereotypically attractive women (read white and young) and often preferred to center or elevate in the press those women who fit this category. Even the media coverage of Kennedy's Colgate-Palmolive protest with NOW did not mention that she was a member of NOW or that she was a feminist.[47] Instead, Kennedy was portrayed as an organizer who was working with NOW and helping them to prepare for the boycott. Later, a scholar followed the lead of the national media when she repeated this mistake and described Kennedy not as a feminist but as an activist "who worked outside of NOW but joined with the organization for certain actions."[48] Despite the fact that the national media ignored Kennedy's participation, the Miss America protest was effective in gaining mass media attention for the women's movement. In fact, Carol Hanisch of New York Radical Women claimed, "Millions of Americans now know there is a Women's Liberation struggle."[49]

Indicating the differences that were emerging among feminists, many members of NOW's national executive committee, including Betty Friedan, neither participated in the planning nor attended the action in Atlantic City. Later, Friedan stated that she admired "the verve and style in the Miss America Protest."[50] She was, however, critical of some of the radicals' tactics and theories, which she described as copying Black Power and communism and as embracing "sex warfare" and "manhatred." She also worried that their actions might seem "more sexy than the NOW actions" because NOW addressed "the concrete social and economic situation of women," which did not grab media attention. She feared that this emerging approach to women's liberation, with its abstract ideas and hippie tactics, was "leading us away from the reality of our movement—and its real possibilities for changing the situation of women."[51] This divide between what constituted "real" or legitimate feminist concerns and appropriate feminist methods of protest, as well as the question of how feminist organizations should be structured, continued to plague the New York chapter of NOW. It finally came to a head a month later during the October 17, 1968, membership meeting. As always, Flo Kennedy was at the center of that controversy.

Leaving NOW and Forming the October 17th Movement

It was not long before Betty Friedan tired of the continued attempts by Kennedy and Ti-Grace Atkinson to radicalize NOW. She deeply regretted her decision a year earlier to support Atkinson as chapter president. Friedan saw Atkinson's fascination with militant radicalism as potentially impeding the feminist cause and thought that the new women's liberation movement was headed in the wrong direction. By the summer of 1968, groups like New York Radical Women and Cell 16 in Boston were holding protests and consciousness-raising groups. Friedan realized that young women were the future of the movement but was critical of some of their tactics and ideas about women's liberation.

Tension between NOW's national leadership and the radical feminists in the New York chapter had been mounting since the Valerie Solanas episode. Friedan was furious because Atkinson and others were continuing to align themselves with controversial causes such as the Solanas case, the complete repeal of abortion laws, and Black Power. The radical feminists in NOW were discussing ways to transform the organization so that it would fight not simply to "get women into positions of power" but to "destroy the positions of power."[52] Determined to stop the "crazies" from taking over the organization, Friedan mobilized votes against Atkinson when she ran for reelection to the presidency. In Friedan's view, once Atkinson knew she would not be reelected, she "came up with a proposal to abolish the office of president and the democratic election of officers . . . [with a] 'drawing lots' anonymous nonleadership scheme that would enable the 'crazies' to take over and manipulate decisions, with no accountability to membership."[53]

Atkinson remembered her suggestion about restructuring the president's position differently: she wanted to see the New York chapter adopt the participatory model of leadership that was circulating among radicals. The participatory democracy model of organizing that was first practiced by the Student Nonviolent Coordinating Committee and then promoted by Students for a Democratic Society strove to create opportunities for all members of a group to make meaningful contributions to decisions and to avoid top-down leadership structures that failed to draw on everyone's insights and energy. Ella Baker and other black women community organizers promoted this practice and helped to make it a part of SNCC's organizing approach.[54] Atkinson argued that her efforts in NOW were largely motivated by the participatory democracy model of organizing and by simple "common sense" about how to get things done efficiently:

> [NOW women] would come in and say, "Something just happened to me," and I'd say, "Great, form a committee." Now I probably learned this from Flo. . . . In the bylaws the president is supposed to form all of the committees. And I'd say, "Stand up, say what you are interested in, and anybody who wants to work on that, they [will] work on that." Because I knew they are going to do better work if this is something

that happened to them. So then you are supposed to appoint the chair. Now when I became president there were like two or three committees, and then there were thirteen standing committees by the time I left. . . . I said, "I'm not at your meetings, how can I appoint a chair? You know who you want. Elect your own chair [and] tell me who it is." To me it was common sense. I wasn't being equitable. It was just common sense. This is going to work better. And it proved it. So what I wanted to do is get rid of the president as this bottleneck and have rotating [presidents].[55]

A few days prior to NOW's October membership meeting, a group of radical feminists met at Atkinson's apartment to discuss ways to push the chapter in a new direction and resolve some of the factional tensions in the organization.[56] Kennedy did not attend the meeting but supported the idea of having rotating presidents. Some of the women even threatened to leave the organization if their motion for rotating presidents did not pass.[57] At the membership meeting, Atkinson remained silent while Kennedy, Carol Goodman, and others "urged an experiment in participatory democracy."[58] At the time, Kennedy described the meeting as being very contentious: some of the leaders of NOW began a litany of "booing and hissing" as the radicals presented their ideas.[59]

Predictably, the motion to have rotating presidents was defeated.[60] Atkinson left the meeting assuming that the other radical feminists would also make good on their threats to leave the organization. She went home and wrote a two-page letter resigning from NOW and a press release criticizing NOW for "advocating hierarchy of offices" and for not understanding that "the fight against unequal power relationships between men and women necessitates fighting unequal power everyplace: between men and women (for feminists especially), but also between men and men, and women and women, between black and white, and rich and poor."[61] Not long after she submitted her resignation, she realized that "as it turned out, I was the only one who resigned." Atkinson recalled Friedan being shocked because she "thought all of the young women were going to leave with [me]." Emboldened by the discovery that the young radical feminists decided to stay in the organization, according to Atkinson, Friedan proceeded to publicly announce that "Ti-Grace left NOW alone."[62] Thus, Atkinson's departure was portrayed as a personal issue rather than a political one.

Kennedy had not promised to leave NOW if the proposal was defeated.[63] She had never wholeheartedly endorsed the approach of NOW's leaders, but she had continued to work with the group, and she had intended to remain in it despite her dissatisfaction with the meeting's outcome. Once Friedan released public statements that were meant to deride Atkinson as marginal and insignificant to the women's movement, however, Kennedy immediately reversed course and resigned. She explained, "I saw the importance of a feminist movement, and stayed in there because I wanted to do anything I could to keep it alive, but when I saw how retarded NOW was, I thought, 'my God, who needs this?'"[64] In her resignation letter, Kennedy outlined the many reasons why she decided to leave NOW. High on her list was the harassment of radical feminists who attempted to push the organization in a more progressive direction.[65] Kennedy was also outraged by Friedan's racism. During a heated discussion at an executive committee meeting where Kennedy offered suggestions for handling NOW's public relations, Friedan warned her not to interfere with the inner workings of NOW and instructed Kennedy to instead "focus her attention on matters of Black Power" and stay out of NOW's organizational business. Last, Kennedy cited NOW's attempts to obstruct her work with Valerie Solanas: "The interference with my clientele and law practice by national and local officers was, to say the least, oppressive."[66]

Oddly, when Atkinson and feminist scholars referred to the "younger dissenting faction" who raised the notion of participatory democracy and then left NOW to form a new radical feminist group, they were in fact referring to Kennedy—a fifty-two-year-old black woman.[67] Atkinson was invested in rewriting the history of the break from NOW so that it centered the story on the younger radical feminists pulling away from the older, more conservative feminists. Perhaps she wanted the October 17th Movement's split from NOW to mirror the widely recognized generational breaks between the Southern Christian Leadership Conference and SNCC or the Old Left and the New Left. By casting the October 17th Movement as an organization of dissident young feminists in NOW, however, Atkinson helped to expunge her mentor from the movement's history.

Atkinson and Kennedy were the only members to officially resign from NOW that fall. The new group they formed was the October 17th Movement, named for the day Atkinson formally resigned. Another key member who joined the October 17th Movement was Kay Lindsey, a black woman writer and producer for Pacifica Radio whose feminist "Poem" would be published in Toni Cade Bambara's seminal anthology *The Black Woman*. Lindsey was instrumental in producing much of WBAI's feminist radio programming in the late 1960s. Her radio programs provided one of the few outlets where black feminists such as Kennedy, Alice Walker, and Eleanor Holmes Norton could articulate a black feminist politics in a public arena at a time when the mass media was ignoring black feminist perspectives.[68]

White feminists such as Charlotte Hill, Nanette Rainone (a broadcaster on Pacifica Radio), Carol Goodman (NOW), and Astrid Bergundaugen also joined the organization.[69] Originally, reflecting Kennedy's three movement commitments, it was slated to be "an action coalition of the student movement, the women's movement and the Negro movement."[70] In contrast to NOW, the October 17th Movement did not have officers, it fully supported participatory democracy, and it advocated the complete repeal of restrictive abortion laws. Members met throughout the winter at their apartments, including Kennedy's, to plan their first major direct action: a demonstration at the New York City Criminal Court to support local abortionist Dr. Nathan Rappaport and to demand the decriminalization of abortion.[71]

While Atkinson's vision for the October 17th Movement resembled Kennedy's, it also departed from hers in significant ways. Atkinson was particularly interested in seeing the October 17th Movement make a commitment to an independent and autonomous women's movement by banning male membership.[72] By the summer of 1969, this new direction was cemented as the organization changed its name: the October 17th Movement became The Feminists.

Leaving The Feminists

During the summer of 1969, Pamela Kearon presented her position paper titled "Man-hating" to the group. In it, Kearon argued that man-hating was a "valid and vital issue" and said she "saw man-hating [as] a subversive and[,] therefore, dangerous sentiment."[73] Atkinson went further, later writing that political women should consider men the enemy and cut off all ties to them. When Atkinson cautioned white women that the "price of clinging to your enemy is your life," she was perhaps echoing a speech she heard Maulana Karenga deliver at the Black Power Conference in Newark. At the conference, Karenga asked, "Any negroes who want to stand up for their white master?," and warned, "We're giving you a chance to die for your white master."[74]

In 1968, Kennedy noticed the early reverberations of this position in women's liberation circles and stated, "I think it's going to be slightly unhealthy, but I can see it happening with women who regard themselves as revolutionary, that they are regarding all men as oppressors."[75] While Kennedy appreciated attempts by The Feminists and other groups to be "militant feminists," she neither advocated women's separatism nor viewed all men as oppressors.[76] Kennedy would continue to see the value in working not only with black men but with white men as well. Later she described herself as a "coalition person," so she did not see the use of closing doors to possible allies. If men tried to usurp power from women in any organization in which she was a member, she argued that just like in her dealings with white feminists, she "could trick [men] first" and keep hold of the reins. Thus, she recognized the limits of working with men of any race and white women, but she saw the possibilities for coalition building as worth the risk. She also saw women of all races and black people as clever enough, given the strength of their own movements, that they could continue to navigate their organizations while benefiting from the outside support.

Kennedy's response to oppression focused mainly on challenging major institutions, which many radicals termed "the establishment," more often than on challenging individual men or even white people as a group. The concept of "men as the enemy" and the strategy of women's separatism, however, became core elements of The Feminists' ideology. Atkinson desperately wanted the emerging movement to be taken seriously and to be regarded as revolutionary. In the late 1960s, white women were attempting to build a distinct radical feminist theory that was unlike that of NOW and that emphasized the particular oppression of women. The Feminists were especially interested in being at the forefront of creating a new radical feminist theory. Much of their early rhetoric relied on the paradigms utilized by Black Power advocates. Black Power spokespersons often looked to revolutionary struggles in the Third World for inspiration and drew parallels between their battles at home and the battles being waged by people of color abroad. Black nationalists frequently invoked the language of making a "revolution" and achieving "liberation" when articulating their struggle, in contrast to the reformist politics of the civil rights movement. Kennedy understood that other political groups looked to black movements for clues about how to frame a collective struggle and resist oppression. Like Black Power advocates, such as the Nation of Islam, who were interested in creating a cosmology that reversed the relationships of power and domination, The Feminists were interested in establishing new concepts that both explained and reversed the relationship between male power and female weakness.

For Kennedy, gender oppression was never the primary contradiction, nor was male supremacy the major form of social domination from which all others originated. She also differed from those white socialist feminists who thought that male dominance was a by-product of capitalism. Kennedy articulated the opinion of a black feminist that racism *and* sexism were the major problems that needed to be overcome. Black feminists such as Fran Beal of SNCC and Patricia Robinson of the Mount Vernon/ New Rochelle group were acutely aware of class domination and often stressed capitalism as an oppressive force as well. While Kennedy saw all oppressions as interrelated, she believed that in the final analysis the legacies of slavery and Jim Crow deeply permeated society, and that therefore challenges to racial inequality always needed to be central. Indeed, as Kennedy worked in predominantly white feminist groups, she continuously maintained that white women should prioritize ending white supremacy and make valuable alliances with black movements. Her approach was also strategic: she thought that major social institutions were all mutually interlocking and could not be transformed without a mass movement involving all oppressed groups fighting against them at once.

Although Kennedy supported black separatism and was "very happy that black people put white people out and said we don't want white people here," it is clear that in her own political organizing, black separatism was not tenable. Kennedy often disrupted Black Power spaces when she insisted on bringing white feminists with her. Similarly, Kennedy was supportive of feminists "putting men out" and forming all-women's groups, but ultimately she did not advocate women's separatism or believe that all-women's organizations were the only, or even the primary, space in which she should organize.[77]

Although Kennedy remained active in The Feminists for several months, by the summer of 1969 she had grown weary of the organization's politics and decided to leave it.[78] The name change also signaled a change in direction, as the organization began to speak less of coalition-building with the Left and black movements and more about working autonomously to end sexist oppression. Other black feminists, including Kay Lindsey, also withdrew from the organization.[79] Although Kennedy's friendship and political alliance with Atkinson would endure, Atkinson understood that The Feminists were far too insular for Kennedy's more expansive politics. "I was beginning to go in a different direction—not talking to men, working with only women. Flo never believed" in this.[80]

In the end, white radical feminists in the October 17th Movement adapted the lessons of the Black Power movement in ways that ignored what black feminists were trying to teach them about interlocking forms of oppression and the importance of coalition building. This rejection shaped the subsequent development of both the predominantly white women's movement and the independent black feminist movement that would develop in the early 1970s. Some histories presume that white radical feminists were never exposed to alternative views that centered on ending racism along with sexism,[81] but Kennedy's example demonstrates that they were in contact with black feminists during the nascent stages of their organizations. Ultimately, the voices and viewpoints of black feminists were ignored.

8

Not to Rely Completely
on the Courts

BLACK FEMINIST LEADERSHIP IN THE

REPRODUCTIVE RIGHTS BATTLES,

1969–1971

On January 14, 15, and 23, 1970, dozens of women packed the thirteenth floor of the federal courthouse in Manhattan to testify about traumatic personal experiences with illegal abortion. During these daylong depositions, women became the expert witnesses in a case seeking to repeal restrictive abortion laws in the state of New York. The women detailed incidents of rape at the hands of sham abortionists, botched procedures that left them infertile or physically damaged, and unwanted pregnancies that rendered them destitute as they struggled to care for children they could not afford to raise.[1] Collectively, they forcefully argued that women should have access to safe, legal abortion procedures and that women, and women alone, should be the ones to decide when and if they wanted to have children. *Abramowicz v. Lefkowitz* was the first case to use women who suffered from illegal abortions instead of physicians as expert witnesses.[2]

Florynce Kennedy was one of the lawyers for this influential suit, which she intended to take on appeal all the way to the Supreme Court in order to radically expand women's reproductive choices by making abortion legal in all fifty states.[3] Indeed, the tactics developed in the *Abramowicz* case—most notably the use of women as expert witnesses—would later be used in *Roe v. Wade*, the landmark 1973 federal case that overturned restrictive abortion laws.[4]

Although Kennedy was a lead lawyer for this case and one of the country's best-known black feminists, her key role in helping to legalize abortion has long been forgotten and is absent from most histories of postwar feminism and the reproductive rights battle.[5] The struggles of women of color to push the predominantly white reproductive rights movement away from a narrow focus on gaining the legal right to abortion and toward a broader agenda that challenged other forms of reproductive injustice are central to emerging scholarship by both activists and scholars.[6] By attaining leadership positions within the predominantly white women's movement, black feminists helped to reshape the abortion rights campaign, introducing issues such as forced sterilization, poverty, and the need for affordable child care. Yet Kennedy's leading role in the legal and political campaign in New York State has been ignored or regarded as merely supportive of the campaign rather than recognized as helping to frame its feminist strategy.[7]

Black women helped to lead the campaign to legalize abortion, which many middle-class white feminists regarded as "the most important goal in the struggle for women's reproductive autonomy."[8] While few black feminists made the legalization of abortion their top priority, they did see it as critical to the struggle for black liberation. As leaders in the abortion rights campaign, they articulated a black feminist agenda as African American women who experienced sexist and racist discrimination in forms that could not be pulled apart and fought separately. Examining the work of Kennedy reveals the central roles that black women played in developing feminist strategies to address this controversial issue.

Kennedy's leadership illuminates the complex but deeply rooted connections between the black and women's liberation movements. Kennedy was in constant negotiation with the Black Power movement. Her feminism did not estrange her from Black Power or lead her to reject it because it was male supremacist; instead, she translated some of the movement's central insights and strategies into forms that feminists could use. Kennedy helped to shape the strategies and tenor of the predominantly white reproductive rights movement and did not simply follow white feminist directives. Indeed, another lawyer for the suit, Diane Schulder, described Kennedy as a seasoned movement attorney and activist who mentored the younger feminist lawyers.[9] Kennedy's central contribution was her keen ability to place the state on trial and to mobilize supporters outside the courtroom, a political strategy she had developed in the Black Power movement.[10]

With the *Abramowicz* case, Kennedy extended her previous legal work and activism in defending Black Power leaders, such as H. Rap Brown of the Student Nonviolent Coordinating Committee, against excessive government surveillance. The *Abramowicz* case became another stage on which she could challenge state-sponsored oppression.[11] She used protests outside the courtroom to ensure that the court could not easily dismiss the demands of the women's movement. In this instance, indeed, she brought women's voices and collective protests directly into the legal proceedings.

Having worked with William Kunstler to defend H. Rap Brown against government repression, Kennedy understood the importance of demonstrations for garnering public support. A year before the *Abramowicz* case, she had organized a bus to bring both feminists and Black Power radicals from New York to Maryland to support Brown and gave speeches criticizing the state for attacking him and the Black Power movement.[12] Kennedy viewed her protests and speeches as part of an effective legal and political defense.

Kennedy's prominence in the reproductive rights struggle placed her at odds with some black nationalists who argued that repealing abortion laws was part of a white genocidal conspiracy against black people. Undeterred by their criticisms, Flo continued to work to decriminalize abortion and challenged black nationalists instead to view the repeated deaths of black and brown women from botched illegal abortions as a form of genocide. Black feminist activism in the late 1960s and 1970s was instrumental in demonstrating that intervening in state discourses on abortion and other methods of birth control was revolutionary and that black liberation could not be won without women securing the right to control their own bodies.

The Courts and Protest

Black legislators had been at the forefront of the battle to end restrictive abortion laws long before the women's movement took up the issue. Percy Sutton, a black New York state assemblyman, supported the legalization of abortion and in 1966 introduced the first bill that would have reformed abortion laws to allow a woman to have the procedure not only when the pregnancy put her in physical danger but also when her mental health was at risk. With little support from other legislators and intense pressure from clergy, that bill was defeated.[13] In 1967, black feminist Shirley Chisholm, then an assemblywoman from Brooklyn, supported a similar abortion reform bill, introduced by Assemblyman Albert Blumenthal. That bill also failed, but Chisholm became known to the burgeoning women's movement as a strong supporter of abortion rights.[14]

Two years later, Redstockings became one of several predominantly white feminist organizations in New York to place a priority on decriminalizing abortion. The group focused on repealing, rather than simply reforming, the state's abortion laws—a goal that represented an important shift from the reform orientation of legislators and feminist organizations such as the National Organization for Women.[15] Abortion law reform would have kept control in the hands of physicians, as it derived from legal arguments that treated restrictive laws as infringements on doctors' right to practice medicine without state interference.

In 1969, several New York legislators, including Chisholm and Blumenthal, together with feminist activists, pushed lawmakers to review the state's statutes on abortion. In response to their agitation, the Joint Legislative Committee on the Problems of Public Health held a hearing on abortion laws. Redstockings members seized the moment, interrupting the proceedings to protest the absence of women witnesses.[16] As the legislators began interviewing "experts," the women attempted to interject testimony about their own experiences with illegal abortions. Security guards quickly ushered the protesters out and the panel continued; however, the committee eventually invited three feminists to testify.[17]

The following month, Redstockings held an abortion speak-out in response to what it viewed as the legislators' token gesture. Over three hundred people crowded Washington Square Methodist Church, many testifying about their unwanted pregnancies and lack of access to safe abortions. Redstockings hoped that women's public statements about their experiences and perspectives would help reverse the stigma and isolation associated with having an abortion and would raise awareness about the need to legalize the procedure.[18]

During the late 1960s, various legislators and feminist organizations were devising ways to challenge the state's restrictive abortion laws. The Women's Health Collective (WHC), a women's group interested in women's interactions with the health system as consumers and workers, began gathering stories of those who had experienced illegal abortions in hopes of filing a suit on their behalf.[19] The WHC discussed this possibility with Nancy Stearns, a staff lawyer for the Center for Constitutional Rights.[20] Realizing that she could not handle this large case alone, Stearns pulled together a group of women lawyers who identified as feminists. Kennedy became a central part of the political team that included Diane Schulder, Carol Lefcourt, Ann Garfinkle, and Emily Goodman.

As the lawyers discussed strategies, Kennedy and Schulder recalled, the Redstockings speak-out "triggered the idea" of having "women testify, as women and as experts, in the federal case to attack the constitutionality of the abortion law."[21] They argued that the case should be linked with the protests that were already occurring in New York City.[22] Like the Redstockings' public speak-outs, the legal depositions could be given in public and made readily available to those who were not yet actively involved with the issue. The lawyers recalled previous civil rights cases in which that had been done. While most depositions were conducted in attorneys' offices away from the media and concerned citizens, Kennedy and Schulder maintained that "public education on a subject that had been kept under wraps for so long was just as important as the court decision in this case."[23]

Stearns, a newly minted attorney with only two years of legal experience, mostly as a researcher on constitutional questions, admitted that she was a bit "green . . . at these types of cases" and that Kennedy was "far better at depositions" because of her previous experience in the courtroom.[24] Other lawyers involved in the case were also fairly recent graduates from law school. Kennedy, however, brought over seventeen years of legal experience, a unique track record of representing plaintiffs and defendants in political trials, and skill in organizing support for those causes outside the courtroom.[25] Kennedy's involvement in the campaign to repeal New York's restrictive abortion laws continued, bridging litigation and movement strategies.

Kennedy and Schulder conducted their preliminary interviews with the plaintiffs in Kennedy's apartment on East 48th Street.[26] As one of the attorneys remembered, "Everyone met at Flo's."[27] Just as Black Power activists and feminists had met in Kennedy's living room to formulate new approaches for challenging the state and gaining media attention for their cause, so too did the plaintiffs in this case. Activists in the women's liberation movement saw their participation in the case as an extension of their feminist organizing.[28]

The final depositions were to be held publicly in the same location as the earlier Redstockings speak-out. But when the state's attorneys arrived at Washington Square Methodist Church, they refused to depose the women, arguing that the atmosphere was more like a circus than a legal proceeding.[29] The judge agreed with the defense, and the depositions were moved to a conference room at the federal courthouse.[30] Perhaps the defense hoped this would prevent the large crowd of outraged women from attending and diminish media attention. But the women were undeterred; they traveled several blocks to the courthouse and packed its small conference room and adjacent corridors. The defense was unable to prevent them from attending the proceedings and testifying as expert witnesses on abortion.

The defense also failed to stop Kennedy from placing the state on trial for dismissing women as the authorities on their own bodies and from using the *Abramowicz* case "as a very definite platform for exploring the extent of the legalized oppression of women."[31] Indeed, Kennedy enlarged the conversation at the deposition by rejecting common legal protocol and forcing the court to engage political questions. While Stearns stressed the constitutional argument, framing the case as a breach of a woman's right to privacy and underscoring the vagueness of the state's legal statutes on abortion, Kennedy made the case a political stage. She used her position to attack the defense as a biased arm of the government.

During the proceedings, Kennedy deposed Lucy Wilcox about her experiences of being young, single, and pregnant.[32] Wilcox described how, during her first pregnancy, she had to move to New York City and live in a home for unwed mothers. Although she wanted an abortion, she was counseled to have the baby and give it up for adoption. During her second pregnancy she lived in New Orleans and aborted her fetus by drinking quinine and castor oil. The state's attorney deemed Wilcox's testimony immaterial and continuously objected on the grounds that she lived in New Orleans during her second pregnancy and that most of her testimony focused on her experience with the adoption process. Among other rebuttals, Kennedy argued that Wilcox's testimony was relevant because it illustrated the lack of abortion options in New York.

A dispute developed between the litigators about the relevance of her testimony and, by implication, that of all women who had sought and been denied legal abortions:

DEFENSE: That's just the problem, because Ms. Kennedy is not bound by relevancy and that's unfortunate, it seems to me, and I think it should be.

KENNEDY: It's quite unfortunate for women that the State of New York is paying people to support religious doctrine . . .

DEFENSE: I'm going to move to strike that statement. There is no testimony to that effect and you haven't come up with any . . .

KENNEDY: . . . Also that the Attorney General's office and apparently other governmental offices have no concern for women's rights or women's feelings and have so indicated in this record, time and again. And I certainly think it relevant politically, if not legally, that the Attorney General is so quick to show his contempt for women and their experiences and ordeals.

DEFENSE: That statement is ridiculous.

STEARNS: The attorneys for the plaintiffs are doing their very best to bring to the court information on an issue which has never really been fully heard by courts before and which is a critical one. And it relates squarely to the constitutional rights of women with respect to this statute. . . .

KENNEDY: Lucy Wilcox is a resident of the state of New York. . . . This issue of whether or not this hypertechnical approach will prevail will be of very great interest to the plaintiffs.

DEFENSE: The question is not the interest to the plaintiffs. The question here is how we can aid the court in reaching a determination with respect to the constitutionality of the state statute. This is not a platform designed to demonstrate or to advertise a particular viewpoint of a particular organization. This is a legal case before a court and let us stick to the issues that are framed within the complaint.

KENNEDY: Let me make it absolutely clear for this record that my concern is for the interest of the plaintiffs. I regard this case as a very definite platform for exploring the extent of the legalized oppression of women and I personally don't, for one second, intend to lose sight of my objectives. That the defendants have no concern for those objectives is now quite apparent.[33]

Throughout the proceedings, Kennedy emphasized that women's voices should be privileged and chastised the state's lawyers for not caring about women's viewpoints. Her audience was neither the judge in this case nor the established legal system but rather the countless women who shared the experiences of the plaintiffs and could therefore understand why restrictive abortion laws should be repealed.

In Kennedy's hands, the legal depositions became an open political tribunal and protest rally. Kennedy did not conceal her intentions; the state's attorneys could clearly see how she was trying to make the case political. Radical attorneys such as Gerald Lefcourt and William Kunstler were utilizing this strategy at the same time to defend Black Power and anti-

Vietnam War protesters.[34] Lefcourt and others credited Kennedy with helping to popularize the technique of supplanting commonplace legal arguments with arguments more familiar to political organizers and with challenging and demystifying the authority of the legal system in order to make a larger political case to the public.[35] Kennedy had little faith that the justice system was just, or even neutral. In fact, she believed that the judicial system was profoundly biased, racist, and sexist and served only "those best able to afford the luxuries" of legal representation and appeals.[36] Through this case Kennedy demonstrated that it was important to utilize the energy of political movements to force the hand of a conservative court. She was acutely aware that legal cases were often won and lost in the court of public opinion. The strong reaction by the defense attorneys against the women's testimony and Kennedy's insistence on politicizing the case suggest that the defense saw this strategy as a serious threat.

Grasping the intricate connections between legal proceedings and political agitation outside the courtroom, Kennedy moved seamlessly between these two spaces. As a member of People to Abolish Abortion Laws, a coalition of feminist groups, she helped to organize a large "Coat Hanger Farewell" protest march to the public Bellevue Hospital on March 28, 1970. The *Abramowicz* case and the various pro-abortion protests during this period helped to make the coat hanger the major symbol of the growing reproductive rights movement because it symbolized the dangerous methods women were forced to use to abort pregnancies on their own. Over fifteen hundred protesters attended the demonstration. In her speech, Kennedy insisted that *all* abortion laws be rescinded, declaring, "There is no need for any legislation on abortion just as there is no need for legislation on an appendectomy."[37] Earlier that day she conducted a smaller "feeder march" to St. Patrick's Cathedral, where she criticized the Catholic Church for influencing abortion laws.[38] As she did routinely, Kennedy encouraged women to utilize their power as consumers and boycott major department stores on the day of the march.[39] She believed that when women stopped buying, those in power would take notice. Kennedy understood that a boycott, a march, and a legal case could be used together as tools to help end restrictive abortion laws.

In speeches and discussions during this period, Kennedy frequently underscored the ways in which the needs of women were ignored in abortion debates and supplanted by the interests of various legislators and the clergy. She wondered out loud how the court's view would change if the position of men and women were reversed and "men could get pregnant"; it struck her that "abortion would be a sacrament!" and a protected right.[40]

On April 3, 1970, only a few days after the protest march and six months after the *Abramowicz* brief was filed, the state legislature unexpectedly legalized abortion for women up to the twenty-fourth week of pregnancy. Consequently, the women no longer had a legal claim and their suit was immediately resolved. Kennedy reasoned that the hundreds of women marching down Fifth Avenue were the final straw that convinced legislators to change the laws. In Kennedy's view, the *Abramowicz* case and the feminist demonstrations against abortion underscored two lessons: "not to rely completely on the courts for anything" and couple all legal actions with organized protest.[41]

Although the state-level victory dashed Kennedy's hope of taking the case to the Supreme Court, the *Abramowicz* case paved the way for other challenges to state abortion laws.[42] The legal arguments the lawyers presented and their strategy of using women as witnesses became the model for other cases challenging restrictive abortion laws, most notably *Roe v. Wade*, which led to the legalization of abortion in all fifty states.[43]

Abortion Rap: Black Feminist Critiques of the "Black Genocide" Theory

Kennedy was disappointed that women plaintiffs in *Abramowicz* would not have an opportunity to testify about their experiences with illegal abortions in a brief that would be presented to the U.S. Supreme Court. Hoping nevertheless that the witnesses would inspire women in other states, Kennedy and Schulder decided to publish a small portion of the women's most damning testimony in *Abortion Rap*, which she described as a "brief to be presented to a people's tribunal."[44] Published in 1971 by McGraw-Hill, the book provided an in-depth synopsis of the class-action suit and highlighted the statements of several women. It also offered an opportunity for Kennedy to challenge antiabortionists, whom she called "fetus fetishists." In later years she pushed to have the Catholic Church's tax-exempt status revoked because of its political activism in funding lobbying and campaigning for antiabortion legislation. Kennedy was especially interested in combating the institutions with the greatest power to limit women's reproductive freedom.[45] The church received much of Kennedy's criticism because she argued that it illegally colluded with the state and attempted to control women's bodies through the "license to fuck. It's called marriage."[46] While she directed most of her energy toward major social and political institutions such as the church and the government, she also criticized activists and organizations that attempted to curtail women's choices. Given her long affiliation with the Black Power movement, she was particularly disturbed by the criticisms of abortion and oral contraception articulated by many black nationalists.[47]

In one chapter of *Abortion Rap*, "Black Genocide," Kennedy takes aim at the black nationalists' argument that legalizing abortion and contraception was a white genocidal plot against black people. Black nationalism of the 1960s and 1970s, like other forms of nationalism, emphasized the role of women as child bearers in assuring the continuity of the nation. As scholars Philip Spencer and Howard Wollman argue, concerns about breeding a nation's subjects can be manifested in a variety of other concerns, ranging from a desire to increase the nation's power by increasing its population to worries about the quality of the populace. They explain that "the association of women with children . . . forms a major plank in nationalist mobilization in times of war when men are expected to be willing to sacrifice themselves while women are expected to sacrifice their male loved one" while taking care of the home and children.[48] The Black Power movement's stress on viewing itself as part of a black and Third World revolutionary war helped to advance masculinist rhetoric that consigned black women to the home and derided the legalization of the pill and abortion as part of the state's plan to reduce the black population and weaken the movement's ability to protect itself against state-sanctioned racist violence, such as police brutality and unjust imprisonment.

Rarely did Kennedy publicly chastise black radicals for perpetuating sexism; she was more likely to scold white feminists when they openly challenged nationalist men for being sexist or labeled black men "the enemy."[49] She argued that black women alone were responsible for critiquing the sexism of black male activists and challenging patriarchal gender norms in their movement. The "Black Genocide" essay in *Abortion Rap* was Kennedy's only published writing that addressed the sexism in the Black Power movement. Contesting black nationalists' arguments against abortion by articulating opinions that black feminists shared, she argued that many black women she encountered desperately needed and wanted access to safe and legal birth control. As black feminist Loretta Ross later explained, black women supported access to abortion and contraception because "we needed to. Necessity was the midwife to our politics."[50]

Using examples of black women who died or suffered from botched abortions and unwanted pregnancies, some of whom she had interviewed for the *Abramowicz* case, Kennedy challenged Black Power–era radicals to view these deaths as a form of genocide. While Kennedy referred to these women in her essay, *Abortion Rap* did not include any of their testimonies.

The black women questioned at Kennedy's apartment were not asked to give public depositions because Kennedy and Schulder feared for their safety. They decided not to invite a woman to speak in the open courtroom if "society might capitalize upon her vulnerability in her personal or family circumstances and damage her in her job or relationships."[51] Early drafts of Kennedy's essay detail black women's experiences with abortion, but the published essay refers only in general terms to the black women they interviewed.[52] While the case and *Abortion Rap* were attempts to privilege women's voices, the voices of black women still had to be protected from hostile responses both within and outside the black community.

One black woman Kennedy and Schulder protected was Florence Rice, feminist and Harlem Consumer Education Council founder. Rice, who was interviewed in Kennedy's apartment for the case, described the two illegal abortions she had endured when she was young, single, and living in Harlem.[53] After one of the procedures, she suffered from an infection, as did many other women who underwent illegal backroom abortions, and "ended up in Harlem Hospital." The nurse was "very nasty" to her because the hospital wanted to know the name of the abortionist. When Rice refused to answer, the nurse snapped, "Oh, well, then you are going to die in this bed" from the infection.[54] Despite her harsh treatment, Rice recovered and years later told her story to Kennedy and Schulder and publicly criticized New York's abortion laws. Although Rice was active in organizing consumers against stores that refused to hire African Americans and that inflated telephone company prices for several years, during the day she cleaned whites' homes and businesses. This form of low-paying employment left her vulnerable to harassment; worse yet, she could be fired if her employers learned of her activism. Yet Rice took these risks every time she participated in a protest. Regardless of Rice's past activism, the legal team must have feared the potential reactions of her employers and some Harlem organizers if they heard of her two illegal abortions. As a result, the attorneys decided that Rice would not share her story during the public depositions.[55] Well aware of Rice's horrific experiences and her work helping to legalize abortion, Kennedy did not ignore Rice's contribution to the reproductive rights battle and cited her in *Abortion Rap* as a black woman activist who did not "equate abortion with Black genocide" and as an ardent supporter of the movement.[56]

Other black women joined Kennedy in publicly supporting legal abortion and opposing black nationalists' call to continue restricting abortions. Her "Black Genocide" essay was part of a small wave of writing by black feminists in the early 1970s challenging claims that contraception was part of a white plot to eliminate African Americans. Frances Beal, Toni Cade Bambara, Pat Robinson, and Kay Lindsey were among those who published poems, position papers, and essays that responded to these arguments.[57] In 1970, Shirley Chisholm, by then a member of Congress representing Brooklyn, published her autobiography, *Unbought and Unbossed*. In it, she described how the stories of many women suffering from "compulsory pregnancy laws" convinced her to actively support the reproductive rights movement.[58] She argued against "label[ing] family planning and legal abortion programs 'genocide,'" characterizing it as "male rhetoric, for male ears" that "falls flat on female listeners and to thoughtful male ones."[59] A year later, in the foreword to *Abortion Rap*, she wrote that "by outlawing these laws we would instead be honoring the basic and individual right of a woman to terminate an unwanted pregnancy."[60]

Black women also pressed their organizations to be more responsive to their reproductive demands. Notably, Denise Oliver, an African American leader in the New York–based Young Lords Party, a predominantly Puerto Rican nationalist group that modeled itself on the Black Panther Party, helped to write a position paper on abortion that argued that "abortions should be legal if they are community controlled, if they are safe, if our people are educated about the risks, and if doctors do not sterilize our sisters while performing abortions."[61] Puerto Rican activists had reason to be especially concerned about the abuse of women on the island because during the 1930s, Puerto Rican women had been targeted by a program that used coercive methods of birth control in order to decrease the rate of population growth in a racist attempt to ameliorate poverty.[62]

Years before the *Abramowicz* case was filed and *Abortion Rap* was published, Kennedy, in her speeches and discussions with black women, repeatedly challenged the notion that having large families was a revolutionary act and the responsibility of black women. She insisted that if black women were to be truly "revolutionary" and play varied and significant roles in the Black Freedom movement, "some of us might want to travel light."[63] Throughout her essay in *Abortion Rap*, her lectures and interviews promoting the book, and her discussions with black women activists during the late 1960s, she seriously engaged the black genocide argument. In doing so, she expressed respect for "the position of black people who regard the pill or abortion as black genocide"; she also shared black nationalists' cynicism about the role played by the U.S. government, health officials, and nongovernmental population-control agencies in funding and supporting racist efforts to limit the growth of communities of color in this country and in Third World nations.[64] Nonetheless, Kennedy consistently maintained that she would not let those criticisms stop her from working actively to repeal abortion laws that led to a disproportionate number of deaths of women of color.

While Kennedy mentioned the sexism of black nationalist groups such as the Nation of Islam, her focus on the Black Panther Party and the Black Power Conference suggests that she was primarily interested in engaging Black Power advocates with whom she had a relationship and for whom she had the most respect.[65] She was particularly critical of an article published in the *Black Panther* newspaper three days after the reformed New York state abortion law went into effect. Brenda Hyson, a member of the Brooklyn chapter, declared that the new law represented a victory only for middle-class white women who wanted smaller families so they could buy more consumer goods and engage in other frivolous pursuits. Black women, she stated, were far less superficial; they "love large families" and had abortions only because they could not afford to raise their children. The real problem was a capitalist system that denied black women the economic opportunities to care for families of any size. Therefore, the only real solution "lies in overthrowing the system and returning the means of production back to the people—Revolution."[66] Hyson echoed a common belief when she expressed suspicion of laws that supposedly helped women but were actually detrimental to them, citing the role of the welfare system and health professionals in sterilizing black women and limiting their government-related benefits. In conclusion, the Panthers implored black women to realize that "[our] revolutionary strength lies in the fact that we outnumber the pigs" and encouraged them to have more children for the revolution.[67]

Kennedy was equally troubled by the 1967 Black Power Conference resolution that declared birth control a means to exterminate African Americans and connected the genocide of blacks in the United States to the genocide of people of color throughout the world. Though she participated in and was a key organizer of the conference, Kennedy did not attend the workshop "Black Women and the Home," which created the anti–birth control resolution.[68] Indeed, her "Black Genocide" essay, written four years later, challenged some of the ideas she heard at the closing session and emphasized that reproductive choice for women was liberating rather than genocidal. Her analysis of abortion, like that of other black feminists, bridged the concerns of three groups: black nationalists, predominantly white pro–abortion rights feminists, and black women who suffered from illegal abortions or unwanted pregnancies and called for safe and inexpensive forms of fertility control.

Kennedy agreed with Hyson that "forced sterilization is not merely a nightmare of the future since it has often been ordered in the case of welfare mothers, and has been used as . . . a precondition for an abortion."[69] For example, in North Carolina during the 1960s, black women were three times as likely as white women to have been sterilized and often had to have their tubes tied in order to receive benefits from Aid to Families with Dependent Children.[70] Kennedy recognized that the state had been instrumental in instituting practices that had sterilized scores of women and men of color. While organizing in Mississippi during the summer of 1964, Kennedy's Wednesdays in Mississippi group had heard stories of unmarried black mothers being forcefully sterilized at the segregated hospital after delivering a second child.[71] Eugenic sterilizations of poor people deemed physically or mentally unfit, especially those in institutions for the disabled, including those who were blind or deaf, was no longer a secret.[72] Nevertheless, she maintained that the legalization of abortion—and white feminists' support of legal abortion—did not signal acceptance or approval of racist policies and practices. Moreover, she argued that legalizing abortion gave all women more control over the ways abortions were practiced. She wondered why black nationalists would support criminalizing the procedure, which allowed for "the continuation of state interference in the personal lives of black people."[73] Legalizing abortion, she maintained, permitted the development of safe, black community–controlled abortion clinics and women's health centers.

Kennedy spoke pointedly of the "silent majority of bleeding women in the emergency rooms of hospitals who could use the help of those espousing black genocide theory."[74] Drawing on the testimonies she had heard from black women in the *Abramowicz* case, she described how black women died or faced severe health and financial problems because of repressive abortion laws. In fact, "teen pregnancy and death from septic abortions were the leading cause of death for black women. Before the legalization of abortions, 80 percent of deaths caused by illegal abortions involved Black and Puerto Rican women."[75] Like Chisholm and Frances Beal, Kennedy asked why black nationalists were not concerned about these black lives.[76] When unsafe abortions took the lives of countless black women, why weren't the laws that caused those deaths viewed as genocidal?

Black feminist activism in the late 1960s and 1970s demonstrated that black women's intervention in state discourses on abortion and other contraceptives was revolutionary and that black liberation could not be won without women securing control of their bodies. For Kennedy and many other black feminists, the black nationalists' call for black women to breed revolutionaries did not sound "too far removed from a cultural past where Black women were encouraged to be breeding machines for their slave masters."[77] This demand had no appeal to the many black women who wanted to limit their families and have greater control over their reproductive health.

Kennedy considered reproductive rights so supremely important that she publicly criticized black nationalists, which she generally refrained from doing. In her essay in *Abortion Rap*, she implored black nationalists to support legalized abortion. Emphasizing that problems arising from the issue should be approached in an "open and dialectical way and not in a mechanical manner" that left no room for women who wanted abortions to have them, she argued that if the legalization of abortion provided new opportunities to use the procedure against black women, both white feminists and black nationalists should oppose these abuses.

Black Feminism and Black Power

Kennedy's participation in the birth-control-as-genocide debate followed earlier black feminist interventions in the Black Power movement. In 1968, in a public conversation on WBAI radio, Kennedy and other black women activists voiced their frustrations about the movement's heightened emphasis on masculinity. Black women saw a connection between the commands of Black Power leaders that women take a backseat to men and the 1965 publication of the government report written by Daniel Patrick Moynihan titled *The Negro Family: The Case for National Action*. Eleanor Holmes Norton of SNCC, a lawyer for the American Civil Liberties Union; Vertamae Smart-Grosvenor, who belonged to the Black Caucus of the National Conference for New Politics; and Peachie Brooks, a black feminist from Brooklyn, all opposed the report's attack on black women. In this profoundly consequential public document, Moynihan, then assistant secretary of labor, described the "tangle of pathology" within the black community that supposedly resulted from female-headed households.[78] Seeking to inform policy makers about the causes of African Americans' problems, Moynihan contended that the "matriarchal structure" of the black family "seriously retards the progress of the group as a whole, and imposes a crushing burden on the Negro male and, in consequence, on a great many Negro women as well."[79]

The black women who spoke out during the radio program were outraged over what they described as a "favorite hustle for white people to write about black people and try to rationalize the system of oppression" so that white supremacy was left blameless for black unemployment and the other hardships facing black communities while black women were found culpable. As Smart-Grosvenor argued, "You got a hustler like Moynihan that comes in and pretends to have a whole lot of insight when in fact all he's doing is blaming Black people for what white people did from the moment [we] came over as slaves."[80] Smart-Grosvenor disagreed with Kennedy on the issue of reproductive choice for black women, however. A heated debate ensued when Smart-Grosvenor declared that she did not think they should direct black people toward the pill and controlling their family size. She also contended that the entire notion of small families derived from a white middle-class culture that was ultimately irrelevant to black people.[81]

The other women who participated in the radio program dismissed the notion that only white middle-class women desired small families; they believed that the pill and abortion gave black women greater control over their bodies and the choice to have children when they wished to do so. Norton exclaimed: "The notion of planned births for black women is [a] far more revolutionary concept than it is for white women. White women have [had] one way or the other [for] controlling their birthing, sometimes imperfectly, before the pill. . . . For black women it was often a case of getting toward middle-class status before one even incorporated that notion. The pill, however, is increasingly being manufactured cheaper and cheaper, which means that you finally have the possibility in this country. . . . This liberating little pharmaceutical miracle may make it possible for black women to do their thing their own way."[82]

Kennedy agreed with Norton but went further, questioning the tendency among some black nationalists to "romanticize the family unit" and favor unlimited childbearing. Kennedy observed that, given the economic reality they faced, black women could not afford the luxury of enjoying large families. Instead, more often than black communities cared to admit, black women had to "walk away from their kids and . . . [send] their kids back home, and . . . have other people caring for their children." She understood that the pill could help alleviate this problem by allowing women to decide if and when they wanted to conceive. Kennedy was disappointed to see some Black Power rhetoric emerging in the mid-1960s that pointed to a subordinate role for black women, gave men "the starring role," and expected black women "to be sorry for anything we ever did to lead the way to anywhere."[83] She was both fascinated and horrified by what she described as the "new" behavior of black women in Black Power meetings. There she witnessed "little girls being nice and quiet and hardly ever . . . interrupting or anything. . . . These cool little girls just sit there in their afros . . . and they just don't say anything, and the men say, 'We are it! And you'll have as many babies as we want you to and you're not going to have any birth control or abortions.'"[84] She found this "quite fascinating" because she came "from the old line"; there "the whole idea was that women were going to take over, and have freedom and . . . were an oppressed group." Women "over fifty are very big on the freedom for women kick"; meanwhile, "younger black women and many of the most political ones are sort of taking the 'let's let the men go ahead now' attitude."[85]

Kennedy saw this change in the way some young black women performed in black political spaces as related to a generational divide between black women who had lived through World War II and were accustomed to fighting against the multiple evils of fascism, racism, sexism, and imperialism and younger women who had not lived through the same conflicts. She wondered why some young black radical women supported the command to take a backseat to black men and stay home to raise a "passel of children" for the impending revolution.[86] This upsurge of oppressive rhetoric differed from what Kennedy perceived as the civil rights movement's openness to black women's leadership. While the civil rights movement was never free of sexism and often propagated conventional gender norms, Kennedy deplored both the Black Power movement's escalating use of rhetoric that criticized black women's leadership as emasculating to black men and any attempts to force black women to recede into the home.

Indeed, Kennedy wondered aloud whether this romanticizing of large black families and the emphasis on women deferring to men was connected to government infiltration into the Black Power movement. She suspected that the CIA was "programming black nationalists to talk like this. . . . If I had a group that was about to withdraw consent to oppression," she reasoned, "I would like nothing better than they should be bogged down in a big family . . . with little kids to run back home to" and much too tired and overwhelmed to engage in political organizing.[87] In seeking to subordinate black women, Kennedy contended, Black Power advocates were, in effect, colluding with the government's efforts to undermine black people by disempowering black women.

Despite her suspicions that the CIA might be responsible for the increased stress on masculinity and the emphasis on the black genocide theory in Black Power rhetoric, Kennedy steadfastly maintained that black nationalists needed to confront their own sexism. She viewed as extremely shortsighted the assertions of Smart-Grosvenor and other black nation-alists that blacks should reject the pill because white people helped to make it available. During this impassioned discussion, she quipped that this type of logic reminded her of a "guy on the subway that has a roach or a bedbug on his shoulder and some white man knocks it off and . . . the [black guy] says, 'You put that back up there. You white people don't let us have anything.'"[88] In response to what she viewed as Smart-Grosvenor's illogic and the narrow reasoning of some black nationalists, Kennedy fre-quently declared that "a burden lifted is a burden lifted."[89]

Throughout her life, Kennedy moved between movements and orga-nizations that we have come to think of as separate in hopes of bridging them and forming more powerful coalitions. In Kennedy's view, the pre-dominantly white women's movement helped to lift a burden from black people by spearheading the battle to legalize oral contraception and abor-tion. She had hoped that the Black Power movement would see the legal-ization of the pill and abortion as a victory for black women and men and as especially important for impoverished single black women, who were the most vulnerable to illegal abortions and the repressive arm of the state. Kennedy suspected that some black radicals were so caught up in rigid ideology and so blind to black women's lived experiences that they promoted new forms of bondage for black women that defeated the over-all mission of the movement by limiting their ability to be active politically.

Kennedy's leadership in helping to legalize abortion reshapes the his-tory of postwar feminism by demonstrating the centrality of black femi-nist activism and theory to this campaign. Kennedy's commitment to this cause was central to her black feminist politics, bridging the concerns of black nationalists who were suspicious of government interventions into the health and lives of women of color, the political views of predomi-nantly white feminists who prioritized the legalization of abortion, and the interests of black women and girls who suffered from illegal abortions or unwanted pregnancies and sought safe and inexpensive forms of contra-ception. As a seasoned movement attorney and activist, she turned the fight to legalize abortion into another way to challenge state-sponsored oppression. Her central contribution was her strategy of combining the use of protests outside the courtroom to ensure that the court could not easily dismiss the demands of the women's movement with the use of litigation to challenge the unjust power of the state. In this instance she brought women's collective protests directly into the legal proceedings. The argument of the *Abramowicz* legal team became the model for other cases that challenged restrictive abortion laws, most notably *Roe v. Wade*.

9

Form It! Call a Meeting!

BUILDING A BLACK FEMINIST MOVEMENT,
1971–1980

Shirley Chisholm, a black feminist and congressional representative from Brooklyn, informally announced on October 3, 1971, during a Southern Christian Leadership Conference event in Chicago, that she would seek the presidency of the United States. Chisholm explained to the audience that "we are tired of tokenism and look-how-far-we-have-comism" that had led to government complacency instead of changing unequal and discriminatory conditions in the United States. It was necessary for "black women to . . . turn this country around," Chisholm argued.[1] From that Chicago stage and throughout her campaign, Chisholm declared that she was "the candidate of the people. My presence before you represents a new era in America's political history. Americans all over are demanding a new sensibility and a new philosophy of government. . . . One where there is freedom from violence and war at home and abroad. Where there is freedom from poverty and discrimination. Where there is a feeling that we are assuring for everyone medical care, employment, and decent housing. Those of you who can now vote for the first time. Those of you who agree with me that the institution of this country belong[s] to all of the people who inhabit it. Those few who have been neglected, left out, or shun[ned] aside for whatever reason."[2] Chisholm positioned herself as representing a broad coalition that included all black people, Latinos, the poor and working class, women of all races, students, and those who wanted to see an end to the protracted war in Vietnam. She promised to place the interests of these groups at the center of her campaign so that they would no longer be taken for granted by the Republican and Democratic Parties.

She was part of a "majority minority" of powerful communities and allies.[3] Indeed, Chisholm promised to be the voice for the "alliance of the alienated" that Florynce Kennedy had theorized and worked toward building throughout her activist career.

Kennedy was thrilled and inspired by Chisholm's presidential campaign and recalled that from the moment she first met the state assemblywoman in the early 1960s, she was "a big fan. Chisholm was right on so many issues that are important to women, blacks, black women."[4] The two worked together to challenge restrictive abortion laws in the state of New York, and Chisholm's introduction to Kennedy and Diane Schulder's book *Abortion Rap* condemned abortion laws as mandating compulsory pregnancy. That same year, despite criticism from other politicians, Chisholm publicly supported the campaign to free Black Panther Angela Davis, who had been arrested on charges of supplying weapons to the Soledad Brothers, who were accused of killing a prison guard.[5] Kennedy, too, had been active in the Free Angela Davis campaign as an organizer and outspoken critic of the federal government, which had aggressively harassed and violently suppressed the black liberation movement, and of the media for their "racist, baiting remarks" and hostile portrayal of the Black Power movement.[6] Chisholm shared many of Kennedy's criticisms and engaged in a full-throated condemnation of U.S. military aggression in Vietnam, voting against every Defense Department appropriation.[7] Moreover, Chisholm had been elected through the backing of a broad coalition of black and Latino women and men. Her presidential campaign promised to extend and strengthen these partnerships on a national stage and with a black feminist at its helm. Indeed, Chisholm's campaign was a striking example for Kennedy of black feminist politics in action. At organizing meetings and during her talks in the fall and spring of 1971 and 1972, Kennedy spoke repeatedly of Chisholm's candidacy and how feminists, students, and antiwar activists should support her for the presidency of the United States.

With the publication of *Abortion Rap* in 1971, Kennedy was busy traveling to promote her book and nurture support for the movement to legalize abortion. During her talks she encouraged young people and various organizers to think about the fight for abortion rights and the battles to defend the black liberation movement from state-sponsored assaults and to elect the first black feminist to the presidency. Kennedy pressed her audience to become a part of the political process and to form "coalitions with the outs of society."[8] The majority of her listeners were young white women students. Just as she had done at National Organization for

Women meetings several years earlier, she advised younger women on a variety of movement tactics and strategies and advocated a comprehensive feminism.

Kennedy encouraged white women students to create an alliance with people of color and to seize political power in their college towns and cities. She wanted students to understand their power not only within but also beyond their campus. "Run for office," she would yell; "do anything to get the needs known. Let's not let this country fall apart under us."[9] Kennedy reminded radical students who tended to think of the nation-state as the enemy and therefore scorned the idea of running for political office that the welfare of masses of people like them and those they cared about depended on changing public policy. Understanding the relationship between power and resistance in the United States, Kennedy argued that oppressed people and especially all women "have at least three kinds of power. Dollar power, to boycott with; vote power, to take over structures with, and maybe even get somebody elected; and body power, to get out and support our friends and make a damned nuisance of ourselves with everybody else."[10]

From her podium in the front of the room, Kennedy frequently hand-picked students from the audience to run for office in a range of places like Iowa City, Iowa, and Oberlin, Ohio. Dressed in a cowboy hat, blue jeans, and numerous buttons that read "Free Angela," "End the War Lords!," and "Ms. Chis for Pres.," Kennedy waved her polished fingernails at students across the room who asked what they could do to change things. She would reply that they could write a woman's column for the school newspaper; boycott what she termed the "jockocrats," the university bureaucrats who spent a fortune on useless athletic programs; or call local television stations and "tell them they are full of shit."[11] Better yet, they "should run for the city school board or for mayor. Challenge white men for their seats" in any college town or city where people disagreed with how things were going in the country. She would command them to "start where you live."[12]

While Kennedy was talking to students and faculty at Queens College in New York in the fall of 1971, she complained to the audience about the electoral process and the lack of feminists in office.[13] One student then said, "I wish the feminists were represented." Kennedy thought for a second, and then the answer dawned on her. The room was filled with young feminists who supported Chisholm, many of whom would be voting for the first time during the 1972 election. Why couldn't this group become the first feminist political organization to support and endorse Chisholm?

Later she explained, "When I thought there could be a feminist party sup-porting Shirley Chisholm, I set it up."[14] That afternoon on the Queens Col-lege campus, Kennedy formed the Feminist Party—an interracial black feminist-led organization in support of black feminist politics and the first black feminist presidential candidate. Of course, the very first step in building an organization, at least in Kennedy's mind, was to begin with publicity: "I just said I will buy buttons and I will set up [my] backpack," and she began working for Chisholm.[15] Having worked to form NOW, Kennedy was impatient with the particulars of officially forming an or-ganization, which would typically involve debate and even disputes over the statement of purpose, a political platform, and tactics. For Kennedy, it was better to just start advertising the Feminist Party, and others could join her.

The most encouraging aspect of Chisholm's campaign, for Kennedy, was the opportunities it offered for forging broad political alliances. Chis-holm's support for expansive coalitions between the women's liberation, antiwar, student, and black liberation movements was at the heart of her campaign. Furthermore, Flo understood Chisholm's candidacy as an opening for the mostly white feminist movement to form important bonds with black women and black movements. Kennedy argued that women had a "natural coalition" and believed Chisholm's campaign would be "one of the procedural project[s] that makes [coalitions] possible. In fact necessary."[16]

By the early 1970s, Kennedy had made a political career of emphasiz-ing the critical linkages among all forms of oppression, especially racism and sexism. She was excited about the growth of the predominantly white feminist movement and its success in legalizing abortion, but she was also disappointed that the struggle did not fully embrace a black feminist posi-tion and challenge racism and sexism simultaneously and continuously. By 1971, Kennedy had redoubled her efforts to create interracial feminist organizations that emphasized a black feminist praxis. Her work during this period was central to building a women's movement that included women of all races as well as an independent black feminist movement.

The Feminist Party and Shirley Chisholm's Campaign

The presidential election in 1972 was the first election in which youth be-tween the ages of eighteen and twenty-one could vote, adding over 11 mil-lion new potential voters.[17] This change was a direct result of activists who pushed for the voting age to be lowered by arguing that since eighteen was old enough to be drafted, then it was certainly the appropriate age to vote. In March 1971, Congress passed the Twenty-Sixth Amendment lowering the voting age to eighteen; in only four months it was ratified by three-fourths of the state legislatures, so it was adopted on July 1. Just as Kennedy was compelled to create the Feminist Party by this new group of voters, Shirley Chisholm's presidential candidacy was inspired by young people. Chisholm recalled that college students began pushing her to run for president during her talks on campus. One undergraduate explained, "We heard from a lot of speakers. None of them dealt with issues the way you have. . . . Don't worry, we will be voting soon and we will support you if you run."[18] Many of these first-time voters, Chisholm explained, were her "earliest and some of my most loyal support."[19]

During the late 1960s, students were demanding to hear radical intellectual voices on their campuses. While the long-established speakers' bureaus boasted of clients who were Nobel laureates and former U.S. presidents whose lectures reflected prevailing public policies, the late 1960s saw the growth of new bureaus that promoted activist clients such as Dick Gregory, a Black Power activist and former presidential candidate for the Peace and Freedom Party; Bill Baird, an abortion rights activist; and Floyd McKissick, the national director of the Congress of Racial Equality. These bureaus answered the demands of the "Student Power" movement and marketed their lectures to those students who governed special events at almost every major college or university. The growth of black and women's studies programs and courses in the late 1960s and early 1970s also allowed a space for a broader diversity of intellectuals and activists to spread their message. So noticeable was the shift in the lecturers who visited college campuses that some administrators lamented the demise of sophisticated intellectual inquiry and dismissed the newer speakers as "kooks" and "entertainers."[20]

In previous years, Kennedy had pressed predominantly white feminist organizations to recognize and challenge the connections among all forms of oppression, especially white supremacy and sexism. Now, when traveling to various newly emerging feminist circles throughout the country, Kennedy no longer had to work within the confines of a small number of local feminist groups. With new feminist forums and the additional financial stability and resources that came from the college honorariums, Kennedy could "start a few fires on [her] own."[21] Now in her mid-fifties and with close to a decade of political organizing behind her, Kennedy had learned that she was at her best when she served as a mentor or catalyst for ideas and actions rather than as a day-to-day member of any one organization. Thus, as soon as Kennedy took up the idea of the Feminist Party, she started persuading students on college campuses and friends within her feminist circles in New York to initiate and lead chapters throughout the state and at universities and colleges all over the country.

By 1971, Kennedy rarely worked as a paid lawyer. She did most of her legal work on cases such as *Abramowicz v. Lefkowitz* pro bono. Working as a lecturer allowed her the financial freedom to take on only those cases that were politically important while giving her more time to organize fund-raisers and protests and to attend meetings on behalf of the Black Power movement. Her prominence as an organizer and movement lawyer followed her into the early 1970s, and she regularly received requests from clients to sue a company for racial or sexist discrimination. Kennedy referred some of these cases to her lawyer friends, such as Bill Kunstler and Gerald Lefcourt.[22] But more often she would advise her would-be clients that "this is not a case to go into the courts" and would suggest that she could instead "form a picket line with you for nothing." Kennedy maintained that as a result of public protests they would be much more likely to see justice and win their demands and that "the courts are not the way to resolve conflicts once the conscience of the society has been made aware of the facts."[23] In her opinion, it was best to go straight to the public so it could hear the case. The courts, Kennedy had long since come to understand, were heavily weighted against oppressed people, especially black people. For Flo, oppressed communities were often better and more immediately served by organizing demonstrations outside the courtroom as a way to force media attention and to attract public support.

The Defense of the Black Panther Party

During the late 1960s and early 1970s, Kennedy's time was consumed with her work to decriminalize abortion, form Feminist Party chapters, and challenge the suppression of the Black Power movement. In 1966, the Black Panther Party (BPP), a socialist-Marxist Black Power group, was formed in Oakland, California, by Huey Newton and Bobby Seale. Both Seale and Newton were students at Merritt Community College and members of its Afro-American Association. The Black Panther's Ten-Point Program critiqued the imbalance in society created by capitalism and demanded decent housing, proper education, an immediate end to police brutality against black people, and the exemption of black men from military service, a direct challenge to the overreliance of the state on black men to fight and die on its behalf in Vietnam. The Panthers also insisted that the justice system live up to its claim of impartiality by having black people be tried in court by a "jury of their peers or people from their black communities, as defined by the Constitution of the United States."[24] The BPP formed armed citizen patrols to protect people against racist police officers in black neighborhoods, as well as establishing a host of community nutrition and health programs. By 1969, the Black Panthers had chapters in cities such as Detroit, Winston-Salem, Los Angeles, Chicago, and New York City.[25] The image of black men carrying guns to defend their communities was highly provocative in the eyes of whites and especially the media. Kennedy argued that the media had a long-standing pattern of blaming black activists for defending themselves against racial violence and white supremacy.

By the late 1960s, the Panthers and the Black Power movement were being forced to fight the majority of their battles in the courtroom. The FBI's covert counterintelligence program illegally stopped Black Power organizers' cars on any pretext, raided their homes, and arrested them arbitrarily. In addition, prosecutors often demanded extremely high bail, even though convictions were not the ultimate goal. Indeed, an unusually large proportion of Black Power activists' trials resulted in acquittals. The strategy was designed to wear the organizers down and divert their time and energy from political organizing to raising bail money and legally defending themselves.[26] At that time, neither Kennedy nor the Panthers knew of the FBI's specific plan to discredit and infiltrate the Black Power movement. Kennedy and the Panthers were well aware of the state's illegal tactics against activists, however. Consequently, Kennedy used the numerous cases of Black Panthers, such as Angela Davis and the Panther 21, as an opportunity to place the government and the media on trial. Her defense of Black Power and the Black Panthers focused on the courts as an illegal arm of the state, and she sought to draw public attention to the fallacy that the justice system treated black activists justly. In her view, the media was also to blame for the attacks on the Black Panthers, and she criticized the "pig press" for its unbalanced coverage of the Black Power movement.[27]

At a press conference Kennedy organized during the summer of 1969, she vehemently condemned the head of the FBI, J. Edgar Hoover, "for directing so much of the investigative energies of the FBI against the BPP instead of directing the FBI's efforts in combatting the spread of addiction among the young people of this county."[28] At other protests, Kennedy critiqued the courts for their insidious role in the repression of the Black Power movement and for indicting twenty-one members of the New York chapter of the BPP on charges of conspiring to blow up numerous department stores, a police station, railroad tracks, and the Bronx Botanical Gardens. Those arrested were held in prison on $100,000 bail each.[29] Comparing Judge John Murtagh, the presiding judge at the Panther 21 trial, to Judge Julius Hoffman, who ordered Black Panther Bobby Seale to be gagged and shackled in court during the trial of the Chicago 8 case, Kennedy argued that "Murtaugh [sic] wanted to set up his own standards of justice." Murtagh's system of justice, she argued, was brutal and prejudiced, and the "Black Panthers could not accept" it.[30]

Black Panther Assata Shakur recalled first meeting Kennedy soon after the Panther 21 were charged. Afeni Shakur, one of the arrested Panther organizers, "spoke highly of Flo," so Assata knew that Kennedy would be a reliable ally in helping to raise funds and rally public support for their defense.[31] The first time Assata visited Flo's apartment, however, she was a bit taken aback. She recalled thinking that Kennedy's address was a bit unusual "because she lived in this apartment in midtown, and black women did not live" on Forty Eighth Street in a mostly white, middle-class neighborhood. She was also surprised to see that Kennedy's apartment served as her legal office and as a central site for an array of organizing campaigns. The two discussed ways in which Flo could support the Panther 21 defense and especially Afeni Shakur, who was pregnant; they worried about Afeni's health and the health of her unborn son, Tupac. Two decades later, Tupac Shakur would go on to become a well-known rapper.[32]

A year later Kennedy continued her work defending the Panthers during the Free Angela Davis campaign, serving as a fund-raiser, organizer, and outspoken critic of the media. During a press conference and rally held with Davis's sister, Fania Davis, in Pittsburg, Pennsylvania, Kennedy reprimanded the "pig press" for its sloppy journalism and for "dumb questions."[33] That same week, Kennedy organized demonstrations in New York City and called for a boycott of all inessential purchasing "until beautiful Angela Davis, Brave Black Woman Freedom Fighter[,] is Free." She asked consumers to donate the money they did not spend to the legal defense funds of Angela Davis; Black Panthers such as Erica Huggins, who had been arrested in New Haven; Panther 21 members Afeni Shakur and Joan Bird; the Soledad Brothers; Michael Maynard, a "marine accused of Vietnam Mutiny"; and the "weatherman and weatherwomen everywhere."[34]

As was Kennedy's practice, she organized picket lines in front of New York's popular department stores and in front of major media outlets with a motley crew of support from Florence Rice, the black feminist, Media Workshop member, and Harlem consumer advocate; black nationalist

Queen Mother Moore; and the Whites Against Racism organization. Each Saturday leading up to Christmas, dozens of men and women marched in front of S. Klein, Macy's, Bloomingdale's, and Gimbels department stores and the office of the *New York Times*. Kennedy argued that consumers should "picket the stores that use your dollars to finance the racist, sexist, New York Times . . . [that] prints PIG REVIEWERS. . . . PICKET THE STORES THAT FINANCE THE RIGHT WING DAILY NEWS."[35] Identifying holiday shopping and the Thanksgiving and Christmas seasons as major occasions for the oppression of women, she asked, "Who needs holidays anyway??? Thanksgiving and XMAS are peak periods for women's oppression." The "cleaning, cooking, buying, frying, baking, mopping" only reinforced women's oppression, so by sacrificing the holidays and donating to the defense fund of political prisoners, women could lighten their own burdens and help to free others.[36]

Kennedy understood only too well that in order for the Panthers and the Black Power movement to win their struggle against the onslaught of unwarranted arrests, costly trials, and the media's extremely negative representations of their movement, they had to create a loud public outcry. Moreover, this battle had to be waged in tandem with their battles inside the courtroom. Broad national defense campaigns in support of the Panthers were created by an alliance of organizers of color alongside white liberals and radicals. These interracial unions, such as the Emergency Citizens Committee for the Defense of the Black Panther Party, the Angela Davis Defense Campaign, the Peace and Freedom Party, and the Westside Committee to Defend the Panthers, generated public support and much-needed funds to help with the release of arrested and jailed Black Panthers.

Kennedy and other black feminists consistently offered support both within and outside these alliances.[37] The Third World Women's Alliance, for example, worked with the Angela Davis legal defense campaign, which was a broad coalition of communists and Black Power activists. In protest rallies and in its newspaper, *Triple Jeopardy*, the Third World Women's Alliance detailed Davis's court hearings, published a letter from Davis as she awaited trial, and featured a drawing of her alongside Puerto Rican independence leader Lolita Lebron on the March 1972 cover of the newspaper.[38] In July 1971, Shirley Chisholm, who was equally outraged over the arrest of Davis, questioned her unjust treatment by the courts. Davis was denied bail and was being held in solitary confinement during her trial. Chisholm argued, "It is shockingly clear that Angela Davis is being denied bail for the reason that she is a black militant fighter for her people and an avowed member of the Communist Party." Chisholm argued that the evidence against Davis was weak and that she strongly supported her release on bail and her ultimate release from jail and warned the courts that "the world, as well as the nation, is watching" to see whether justice would prevail.[39]

The FBI intensified its surveillance of Kennedy in the late 1960s and noted that she had "been doing little legal work, but is occupied with the defense of the BPP and the women's liberation movement."[40] By 1972, Kennedy was using her position as a lawyer to criticize the injustices of the legal system, which was stacked against black and brown people and their movements. Kennedy spoke frequently about her expansive black feminist concerns during her lectures alone and with her coauthor Diane Schulder, as well as with her other speaking partner, *Ms.* magazine founder Gloria Steinem.

Reaching Feminists on Campus

Gloria Steinem recalled first seeing Kennedy on a TV show along with Anselma Dell'Olio and Ann Koedt, author of "The Myth of the Vaginal Orgasm." "I had never heard women tell the truth in public about sex before," she said, and Steinem immediately "called up the station to find out about these women." She remembered being particularly impressed by Kennedy, who struck her as "an outrageous, effective, and unique woman": "I was magnetized by her from the beginning."[41] Steinem and Kennedy became friends as they worked together at organizing meetings and fund-raisers throughout the city. Eventually they became speaking partners, traveling from campus to campus across the country, widening feminist conversations and amassing new recruits.

The former Media Workshop member Dorothy Pitman Hughes had been Steinem's initial speaking partner. By the late 1960s, Hughes was deeply involved in organizing day care centers in New York City for low-income families of color and was an advocate of affordable child care. Later she would also start one of New York City's first shelters for battered women.[42] During their talks, Hughes and Steinem advocated a multiracial, cross-class feminist movement and as a result attracted a much broader audience than when Steinem spoke alone. In 1970, when Hughes became pregnant and could no longer travel, Kennedy agreed to fill in for her.[43]

Steinem recalled that, "by speaking together at hundreds of meetings," she and Hughes and Kennedy "hoped to widen the public image of the women's movement."[44] Flo and Gloria lectured on topics ranging from

"Women's Liberation: What Is It All About?" to "Abortion and Choice" at universities such as Yale, Texas A&M, and the University of Wisconsin–Green Bay.[45] They helped to enlarge the public image of the women's movement not simply by having a black feminist speak on behalf of the movement but also through Kennedy's expansive definition of feminism as a political tool that could challenge all forms of domination.

It was customary for Steinem to begin these talks and for Kennedy to follow her. At times Steinem joked, "If I don't speak first I'm a real anti-climax after Flo. Sometimes she makes me look like I've been standing still."[46] While commenting on Kennedy's ability to captivate an audience, Steinem was also pointing to Kennedy's capacious feminist politics, which often made the younger Steinem feel as though Kennedy had surpassed her intellectually and politically. Perhaps Steinem's assessment of Kennedy's lectures was based on the fact that Kennedy never addressed the oppression of women in isolation but always connected it with other forms of injustice. In so doing, she expanded the boundaries of what was conventionally considered second-wave feminists' concerns. Kennedy also expanded the boundaries of what the media presented as the primary concerns of second-wave feminists. Steinem was a darling of the media, in part because of her long hair and slim figure that allowed her to work undercover as a Playboy bunny in the early 1960s and in part because of the media savvy she had developed as a journalist. While newspapers often focused on her as a major spokeswoman for feminism, having Kennedy and her brand of black feminism voiced at these lectures challenged the media's limited agenda.

In her talks and protests, Kennedy insisted that white feminists go beyond the current framing of women's issues and address all forms of domination, which meant challenging the state. "To give a whole speech about crotch control doesn't make any sense to me," she argued.[47] Reproductive and sexual freedom, while essential, was not the only right that women needed to secure; indeed, women should not allow themselves to be reduced to their bodies but should claim their full rights as citizens. In a later speech, Kennedy critiqued women's liberation advocates for their narrow vision of feminist politics and their failure to criticize the government for its misplaced priorities. To this veteran antiwar activist, wasting money on the military while cutting social programs that served impoverished women and children should have concerned all feminists. But "feminists don't even deal with Pentagonorrhea, right. We deal with rape. We deal with abortion. But you see, if we started dealing with Pentagonorrhea, they'd give us the abortion laws."[48] In Kennedy's distinctive lexicon, she likened the U.S. Defense Department to a venereal disease: Pentagonorrhea signified the shameful government misspending that occurred in Washington to prop up U.S. imperialism and support reactionary regimes around the world. Commenting on charges that programs serving the inner cities failed to account for public funds, she protested, "It's only the heads of poverty programs that have to answer for [a] fifteen thousand dollar discrepancy" in their books. "Nobody ever hardly hears of any generals or any of the people that spread the major social disease that America spreads throughout the world [being indicted] . . . I call [this] Pentagonorrhea." Kennedy maintained that if feminists started raising the broader issue of "Pentagonorrhea," the government would be forced to concede to their demand for Medicaid funding of abortions for poor women.[49]

"Slippery Dick [Nixon]," "Move on Over or We Will Move on Over You," and "Attica Amerika" were some of the songs Kennedy sang at the beginning of her lectures and demonstrations. The lyrics criticized the government and the media for their role in oppressing all women, children, blacks, students, and prison inmates. When Flo referred to prison inmates, she was speaking not only about the imprisoned leaders of the BPP but also of the prison rebellion that occurred in Attica, New York, in September 1971, when the mostly black and brown inmates took over the maximum-security prison to demand more humane living conditions. Despite ongoing negotiations, Governor Nelson Rockefeller ordered an armed assault that led to the killing of forty-three people, including thirty-three inmates. Kennedy described the oppression and murder of prisoners as a form of genocide and condemned Rockefeller for "bringing VIETNAM to NEW YORK."[50] Frequently she also labeled the United States "Attica Amerika . . . a society where an oppressive system has ripened into maturity [and where] every level is oppressed in varying degrees."[51] Kennedy regarded her speeches, whether given alone or with Steinem, the same way she did her demonstrations on the streets of New York City: as opportunities to grab the audience's attention and educate them about connections between all forms of oppression and about the alliances students were primed to help build and sustain.[52]

Administrators at times complained when Kennedy was invited to their campuses. They thought that she would talk only about women's issues, but their definition of women's issues was much narrower than hers. "Kennedy," they protested, "addressed herself to minority women's rights not women's rights in general, as she was contracted to do."[53] Kennedy's basic message to white people had not changed in over twenty years;

white women and men and especially white feminists should form coalitions with African Americans and other oppressed communities. By the fall of 1971, however, Kennedy was also asking that white feminists support a black woman as the leader of that alliance.

In the months leading up to the Democratic National Convention in Miami, Kennedy helped to establish over twenty Feminist Party chapters at colleges such as Florida Atlantic University, the University of Missouri–Columbia, and Purdue University in support of Shirley Chisholm's run for the presidency. Feminist Party newsletters described how chapter members were working to "reorder national priorities on war, taxation, child care, racism, sexism, and genocide."[54] Several white feminists remember joining the Feminist Party and identifying as feminists only after Kennedy visited their campus and recruited them.[55] Thus, black feminism became the conduit for their initial understanding of how to be active politically and intellectually as feminists.

While speaking to a group of students at Texas A&M with Steinem, Kennedy went about the business of recruiting students to form a chapter on their campus. She explained that the Feminist Party was "not absolutely limited to supporting Shirley Chisholm" but that "most of the chapters" were doing so because her campaign was "the most exciting, most dangerous, the most likely . . . to blow the minds of [the] various parts of the establishmentarians."[56] Kennedy believed that Chisholm's candidacy frightened "the establishment" because it promised to place in a position of power "a fighting black woman who doesn't accept the sexist, racist, pro-war bull."[57] After hearing Flo and Gloria speak, one faculty member formed a Feminist Party chapter at the local community college a few miles away and was very proud to host the "college's first interracial organization."[58]

At home in New York City, Kennedy encouraged friends and other feminists, many of whom she met in the fight to legalize abortion, to join the Feminist Party and become delegates for Chisholm. Feminists from her New York circles, including Rosalyn Baxandall (New York Radical Women), Sandra Hochman (poet), and Irene Davall (media producer), became active in the party through Kennedy's assertive and repeated "nudging."[59] Baxandall was head of a local New York chapter and Davall became the Feminist Party's director. Poet Sandra Hochman had originally been asked to be a delegate for Senator George McGovern, who was the forerunner for the Democratic nomination, but became a delegate for Chisholm once Kennedy convinced her that "it was easy to be for McGovern" and that supporting Chisholm was "much more radical."[60] Kennedy and Hochman both served as Chisholm delegates and cosponsored several fund-raisers to benefit the campaign.[61] They became closer friends and allies through their work on the campaign, and it was through Kennedy that Hochman recognized the importance of black feminist leadership and a black feminist message.

Kennedy was equally outspoken in support of Chisholm's campaign at NOW's national conference in February 1972. Local and regional NOW groups endorsed Chisholm, and many of their members were her delegates.[62] Kennedy reinforced this support, and she reminded NOW members who were McGovern delegates that Chisholm was a founding member of NOW and they had helped her successful run for Congress in 1968. Flo explained that "actions of women must involve the empowerment of those who relate to feminist politics." As she did in her talks with college students, she encouraged NOW women to become powerful allies of progressive candidates or, where there were none, to enter politics themselves.[63] "In an electoral year the focus must be on the electoral process," Kennedy stated. "The choice is wide. You can run for office yourself, support the candidacy of Shirley Chisholm for President, work for Linda Jenness of the Socialist Workers Party, raise feminist issues and when the media refuses to cover your actions, you can use your dollar power to take consumer action against the media in your area and their advertisers."[64]

The Feminist Party was instrumental in helping members of college and university chapters travel to Miami in July for the 1972 Democratic National Convention, the first at which women constituted 40 percent of the delegates.[65] This was a dramatic increase from the previous convention in 1968, where women made up only 16 percent of delegates. This increase was largely due to feminist movement organizing. In the fall of 1971 the newly created National Women's Political Caucus lobbied the Democratic Commission on Party Structure and Delegate Selection to amend its guidelines to ensure proportional demographic representation of women at the 1972 convention and threatened to engage in a mass protest if the commission refused. The commission finally conceded to the women's demands, and hundreds of women delegates attended the convention.[66]

The National Women's Political Caucus was founded in 1971 to increase women's political participation as elected and appointed officials, as delegates to national party conventions, as judges in the state and federal courts, and as lobbyists, voters, and campaign organizers. The founders included Betty Friedan, Shirley Chisholm, Gloria Steinem, and Bella Abzug.[67] Abzug, Chisholm's colleague in the House and an outspoken feminist, did not support Chisholm's nomination on the grounds that she could not win the general election.[68]

According to Steinem, some of the caucus founders were reluctant to invite Kennedy to the group's first conference because they feared that she would "Mau Mau us."[69] Despite these objections, Steinem invited Kennedy to attend. Kennedy did not care whether she had an official invitation or was intentionally left off the list; women were organizing politically, so she had to be there. By this time some white feminists regarded Flo as a thorn in their side because she always brought up the issue of racism and imperialism, no matter the meeting's agenda, and because she seemed far too brash, aggressive, and uncompromising. Although Kennedy inspired some white feminists, she turned others off. Various white feminists thought it was essential to appear "reasonable" rather than angry and to behave politely. Kennedy was not their kind of woman. Not surprisingly, she embraced her role as an irritant to liberal white feminists.

When Kennedy and the Feminist Party traveled to the Democratic National Convention in Miami, she was equally excited to be a steady nuisance to the media for excluding Chisholm and her antiracist, antisexist, and antiwar politics from the national debate. Feminist Party chapters in Boca Raton and West Palm Beach hosted students in campus dormitories, and a few black families in Miami opened their homes to members.[70] Despite media representation to the contrary, here, as in the 1968 Miss America protest in Atlantic City, black communities were supportive of feminists, especially the feminists Kennedy's organization brought to their doorstep. The Feminist Party organized dozens of feminists from New York and throughout the country to travel to Miami.[71]

As Kennedy saw it, drawing the media's attention to Chisholm's message should be their first step. The Feminist Party argued that Chisholm was continuously battling a "media white out," as the major networks failed to take her campaign seriously and ignored or dismissed her presence on the campaign trail.[72] In fact, several months before Chisholm arrived in Miami she was forced to file a lawsuit against NBC, CBS, and ABC in order to be included in their televised presidential debates.[73] Again and again, the media paid more attention to the white male candidates whom Chisholm had "already won against" than to Chisholm.[74] The erasure of Chisholm's candidacy peaked during the Miami convention.[75]

Infuriated, Kennedy and the Feminist Party planned a surprise demonstration to gain the media's attention. Kennedy suggested to Sandra Hochman that a group of women "march on the bullshit media" during their final televised media roundup. Flo was convinced that the major networks "are going to leave out Chisholm . . . they are going to leave out the women . . . they are going to make us invisible."[76] With Kennedy at the head, Feminist Party members, as well as several women Hochman had employed to film the convention, marched into the auditorium singing, "Move on over or we will move on over you!" and "Revolution, revelation, we live in a cuckoo nation!"[77] Journalists could not help but notice the group of women as they marched around the auditorium, some wearing Mickey Mouse masks and others crocodile masks. Hochman had suggested that the women wear costumes to "poke fun" at the media and politicians for supporting the war in Vietnam.[78] The protesters disrupted the broadcasts by chanting, "No one comes to ask our opinion!" and "Crimes of the media against women!" while Kennedy was yelling, "White out of Shirley, totally racist!" As some reporters attempted to leave the auditorium and others tried to ignore the demonstration, Kennedy loudly demanded that the male reporters listen to them because the media depended on women consumers: "We are women with money! We pay your salaries! Buy your bullshit soap! We finance your whores! . . . You work for us! You are going to listen to us!"[79]

The auditorium was filled with tension as the women forcefully demanded that the newsmen stop the erasure of Chisholm. Quickly, a security guard came to usher the women out of the building. Even when threatened with arrest, the women refused to leave. A white male guard then tried to convince Kennedy to leave, but she ignored him. Finally, the guard tried to physically expel her. Surprising both the officer and the other demonstrators, Kennedy began fighting back. She snapped forcefully, "Get your hands off of me!" and fired several rapid punches directly into the guard's chest.[80] She then moved out of his reach and continued chanting, "White out of Shirley, totally racist!"[81] The women protesters looked excited, impressed, and even stunned by Kennedy's bravery.[82]

To their surprise, the women were not arrested but were eventually forced to leave the auditorium after Hochman cut the electricity cable to one of the network's cameras.[83] Their spontaneous battle with the newsmen underscored Kennedy's central message that organizers should protest "the media for selling you chocolate covered bullshit."[84] She later explained that if the media paid more attention to the political interests of all women and black people, she would not have to be so "loud and crazy." "You could have reasonable people" on television, but since there "is an eeny meeny miney mo, one in every sixty-four . . . [then] we have to be a little loud and a little crazier" to get the media's attention on the issues that were central to oppressed people.[85]

In the end, Shirley Chisholm did not win the Democratic Party's nomination and amassed only a negligible sum of delegates, falling short of the political leverage she had hoped to gain during this pivotal election year.[86] By Chisholm's own account the campaign had very few financial resources and was mostly a volunteer effort.[87] Although Chisholm had the support of many white feminists, especially those Kennedy recruited through the Feminist Party, she was disappointed that other white women "held on but they couldn't go all the way." Many publicly recognized white feminists who campaigned for Chisholm ended up supporting McGovern in the final hours.[88]

Chisholm was equally disappointed by black male politicians who had refused to take her campaign seriously because she was a woman. A few months before the Democratic National Convention, Kennedy attended the first National Black Political Assembly in Gary, Indiana (more commonly known as the Gary Convention). There, she saw firsthand that black male politicians would not seriously engage with Chisholm's candidacy and failed to endorse her.[89] Amiri Baraka claimed that it was Chisholm's failure to appear at the convention that prompted many to reject her candidacy.[90] Kennedy, however, came to understand that most activists—whether they were white women or black men—were not ready for a black woman to lead a coalition of all oppressed groups: "The Chisholm candidacy not only freaked out the Establishment and the niggerizers, but it also confused and unsettled the niggers—and by niggers, I don't mean just the black niggers, but also the student niggers and the woman niggers and the poor niggers—plus a whole lot of other people who thought they were revolutionaries but discovered they couldn't dig her wig."[91] Kennedy used Chisholm's well-recognized wig as a metaphor for black women. While white women and black men claimed they wanted to disrupt white male political hegemony, they ultimately would not support the candidate who best represented that mission.

Chisholm remarked that the only people who stood by her in the end were black and brown women. "They did not have the one problem with my candidacy that many white women did; the whites knew I couldn't be elected, and so their support, even when it was given, seemed a little tentative, because they felt they were fighting for a lost cause. But women like Fannie Lou [Hamer], Lupe [Anguiano] and the rest, having been long active in the civil rights movement and other minority causes, were used to taking up seemingly impossible challenges."[92]

Kennedy, too, understood that it was unlikely that Chisholm would win the Democratic nomination, much less the presidency. For Kennedy, however, this was far from the point. To the press and in her speeches she demanded that the media value the accomplishments of Chisholm's campaign despite its lack of resources and the tidal wave of opposition. Chisholm's campaign demonstrated how "you don't need to win to have influence."[93] Indeed, the campaign made a place for a black feminist message in the national political dialogue. Later, commenting on similar feminist goals that at the outset seemed impossible to achieve, Kennedy explained, "I don't care whether we lose or win. The struggle is what's important."[94]

The Limits of White Feminist Support of Black Women

Like Chisholm, Kennedy came to realize that white feminist support of black women had its limits. In the same year as the Democratic National Convention, Kennedy was quoted criticizing white feminists for not being "prepared to struggle for anything besides their own liberation. . . . There are definitely projects that are ideally suited to fight racism and sexism, but white women are not as prepared as they say they are to help minority groups."[95] Several years later Kennedy reflected on the failure of the predominantly white feminist movement to live up to its radical potential of challenging racism alongside sexism and described how black women had grown tired of unfulfilled promises to fight for the liberation of all women. They were not impressed by white feminists who did not address issues that were central to the black community: "You are not saying anything about the [Black Power movement's] New York Eight, or anything that black women are into. They want to see feminists come in where women are involved in the black community, whether it is about a feminist issue or not. See that's what they can understand and see getting together with."[96] Kennedy understood that alliances meant working on more than just the issues that individuals had in common with their allies, such as sexism; it also meant making their issues one's own. If black women were defending black men against the state, then white feminists ought to support them in doing so. In 1971, when some white feminists refused to support black and Latino prisoners involved in the Attica rebellion for better living conditions because they were men, Flo was furious, remembered Naomi Jaffe of the Weather Underground. Kennedy flatly told Jaffe, "We don't support Attica! We *are* Attica! We are Attica or we are nothing!"[97]

Kennedy was especially frustrated with white feminists who approached black feminists only when they needed them or as tokens and then failed to join with black women "when the issues are simple and simple numbers could make all the difference." She explained, "I still work with white women because I think they're important and I understand the pathology, but there's no reason for black women to be with you guys."[98] One technique that white feminists used in a misguided attempt to recruit black women was criticizing the sexism of black men. At every turn, Kennedy confronted this approach and instructed white feminists to stop it immediately. "Don't try to recruit black women into the women's movement on the basis of sexism of the black male. Recruit black women by attacking the racism of white females."[99] Flo argued that black women were "angrier about the sexism of black men" than white feminists were and that black women needed to be left alone to challenge sexist oppression in their own communities.[100] White feminists should challenge the racism of other white feminists and of white women throughout the country if they were interested in sisterhood with black women:[101] "Call a press conference and announce that the *racist women* who are active, not just in South Boston but in Detroit . . . in New York . . . *are unacceptable as sisters.*"[102] She realized that some white feminists were attempting to address racism and acknowledged, "I know that racism is lower among feminists," but she urged white feminists to redouble their commitment to ending racism throughout the dominant society and in the movement.[103]

Although Kennedy was impressed by some individual white feminists who were focusing on challenging racism, she was disappointed that by the mid-1970s the women's movement was still not making the fight against white supremacy a priority. The movement's failure to make significant strides in this direction made Kennedy weary of white feminists' continual pleas for her to recruit black women. Speaking to both white and black audiences, Kennedy rejected the position of black feminist recruiter and flatly told white women "to leave black women alone!"[104] In fact, she often discouraged black women from joining predominantly white feminist organizations on the grounds that their voices would not be heard and issues of importance to them and their community would be ignored.

The late 1960s and early 1970s witnessed the continued repression of Black Power leaders. Black women were among those targeted by the state. In response, Kennedy advised black women to join in the defense of the black liberation movement. Having worked in the defense of Angela Davis and the Panther 21, she became one of Assata Shakur's lawyers in 1973 after her arrest on numerous charges ranging from bank robbery to murder. Kennedy saw firsthand how the courts ignored the rights of Black Power advocates and how the government frequently and "deliberately . . . infiltrate[d] black groups."[105] "As far as black women are concerned," she said, "I would certainly be most appalled if they all rushed into the women's movement. It's clear that most black people should be involved with the problems of the black liberation struggle."[106]

Kennedy's major efforts in the late 1960s and early 1970s to build coalitions demonstrate that she was far more interested in seeing white feminists form alliances with black-led movements or form feminist organizations with a black feminist agenda than in bringing black women into the mostly white feminist movement. At the same time, she encouraged the formation of autonomous, black-led feminist organizations.

The National Black Feminist Organization

Black feminists in New York City, such as Margaret Sloan, formerly of CORE and SCLC and a *Ms.* magazine editor, and Jane Galvin-Lewis, also a writer and editor at *Ms.*, were eager to create an organization that challenged racism and sexism as interlocking oppressions. By 1973, Kennedy's organizing and speaking calendar was full and she no longer had time to lecture with Steinem, so Sloan and Galvin-Lewis went on speaking tours with Steinem. By traveling to college campuses speaking about feminism, Kennedy, Galvin-Lewis, and Sloan became aware of the numerous young black women outside New York who identified as black feminists. One by one these young women, usually one of only a few on their campus, would run up to them after their talks and say that they too were black feminists. Galvin-Lewis remembered, "They were so happy to see another [self-identified] black feminist."[107] Much like the Black Power Conference and the New Politics conference of the 1960s, their college lectures became sites for organizers to find each other and to form networks of support.

During the summer of 1973, a small group of black women, including Sloan and Galvin-Lewis, visited Kennedy's apartment to discuss what they had witnessed in other cities and towns and the possibility of creating a national black feminist organization. It was obvious that there were black feminists across the country hungry for an organization, they argued. Sunday after Sunday they would walk up the three flights to Kennedy's apartment and then lament black women's erasure from the media's coverage of the feminist movement, discuss the myriad problems facing black women, and consider how they could meet other black women interested in feminism. Later, feminists remembered that "Flo always has these salons . . . she has everyone over" to vent and talk politics.[108] As Flo had done for over a decade, she would serve Entenmann's yellow cake with chocolate frosting, and no matter how many people were in the room Flo would make sure everyone had a share, "cutting up the cake in small, small pieces."[109] As black feminists sat in Kennedy's living room, they hashed out the obstacles they were up against. Galvin-Lewis explained that black women "were facing problems in pay [and] proper child care," issues that were being left off the agendas of both the Black Power and the mostly white feminist movements. After sitting on Kennedy's sofa talking about the vital need for a black feminist organization, "we would get outside and say, 'Well, I don't know, [this might] get a little scary.'"[110]

Despite their anxiety, they would return to Kennedy's apartment the next Sunday and resume their discussion. Finally, Flo became "fed up" with "talking and talking" instead of taking action. Galvin-Lewis explained that Kennedy pushed the women to move forward. She barked, "I'm so sick and damn tired of hearing you bitches running around here, talking about you're going to form something. Form it! Call a meeting!" She threatened not to let them back into her apartment unless they actually started a group and encouraged them to call a press conference "to let people know you are there!" If they were upset that the media ignored them, they should force the press to take notice and gain the attention of black women nationally. Galvin-Lewis remembered thinking they had run out of excuses; "we had to do it." The National Black Feminist Organization (NBFO) was founded that Sunday in Kennedy's living room.[111]

On August 15, 1973, the nascent NBFO held a press conference and invited the lawyer and head of New York's Human Rights Commission, Eleanor Holmes Norton, to give a statement announcing its formation. Sloan told reporters from the *New York Times*, the *Chicago Tribune*, and the *Village Voice* that the new organization would challenge both the "racism killing us from outside the black community" and the sexism that was killing women "from within the community."[112] Soon the NBFO's phone would not stop ringing. Black women from all over the country were interested in joining the group and starting chapters in their own cities and towns. The women in New York soon had enough members to meet regularly in a room behind a Harlem beauty parlor. The group grew so quickly that they had to move their meetings to a school auditorium. The flood of new members demonstrated that more black women were interested in feminism than many had assumed.[113]

Margo Jefferson (journalist), Faith Ringgold (artist), Ringgold's daughter Michelle Wallace (writer), and Doris Wright (writer) were a few of the other black feminists who attended meetings during the organization's early days, and some became its leaders.[114] These women were part of the small wave of black feminist writers and artists whose works articulated a pronounced challenge to the intersections of racism and sexism.[115] These and other women worked to define the specific oppression of black women and to decide the group's priorities. Scholar Kimberly Springer found that the NBFO worked mainly to raise consciousness and planned a national conference in New York that winter.[116]

Kennedy attended some of the early NBFO meetings and was a keynote speaker at its first national conference, held in New York City on December 1–3, 1973. The other two keynote speakers were Shirley Chisholm and Eleanor Holmes Norton. Numerous workshops offered strong opinions on issues ranging from affordable child care to alternative government-funded drug rehabilitation programs for black women. Black feminists Alice Walker, Florence Rice, and sisters Beverly and Barbara Smith and numerous college students made up the approximately four hundred black women who attended the conference.[117] This strong showing, when the group had just announced its formation, testified to the fact that black feminists existed; bringing them together was the real task. In fact, during the period when the NBFO was formed, the Louis Harris Polling Agency and Virginia Slims, a tobacco manufacturer, conducted a series of "American Women" polls to measure the political affinities of women consumers. The polls in 1970 and 1972 demonstrated that black women were more sympathetic to the feminist movement than white women. Yet black women did not join predominantly white feminist organizations in any significant numbers. The creation of a national black feminist group provided black women with an opportunity to join a group that addressed their political concerns as feminists.[118]

At the NBFO conference Shirley Chisholm argued that a black feminist organization was necessary in order to place black women's concerns on the political and social agenda. She distinguished the concerns of black feminists from the contemporary preoccupations of white feminists: "Black women don't exactly see themselves as hung up in desexing all-male bars. We aren't hung up in defining ourselves Ms., Mrs., or Miss. This is just another label to us." Chisholm emphasized that black women are "just concerned about day-to-day survival, which has to do with such things as the fight for day care centers and the minimum wage."[119]

Kennedy addressed similar concerns. Like many of the other speakers, she voiced her frustration with the limits of white feminists' support for black women. But she did not end her comments there. Kennedy insisted that black women had power and that they could "run for office, take charge. We know everything and we're going to tell it." As Kennedy saw it, black women knew a great deal about sexism, racism, and other forms of oppression through their own experiences and were in a unique position to educate others. Moreover, she insisted, black women should do so from a leadership position and not from the sidelines. She was clear that some of their independence was involuntary; being abandoned by a husband or boyfriend and "being left with kids" was "not liberation, don't let no motherfucker tell you it is." But despite these heavy burdens, black women were far from powerless. Although they were at the bottom of the socio-economic and political ladder, all they had witnessed from this position had given them insight into the complexities of oppression. "You have a lot of power because of it," she reminded them.[120]

The press pointed out that "throughout her speech, Kennedy made sharp digs at the establishment." She called for "pigs out of the white house" and promised to "personally drag sticky Dick's [Nixon's] ass out of there."[121] She berated the media, her favorite whipping boy, for vapid programming and lambasted the Nielson TV rating system as racist and sexist.[122]

Speaking directly to black women, Kennedy insisted that this new black feminist organization recognize and embrace black lesbians. Implicitly, she was contrasting her position with that of NOW's president Betty Friedan, who in 1969 labeled lesbian feminists the "lavender menace" and said that their presence in the movement threatened to distract and derail the struggle for women's rights.[123] "There will be no problem" with lesbians, Kennedy commented. "Cupcakes and lesbians don't go together, daddy told us, but we are not daddy's little cupcakes anymore." Kennedy often used the term "cupcake" to describe women who did as they were told by their family, religious institutions, and the dominant society in general. Frequently, Flo suggested that feminist protesters perform "cupcakeville" or "cupcake" in order to go unnoticed into churches or government buildings and then surprise those in charge with street theater protests once inside.[124] She would challenge women who were especially confined by notions of acceptable appropriate behavior to shatter the confining image of the well-trained and obedient good girl. Black feminist organizations and a larger movement were not going to make the mistakes of some other feminists by insisting on heterosexual conformity.[125]

Kennedy's speech and the NBFO's conference received critical reviews by two of the women in attendance. Anne Williams, a white feminist writer for *off our backs*, judged Kennedy's feminism as inconsistent when she told white feminists to stop criticizing the chauvinism of black men and thereby privileged "racism and classism" over sexism.[126] This advice to white feminists was a staple of Kennedy's speeches, and she hoped they would eventually heed her suggestions if they were interested in aligning with black women.

African American Brenda Verner, a writer for *Encore*, was also sharply critical of Kennedy and the NBFO, arguing that the new black feminist organization was merely imitating white feminism and Flo was simply a modern-day mammy. Likening Kennedy's speech to those given by nineteenth-century black feminist-abolitionist Sojourner Truth when she spoke in front of white women abolitionists, Verner described Kennedy as "the antebellum image of [the] African woman as protector of the master's house and his children—only now, she is helping to protect the interests of the master's *wife*."[127]

Black women's mission to create their own independent black feminist organizations and movement was greeted by several articles that questioned black feminism's usefulness and contended that "few persons [are] . . . viewed with as much curiosity, suspicion or hostility as black feminists."[128] Kennedy was disappointed that some black women and men saw black feminism as traitorous in the fight for black liberation.[129] Despite these criticisms, Flo did not make responding to critics of the nascent struggle a fixture of her talks.[130] She no doubt saw her own black feminist work as valuable and necessary and therefore did not bother with black feminism's detractors. She cared deeply about what her younger sisters, Joyce and Faye, thought; they supported her black feminism and had developed into outspoken writers and community advocates in their own rights by the mid-1970s.[131] Similar to her interactions with Black Power advocates over sexism in the Black Freedom movement, Kennedy rarely publicly engaged black women's criticisms against black feminism. Her main targets were always the government, the church, corporations, and the media.

The response to Verner's article by the NBFO's chair, Margaret Sloan, and another key member, Margo Jefferson, demonstrates Kennedy's political influence over the organization. Both women wielded Kennedy's terminology and theories to directly confront criticism that black feminists were simply white feminists in blackface, identifying Verner's comments as "horizontal hostility" and thus "allowing the powers that be to stroll away with the real political, economic, and cultural power still in tow." In addition, they pointed to the fact that NBFO's platform centered on an intersectional analysis of oppression that was equally committed to ending sexism and racism.[132]

The Limits of Kennedy's Organizing

During the early months of the NBFO, Kennedy served as a mentor and catalyst rather than as a day-to-day member, often giving advice and bringing people together in one room to think, talk, and organize. As one member put it, Kennedy would "throw out an idea" and then "move on."[133] By the end of 1973, Kennedy was traveling frequently, and her schedule did not allow her to be actively involved in the new organization. She counseled Sloan and Galvin-Lewis on how to respond to critics of their growing movement and reminded them to continue enjoying the bonds they were building and the gates they were shattering. The group quickly grew from a handful of women meeting at Kennedy's apartment to an organization with several chapters across the country and a sizable group at its national headquarters in New York.[134] When Kennedy met black women at talks and political meetings throughout the country, she encouraged them to join the NBFO and often passed out two organizing lists after her lectures. One was titled "NBFO for black women only"; another, "Feminist Party," was open to anyone.[135]

The outpouring of interest in the NBFO amazed and overwhelmed the founders. Without a solid organizational structure or any way to manage the flood of responses, they were unable to provide the many women who contacted them with guidance on how to start a local chapter in their community. Not long after the first conference in New York, the NBFO chapters in Boston and Chicago broke off and formed their own black feminist organizations, the Combahee River Collective and the National Alliance of Black Feminists.[136]

The strategy the NBFO used—calling a press conference first and setting up a functioning organization second—was one Kennedy often used when she created a new group or wanted to gain media attention for an issue. However, increasing media visibility for a cause was not always an effective way to start and sustain a national organization. When Kennedy created smaller organizations, such as the Feminist Party, on college campuses, this technique was useful for making a small organization appear much larger than its actual numbers. This strategy also worked well because Kennedy was not in charge of the individual Feminist Party chapters and the local chapters organized their programs and direction. When she was arguing the Valerie Solanas case, Flo had called a press conference to help build support for a feminist heroine and fuel a budding women's liberation movement. Through these press conferences Kennedy forced the media to recognize an issue they might normally ignore. Indeed, during

NOW's formative years, the organizers were extremely skilled at using the media to create the impression that NOW was much larger than it in fact was and that it spoke for a mass power base.[137] In this case, however, forming a national organization of black feminists when they already existed across the country required a more developed infrastructure.

Black feminists had emerged through many different forms of activism, and what was needed was an organization to coordinate them. This was not a nascent movement after all. Unprepared to harness the hundreds of calls and inquiries it received, the NBFO was ill-equipped to sustain and build connections with black feminists in other locations. In this way, Kennedy's guidance that focused on media attention instead of on building a viable foundation for the organization disadvantaged the nascent group from the start. Unlike their white feminist counterparts, young black feminists in the NBFO received far less of Kennedy's day-to-day support and advice. Despite the difficulties with coordinating the NBFO's national office, the organization functioned for two years and helped to inspire the creation of other black feminist organizations and a black feminist movement.

Building a Black Feminist Coalition against Racism and Sexism

When the NBFO disbanded in 1975, Kennedy was more deeply ensconced in the black feminist struggle and helped to create and support several new black feminist organizations. In 1975, Kennedy founded a black feminist organization called the Coalition Against Racism and Sexism (CARS), insisting that "racism and sexism are two of the most virulent maladies of our society" and that an organization was needed to bring together a broad alliance of activists to challenge these interlocking systems of oppression.[138] Realizing that white feminists had failed to fully tackle racism alongside sexism, she still believed that the movement had the potential to do so. Her work in black feminist groups did not mean she had given up on white women: "I'm not saying feminism is unimportant, but it is a basis for [a] coalition, and . . . it is [time] to call it." As before, when Kennedy perceived a need and opportunity for a new group, she assembled one. CARS was a "coalition of Blacks, women, Hispanics, Bronx youth, gays, Republicans, rank and file workers, socialists, anti-Moynihan Democrats and others."[139] The small group brought together many of Kennedy's longtime friends and organizers, including black men from the Media Workshop, such as Jim Haughton; black feminists, such as Florence Rice and Jane Galvin-Lewis; and white feminists, such as Irene Davall.[140]

Kennedy continued to believe that she was best able to attack racism and sexism when she targeted the media. The group's first action in January 1975 was similar to the actions she had called for with the Media Workshop years earlier: members organized a boycott to challenge major New York City TV networks for the "trend toward racist, sexist deterioration" in programming. Specifically, CARS demanded that the Federal Communications Commission withhold license renewal for most of the major TV stations in New York City. Its main grievance was that the media consistently held a "whiteout of press conferences [and] planning sessions" that were organized to challenge racism and sexism. Members protested what they saw as a trend toward casting black people, women of all races, and youth "as undercover cops and/or collaborators" and the failure of media outlets to hire a sizable number of "paid consultants, advisory groups, producers, writers and news personnel competent to deal with the serious issues [of] racism, sexism, government and business delinquency in the news and public affairs."[141] Finally, they objected to the spread of useless TV game shows and sports in prime time, which served to distract people from the problems in society.

In 1976, CARS formed a subcommittee called the "Coalition for the Benign Neglect of Moynihan," which held a press conference and circulated a petition protesting the Democratic senatorial nomination of Daniel Patrick Moynihan, the author of *The Negro Family: The Case for National Action*, also known as the notorious Moynihan Report, which blamed "black matriarchy" for the problems impoverished black families faced and called for the "benign neglect" of poverty, that served as the rationale for conservative attacks on social welfare programs. That same year, Kennedy described Daniel Patrick Moynihan as "Nigger expert No. 1. He rose to prominence on the back of the Black family. He started out telling you about the matriarchal Black family headed by women, abandoned by men. He didn't tell you that racism played the major role."[142] Members of the black feminist organization "collected signatures in Geneva-Rochester, Bronx, Rockland County, Nassau County, Westchester and Queens area of persons interested in a coalition against continued heavy military arms spending and the scapegoat[ing] of the unemployed and welfare recipients." CARS called on voters to support Jewish Marxist historian Herbert Aptheker, the U.S. senatorial candidate for the Communist Party (USA), instead.[143] Aptheker was a longtime opponent of racism who documented numerous revolts of enslaved African American people. Kennedy identified CARS as part of the black feminist movement, but she was clearly not interested in black feminist organizations remaining all women, or even all black.

Over the next decade, Kennedy continued to work with and establish a range of black feminist organizations throughout the country. As black feminism continued to expand and gain popularity in various spaces, she was often called on to help black women frame their new organizations' message and goals. Sometime between 1974 and 1976, Kennedy founded a local black feminist group, Black Women United for Political Action (BWUPA).[144] The organization was based in the predominantly black neighborhood of Bedford-Stuyvesant, Brooklyn. In 1964, Harlem and Bed-Stuy were sites of intense urban unrest, and in the late 1960s, the Brownsville area of Bedford-Stuyvesant experienced controversy over community control of schools.[145] Its early members included Beulah Sanders of the National Welfare Rights Organization and Florence Rice, a Harlem consumer rights activist. The organization hosted a National Black Convention on International Black Women's Day in 1978 and numerous panels and consciousness-raising sessions.[146] While Kennedy was listed as the founder, the DWUPA was primarily maintained by the acting chairwoman and local Brooklyn community organizer M. A. Terry.

Kennedy's support of new black feminist organizations extended to Connecticut as well. In the spring of 1980, she was invited to speak to a recently formed women's group in New Haven called the African American Women's Salon. She was the group's inaugural speaker and kicked off its drive to attract more members. The Salon, whose members were "90 percent black with the rest Spanish" (Latina), was committed to "ending sexism and racism in our community" and "supporting each other in all of our endeavors." Some members were pursuing graduate and professional degrees and others were "working in theatre or starting nonprofits." Linda Randolph joined the group after hearing Kennedy speak and was captivated by her humor and the advice she gave the women. Randolph remembered Kennedy giving a speech to a room filled with mostly black and brown women that encouraged them to continue to engage politically with their local communities. "The women were on fire when she left," and they continued to discuss and plan what they "were going to do next."[147] Later, Randolph went on to become the treasurer of the organization, while playwright and *New York Amsterdam News* writer Theresa McGriff served as the chair. The Salon was a study and support group where black and brown women would go to "become more politically aware." The women met at each other's homes to read and discuss and debate ideas about local and national politics. In reflecting on why they did not label themselves feminists while they supported black feminist philosophies, Randolph said, "I don't think we thought that was important. . . . We thought sharing ideas," educating each other, and supporting each other "as black women" was most central. A feminist or black feminist title did not occupy their agenda.[148] Many of them were active professionally and/or politically in other organizations and needed the support and aid of other black and brown women to help them balance all that they were attempting to achieve and to continue to validate their ongoing and manifold work and activism.

By the early 1970s, Kennedy had made a political career of emphasizing the critical linkages among all forms of oppression, especially racism and sexism. She redoubled her efforts to create interracial feminist organizations that emphasized a black feminist praxis. Her work during this period was central to building both a women's movement that included women of all races and an independent black feminist movement. The growth of the black feminist movement, in turn, raised her profile. Throughout the mid-1970s and early 1980s, numerous black feminist organizations formed across the country. Many of them called on Kennedy for her help as they attempted to shape a black feminist agenda in their own communities.[149] The vast majority of these groups gained little or no media attention for their actions in organizing women's consciousness-raising sessions or creating child-care programs. Nor did many other organizers know of them beyond the neighborhoods and communities in which they worked. Most of these small groups did not label their organizations as feminist or black feminist, but they identified with the black feminist politics articulated by Kennedy and were working against sexism and racialized classism in their own communities. Years later, Flo remembered assisting these and other black feminist groups and noting that so much was happening with black feminists all over the country that she could not possibly be everywhere or take advantage of all of the places where black feminism was emerging.[150]

Kennedy saw black feminism as a praxis created and led by black women but available to everyone. She provided activists of all stripes with a theory and practice that centered on challenges to racism and sexism but expanded widely to include challenges to all forms of oppression. The organizers Kennedy mentored in the 1960s and 1970s applied her lessons to a broad variety of movements and actions. As a teacher, leader, and intellectual, she found imaginative ways to tie movements together and form more powerful coalitions. Although often the organizations she founded did not endure, the incisive views she articulated and the political connections she forged raised the consciousness of organizers and broadened the agendas of movement organizations. Kennedy's insistence on a comprehensive black feminist praxis had transformative consequences.

Epilogue

UNTIL WE CATCH UP

The Struggle Continues

In July 1977, 60 Minutes aired a segment featuring Florynce Kennedy that included part of a speech she gave to college students, her favorite audience. Standing at the podium dressed in her trademark hat and sporting bright nails and long false eyelashes, Kennedy responded to the backlash against affirmative action for African Americans, women, and other groups that have suffered from discrimination. Showing the absurdity of the contention that the law constituted discrimination against those who took their privileges for granted, she argued: "You cannot have reverse discrimination until we catch up. Until black people have lynched as many white people as white people have lynched black people. Until women . . . have raped as many men as men have raped women. Until women and black people and homosexuals and farmworkers and domestic workers and handicapped people and old people and kids have been able to be in charge of discrimination to the same degree as the people who keep them out."[1] Kennedy, now sixty-one years old, challenged the idea that women and black people were no longer oppressed by racism and sexism and that state-sanctioned discrimination and violence now served the interests of those who had previously been oppressed. Kennedy had spent most of her adult life protesting discrimination; now she confronted the false and misleading argument that the hard-won gains made by black and women's movements had come at the cost of white men and threatened their institutional power. This reactionary stance had been familiar to her since the end of World War II, when black people and white women were depicted in the media as "getting all the best jobs" and "'taking over'

215

the theatre."[2] Once again, Kennedy responded to criticism of women and black people that erupted when they began to enter fields that were once closed to them. She used her sharp wit and sarcastic analogies to underscore that systems of power such as racism and sexism had been neither overturned nor reversed. Flo had recently spoken out against the illegal imprisonment and murder of Black Power advocates and the rape of incarcerated women by prison guards—crimes that were repeatedly disregarded and legally protected.[3] Kennedy told her audience bluntly, "You cannot have reverse discrimination until we catch up."

Florynce "Flo" Kennedy demonstrates that for Kennedy, the "we" was not just women or just black people or, for that matter, just black women. Kennedy's black feminist politics championed more than the identities she embodied. The "we" was expansive, for it included the many different groups that were marginalized by the dominant structures of economic and political power. The parallels Kennedy drew between different forms of oppression began with racism and sexism but did not end there; she understood that all forms, from ableism to heterosexism, were linked and that abuse was insidious, contagious, and far-reaching. Discrimination was exercised against all those whose bodies were mistreated and whose voices were ignored: the elderly, children, and laborers—especially those in domestic and agricultural work, who were often women, immigrants, and persons of color. At the time of her *60 Minutes* appearance, discrimination against the disabled and against gay, lesbian, bisexual, and transgendered people had not yet been outlawed, but their movements were gaining momentum by the mid-1970s. Until these groups and others wielded power "to the same degree as the people who keep them out," the notion of reverse discrimination would be a myth propagated by the media and endorsed by the U.S. Supreme Court that was deployed for the benefit of those who retained institutional power.[4] Kennedy's main objective was to build pragmatic coalitions of the "outs in society," an "alliance of the alienated."[5]

The host of *60 Minutes*, Morley Safer, described Kennedy as "never at peace" although the United States was now "at peace with itself and the rest of the world." Safer contrasted the "silent seventies" with the riotous sixties.[6] However, Kennedy and the groups she organized with knew far too well that black people, gender and sexual minorities, and prisoners still faced biased media coverage, police harassment, and systemic limitations on their rights and freedoms and could not afford to be silent amid such complacency. During an interview in the 1980s, Kennedy was asked how she could keep on organizing and never burn out. Flo responded, "I really don't understand why people get burned out politically. I should think if they really believed in what they are doing, they would know that they have the best thing going for them."[7]

Kennedy died on December 23, 2000, at the age of eighty-four. Until she became severely ill in the early 1990s, she continued to work on social and political issues that expressed her commitment to a comprehensive black feminist politics, from legalizing sex work to publicly implicating the U.S. government in the assassination of black leaders like Martin Luther King. Indeed, even toward the end of her life, when she was confined to her apartment and bedridden, Kennedy managed to create makeshift fliers calling for the freedom of imprisoned Black Panther Party member Mumia Abu-Jamal and the end of apartheid in South Africa.[8]

Two years before the *60 Minutes* feature was aired, Kennedy traveled to Mexico City to participate in the United Nations' International Year of the Woman. From June 19 to July 2, 1975, hundreds of women and men from around the world met to develop a global ten-year plan of action to improve the status of women and advance "equality, development and peace."[9]

More than twenty miles separated the official conference, which was attended by delegates chosen by their national governments, from the unofficial conference, or "Tribune," which drew activists with more radical views. The UN's division for nongovernmental organizations ensured that the Tribune was open to the public, and it attracted nearly five thousand women and men, mostly from nongovernmental agencies and advocacy groups.[10] Vietnamese women's union leader Lê Thị Xuyến and Nigeria's chief nursing officer, Victoria Mojekwu, participated, as did such U.S. women as Angela Davis, Betty Friedan, and Kennedy.[11] Many of the women at the conference criticized UN officials for deliberately keeping the two meetings a vast distance apart and for limiting feminist participation at the official UN conference.[12] Nonetheless, Kennedy and others utilized the Tribune to share ideas and forge new collaborative relationships.[13]

In addition to attending the Tribune panels, Kennedy held informal conversations in her hotel room to discuss the issues that particularly concerned her at home, from decriminalizing sex work to the persecution of black liberation leaders such as Assata Skakur.[14] Always attuned to the media's ability to inform public opinion, Kennedy organized a group of demonstrators who stood outside the Tribune's halls and within earshot of the press. With Flo at the helm wearing her "Nixon Knew" button, the group chanted songs that derided the United States and altered the lyrics of "The Star-Spangled Banner" from "Oh say, can you see, by the dawn's early light" to "Oh say can you see any heel marks on me?"[15] Kennedy's disaffected ballad continued:

> My country 'tis of thee
> Sour land of bigotry
> Of thee I sing.
> Land of Indian massacre
> Land of Black slavery
> Land of hypocrisy
> Of thee I sing.[16]

The lyrics affirmed the criticisms made by women from developing countries who condemned imperialism for creating a severe imbalance in access to the world's resources, for promoting restrictive understandings of women's place in society, for provoking political conflicts that escalated into violence, and for deepening poverty.[17] In this view, women's concerns went far beyond what Kennedy described as typical "crotch issues." Years later, Kennedy remarked that the UN women's conference organizers did not fully support political discussions outside the purview of recognized female concerns, such as reproductive health and the family: "Women are not going to be encouraged to talk about South Africa apartheid, [the causes of severe famine in] Ethiopia, certainly not the Arab/Israel scene and so there again women are being silenced."[18]

The links Kennedy made in Mexico City with women who shared her politics were far-reaching. She forged close ties with both white and aboriginal delegates from Australia, who invited her to attend a women's conference to be held two months later in Canberra. In August, Kennedy arrived at the Women in Politics Conference to deliver a talk focused on the media and feminism. Much to the frustration of a few of the white women in the audience, Kennedy did not stick to the announced topic. Instead, she traced the direct connections among racism, imperialism, colonialism, and sexism and contended that "the pathology of oppression was the same old stuff found in Australia and America, and other parts of the sexist, racist, imperialist, colonialist world."[19] Meeting with aboriginal women, Kennedy no doubt heard of the numerous—and familiar—injustices that native communities faced: constant policing and arrests for petty offenses, laws that regulated their drinking, and other regulations that allowed businesses to pay them less than the legal minimum wage.[20] One observer interpreted the connections Flo made as "demanding a society based not upon merit" but upon feminism and antiracism and called Kennedy a "menace and an insult to womanhood."[21]

But this criticism did not represent the views of some of the other white women at the conference. Kennedy's centering of the links between racism and sexism held strong appeal for labor organizers and aboriginal women organizers, while radicals were inspired by her insistence that the women's movement offered a "smorgasbord of ideas." Speaking from her own experience as a black feminist, Kennedy argued that there was more than one valid way to confront injustice and that "we must not let any seeming difference be division for us."[22] Kennedy described what she called a "testicular approach" to organizing: "There's a little story I have been telling about strategy, and it applies to the church, to the media, to the police, the government, business, everyone. It's the story of the woman who's at the dentist, and she is leaning back in the chair. She's a very square lady. . . . So she's leaning back in the chair and the dentist has worked on her for about three minutes and all of a sudden he realizes she has managed to obtain a very tight grip on his testicles, and she is squeezing just short of agony. So he stops and she says, 'We are not going to hurt each other, are we, doctor?'"[23] Kennedy's story underscored the fact that power exists at the most basic level and is exercised routinely. It can even be wielded by those who society might assume are the least willing or able to resist. Kennedy often concluded this anecdote with the acknowledgment that "when you apply the right kind of pressure to the appropriate sensitive area, people become even more concerned than you are about your progress and happiness."[24] The white woman who led the Australian Labor Party, Jean Roberts, found Kennedy's suggestion particularly valuable in helping her to understand how to work with other activists and appreciated Kennedy's insistence that "political power is available to you." "I keep thinking of Flo Kennedy saying about her testicular reach, that if anything is near enough to reach you, then you are just as near to it."[25]

During the International Year of the Woman conferences in Canberra and Mexico City, Kennedy made sure to support an issue that drew most of her time and energy at home: the decriminalization of sex work. Having organized with COYOTE (Call Off Your Old Tired Ethics) since former sex worker Margot St. James founded the group in 1973, Kennedy saw the decriminalization of sex work as an important feminist issue, arguing that the government and the church controlled the "license to fuck" and thus held power over women and their bodies. Their control was maintained by an unconstitutional alliance of church and state, which set up the legal and religious validation and licensing of heterosexual marriage in tandem with the policing and prosecution of sex workers.[26] In the 1970s, Kennedy articulated a clear understanding of the deployment of heteropatriarchy that connected the everyday housewife to the hometown "hooker."[27]

In an interview given at the end of the Canberra conference, Kennedy described how women were relegated to low-paying occupations, offering marriage and clerical work as prime examples of the poorly paid jobs available to women in the United States. In Kennedy's assessment, marriage was scrubbed free of its romantic or affectionate associations and was defined by the wife's economic dependence on her husband. Kennedy argued that "prostitutes in the United States could earn $100 a night and file clerks $100 a week, while housewives got nothing for sex, filing, nurse maiding, and hundreds of other jobs." "If the government cannot provide full employment," she contended, "it has no right to criminalize one of the best paying jobs, prostitution."[28] She distinguished this position from advocacy of the legalization of prostitution, which would make it state-regulated. In other talks, Kennedy advocated the unionization of sex work so that women themselves, rather than pimps or organized crime, could control their income and the ways in which one of the only highly paid, female-dominated occupations was practiced.

Intent that the legalization of sex work be a part of an international conversation on women's rights during the Mexico City conference, Kennedy and St. James presented a resolution for the "recognition of 'prostitutes' rights,'"[29] which asserted that sex workers had the right to organize and control their labor and not be harassed and arrested by the police. As one reporter remarked, their objective "collides head on with the stated UN objective of wiping out prostitution everywhere in the world."[30] The final UN report compared sex work, rape, mental cruelty, and child marriage and argued that "prostitution is one of the most grievous offenses to the dignity of women."[31] The report showed that girls and young women in developing countries are often forced into prostitution because of the lack of economic opportunities.[32]

Kennedy did not condone women or children being forced into sexual slavery. She was, however, compelled to point out the parallels between marriage and prostitution. Stressing the hypocrisy of arguments against sex work that ignored marriage as a legal and socially acceptable form of women's servitude, she argued that a wife's dependence on an abusive husband was all too often one of the only ways for her to make ends meet and support her children.[33] Kennedy recommended the legalization of sex work as a short-term remedy; a long-term solution required the expansion of opportunities for women to become financially independent of their sexual relationships with men. Sex workers did not need their dignity saved by the UN, Kennedy contended.[34] In response to those who labeled sex work as an offense to women's dignity, she reasoned that they were not fallen women and that sex work was a noble profession, no worse than nursing. "What am I going to say, 'they are bad women'?" Kennedy retorted. "I don't care what feminists say about whores; I wish you would hear what some of the whores say about the feminists."[35]

Exhibiting her willingness to take on unpopular causes in the face of power, Kennedy served as a defense lawyer for the brother of James Earl Ray, the man who was convicted of killing Martin Luther King. In 1976, the U.S. House of Representatives Select Committee on Assassinations began investigating the murders of King and John F. Kennedy. Mark Lane, the lawyer who had represented James Earl Ray, argued that additional evidence proved Ray's innocence. A police detective in Memphis at the time of King's death also came forward with new details in the case.[36] For two years, the House subcommittee chaired by Representative Louis Stokes (D–Ohio), an African American lawyer, held hearings assessing these and other reports of conspiracies to murder King and Kennedy.

Flo Kennedy and William Pepper served as the attorneys for James Earl Ray's brother, Jerry Ray, during the subcommittee's Washington hearings in November 1978. Jerry Ray received immunity for testifying about his involvement in the case.[37] Using her signature strategy, Kennedy attempted to turn the tables and place the government on trial for the murder of black civil rights leader Martin Luther King. Reporters observed that she vehemently contested opposing counsel's evidence that Jerry Ray had assisted in his brother's escape and instead pointed toward a government cover-up.[38] In a later speech, Kennedy explained her rationale for defending Jerry Ray: "They were attempting to cover up the conspiracy in the Martin Luther King case. They were accusing Jerry Ray of having robbed a bank, along with his brother James, in order to account for the money the FBI or police or Ku Klux Klan or whoever was really in on it had given him. It was obvious. You know, small time criminals do not have their nose fixed and get passports and go to London. That's strictly the CIA's *modus operandi*."[39] Kennedy argued that the bank's surveillance tape cleared Jerry Ray of the robbery and that there was no other satisfactory explanation for how James Earl Ray garnered the funds and high-level connections that enabled him to escape from prison the year before King's death, travel to Memphis when King was organizing sanitation workers there, go undetected by the police and the FBI even though King was under intense government surveillance, and then after the assassination speedily receive a passport and flee to Europe.[40] She was frustrated that the "subcommittee was going to use that bank robbery story as a cover up even though they knew the brothers were not guilty." "If [James Earl] Ray killed King," Kennedy contended, "he did not do it alone"; the FBI, CIA, and other federal agencies must have been involved.[41]

The day Kennedy was scheduled to appear as Jerry Ray's attorney, she contemplated the criticism she was bound to hear from others in the black community, starting with her sister Joyce, and made a list of the reasons why they would disapprove of her defending a man she recognized as "a redneck racist."[42] In the end, Kennedy concluded, the evidence against James Earl Ray and Jerry Ray "rest[ed] largely on writings, statements and/ or connections of ex-cons or others having an interest in showing up the guilt of James Earl Ray."[43] For Kennedy, the hearing was an opportunity to focus attention squarely on what she described as a government conspiracy to destroy black movements and their leaders. She compared the suppression of information during the hearing to the tactics utilized by former President Richard Nixon when he was under investigation for the Watergate scandal: he gave "the FBI just enough to keep them off his back" but left out key details.[44] Both Pepper and Kennedy charged the committee with "being ignorant of any information that may exonerate the Rays" and allowing unsworn and unverified allegations to be entered into the official record.[45] Kennedy maintained that "the real point" of her serving as Jerry Ray's lawyer "was not to permit them to cover up the story" of a conspiracy and to keep public scrutiny on the government's part in the devastation of black and other radical movements.[46] In the end, the committee concluded that James Earl Ray could not have acted alone but ruled out the involvement of the U.S. government.[47]

In the late 1970s and early 1980s, deeply frustrated with government cover-ups and public hypocrisy, Kennedy continued to argue that black people should be at the vanguard of leadership. In the United States, she maintained, white supremacy was central to perpetuating hierarchies of wealth and power, and society would have to look to black women and men for political direction "because it can't get morally straight until it understands [that racism is] the country's pathology."[48] Kennedy located racism as fundamental to understanding oppression writ large.

In 1983, when Kennedy was in her late sixties, Reverend Jesse Jackson announced that he would seek the Democratic Party's nomination for the presidency. Having worked as an activist in the Southern Christian Leadership Conference since 1965, Jackson formed Operation PUSH in 1971 to help address poverty both in his local Chicago community and throughout the country. Although the media portrayed him as the black candidate, as it had done with Shirley Chisholm over a decade earlier, Jackson's platform advocated the interests not only of black people but also of a wide array of citizens, offering an opportunity for black leadership for those left out by the Republican Party's conservative agenda.[49] He described his campaign as representing "the damned, the disinherited, the disrespected and the despised . . . the white, the Hispanic, the black, the Arab, the Jew, the woman, the native American, the small farmer, the businessperson, the environmentalist, the peace activist, the young, the old, the lesbian, the gay, and the disabled" to make up what he called a Rainbow Coalition to defeat President Ronald Reagan's bid for reelection.[50]

Kennedy was thrilled by the Rainbow Coalition's appeal to a wide base of support and utilized her waning energy to promote Jackson's candidacy. By the late 1970s, she was hosting *The Flo Kennedy Show* on Manhattan Cable Television, interviewing activists, many of whom were her longtime friends, such as Bill Kunstler, Diane Schulder Abrams and Queen Mother Moore.[51] In 1984 her show supported Jackson's Rainbow Coalition, and on July 24, Kennedy organized a "Freedom, Justice and Equality" rally in Harlem to "demonstrate black solidarity and to reaffirm full support for the Rev. Jesse Jackson."[52] The rally was aired on her show alongside numerous endorsements of Jackson's candidacy. This backing was especially important as Jackson faced mounting criticism for supporting an independent Palestinian state and because he refused to denounce Nation of Islam leader Louis Farrakhan.[53]

When Jackson did not win the Democratic nomination, Kennedy was not surprised, but nonetheless she was disappointed that more white women, especially feminists, had not joined the Rainbow Coalition. She argued that white "feminists generally are not aware of the value of black men to the feminist community." While Kennedy did not see the failure to unite around a common agenda as a problem unique to white feminists, she was profoundly disappointed that the white feminist struggle had not embraced new allies. In 1984 she still believed in the value of "a coalition of black men and black women with white women."[54]

Kennedy's advocacy of inclusive coalitions, especially those among white women, black women, and black men, had been part of her politics since the 1950s, and she worked in myriad organizations and movements to advance this agenda. Despite Kennedy's years of challenging sexism and other forms of institutional oppression in the courts, Lucy Komisar, the former vice president of the National Organization for Women, dismissed Kennedy in her interview with *60 Minutes*, arguing that Kennedy was not "really a part of the women's movement" or among the "real feminist leaders." "What has she done to attract attention to real problems? We know in this country what the problems are. The steps that the real feminist leaders are doing now is seeking to get legislation passed or to win court cases, to change the actual practices."[55] Komisar's limited definition of feminist activism echoed what some of her feminist colleagues deemed the primary effort of a feminist struggle: working within the courts and formal politics to advocate for women's rights. By the mid-1970s, however, feminists of color, as well as many white radical and socialist feminists, had demonstrated that this definition was too narrowly constructed and focused too heavily on reform.[56]

Kennedy's success in gaining the spotlight for herself and her causes disturbed some feminists. Her approach often ran counter to ideas and practices that promoted leaderlessness as the key to equalizing relations of power within the women's liberation movement.[57] Moreover, Kennedy utilized a model of organizing that relied on charismatic leadership to place her black feminist agenda at the center of the media's gaze. She sought to control her image and often spoke past her interlocutors and ignored their questions in order to communicate her radical message directly to a receptive audience.

Kennedy's contribution over her long political life cannot be reduced to that of performer or, worse yet, "not a real feminist leader." Kennedy was active in numerous feminist organizations, included those overwhelmingly made up of white women, and worked on many of the key issues that were the prime targets of feminists like Lucy Komisar, such as the legalization of abortion and the ratification of the Equal Rights Amendment. Her experience as a lawyer, however, had taught her that focusing on the law was a slow, "one-ass-at-a-time proposition" with limited opportunities for making significant gains when "what we have to do is stop the wringer."[58] Kennedy had found that for most black people, the poor, and women, the courts were the last place to seek justice. "The practice of law in this system has nothing to do with justice! . . . If there's a case where the Establishment has an interest, forget it."[59] In organizing street theater actions and creating numerous organizations, Kennedy moved beyond the courts to challenge discrimination and affirm a black feminist praxis.

In the end, critics like Komisar have dismissed Kennedy's intellect and influence and reduced her to a mere "entertainer," critiquing Flo's use of humor and street theater protests to make her political points and attract media attention. Kennedy's multifaceted politics and her flamboyant self-presentation have puzzled some organizers and scholars. In part, this confusion accounts for some of the reasons why Kennedy has been largely ignored and why her theoretical and strategic insights have not been incorporated into radical political perspectives of feminist and Black Power histories. Those who do not see the connections among various forms of oppression find it difficult to categorize a black woman activist and theorist who was a founder of predominantly white feminist organizations; argued that the Black Power movement should be at the vanguard of progressives; encouraged gender-integrated, multiracial coalitions at a time when most organizations and their leaders were moving in the opposite direction; challenged the mainstream media; and used her sharp wit to devastating effect. Others had difficulty comprehending a well-trained practicing lawyer who called herself an antiestablishmentarian. Flo Kennedy's black feminist praxis bewildered those whose minds remained fixed by the dominant society's logics. Her thoughts and actions were impossible to organize into neat, mutually exclusive categories—especially when feminists were generally imagined as white and Black Power leaders were frequently portrayed as male.

To the people who worked with and learned from Florynce "Flo" Kennedy, she was a teacher, a catalyst, a lawyer, a cheerleader, a bridge to other organizers and to expansive and broad concepts, an exacting critic, a complex thinker, and a sharp leader who animated political engagement and made political organizing less intimidating and far more appealing. Kennedy had the rare ability to pivot from playful to serious, to reframe quotidian details as profound revelations, and to generate insightful metaphors. She used humor as both a weapon and a salve, slicing through racist-sexist logic and easing and heightening tension all in the same breath.

Kennedy's black feminism in many ways anticipated scholar Cathy Cohen's framing of a radical black queer politics. Cohen "envisions a politics where one's relation to power . . . is privileged in determining one's political comrades. I'm talking about where the *nonnormative* and *marginal* position of punks, bulldaggers, and welfare queens, for example, is the basis for progressive transformative coalition work."[60] Kennedy saw those who stood on the margins, from sex workers to prisoners, as armed with political tools and central to creating successful movements. Never embracing a single-issue framework or an analysis that emphasized only one axis of oppression, Kennedy borrowed ideas from organizers and struggles, added her own opinions, and then consciously and generously spread those ideas to other movements and activists. Her black feminist intersectional analysis enlarged the scope of possible alliances and both broadened and deepened the promise of radical social transformation.

Notes

BHC	Billie Holiday Collection, Manuscript, Archives, and Rare Book Library, Emory University, Atlanta, Ga.
FKP	Florynce Kennedy Papers, unprocessed manuscript collection in possession of Joyce Kennedy-Banks, East Orange, N.J.
FRK/FBI	Florynce Rae Kennedy Federal Investigative Report, Federal Bureau of Investigation
NAACP Records	National Association for the Advancement of Colored People Records, Manuscript Division, Library of Congress, Washington, D.C.
NCNWP	National Council of Negro Women's Papers, National Archives for Black Women's History, Mary McLeod Bethune Council House National, Washington, D.C.
NOW: NYC	National Organization for Women: New York Chapter Papers, Tamiment Library, New York University, New York, N.Y.
PBF	Papers of Betty Friedan, 1933–1985, Arthur and Elizabeth Schlesinger Library on the History of Women in America, Radcliffe Institute for Advanced Study, Harvard University, Cambridge, Mass.
PFK	Papers of Florynce Kennedy, Arthur and Elizabeth Schlesinger Library on the History of Women in America, Radcliffe Institute for Advanced Study, Harvard University, Cambridge, Mass.
TGAP	Ti-Grace Atkinson Papers, in the possession of Ti-Grace Atkinson, Cambridge, Mass.

INTRODUCTION

1. Florynce Kennedy, born Florence Rae Kennedy, changed her name before the spring of 1933. Although I did not find a record of a legal change of name, she became known in her professional and social life as Florynce Kennedy. Florynce Kennedy Metropolitan Life Insurance Company application, April 9, 1933, box 12, FKP.

2. Kennedy used this quote or a variation of this quote in numerous speeches throughout the 1970s and early 1980s. Kennedy, audiotape of interview for *Speaking for America*.

3. Breines, *Trouble between Us*; R. Rosen, *World Split Open*; Evans, *Tidal Wave*; Ruth Rosen, "Refugees of the Fifties," keynote address at the conference A New Insurgency: The Port Huron Statement in Its Time and Ours, University of Michigan, Ann Arbor, October 31, 2012.

4. Ward, "Third World Women's Alliance"; Springer, *Living for the Revolution*; Roth, *Separate Roads to Feminism*; Harris, *Black Feminist Politics*. Some works on the welfare rights movement demonstrate that black women's organizing predated the predominantly white second-wave feminist movement; see especially Nadasen, "Expanding the

Boundaries of the Women's Movement," and Nadasen, *Welfare Warriors*. Orleck, *Storming Caesars Palace*, examines the welfare rights movement in Las Vegas as a struggle organized by African American women against the intersections of racism, sexism, and capitalism. McGuire, *At the Dark End of the Street*, chap. 3, argues that the Montgomery, Alabama, bus boycott of 1955 should be viewed as an African American women's movement against rape and other forms of racist and sexist violence that predates the second-wave feminist movement.

5. Most scholarship on postwar feminist organizing views black feminism as emerging largely in protest against exclusion by white feminists or in opposition to Black Power's sexism; see, for example, Roth, *Separate Roads to Feminism*; Nelson, *Women of Color*; and Springer, *Living for the Revolution*. Examples of previous scholarship on the Black Power movement that overlook black feminism and do not fully examine black women in the movement as central leaders and intellectuals include Singh, *Black Is a Country*; Joseph, *Waiting 'til the Midnight Hour*; and Swan, *Black Power in Bermuda*. For works that address black women's centrality to the Black Power movement as key thinkers and leaders, see, for example, Nelson, *Body and Soul*; Fernández, "Denise Oliver and the Young Lords Party"; Williams, "Black Women, Urban Politic, and Engendering Black Power"; and Williams, *Concrete Demands*. For examples of works that explore Black Power's influence on feminism and feminist connections to Black Power, see Ward, "Third World Women's Alliance"; Thompson, *Promise and a Way of Life*; Valk, *Radical Sisters*; and Breines, "Sixties Stories' Silences."

6. Crenshaw, "Mapping the Margins"; Collins, *Black Feminist Thought*. Collins utilizes the term "interlocking systems of oppression" to explain such systems based on race, class, and gender. Over the past decade, studies of feminism from a range of disciplines utilize theories of intersectionality as part of their analysis of not only race, class, and gender but also, for example, ability, sexuality, and various other hierarchies of difference and power. Hewitt, *No Permanent Waves*, 74, 102; Mann and Huffman, "Decentering of Second Wave Feminism"; Banet-Welser, "What's Your Flava?," 209; Valentine, *Imagining Transgender*, 11. For works on black women's activism in the civil rights movement, see, for example, Ransby, *Ella Baker and the Black Freedom Movement*; McGuire, *At the Dark End of the Street*; Greene, *Our Separate Ways*; Lee, *For Freedom's Sake*; Charron, *Freedom's Teacher*; Theoharis, *Rebellious Life of Mrs. Rosa Parks*; Robnett, *How Long? How Long?*; Feldstein, *How It Feels to Be Free*; and Crawford, Rouse, and Woods, *Women in the Civil Rights Movement*.

7. "Old Black Flo," episode of *60 Minutes*.

8. Kennedy, "It's Damn Slick Out There," interview with Sohnya Sayres, 347.

9. Roth, *Separate Roads to Feminism*, 83–85; Echols, *Daring to Be Bad*, 49–50.

10. Echols, *Daring to Be Bad*; Rosen, *World Split Open*; Davis, *Moving the Mountain*; Evans, *Tidal Wave*.

11. While several histories of the predominantly white postwar feminist movement briefly list Kennedy, they typically note her and other black feminists who worked in the movement as the exceptions or as some of the few early members but offer little or no examination of their influence on the movement. In addition, when Kennedy is mentioned, she is noticed for making white feminists laugh or for her role in helping to form the National Black Feminist Organization. Echols, *Daring to Be Bad*, 291, 383. Echols also

notes Kennedy's membership in NOW and some of her feminist protests, especially with Ti-Grace Atkinson. Breines, *Trouble between Us*, 119; Evans, *Tidal Wave*, 78. For examples that give a bit more detail of Kennedy's activism, see Cohen, *Sisterhood*; Roth, *Separate Roads to Feminism*; and Kelley, *Freedom Dreams*.

12. Springer, *Living for the Revolution*; Roth, *Separate Roads to Feminism*; Ward, "Third World Women's Alliance."

13. Kennedy, *Color Me Flo*, 52. See Hicks, *Talk with You Like a Woman*, 159–71, for a history of the ways the courts criminalized black women.

14. Kennedy interview with Marcia Cohen, 3. The transcriber was not sure if Kennedy said "that" or "them."

CHAPTER 1

1. Florynce Kennedy, detailed handwritten reminiscence, November 23–December 5, 1956, box 2, folder 10, PFK.

2. Ibid.

3. Kennedy, detailed handwritten reminiscence, November 7, 1956, box 2, folder 10, PFK.

4. Ibid. Kennedy speculates that her father might have been at work or sleeping downstairs when the white mob arrived. In the version of the story she originally heard, her father confronted the men at the door. In these notes, Kennedy attempted to reconcile this information with the new details about her mother's role in the confrontation.

5. Kennedy, detailed handwritten reminiscence, November 23–December 5, 1956, box 2, folder 10, PFK; entry for Lucy Jackman, *R. L. Polk and Co.'s Kansas City, Missouri, Directory*, 1913.

6. Kennedy, detailed handwritten reminiscence, November 23–December 5, 1956, box 2, folder 10, PFK.

7. Ibid.

8. Ibid.

9. Ibid.

10. For a detailed study of the ways in which rape was used as a weapon of terror against black women during the civil rights era, see McGuire, *At the Dark End of the Street*.

11. H. Rosen, *Terror in the Heart of Freedom*, 207.

12. Kennedy, "Color Me Flo" original transcript, box 5, tape 2, p. 6, FKP; Kennedy interview with Marcia Cohen.

13. Kennedy, "Color Me Flo" original transcript, box 5, tape 2, p. 8, FKP.

14. Kennedy interview with Jacqueline Ceballos.

15. Kennedy interview with Diane Schulder Abrams as the guest host of *The Flo Kennedy Show*, February 21, 1985, PFK; Kennedy interview with Diane Schulder Abrams on the *Diane Abrams Show*.

16. Kennedy interview in *The First Time*. In Lizzie Borden's 1983 feminist science fiction film *Born in Flames*, Kennedy plays the character Zella Wiley. The film presents an alternative feminist United States in which sexism, racism, heterosexism, and classism are challenged.

17. Manuscript census returns, population, Elm Bluff, Dallas County, Alabama, Tenth

Census of the United States (1880), microfilm series T3, roll 11, p. 392; manuscript census returns, population, Huntsville, Madison County, Alabama, Twelfth Census of the United States (1900), microfilm series T623, roll 28, p. 328.

18. Watkins, *King Cotton*, 137.

19. Flynt, *Alabama in the Twentieth Century*, 318.

20. Manuscript census returns, population, Huntsville, Madison County, Alabama, Twelfth Census of the United States (1900), microfilm series T623, roll 28, p. 328.

21. Kelley, *Thelonius Monk*, 11.

22. Manuscript census returns, population, Huntsville, Madison County, Alabama, Twelfth Census of the United States (1900), microfilm series T623, roll 28, p. 328. African American men in Madison County are listed primarily as day laborers and farmhands.

23. Schirmer, *City Divided*, 28.

24. Ibid., 29.

25. Ibid., 27–28; Painter, *Exodusters*, 4.

26. Manuscript census returns, population, Kansas City, Jackson County, Missouri, Thirteenth Census of the United States (1910), microfilm series T624, roll 787, p. 12A; Wiley Choice Kennedy, World War I draft registration card, 1917–1918, Jackson County, Missouri, serial 1153, order number 1252, roll 1683383, draft board 10, U.S. Selective Service System Draft Registration Cards, 1917–1918, Records of the Selective Service System, RG 163, National Archives, Atlanta, Ga.; Kennedy, detailed handwritten reminiscence, October 17, 1956, box 2, folder 10, PFK. For the White Hotel, see Isaacson and Wallace, *Kansas City in Vintage Postcards*, 36. The White Hotel lost prestige when its Blue Goose Café became a speakeasy during prohibition.

27. Johnson, "Beyond Freedom," 123. On the respected position that waiters, most notably Julius Avedorph, enjoyed within the black community, see Best, *Passionately Human*, 35–36.

28. Kennedy, *Color Me Flo*, 24.

29. Hughes-Peterson, *Anthology of Respect*; Kennedy, "Color Me Flo" original transcript, box 5, tape 3, p. 4, FKP.

30. See Bates, *Pullman Porters*.

31. Kennedy, "Color Me Flo" original transcript, box 5, tape 3, p. 4, FKP.

32. Kennedy, *Color Me Flo*, 24.

33. Ibid., 24; Kennedy, "Color Me Flo" original transcript, box 5, tape 3, p. 14, FKP.

34. Manuscript census returns, population, Frankfort, Franklin County, Kentucky, Tenth Census of the United States (1880), microfilm series T9, roll 414, p. 166; manuscript census returns, population, Kansas City, Jackson County, Missouri, Tenth Census of the United States (1880), microfilm series T9, roll 692, p. 176; manuscript census returns, population, Kansas City, Jackson County, Missouri, Twelfth Census of the United States (1900), microfilm series T623, roll 863, p. 5A; Fifth U.S. Colored Calvary, U.S. Colored Troops Military Service Records, 1861–1865, Compiled Military Service Records of Volunteer Union Soldiers Who Served with the United States Colored Troops, Records of the Adjutant General's Office, 1780's–1917, RG 94, National Archives Microfilm Publication M1817, roll 68, Camp Nelson, Enclosure 22; Kennedy, "Color Me Flo" original transcript, box 5, tape 2, pp. 4–5, FKP.

35. Joyce Kennedy-Banks, "Kansas City Kennedys," manuscript, box 11, FKP.

36. Ibid.; Flo Kennedy, "Growing up Black (and Precious)," box 10, FKP; Kennedy, "Color Me Flo" original transcript, box 5, tape 3, p. 4, FKP.

37. Wiley Kennedy and Zella Jackman marriage license, Kansas City, Jackson County, Missouri, October 7, 1912, Bureau of Vital Records, Missouri Department of Health, Kansas City, Missouri.

38. Lucy Simpson Jackman's U.S. Veterans and Adjudication Pension Appeal, Application number (Missouri) 410624 and (California) 1225385, Department of Veterans Affairs, Washington, D.C. Lucy Jackman appealed to the Veterans Administration to gain access to William Jackman's Civil War pension. Several of the appeal documents describe her husband's abandonment and Lucy Jackman's struggle to gain the pension she argued she deserved. In contrast, William Jackman testified that he left his wife because she cheated on him. As a teenager, Flo helped find supporting documents of Lucy and William's marriage.

39. Manuscript census returns, population, Kansas City, Jackson County, Missouri, Thirteenth Census of the United States (1910), microfilm series T624, roll 787, p. 11A.

40. See entries for Lucy Jackman, *R. L. Polk and Co.'s Kansas City, Missouri, Directory*, 1910, 1911, and 1912. The Kansas City directory demonstrates that Lucy Jackman returned to domestic work in 1915. Years later, Joyce Kennedy-Banks stated that at one point her grandmother operated a laundry business "which employed as many as seven people." If this information is true, Lucy Jackman kept this business off the books and away from local and federal officials. Kennedy-Banks, "Kansas City Kennedys," manuscript, box 11, FKP.

41. Schweninger, *Black Property Owners*, 180.

42. Florynce Kennedy, detailed handwritten reminiscence, November 23, 1956, box 2, folder 10, PFK; Kennedy, "Color Me Flo" original transcript, box 5, tape 2, pp. 6, 27, FKP.

43. "A Negro Home Wrecked," *Kansas City Star*, November 12, 1911; Schirmer, *City Divided*, 42, 74–75; M. W. O. memorandum to J. R. S. re Kansas City Missouri Segregation, May 26, 1919, box C404, folder 14 "Segregation-Residential-Kansas City, Mo., May 7–May 29, 1919," Kansas City, Missouri, Branch Records of the NAACP, Manuscript Division, Library of Congress, Washington, D.C.

44. Schirmer, *City Divided*, 42.

45. Williams, *Torchbearers of Democracy*, 225.

46. Schirmer, *City Divided*, 102.

47. NAACP secretary, Kansas City, Missouri, Branch, to the mayor of Kansas City, May 29, 1919, box C404, folder 14; NAACP secretary, Kansas City, Missouri, Branch to NAACP National Headquarters, May 20, 1919, both in NAACP Records.

48. Schirmer, *City Divided*, 101.

49. "Warn Negroes to Stay Out of Eastside," *Kansas City Journal*, April 18, 1919.

50. Quoted in Schirmer, *City Divided*, 101.

51. Ibid., 152; Claude A. Barnett, "Some Impressions of Greater Kansas City," *Chicago Defender*, January 19, 1918, 3; Coulter, *Take Up the Black Man's Burden*, 52.

52. Jones, "Politics of the Ku Klux Klan," 7; Kirkman, *Forgotten Tales of Kansas City*, 91–92; McVeigh, *Rise of the Ku Klux Klan*, 19–20, 67; "Wizard Says 'Let's Quit'"; "Fiery Cross Flames as in the Days of Old."

53. Kirkendall, *History of Missouri*, 94.

54. Coulter, *Take Up the Black Man's Burden*, 53; J. Taylor, *Freedom to Serve*, 42.

55. Kelley, *Race Rebels*, 45.

56. Coulter, *Take Up the Black Man's Burden*, 53.

57. Schirmer, *City Divided*, 101.

58. E. G. S. memorandum to J. R. S. re Kansas City, Missouri, Branch Segregation Problem, May 13, 1919, box C404, folder 14, NAACP Records.

59. Kennedy, detailed handwritten reminiscence, November 23, 1956, box 2, folder 10, PFK.

60. Schirmer, *City Divided*, 102.

61. Kennedy, detailed handwritten reminiscence, November 11–18, 1956, box 2, folder 10, PFK. Grayce Kennedy was born Grace. In later years, following Flo's example, some of the sisters placed the letter "y" in their name.

62. Kennedy, detailed handwritten reminiscence, November 1, 1953, box 2, folder 10, PFK.

63. Kennedy, *Color Me Flo*, 27. "Peckerwood" was a slur used by both blacks and upper-class whites for "cracker" or "poor white trash."

64. Ibid.

65. Kennedy interview with Jacqueline Ceballos.

66. Kennedy, *Color Me Flo*, 26.

67. Kennedy-Banks, "Kansas City Kennedys."

68. Kennedy, detailed handwritten reminiscence, November 1, 1953, box 2, folder 10, PFK.

69. Kennedy, "Growing up Black (and Precious)."

70. Kennedy, detailed handwritten reminiscence, November 1, 1953, box 2, folder 10, PFK.

71. Kennedy, *Color Me Flo*, 27; Kennedy, "Color Me Flo" original transcript, box 5, tape 2, p. 8, FKP.

72. Kennedy, detailed handwritten reminiscence, November 1, 1953, and October 17, 1956, box 2, folder 10, PFK.

73. For an example of childrearing ideas in the early twentieth century, see Maris, *Essays on Duty and Discipline*.

74. Kennedy, detailed handwritten reminiscence, October 23, 1956, box 2, folder 10, PFK.

75. Kennedy-Banks, "Kansas City Kennedys"; Kennedy-Banks interview with author, October 16, 2004; Kennedy, *Color Me Flo*, 31.

76. Kennedy, *Color Me Flo*, 25.

77. Hunter, *To 'Joy My Freedom*, 234; Amott and Mattaei, *Race, Gender, and Work*, 158.

78. Kennedy, "Color Me Flo" original transcript, box 5, tape 3, pp. 13–14, FKP. By 1915, William Jackman was living in California; he eventually moved into the Pacific Branch National Home for Disabled Volunteer Soldiers in Los Angeles. Lucy Jackman was in Los Angeles visiting her son. She may have also been attempting to claim her share of her husband's Civil War veteran's pension. There was confusion over who deserved his pension. William Jackman was married to Mary Jackman in 1880, but he may not have been legally divorced from his first wife, which could explain why the second Mrs. Jackman did not make a formal claim for his pension until the 1930s. It is also possible that the government was attempting to avoid paying Lucy Jackman what was owed her as a

veteran's widow and used the first marriage as an excuse to do so. Lucy Simpson Jackman, U.S. Veterans and Adjudication Pension Appeal; manuscript census returns, population, Kansas City, Jackson County, Missouri, Tenth Census of the United States (1880), microfilm series T9, roll 692, p. 176. Historian Brandi Brimmer demonstrates that African American women were especially vulnerable to being turned away because the government claimed that they were not legitimate wives and widows. Despite being rebuffed, many black women continued to make claims on the state as widows and citizens. Brimmer, "'Her Claim for Pension Is Lawful and Just.'"

79. Kennedy, detailed handwritten reminiscence, October 17, 1956, box 2, folder 10, PFK, 1; Kennedy, "Color Me Flo" original transcript, box 5, tape 13, p. 14, FKP.

80. Kennedy-Banks interview with author, October 16, 2004; Kennedy interview with Jacqueline Ceballos, 19; Kennedy, detailed handwritten reminiscence, October 19, 1956, box 2, folder 10, PFK.

81. Kennedy interview with Jacqueline Ceballos.

82. Ibid. Flo states, "Zella was so ambitious. We picked up her ambitiousness." Kennedy, "Color Me Flo" original transcript, box 5, tape 2, p. 14, FKP; Kennedy-Banks interview with author, October 16, 2004.

83. Sides, L.A. City Limits, 15.

84. Ibid., 16, 18; Flamming, Bound for Freedom, 68.

85. Kennedy, "Color Me Flo" original transcript, box 5, tape 1, p. 3, FKP.

86. Ibid.

87. Ibid., tape 2, p. 20; Florynce Kennedy interview with author.

88. Kennedy, detailed handwritten reminiscence, October 19, 1956, box 2, folder 10, PFK.

89. Kennedy, "Color Me Flo" original transcript, box 5, tape 2, p. 16, FKP. Los Angeles was marked by racial segregation; the South Central neighborhood where Kennedy lived later became predominantly black and Mexican. Sides, L.A. City Limits, 18.

90. Kennedy interview with Diane Schulder Abrams on the *Diane Abrams Show*; Kennedy, "Color Me Flo" original transcript, box 5, tape 3, pp. 13–14, FKP.

91. Kennedy, detailed handwritten reminiscence, October 19, 1956, box 2, folder 10, PFK; Kennedy, "Color Me Flo" original transcript, box 5, tape 3, p. 14, FKP.

92. Kennedy interview in *The First Time*, 145.

93. Kennedy, *Color Me Flo*, 31.

94. Kennedy, "Color Me Flo" original transcript, box 5, tape 2, p. 14, and tape 3, p. 8, FKP.

95. Kennedy, detailed handwritten reminiscence, October 19, 1956, box 2, folder 10, PFK.

96. Kennedy, *Color Me Flo*, 30.

97. Manuscript census returns, population, Kansas City, Jackson County, Missouri, Sixteenth Census of the United States (1940), microfilm series T627, roll 2168, p. 2B.

98. Hall and Ferguson, *Great Depression*, 4.

99. Greenberg, *To Ask for an Equal Chance*, 27.

100. Jones, *Labor of Love, Labor of Sorrow*, 196–200; Gore, *Radicalism at the Crossroads*, 18.

101. Coulter, *Take Up the Black Man's Burden*, 274.

102. Kennedy, *Color Me Flo*, 31.

103. Entry for Zella Kennedy, *Los Angeles, California, City Directory* (Los Angeles City Directory Company, 1925).

104. Kennedy, *Color Me Flo*, 31.

105. Ibid.

106. Kennedy interview with Abrams, PFK; Pasternak and Sydell, "Flo Kennedy Still 'Kicking Ass' at 75."

107. Kennedy, *Color Me Flo*, 34.

108. Entry for Florence Kennedy, *R. L. Polk and Co.'s Kansas City, Missouri, Directory*, 1933, 1938; Florence Kennedy Metropolitan Life Insurance Company application, box 6, FKP.

109. Kennedy, "Color Me Flo" original transcript, box 5, tape 3, p. 2, FKP. Nearly 20 million families turned to public and private agencies for help.

110. Kennedy, *Color Me Flo*, 34; entry for Florence Kennedy, *R. L. Polk and Co.'s Kansas City, Missouri, Directory*, 1942.

111. Kennedy, *Color Me Flo*, 34.

112. Kennedy, "Color Me Flo" original transcript, box 5, tape 3, p. 8, FKP.

113. Kennedy, *Color Me Flo*, 32; Kennedy, "Color Me Flo" original transcript, box 5, tape 2, p. 12, FKP.

114. Moore, *Leading the Race*, 43–44.

115. Kennedy, *Color Me Flo*, 33; Kennedy, detailed handwritten reminiscence, October 17, 1956, box 2, folder 10, PFK.

116. Kennedy, *Color Me Flo*, 32; Kennedy, "Color Me Flo" original transcript, box 5, tape 3, p. 8, and tape unknown, p. 7A, FKP.

117. Kennedy, "Color Me Flo" original transcript, box 5, tape 2, pp. 4–5, 18, FKP.

118. Kennedy interview in *The First Time*, 144; Kennedy, detailed handwritten reminiscence, October 20, 1956, box 2, folder 10, PFK.

119. Kennedy interview in *The First Time*, 144.

120. Ibid., 150.

121. Ibid., 145.

122. Kennedy, *Color Me Flo*, 33.

123. Kennedy-Banks, "Kansas City Kennedys."

124. Kennedy interview in *The First Time*, 150.

125. Kennedy, *Color Me Flo*, 32.

126. Kennedy interview in *The First Time*, 150.

127. Ibid., 149.

128. Ellen K. Rothman called this practice of white women the "invention of petting." Young women could pet without being in a serious courtship. Young white working-class women living away from their families in industrial towns at times engaged in this practice. Rothman, *Hands and Hearts*, 54; Peiss, *Cheap Amusements*, 112. Urban working-class white women who did not know about or use birth control expected that their partner would marry them if they became pregnant. Illegitimacy rates rose, but rates of premarital conception rose more sharply. Kennedy engaged in petting and laid claim to her own sexual desires while still living at home. Few histories have attempted to understand how black women exerted their right to this practice.

129. Kennedy, "Color Me Flo" original transcript, box 5, tape 3, p. 4, FKP.

130. Engelman, *History of the Birth Control Movement*, 143.

131. Manuscript census returns, population, Kansas City, Jackson County, Missouri, Fifteenth Census of the United States (1930), microfilm series M1930, roll 1199, p. 17A.

132. Kennedy, *Color Me Flo*, 35.

133. The Kansas City, Missouri, NAACP branch records provide only limited details of boycotts and other protests during the 1930s. See Kansas City, Missouri, Branch Records of the NAACP, boxes G107, G108, and C401, Manuscript Division, Library of Congress, Washington, D.C.

134. Kennedy, *Color Me Flo*, 35.

135. Kelley, *Race Rebels, 1–2, 36*.

136. Florynce Kennedy to Whom It Concerns, May 5, 1946, box 8, FKP; Kennedy, *Color Me Flo*, 35.

137. Kennedy, *Color Me Flo*, 35; Florynce Kennedy, unorganized notes, FKP.

138. Kennedy to Whom It Concerns.

139. Van Deburg, *Modern Black Nationalism*, 175.

140. Kennedy, *Color Me Flo*, 34; Florynce Kennedy's adult insurance photos demonstrating her injured back, box 1, FKP.

141. Bay, *To Tell the Truth Freely*, 48.

142. Theoharis and Woodard, *Freedom North*, 7.

143. Kelley, "'We Are Not What We Seem,'" 37.

CHAPTER 2

1. Coontz, *Marriage, a History*, 221.

2. Kennedy, unorganized notes, FKP; Kennedy, *Color Me Flo*, 38; Kennedy, "Color Me Flo" original transcript, box 5, tape 5, p. 4, FKP.

3. Kennedy, *Color Me Flo*, 37.

4. Wilkerson, *Warmth of Other Suns*, 251; Kasinitz, *Caribbean New York*, 26.

5. Biondi, *To Stand and Fight*, 3–5.

6. Kennedy interview with Jacqueline Ceballos.

7. Maurrasse, *Listening to Harlem*, 21; Mallory, *Harlem in the Twentieth Century*, 31.

8. Kennedy interview with Jacqueline Ceballos.

9. Kennedy, "Color Me Flo" original tape transcript, box 5, tape 4, p. 3, FKP.

10. Kennedy would use this same legal tactic when she moved into her next New York apartment. See legal documents related to 8 East Forty-Eighth Street, Suite 3C, New York, New York, box 1, FKP.

11. Gregory, *Black Corona*, 25.

12. Kennedy, *Color Me Flo*, 35.

13. Ibid., 61.

14. J. Gordon, *Black Leadership for Social Change*, 126; Powell, *Adam by Adam*, 81.

15. For an example of blacks outside New York writing to Powell for help, see Tyson, *Radio Free Dixie*, 73.

16. Florynce Kennedy to Whom It Concerns, May 5, 1946, FKP.

17. Ibid.

18. Theoharis and Woodard, *Freedom North*, 7.

19. Kennedy, unorganized notes, FKP.

20. Kennedy to Whom It Concerns; Kennedy, "Color Me Flo" original transcript, box 5, tape 5, p. 4, FKP.

21. Stolzfus, *Citizen, Mother, Worker*, 99; Hartmann, *The Home Front and Beyond*, 53–70.

22. Jones, *Labor of Love, Labor of Sorrow*, 234.

23. Wynn, *African American Experience during World War II*, 67–68.

24. Ibid.

25. Ibid., 68.

26. Kennedy, "Color Me Flo" original transcript, box 5, tape 5, p. 1, FKP.

27. Ibid., box 5, tape 5, p. 3.

28. D. O'Brien, *Constitutional Law and Politics*, xxi, 1386, 1389.

29. Grothaus, "'Inevitable Mr. Gaines'"; Greene, Kremer, and Holland, *Missouri's Black Heritage*, 168.

30. Kennedy, "Color Me Flo" original transcript, box 5, tape 5, p. 4, FKP.

31. "Our History," City College of New York, http://www.ccny.cuny.edu/about/history .cfm, accessed November 4, 2014.

32. Kennedy, "Color Me Flo" original transcript, box 5, tape 5, p. 5, FKP.

33. Columbia University Office of the Registrar to author, June 20, 2014, in author's possession.

34. In 1945, women at Columbia received 2,407 undergraduate and graduate degrees, while only 984 degrees were conferred on men. *Columbia University in the City of New York*, 1945.

35. Burrell, *History of Adult Education*, vii–x, 94–97; *Columbia University in the City of New York*, 1936, 1937, 1938, 1939. The Office of the Registrar did not publish records of the non-matriculating or matriculating women enrolled in the university's undergraduate program until the late 1940s; only the women who graduated from the program were listed. As a result, it is hard to determine the exact number of women enrolled in the program before the late 1940s.

36. Farmer, "College Marks 25 Years of Coeducation."

37. McCaughey, *Stand, Columbia*, 329.

38. Kennedy, "Color Me Flo" original transcript, box 5, tape 5, p. 5, FKP.

39. Columbia School of Engineering began to admit undergraduate women during World War II. However, during this period women students had to take their non-engineering classes at other schools in the university.

40. Rosenberg, *Changing the Subject*, 4–5, 7.

41. Ibid., 179–88.

42. "Draft Women?"; "'Women in the War' Meeting Subject"; "Grumman, Columbia Plan Training for Women."

43. Jones, *Labor of Love*, 234–35; Amott and Mattaei, *Race, Gender and Work*, 131.

44. Kennedy, "Color Me Flo" original transcript, box 5, tape 4, p. 3, FKP; Columbia University Office of the Registrar to author, June 20, 2014.

45. Kennedy, *Color Me Flo*, 38.

46. Moya B. Hansen, "'Try Being a Black Woman!,'" 219; Shaw, *What a Woman Ought to Be and Do*, 2–3; "Negro Women Offered Big Opportunities in Nursing."

47. Kennedy to Whom It Concerns.

48. Kennedy interview in *The First Time*, 145.

49. Kennedy to Whom It Concerns.

50. Florynce Kennedy, "Autobiographical Sketch . . . September 1947," box 8, FKP.

51. Kennedy, "Color Me Flo" original transcript, box 5, tape 4, p. 1, FKP.

52. Ibid.

53. Kennedy to Whom It Concerns.

54. D. Campbell, "The War and Beyond," 288.

55. Tuttle, *Daddy's Gone to War*, 19–20.

56. "Barnard Girls Stronger, More Fertile—Dr. Alsop."

57. Ibid.

58. Ibid.

59. "Atlanta Council of Negro Women Will Meet Thursday"; "Negro Women Offered Big Opportunities in Nursing"; "Educators Urges Women to Prepare as Homemakers."

60. Kennedy to Whom It Concerns.

61. Ibid.

62. Kennedy, "Autobiographical Sketch . . . September 1947."

63. Stansell, *American Moderns*, 225–27.

64. McGuire, *At the Dark End of the Street*, 47.

65. "Barnard Girls Stronger, More Fertile—Dr. Alsop"; "Educator Urges Women to Prepare as Homemakers"; "Young Women Warned of Wartime Marriage Hysteria."

66. Ladd-Taylor, *Mother-Work*, 120.

67. Curwood, *Stormy Weather*, 51.

68. Kennedy, "Autobiographical Sketch . . . September 1947."

69. Kennedy-Daly interview with author; Kennedy-Banks interview with author, October 16, 2004.

70. Florynce Kennedy, "Poisoned Soup," May 1, 1945, undergraduate papers folder, box 8, FKP.

71. Coontz, *Way We Never Were*, 31.

72. Anderson, "Last Hired, First Fired"; Claudia Jones, "An End of the Neglect of the Problems of the Negro Woman!," *Political Affairs* (1949), reprinted in Guy-Sheftall, *Words of Fire*, 109–11.

73. Biondi, *To Stand and Fight*, 14–16; G. O'Brien, *Color of the Law*, 35–36.

74. Burrell, *History of Adult Education*, 95.

75. *Columbia University in the City of New York*, 1946 and 1947.

76. Flo Kennedy, "A Comparative Study: Accentuating the Similarities of the Societal Position of Women and Negroes," reprinted in Kennedy, *Color Me Flo*, 120–24.

77. Ibid., 121.

78. Dwight D. Eisenhower, "Females 'Slupping' in Den Chided by Frosh Buddies," letter to the editor, *Columbia Daily Spectator*, April 1, 1949.

79. Kennedy, "Comparative Study," 121.

80. Ibid.

81. Kennedy to Whom It Concerns.

82. Ibid.

83. Bentley, *Thirty Years of Treason*.

84. Biondi, *To Stand and Fight*, 7.

85. Kennedy to Whom It Concerns.

86. Flo Kennedy personal profile, 1951, box 8, FKP.

87. Kennedy, "Autobiographical Sketch . . . September 1947."

88. Ibid.

89. Stern, *Understanding the Russians*; Stern and Locke, *When Peoples Meet*.

90. Price, *Threatening Anthropology*, 137.

91. Kennedy, *Color Me Flo*, 40.

92. Ibid.

93. Price, *Threatening Anthropology*, xiv, 136–38. Price also wrote for the popular press under a pseudonym. He wrote one of the first studies in medical sociology (1927), worked as an anthropologist with Native Americans in the state of Washington, and with Alain Locke coedited a collection of essays on cross-cultural and interracial encounters among diverse peoples.

94. T. Morgan, *Reds*, 442.

95. Investigative Report 0977697, New York, New York, March 12, 1945, FRK/FBI.

96. Kennedy, "Autobiographical Sketch . . . September 1947."

97. *Columbia University Bulletin of Information . . . 1947–1948*, 14; Columbia University Office of the Registrar to the author, June 20, 2014.

CHAPTER 3

1. Kennedy, *Color Me Flo*, 39.

2. Ibid.

3. Devine, *Henry Wallace's 1948 Presidential Campaign*, 16, 236; Castledine, *Cold War Progressives*, 6–8.

4. Flo Kennedy, "Nigger Control: The ConGame Continued," essay in "Politics of Oppression," unpublished manuscript, folder POO, box 13, FKP.

5. Flo Kennedy interview in Dreifus, *Radical Lifestyles*, 107.

6. Ibid.

7. Ibid.; Kennedy, *Color Me Flo*, 39; Pasternak and Sydell, "Flo Kennedy Still 'Kicking Ass' at 75."

8. Kennedy, *Color Me Flo*, 52. See Hicks, *Talk with You Like a Woman*, 159–71, for a history of the ways the courts criminalized black women at the turn of the century.

9. Mack, *Representing the Race*, 2.

10. Kennedy interview with Doon Arbus.

11. Staff of the Foundation for Research in Legal History, *History of the School of Law*, 291; "A Brief History of Women at C[olumbia] L[aw] S[chool], Part 1," http://www.law .columbia.edu/law_school/communications/reports/Fa112002/brief/, accessed October 28, 2014.

12. Staff of the Foundation for Research in Legal History, *History of the School of Law*, 348–59.

13. Motley, *Equal Justice under Law*, 56. In 1945, Elreta M. Alexander-Ralston was the first black woman to graduate from Columbia Law School. She became the first practic-

ing black woman lawyer in her home state of North Carolina and eventually served on the bench.

14. Ibid.; *Columbia University Bulletin of Information . . . 1947–1948*, 4; Kennedy, *Color Me Flo*, 39. As Kennedy was attending undergraduate classes at night and Baker (Motley) attended law courses during the day, it does not appear that they knew each other at Columbia.

15. *Columbia University Bulletin of Information . . . 1947–1948*, 5.

16. "Veterans Boost Enrollment 67%." Seven of the women admitted to Columbia School of Law were veterans who most likely served in the military as nurses or clerical workers.

17. Honey, *Creating Rosie the Riveter*, 97–98.

18. Some of the few women admitted were daughters of famous white men, such as Columbia's own Nobel Prize–winning physicist, I. I. Rabbi.

19. *Columbia University Bulletin of Information . . . 1947–1948*, 14, 47–48; "Entering Class of 205 Marks Return of School to Normalcy"; Kennedy interview in Dreifus, *Radical Lifestyles*, 107.

20. *Columbia University Bulletin of Information . . . 1947–1948*, 14, 47–48.

21. Pasternak and Sydell, "Flo Kennedy Still 'Kicking Ass' at 75."

22. See also Fuccio Louis's student admissions card, dated September 1949. Louis gained admission with a B average from Columbia College. Even male students from other universities gained admission with grade point averages that were lower than Kennedy's. For example, James Carr from Notre Dame gained admission with a C+ average and Joseph Flynn from Yale College gained admission with a C average; see School of Law Admission Cards Collection, 1940–1950, Columbia University School of Law Library, New York, New York. Kennedy's admission card was missing from the Columbia University School of Law Library.

23. Kennedy, *Color Me Flo*, 39; Kennedy interview in Dreifus, *Radical Lifestyles*, 107.

24. "Oklahoma School Bars Negro Again"; "6 Negroes Test Oklahoma Race Law"; "Court Orders School for Negro."

25. Flo Kennedy, "A Comparative Study: Accentuating the Similarities of the Societal Position of Women and Negroes," reprinted in Kennedy, *Color Me Flo*, 120–24.

26. Ibid.

27. Gore, *Radicalism at the Crossroads*, 39.

28. "Brief History of Women at C[olumbia] L[aw] S[chool], Part 1." Some women law students described experiencing support from the male law students and professors.

29. "Entering Class of 205 Marks Return of School to Normalcy."

30. "Brief History of Women at C[olumbia] L[aw] S[chool], Part 1."

31. Ibid.; Kennedy, "Nigger Control: The ConGame Continued."

32. Kennedy interview in Dreifus, *Radical Lifestyles*, 108.

33. Kennedy, *Color Me Flo*, 40.

34. Kennedy, "Nigger Control: The ConGame Continued."

35. Kennedy interview in Dreifus, *Radical Lifestyles*, 108; Florynce Kennedy, "Paper #VI—Three Periods—Period," Law in Society exam, January 2, 1951, PFK; Florynce Kennedy, "On the Good, the True, the Beautiful, in Law, i.e. Cardozo," paper no. V, PFK.

36. Kennedy, *Color Me Flo*, 39.

37. Kennedy interview with Doon Arbus.

38. Kennedy, *Color Me Flo*, 40.

39. Kennedy, "On the Good, the True, the Beautiful, in Law, i.e. Cardozo"; Kennedy, "Paper #VI—Three Periods—Period."

40. Kennedy, *Color Me Flo*, 40.

41. Kennedy, "On the Good, the True, the Beautiful, in Law, i.e. Cardozo," 1, 3, 4.

42. "Karl Llewellyn, Law Expert, Dies," *New York Times*, February 15, 1962, 29; N. Hull, *Roscoe Pound and Karl Llewellyn*, 2–3.

43. "'Law In Society,' a New Approach," *Columbia Law School News*, March 13, 1950, 3.

44. Kennedy, "On the Good, the True, the Beautiful, in Law, i.e. Cardozo."

45. Ibid., 2.

46. Kennedy, *Color Me Flo*, 39.

47. Ibid., 40.

48. *Columbia University Bulletin of Information . . . 1947–1948*, 40–46. In 1933, Howard University School of Law officially announced a program focusing on civil rights law. Mack, *Representing the Race*, 44; McNeil, *Groundwork*, 84. Howard Law–trained Thurgood Marshall helped to define the strategy and litigate the NAACP cases that overturned *Plessy v. Ferguson*.

49. Motley, *Equal Justice under Law*, 58. Kenneth Mack describes how Thurgood Marshall recalled a story in which he was refused admission into his state's law school and how this rejection fueled his desire to end Jim Crow segregation. For Mack, this legend is a convention in the language and literature of black attorneys of the Jim Crow era. Mack, *Representing the Race*, 1–6.

50. Kennedy, "Comparative Study," 121.

51. The FBI notes that Kennedy was eligible for aid because of a physical disability and was "assisted with her legal training at Columbia"; Investigative Report, date unknown, place unknown, FRK/FBI. See also Kennedy interview with Jacqueline Ceballos.

52. "Women's Law Society Founded, Dorothy Beck Elected Chairman."

53. Ibid.

54. "Women's Society Welcomes Frosh."

55. Biondi, *To Stand and Fight*, 164.

56. "Revelry, Relaxation Keynote Kent Lounge"; Kennedy, "On the Good, the True, the Beautiful, in Law, i.e. Cardozo."

57. Stollman interview with author.

58. Kennedy, "Law in Our Society," 2, undergraduate papers folder, box 8, FKP.

59. The New York City Bar Association excluded lawyers who were in private practice or at small firms. Because most African Americans and women of all races were not typically hired at large New York City law firms, they could not join the New York City Bar Association.

60. *Columbia University, Report of the Registrar*, 24; *Columbia University Bulletin of Information . . . 1950–1951*, 5; *Martindale-Hubbell Law Directory*, 8th–9th annual ed., 1957, 2:1744.

61. "Job Outlook Excellent for June Graduates."

62. Kennedy interview in Dreifus, *Radical Lifestyles*, 108.

63. Ibid.

64. Kennedy, *Color Me Flo*, 41. Dean Reese was also the head of Legal Aid in New York City. Kennedy's earlier protest against the dean was probably not far from his mind when her application came across his desk. Kennedy then had several strikes against her: she was black, she was a woman, and she was a troublemaker.

65. McLeod, *Life of Judge Jane Bolin*, 28.

66. Morello, *Invisible Bar*, 197.

67. McLeod, *Life of Judge Jane Bolin*, 20.

68. Bolin, whose father was a lawyer, was the first African American woman to graduate from the Yale University School of Law. Bolin practiced briefly with her father and then her husband. She was appointed in 1939 to a judgeship on the Domestic Relations Court of New York.

69. Kennedy interview in Dreifus, *Radical Lifestyles*, 108.

70. McLeod, *Life of Judge Jane Bolin*, 28–29.

71. Kennedy interview in Dreifus, *Radical Lifestyles*, 109.

72. Kennedy, *Color Me Flo*, 41.

73. Paula Moore and Mildred Mebel were associates at Hartman, Sheridan and Tekulsky during Kennedy's tenure.

74. Millen, "Blanche Goldman Etra, 1915–1995."

75. Stollman interview with author.

76. Weiss, *Always in Trouble*, 13.

77. Stollman interview with author.

78. McLeod, *Life of Judge Jane Bolin*, 28; *Martindale-Hubbell Law Directory*, 1951, 1952, 1953, 1954, 1955; J. Smith, *Rebels in Law*, 43.

79. Kennedy, *Color Me Flo*, 41.

80. Ibid.; Kennedy, "Color Me Flo" original transcript, box 5, tape 6, p. 4, FKP.

81. Kennedy-Banks interview with author, October 17, 2004.

82. Ibid.; Kennedy, *Color Me Flo*, 41.

83. Kennedy-Banks interview with author, October 16, 2004; Kennedy, "Color Me Flo" original transcript, box 5, tape 6, p. 5, FKP.

84. Flo Kennedy, notes on George Morris property damage case, FKP; George Morris, 1956 file, 9.12, PFK.

85. *Martindale-Hubbell Law Directory*, 1957, 1958.

86. "History," Phillips Nizer website, http://www.phillipsnizer.com/about/history.cfm, accessed October 28, 2014.

87. Kelley, *Thelonious Monk*, 156.

88. Kennedy, *Color Me Flo*, 44.

89. Ibid., 32.

90. Kennedy-Daly interview with author.

91. Stollman interview with author.

92. *Martindale-Hubbell Law Directory*, 1958, 1959. Like Kennedy, Fields was an outsider in the legal profession because he was disabled early in life, most likely from polio, and used crutches to walk.

93. Quoted in Weiss, *Always in Trouble*, 13.

94. Stollman interview with author. After he worked at Kennedy's firm, Stollman cre-

ated ESP-Disk', an independent record label, and represented artists, even though he did not have even a basic appreciation for jazz music.

95. Charles D. Dye and Florynce R. Kennedy, Certificate of Marriage Registration, November 30, 1957, The City of New York Office of the City Clerk, New York, New York.

96. Rich, *C. M. Kornbluth*, 139, 163; Merril and Weary, *Better to Have Loved*, 95.

97. Kennedy, *Color Me Flo*, 44.

98. Ibid.; Charles Dye to Rita Dragonette-Dye, 1946, box 5, folder 13, PFK; Kennedy, *Color Me Flo*, 44. George Stark was elected to New York City's Municipal Court in 1951 and became a justice on the New York State Supreme Court in 1968. Graphic artist Ronald Clyne was best known for designing the album covers for Folkway Records. Science fiction writer David Kyle founded Gnome Press in 1948.

99. Charles D. Dye and Florynce R. Kennedy, Certificate of Marriage Registration, November 30, 1957, The City of New York Office of the City Clerk, New York, New York.

100. Kennedy, "Color Me Flo" original transcript, box 5, tape 15, p. 3, FKP.

101. Kennedy, "Color Me Flo" original transcript, box 5, tape 15, FKP.

102. Flo Kennedy to Charlie Dye, date unknown, FKP.

103. Florynce Kennedy, "Heights Holiday," 2.11, PFK; Kennedy, "Color Me Flo" transcript, box 5, tape 15, p. 1, FKP.

104. When women married, their names were changed automatically unless they objected. Civil rights leader Ella Baker did not change her name after she married and kept her marriage private from most organizers. Ransby, *Ella Baker and the Black Freedom Movement*, 102. Wilkes, Kennedy and Fields stationary, box 7, FKP. Kennedy's last name on the firm's letterhead remained Kennedy.

105. Kennedy, *Color Me Flo*, 39.

106. Charlie Dye worked as a security guard during the day.

107. Flo Kennedy to Charlie Dye, date unknown, box 4, FKP.

108. Kennedy-Banks interview with author, October 16, 2004.

109. Kennedy, *Color Me Flo*, 43.

110. Florynce Kennedy to Charlie Dye, May 2, 1958, FKP.

111. Kennedy, "Heights Holiday."

112. Florynce Kennedy to Charlie Dye, September 14, 1959, box 4, FKP.

113. "When he finally would come after me, he'd show up with a big grin on his face and a royalty check in his hands. He'd take me out to dinner and then we would go to Birdland. He'd cry and say how much he missed me," Kennedy recalled. Like other battered women, she admits, she would relent and "would go back." Kennedy interview in Dreifus, *Radical Lifestyles*, 112. See also Motz, *Toxic Couples*, 132.

114. Florynce Kennedy to Charlie Dye, September 21, 1959, box 4, FKP.

115. Kennedy, *Color Me Flo*, 43.

116. Imber-Black, *Secret Life of Families*, 69.

117. William Dufty, "'Ghost Writer' for Billie Holiday Describes Scene at Last Curtain," *Daily Defender* (Chicago), July 22, 1959, 19.

118. Vail, *Lady Day's Diary*, 200.

119. Kelley, *Thelonious Monk*, 157.

120. Kennedy, *Color Me Flo*, 47.

121. Ibid., 48; Griffin, *If You Can't Be Free*, 42; Nicholson, *Billie Holiday*, 159.

122. Griffin, *If You Can't Be Free*, 41.

123. Chevigny, *Gigs*, 4–5; Dan Wakefield, "Dope on the Downbeat," *Nation*, August 31, 1957, 92–93.

124. Chevigny, *Gigs*, 59–61.

125. Kennedy, "Color Me Flo" original tape transcript, box 5, tape 17, p. 4, FKP.

126. On "race women," see Angela Davis, *Blues Legacies and Black Feminism*, 162; and Margolick, *Strange Fruit: The Biography of a Song*.

127. Kennedy, *Color Me Flo*, 48.

128. Perucci, *Paul Robeson*, 14.

129. Griffin, *If You Can't Be Free*, 54. On Holiday being forced by the FBI to stop singing other political songs, such as "communist anti-war songs," see Angela Davis, *Blues Legacies and Black Feminism*, 162; and Margolick, *Strange Fruit: Billie Holiday, Cafe Society, and an Early Cry for Civil Rights*.

130. Blackburn, *With Billie*, 111.

131. Griffin, *If You Can't Be Free*, 54.

132. Kennedy, *Color Me Flo*, 47. Kennedy was particularly outraged that Holiday's agents had not affiliated her with any of the performing rights societies; see "Color Me Flo" original transcript, box 5, tape 16, p. 17, FKP.

133. Griffin, *If You Can't Be Free*, 42.

134. Nicholson, *Billie Holiday*, 224.

135. William Dufty, "The True Story of Billie Holiday," *New York Post*, July 22, 1959, 4, 22.

136. Florynce Kennedy, "It's Damn Slick Out There," original essay and interview, FKP.

137. Kennedy, "Color Me Flo" original transcript, box 5, tape 6, p. 5, FKP.

138. Kennedy, *Color Me Flo*, 45; *Joseph Vallelunga v. Thurman Gardens Inc.*; *Willie M. Plummer et al. v. Christopher McHale et al.* For information on Wilkes's disbarment, see *The Record of the Association of the Bar of the City of New York, Committee Reports 1960–1961* 16, no. 7 (October 1961): 34; and *In the Matter of Donald E. Wilkes, an Attorney and the Association of the Bar of the City of New York*, June 21, 1961.

139. *Vallelunga v. Thurman Gardens Inc.*

140. Kennedy, "Color Me Flo" original transcript, box 5, tape 15, p. 7, FKP.

141. Kennedy interview in Dreifus, *Radical Lifestyles*, 110.

142. Ibid.

143. *Vallelunga v. Thurman Gardens Inc.*

144. Kennedy, "Color Me Flo" original transcript, box 5, tape 15, pp. 7–9, FKP.

145. Ibid.; *The Record of the Association of the Bar of the City of New York, Committee Reports 1960–1961* 16, no. 7 (October 1961): 34; *In the Matter of Donald E. Wilkes*.

146. Kennedy, *Color Me Flo*, 46.

147. Kennedy, "Color Me Flo" transcript, box 5, tape 15, p. 11, FKP.

148. *The Record of the Association of the Bar of the City of New York, Committee Reports 1960–1961* 16, no. 7 (October 1961): 34; *In the Matter of Donald E. Wilkes*.

149. Kennedy, *Color Me Flo*, 46; *In the Matter of Donald E. Wilkes*.

150. Donald Wilkes Jr. to author, June 5, 2013, and June 7, 2013, in author's possession. Wilkes described how his father abandoned the family and never paid child support, although his mother fought in court to obtain it. Wilkes Sr. eventually moved back to Florida and attempted to practice as a lawyer again. His petition, however, was denied.

151. Kennedy interview in Dreifus, *Radical Lifestyles*, 111.

152. *The Record of the Association of the Bar of the City of New York, Committee Reports 1960–1961* 16, no. 7 (October 1961): 34; *In the Matter of Donald E. Wilkes.*

153. Kennedy interview in Dreifus, *Radical Lifestyles*, 110.

154. Kennedy, *Color Me Flo*, 46.

155. Ibid., 46–47.

156. Florynce Kennedy to Charlie Dye, September 14, 1959, box 4, FKP.

157. Riley, *Divorce: An American Tradition*, 157.

158. In the late 1960s and 1970s, Kennedy listed Diane Schulder and Carol Lefcourt as her legal partners. Kennedy was not practicing with these women; she added their names to her letterhead to help these new women attorneys succeed.

159. Interviews and off-the-record conversations with Kennedy's feminist friends and members of their families revealed very little about Flo's personal life. For example, Peg Brennan's daughter, Pam Brennan, asserted that Kennedy was "asexual." Perhaps because Kennedy was in her late forties and fifties when she shared a summer home with the Brennan family and Kennedy was publicly unattached, Pam, then a teenager, mistakenly assumed that Kennedy did not have sexual desires. Kennedy's sisters said that Kennedy had romantic relationships with men but talked about them only with her sisters, especially Joyce. Kennedy did not disclose much information about her romantic and sexual relationships with her friends and her personal papers had been handled before they reached me, so it is difficult to say anything definitive about her romantic relationships except that she had them. Pam Brennan conversation with author, March 7, 2008; Peg Brennan conversation with author, March 7, 2008; Atkinson interview with author, October 21, 2013; Cellabos interview with author; Dell'Olio interview with author; Kennedy-Banks interview with author, October 16, 2004.

CHAPTER 4

1. *Martindale-Hubbell Law Directory*, 1960.

2. Steinem, "The Verbal Karate of Florynce Kennedy, Esq."

3. Kennedy, *Color Me Flo*, 52.

4. Emil K. Ellis to Florynce Kennedy, February 28, 1961, folder 18, box 1; Louis McKay to Mr. Halperin, October 6, 1961, folder 3, box 2, BHC.

5. Kennedy, *Color Me Flo*, 48.

6. Ibid.

7. Florynce Kennedy to Whom It Concerns, May 5, 1946, FKP; Florynce R. Kennedy to Whom It May Concern, August 11, 1961, folder 18, box 1, BHC.

8. Kennedy, *Color Me Flo*, 48.

9. "Notice to the Trade," *Variety*, November 23, 1960, 52; Estate Disbursement, November 1960–July 1961, Charlie Parker folder, box, 6, FKP.

10. Kennedy, *Color Me Flo*, 52.

11. Ibid.

12. Graham, "Negro Artists Warned to Use Care in Contract with AGVA."

13. Kennedy, "Color Me Flo" original transcript, box 5, tape 21, p. 6, FKP; Kennedy, *Color Me Flo*, 52.

14. "Notice to the Trade."

15. Ibid.

16. Graham, "Negro Artists Warned to Use Care in Contract with AGVA"; Stollman interview with author.

17. Graham, "Negro Artists Warned to Use Care in Contract with AGVA."

18. Ibid.

19. Haygood, *King of the Cats*, ix–xx.

20. Many documents in the Billie Holiday Collection detail Kennedy's work to safeguard Louis McKay's share of Billie Holiday's profits. Several folders and documents are mislabeled Louis McKay's writings when in fact they are Kennedy's legal notes and writings. See Florynce Kennedy to Louis McKay, December 31, 1963, folder 18, box 1; and Florynce Kennedy to Associated Booking Corporation, October 12, 1962, folder 18, box 1, both in BHC.

21. Kennedy, *Color Me Flo*, 42; Chase Manhattan bank statements for February 1962, March 1963, and April 1966, estate of Eleanora McKay, folder 22, box 1, BHC.

22. Kennedy, *Color Me Flo*, 42.

23. Steinem, "The Verbal Karate of Florynce Kennedy, Esq."

24. Kennedy, *Color Me Flo*, 52.

25. Ibid., 49.

26. Ibid., 52.

27. Ibid.

28. Parker, *My Life in E-Flat*, 40–57; "Chan Parker, 74, Known as Jazzman's Wife," *New York Times*, September 19, 1999.

29. Quoted in Weiss, *Always in Trouble*, 13.

30. Stollman interview with author.

31. Petition to the Surrogate Court of New York, May 11, 1961, index no. A.670/1956, Florynce Kennedy for Doris Parker; "Yardbird's Widow Challenged," *Jet*, January 25, 1962, 58.

32. Stollman interview with author.

33. Ibid.; Weiss, *Always in Trouble*, xiii–xiv, 13–15.

34. Parker, *My Life in E-Flat*; Chan Parker to Doris Parker, date unknown, FKP. Chan argued that Doris and Charlie's marriage in Mexico was not valid. She also alleged that Doris tried to divorce Charlie, and finally she questioned whether Parker had ever divorced his first wife and the mother of his eldest son.

35. "Inside Stuff—Music," *Variety*, January 11, 1961, 48.

36. "Notice of Claim: In the Matter of Charles Parker," September 10, 1962, Surrogate Court of New York.

37. Ibid.; "Inside Stuff—Music."

38. "Inside Stuff—Music"; Stollman interview with author.

39. Stollman interview with author.

40. Louis McKay to Maely Dufty of *Jazz Day* magazine, June 19, 1961, folder 2, box 3, BHC.

41. *McKay v. Columbia Broadcasting System, Inc., James E. Allen, Claire Roskam, John Butler, Carmen De Lavallade and William Dufty*, 324 F. 2nd 762 (2d Cir. 1963), "Legal Proceedings McKay/Holiday Estates vs. Columbia Broadcast Co. 1962" folder, box 1, BHC.

42. O'Meally, *Lady Day*, 185.

43. Blackburn, *With Billie*, 236. Years later, during Bill and Maely Dufty's divorce proceedings, Bill accused Maely of having an affair with Lou McKay.

44. Stollman interview with author.

45. Opening Statement by Kenneth A. Cox, Chief Broadcast Bureau, Federal Communications Commission, Public Proceedings in Overall Program Inquiry: Docket No. 12782, June 20, 1961, folder "Piracy of Ideas," box 12.5–12.6, PFK; Kennedy notes, June 23, 1961, *The Ann Sothern Show*, box 12.5–12.6, PFK; *Commerce: Business, Patents, Trademarks and Foreign Trade*.

46. Kennedy, *Color Me Flo*, 53.

47. Kennedy, "Color Me Flo" original transcript, box 5, tape 21, p. 8, FKP.

48. Kennedy, *Color Me Flo*, 53.

49. Alexander Rauso to Florynce Kennedy, May 24, 1960, box 3, FKP; Florynce Kennedy to Gentleman re: FCC Inquiry into Network Activity in Television, January 27, 1962, box 12.5–12.6, FKP; "NBC, MCA Defendants in 100G Suit over Use of 'Suspicion' Title," *Variety*, April 19, 1961, 50.

50. Florynce R. Kennedy to Joseph E. Quinn, January 3, 1962, folder "Piracy of Ideas," box 12.5–12.6, PFK.

51. Flo Kennedy notes, June 23, 1961, folder "Piracy of Ideas," box 12.5–12.6, PFK; Bennet Olan to Florynce Kennedy, February 24, 1960, box 12.5–12.6, PFK; Florynce Kennedy to Bennet Olan, April 4, 1960, box 12.5–12.6, PFK.

52. Florynce Kennedy to Peter Megargee Brown, October 13, 1961, box 8, FKP.

53. Ibid.

54. Ibid.

55. Ibid.

56. Ibid.

57. G. Hull, *Music Business*, 123.

58. Ibid., 2.

59. Ibid., 234.

60. Kennedy to Peter Megargee Brown, October 13, 1961.

61. Kennedy to Quinn, January 3, 1962. The phrase "piracy of ideas" has been in use since the nineteenth century. Lawyers used the term to discuss copyright disputes between visual artists. Underdown, *The Law of Art Copyright*, 183–84. Kennedy used the term to refer specifically to corporations' theft of the ideas and work of individual artists.

62. "NBC, MCA Defendants in 100G Suit over Use of 'Suspicion' Title."

63. Kennedy to Peter Megargee Brown, October 13, 1961.

64. Kennedy, *Color Me Flo*, 49.

65. Kennedy to Peter Megargee Brown, October 13, 1961.

66. Zak, *I Don't Sound Like Nobody*, 25.

67. Quoted in ibid.

68. *Directory of U.S. Negro Newspapers and Magazines*.

69. Schecter, *Ida B. Wells Barnett*, 188.

70. Kennedy, unorganized notes, FKP.

71. Rowland Evans Jr., "Cuba Fiasco Heightens Pressure for CIA Rein: White House Disturbed Give Candid Accounts," *Washington Post*, May 3, 1961, A19; Statler, *Replacing France*, 183–218.

72. McCann, *Terrorism on American Soil*, 104–5.

73. Florynce Kennedy, "Once Upon a Week," *Queens Voice*, June 5, 1964.

74. Milton Galamison was a Presbyterian pastor in Bedford-Stuyvesant, Brooklyn. In 1964 and 1965 he was also the chair of the Citywide Committee for School Integration. He led numerous boycotts and sit-ins challenging segregation in New York and was frequently arrested. The tactics the Brooklyn chapter of CORE used included dumping trash on the steps of Borough Hall to protest inadequate garbage collection in black neighborhoods. In 1964, Brooklyn CORE activists targeted the opening day of the 1964 World's Fair with a "stall-in" that tied up traffic. See Purnell, *Fighting Jim Crow*.

75. Florynce Kennedy, "Once Upon a Week," *Queens Voice*, July 3, 1964.

76. Ibid., May 22, 1964.

77. Ibid.

78. Reid, *Redefining Black Film*, 23–24.

79. Kennedy, "Once Upon a Week," *Queens Voice*, May 5, 1964.

80. Ibid., May 22, 1964.

81. Wolfgang Saxon, "Eric F. Goldman, 73, a Historian and Presidential Consultant, Dies," *New York Times*, February 20, 1989, A16.

82. Kennedy, "Once Upon a Week," *Queens Voice*, May 22, 1964.

83. Ibid.

84. Ibid.

85. Reagan, *When Abortion Was a Crime*, 201.

86. C. White, "Integrated Teams of Women Report Fear of Progress in Mississippi."

87. Height, *Open Wide the Freedom Gates*, 157.

88. Ibid., 168. For a more detailed discussion of Height's opinion of interracial coalitions, see Height, *Step by Step with Interracial Groups*.

89. Harwell, "Wednesdays in Mississippi," 634; Mrs. Richard Dammann, Report Team 5, p. 11, NCNWP. See also Harwell, *Wednesdays in Mississippi*.

90. Harwell, "Wednesdays in Mississippi," 617; "WIMS Team #5 1964, Mississippi Review, Team 5 New York to Ruleville," transcript and audiotapes 001-S15-ss5-f18-S1, 001-S15-ss5-f18-S2, and 001-S15-ss5-f18-S3, NCNWP. Please note that the NCNWP transcriptions were incomplete at the time of my research and some of Kennedy's comments were not correctly identified by the transcriber. Future researchers should listen to the audiotapes.

91. By 1963, according to Cowan's daughter, Trude Lash was working with Pauli Murray to promote women's participation in the civil rights movement. She was an anti-Nazi German immigrant (her maiden name was Wenzel) who, through her husband, became friends with Eleanor Roosevelt and later worked with her at the UN. She, like Cowan, was identified with the New York Citizens Committee for Children. Marjorie Spiegel Dammann was a professional social worker who established agencies for troubled families in Westchester County. She married Richard Weil Dammann, a Harvard Law School graduate, in August 1935; *Herald Statesman* (Yonkers, New York), August 24, 1935. It is unclear whether Polly Spiegel Cowan was a relative of Marjorie Spiegel Dammann, but it is clear that they had a lot in common as Jews of German descent who grew up in Chicago and its suburbs, went to Seven Sisters colleges, lived in New York City, and were advocates of social services for children and civil rights.

92. See the registration forms for Wednesdays in Mississippi: Marie C. Barksdale, Mrs. Richard W. Dammann, Frances H. Haight, and Florynce Kennedy, all in NCNWP.

93. Chalmers, *Crooked Places Made Straight*, 27.

94. "WIMS Team #5 1964, Mississippi Review, Team 5 New York to Ruleville."

95. Ibid.

96. Ibid.

97. The next summer, several white southern women offered their homes to the northern WIMS members.

98. Harwell, "Wednesdays in Mississippi," 625.

99. Ibid., 634.

100. Ibid.

101. Ibid., 618.

102. "WIMS Team #5 1964, Mississippi Review, Team 5 New York to Ruleville."

103. Ibid.

104. Ibid.

105. Hamer, "Federal Trial Testimony," 7–14; Lee, *For Freedom's Sake*, 1–2.

106. "WIMS Team #5 1964, Mississippi Review, Team 5 New York to Ruleville."

107. Ibid.

108. Florynce R. Kennedy, "Once Upon a Week," *Queens Voice*, November 13, 1964, 14.

109. Marjorie Spiegel Dammann's Final Report, Team 5, NCNWP.

110. Ibid.

111. "WIMS Team #5 1964, Mississippi Review, Team 5 New York to Ruleville."

112. Schultz, *Going South*, 111–12; Height, *Open Wide the Freedom Gates*, 161–62, 193–94.

113. Kennedy, "Color Me Flo" original transcript, box 5, tape18, p. 1, FKP.

114. Height, *Open Wide the Freedom Gates*, 161.

115. For more information on Thelma Sanders and her other work in Woman Power Unlimited, see Morris, "Local Women and the Civil Rights Movement in Mississippi," 200.

116. Kennedy, "Color Me Flo" original transcript, box 5, tape 18, p. 1, FKP.

117. Tyson, *Radio Free Dixie*, 308. Also see Umoja, *We Will Shoot Back*.

118. Kennedy, "Color Me Flo" original transcript, box 5, tape 18, p. 1, FKP.

119. "WIMS Team #5 1964, Mississippi Review, Team 5 New York to Ruleville."

120. Ibid.

121. Ibid.

122. Ibid.

123. Ibid.

124. Ford, "Soul Generation," 24.

125. "WIMS Team #5 1964, Mississippi Review, Team 5 New York to Ruleville."

126. Dick Schaap, "Secret Project in Mississippi: Interracial Meetings of Women," *New York Herald and Tribune*, August 30, 1964; Height, *Open Wide the Freedom Gates*, 168; Sargent, *Civil Rights Revolution*, 98–99.

127. Marable, "Time for Another Freedom Summer."

128. Kennedy, "Once Upon a Week," *Queens Voice*, November 13, 1964, 14.

129. "Suggested Highlights from WLIB'S Public Service Programming," August 6, 1966, box 8, FKP.

130. Investigative Report, New York, New York, July 28, 1964, November 6, 1964, November 15, 1964, February 5, 1965, January 19, 1965, February 2, 1965, FRK/FBI.

131. Investigative Report, location unknown, January 19, 1965, New York, FRK/FBI, 24. The Workers World Party consistently supported many civil rights and Black Power organizations, especially the Black Panther Party.

132. Florynce R. Kennedy to Sir, February 21, 1960, box 12.5–12.6, PFK.

133. "Lady Lawyer Cries Police Brutality."

134. "Woman Attorney Requests $500,000 from New York."

135. *The People of the State of New York, Respondent, v. Florynce Kennedy, Appellant*, decided April 6, 1967.

136. "Lady Lawyer Cries Police Brutality."

137. Ibid.

138. Ibid.

139. Ibid.

140. Kennedy-Banks interview with author, October 16, 2004.

141. "Lady Lawyer Cries Police Brutality."

142. *The People of the State of New York, Respondent, v. Florynce Kennedy, Appellant.*

143. "Woman Attorney Requests $500,000 from New York."

144. Kennedy-Banks interview with author, October 16, 2004.

CHAPTER 5

1. Garrow, *Bearing the Cross*, 475–88; *Eyes on the Prize: America's Civil Rights Movement, 1964–1985*, episode "Power! (1966–68)."

2. James Meredith served in the U.S. Air Force and, after filing suit with the support of the NAACP, was the first black student to enroll in the University of Mississippi. At the time of the march, Meredith had earned a master's degree in political science in Nigeria and was a law student at Columbia. He was not killed by the gunman and recovered enough to rejoin the march when it ended in Jackson.

3. Garrow, *Bearing the Cross*, 476–77.

4. In 1964, the group that would become the Deacons for Defense and Justice formed in Jonesboro, Louisiana, to protect civil rights organizers against violence from the Ku Klux Klan and other white vigilantes. L. Hill, *Deacons for Defense*, 2.

5. "SNCC to Use March as a Vehicle for Power"; "Black Power Concept Hit by Roy Wilkins"; Handler, "Wilkins Says Black Power Leads Only to Black Death."

6. "Black Power Insurgent Disturbing."

7. "Powell Tells Howardites to Seek Audacious Power."

8. Although Floyd McKissick, the executive director of CORE, was not present, he was also announced as one of the lead conference organizers. B. Washington, "Leaders to Build Up Black Power Concept."

9. Ibid.

10. Lardner, "Black Power Still Undefined after Meeting."

11. Morris, "Powell Confers on 'Black Power.'"

12. Ibid.; Lardner, "Black Power Still Undefined after Meeting." Carmichael and McKissick did not attend the planning meeting in Washington. Reports conflict as to why

they failed to attend. Powell explained to reporters that they were busy doing fundraising and organizing meetings. The US Organization was formed in Los Angeles after the Watts uprising. At the time of the Black Power Conference, Karenga was working on a Ph.D. in African linguistics at UCLA. In 1966, the US Organization and Karenga created the Kwanzaa holiday as an alternative to Christmas. Brown, *Fighting for US*, vii, 69–70.

13. Quoted in "The Sexes: Blacks v. Feminists."

14. McDuffie, *Sojourning for Freedom*, 93.

15. Kennedy interview with Jacqueline Ceballos.

16. Roth, *Separate Roads to Feminism*, 83–85; Echols, *Daring to Be Bad*, 49–50.

17. Ward, "Third World Women's Alliance"; White, *Dark Continent of Our Bodies*; Countryman, *Up South*, 258–94; Thompson, *Promise and a Way of Life*; Valk, *Radical Sisters*.

18. "Suggested Highlights from WLIB's Public Service Programing," *WLIB: Harlem Radio Center Newsletter*, August 6, 1966, FKP.

19. Kennedy, *Color Me Flo*, 53.

20. Investigative Report, New York, New York, May 30, 1966, FRK/FBI; Crosby, "For Vietnam Withdrawal"; Douglas Robinson, "Women March Here to Protest the Vietnam War," *New York Times*, May 8, 1966, 2.

21. Kennedy, *Color Me Flo*, 53.

22. Ibid.

23. In 1959, James Haughton founded the American Negro Labor Council to help organize independent black workers to battle racism in the "house of labor, racism in the government, and in the industry." "James Haughton on the House of Labor," interview with Janine Jackson, 1999, History Matters, http://historymatters.gmu.edu/d/7038/, accessed October 29, 2014. The American Negro Labor Council disbanded in 1963, and in 1964 Haughton formed the Harlem Unemployment Center to challenge racial exclusion in the skilled, unionized building trades. In 1971, the center was renamed Fight Back. See Golland, *Constructing Affirmative Action*, 144.

24. In 1965 Dorothy Pitman (Hughes) produced the John Killens musical *Ballad of the Winter Soldier*, starring black actors Ossie Davis, Diahann Carroll, and Sidney Poitier. Proceeds from the play were donated to CORE. Pitman was also a leader in African Americans Against the Vietnam War and in the West Side Unified Action Council, an interracial group. Florence Rice was the founder of the Harlem Consumer Education Council and the Ladies Garment Workers Union. The Harlem Consumer Education Council helped educate low-income blacks and Latinos about their rights as consumers and conducted boycotts. Edna Slatkin was a garment industry trade union coordinator. In 1964 she was also part of a group of white parents from New York City called EQUAL, which held vigils and took out newspaper advertisements protesting segregated and unequal public schools. Harry Halsey was a shop steward in New York City's garment industry. Joan Hamilton of YAWF was also a member of the West Side Unified Action Council. "Here Is List of Vigil Keepers: Walking around the Clock in Racial Harmony!"; EQUAL advertisement, *New York Times*, June 19, 1964, L15.

25. Edna Slatkin and Harry Halsey to Trade Unionists and Friends, September 1966, box 126, folder 1548, PBF.

26. Neubeck and Cazenave, *Welfare Racism*, 129; Gilens, "How the Poor Became Black."

27. "Benton and Bowles' Liberal Front Sugar Coats Latent Racism," Media Workshop flier, box 126, folder 1548, PBF.

28. "Media Workshop Joins Powell Week Boycotts," press release, January 8, 1967 (date misprinted on flier as 1966), box 126, folder 1548, PBF.

29. Slatkin and Halsey to Trade Unionists, September 1966; Florynce Kennedy, "Once Upon a Week," *Queens Voice*, July 3, 1964.

30. "Media Workshop Joins Powell Week Boycotts."

31. "Negro Consumer: He Is Getting More Attention from Big National Advertisers," *Wall Street Journal*, June 30, 1961.

32. Meier and Rudwick, "Origins of Non-violent Direct Action in Afro-American Protest." Meier and Rudwick note that during the Depression, "Don't buy where you can't work" campaigns were formed in numerous northern and midwestern cities. Through organizations such as the Urban League, CORE, and the NAACP, blacks consistently used the consumer boycott as a way to gain employment. See Weiner, "Negro Picketing"; Weems, "African-American Consumer Boycotts"; and Sewell, "'Not-Buying Power' of the Black Community." For an excellent study of how black women on welfare understood their buying power as consumers, see Kornbluh, "Black Buying Power."

33. Flo Kennedy to Media Workshoppers, October 26, 1966, box 126, folder 1548, PBF.

34. Media Workshop Statement of Its Role, Objectives and Demands, box 126, folder 1548, PBF.

35. Slatkin and Halsey to Trade Unionists, September 1966; "Benton and Bowles' Liberal Front Sugar Coats Latent Racism"; Kennedy, *Color Me Flo*, 53.

36. Kennedy, *Color Me Flo*, 53.

37. "B&B Gets a Mickey Finn."

38. Slatkin and Halsey to Trade Unionists, September 1966; "Benton and Bowles' Liberal Front Sugar Coats Latent Racism."

39. Allen, *Speaking of Soap Operas*. General Foods was a conglomerate that owned such popular products as Kellogg's Corn Flakes, Jell-O, and Birds Eye frozen foods. The merger of the Philip Morris Tobacco Company and Kraft with General Foods came later, but Benton and Bowles was already Kraft's ad agency. Shepherd Meade, who wrote the best-selling self-help manual *How to Succeed in Business without Really Trying: The Dastard's Guide to Fame and Fortune* (1952), was one of its vice presidents. Its cofounder, Chester Bowles, was the head of Franklin Delano Roosevelt's wartime price administration board and served as secretary of state under John F. Kennedy. So this agency was not only financially successful but also politically important. For more details, see "Benton and Bowles," *Advertising Age*, September 15, 2003.

40. Slatkin and Halsey to Trade Unionists, September 1966.

41. Kennedy, *Color Me Flo*, 53.

42. Consumer Education Council flier, date unknown, unorganized Florence Rice Papers, Schomburg Center for Research in Black Culture, New York.

43. Slatkin and Halsey to Trade Unionists, September 1966.

44. Kennedy, *Color Me Flo*, 53.

45. George Palmer, "Tavern Topics," *New York Amsterdam News*, January 21, 1967, 19.

46. Flo Kennedy notes on article in *Advertising Age*, box 8, folder "Media Workshop, Black GIs," FKP; "B&B Gets a Mickey Finn."

47. Feehery, "Negro Has Precarious Foothold in Agency Field, 3 City Survey Shows"; "Negro Has Precarious Foothold in Agency Field, 3 City Survey Shows," Media Workshop flier, box 8, folder "Media Workshop, Black GIs," FKP. The Media Workshop flier is a reprint of the *Advertising Age* article with the Media Workshop's protest underlined and the group's name and Kennedy's address on the bottom of the page. Kennedy frequently redistributed noteworthy articles in this manner and labeled them organizing newsletters.

48. "Media Workshop Roundtable Proposal," box 126, folder 1548, PBF.

49. "B&B Gets a Mickey Finn." For a study of similar efforts to create and produce black alternative media during this period, see Heitner, *Black Power TV*.

50. Hamilton, *Adam Clayton Powell Jr.*, 33.

51. Douglas Martin, "Sam Gibbons, Democrat of Florida, Dies at 92," *New York Times*, October 10, 2012.

52. Hamilton, *Adam Clayton Powell Jr.*, 32.

53. Musgrove, *Rumors, Repression, and Racial Politics*, 28.

54. Ibid., 29.

55. Hamilton, *Adam Clayton Powell Jr.*, 420.

56. Kennedy, *Color Me Flo*, 61.

57. Flo Kennedy, telegram to Representative Sam Gibbons, September 18, 1966, box 126, folder 1548, PBF.

58. Musgrove, *Rumors, Repression, and Racial Politics*, 31.

59. Hamilton, *Adam Clayton Powell Jr.*, 233–35.

60. "Media Workshop Joins Powell Week Boycotts."

61. Bolton, *Counting-Out Rhymes of Children*, 105. Since the civil rights movement, an alternative version, "Catch a tiger by the toe," has been used instead.

62. "Media Workshop Joins Powell Week Boycotts." The S. Klein department store was known for its bargains and appealed to customers who were less affluent than Macy's customers. Its stores in Union Square in New York City and Newark, New Jersey, served many black consumers.

63. "Powell Bars Heading Black Power Talks."

64. Wright, *Let's Work Together*, 146.

65. For studies that demonstrate the longer history of Black Power, see Tyson, *Radio Free Dixie*; Theoharis and Woodard, *Freedom North*; and Countryman, *Up South*.

66. Caldwell, "Two Police Inspectors from Here among the Newark Delegates."

67. Ibid.

68. Kennedy, unorganized notes, FKP.

69. "WIMS Team #5 1964, Mississippi Review, Team 5 New York to Ruleville," transcript and audiotapes 001-S15-ss5-f18-S1, 001-S15-ss5-f18-S2, and 001-S15-ss5-f18-S3, NCNWP.

70. Kennedy, unorganized notes, FKP.

71. Baxandall and Gordon, *Dear Sisters*, 11.

72. Kennedy interview with Diane Abrams on the *Diane Abrams Show*; Kennedy interview with Jacqueline Ceballos, 10.

73. Jean Faust was an environmental aide to Congressman William F. Ryan; Cynthia Epstein was a graduate student at Columbia University; Ti-Grace Atkinson was a gradu-

ate student at Columbia; and Shepard Aronson was a doctor. While Friedan described herself in *The Feminine Mystique* and to the media as a typical housewife and mother, she had worked as a labor journalist during and after college. See Horowitz, *Betty Friedan*.

74. Carden, *New Feminist Movement*, 104.

75. "NOW First Meeting," Ti-Grace Atkinson's meeting notes, February 6, 1967, and NOW's statement of purpose. Other issues discussed at the first meeting included "divorce laws, equal employment opportunities, civil rights for women in the U.S. constitution—Set up committees—Image of women, Social Innovations, Employment, Finances," TGAP.

76. NOW's statement of purpose.

77. Epstein interview with author.

78. Kennedy interview with Jacqueline Ceballos.

79. Kennedy, *Color Me Flo*, 62.

80. Ibid.; *Making Policy, Not Coffee*, in author's possession.

81. Atkinson interview with author, October 21, 2013.

82. Ibid.; Kennedy, *Color Me Flo*, 62.

83. Kennedy, *Color Me Flo*, 62.

84. Atkinson interview with author, October 21, 2013.

85. "NOW Meeting attendance sheets," February–December 1967, NOW: NYC.

86. Atkinson interview with author, October 28, 2006; Brennan interview with author.

87. Swanteck, "Florynce Kennedy Says It Loud about Abortion, Church, Calley."

88. Atkinson interview with author, October 28, 2006.

89. Anselma Dell'Olio was a journalist. Kate Millet was an artist and graduate student at Columbia. Millet's dissertation critiqued the sexism and heterosexism of various popular male authors and was the basis for her popular 1970 book, *Sexual Politics*. Catharine Stimpson was a recent Ph.D. graduate from Columbia University.

90. NOW meeting attendance sheets, February–December 1967, NOW: NYC.

91. In the group's second year, Kennedy was elected to the advisory committee. Like the advisory committees of many organizations, however, it never met in any official capacity or held formal power in the decision-making process. Kennedy's name appeared alongside those of other notable women and men on some of NOW's publicity.

92. Muriel Fox to Betty Friedan, box 126, folder 1548, PBF.

93. Flo Kennedy with briefcase, photo, The Sixties Collection, 1969, Richard Avedon Foundation Archive, New York, New York; Brennan interview with author; Atkinson interview with author, May 15, 2009.

94. Stone, "National Conference on Black Power," 189.

95. Woodard, *Nation within a Nation*, 86.

96. Quoted from the National Black Power Conference pamphlet in Allen, *Black Awakening in Capitalist America*, 158.

97. Van Deburg, *New Day in Babylon*, 26.

98. Flo Kennedy, "Chicago's Black Power Conference," *Islamic Press International News Gram*, October 17, 1967, box 8, FKP. For other movements that were influenced by Black Power, see Ogbar, "Rainbow Radicalism"; and Thomas Blood McCreary, conversation with author, New York, New York, September 28, 2008.

99. Kennedy, "It's Damn Slick Out There," interview with Sohnya Sayres, 357.

100. Wright, *Let's Work Together*, 146. See also Rogers, "Angry Black Power Militants Seize Control of Conference"; and Holstrom, "'Black Power' Parley in Newark."

101. Kelley, *Freedom Dreams*, 199.

102. Atkinson interview with author, October 28, 2006. Peg Brennan was a feminist and antiwar activist who had attended some of the early NOW–New York chapter meetings.

103. Ibid.; Investigative Report, Newark, New Jersey, July 27, 1967, FRK/FBI.

104. Investigative Report, Newark, New Jersey, July 27, 1967, FRK/FBI.

105. Atkinson interview with author, October 28, 2006.

106. Ibid.

107. Ibid.; Brennan interview with author. Quotation from Ti-Grace Atkinson to author, July 23, 2007, in author's possession.

108. Bender, "Valeria Solanis [*sic*] a Heroine to Feminists."

109. Kennedy, "Color Me Flo" original transcript, box 5, tape 11, p. 13, FKP.

110. Woodard, *Nation within a Nation*, 84.

111. Ransby, *Ella Baker and the Black Freedom Movement*, 3; Kennedy, audiotape of interview for *Speaking for America*.

112. Kennedy, "It's Damn Slick Out There," interview with Sohnya Sayres, 352, 357; Woodard, *Nation within a Nation*, 196.

113. Mayeri, *Reasoning from Race*, 3–4.

114. Kennedy, unorganized notes, FKP.

115. Kennedy, audiotape of interview for *Speaking for America*.

116. "A Message for White Radicals," in *Reconstruction* (date unknown), reprinted in Kennedy, *Color Me Flo*, 58.

117. *Don't Mourn for Us . . . Organize. The Call of the National Conference for New Politics Organize*, pamphlet, National Conference for New Politics vertical file, Tamiment Library, New York University.

118. Maier, *Dr. Spock*, 285.

119. Atkinson interview with author, October 28, 2006.

120. Hall, "'On the Tail of the Panther,'" 65.

121. Forman, *Making of Black Revolutionaries*, 498; Investigative Report, Chicago, Illinois, September 31, 1967, FRK/FBI.

122. Broder, "Negroes Push Left to 'Genocide' Black."

123. Goodman, "Yessir, Boss, Said the White Radicals: When Blacks Run the New Left"; Wechsler, "No Winners."

124. Bloom and Martin, *Black against Empire*, 86–87; Hayden, *Rebellion in Newark*.

125. Kennedy, "Chicago's Black Power Conference."

126. "National Conference for New Politics Final Resolutions," 11, National Conference for New Politics vertical file, New York University, Tamiment Library.

127. Echols, *Daring to Be Bad*, 48.

128. Ibid., 47–48.

129. "National Conference for New Politics Final Resolutions," 22–23.

130. Echols, *Daring to Be Bad*, 49.

131. Ibid.; Evans, *Personal Politics*, 198–99.

132. Atkinson, *Amazon Odyssey*, 97–98. Atkinson credits their statement with forc-

ing the creation of the Women's Workshop. Her description conflicts with the NCNP's printed resolutions, which detail how the Women's Workshop was planned before the convention started. See "National Conference for New Politics Final Resolutions."

133. Atkinson interview with author, October 28, 2006.

134. Ibid.; Brennan interview with author.

135. Atkinson interview with author, October 28, 2006.

136. Florynce Kennedy and Ti-Grace Atkinson to New Politics Women, September 1967, box 5, folder 3, NOW: NYC.

137. Ibid.

138. Ibid.

139. Kelley, *Freedom Dreams*, 137.

140. Atkinson interview with author, October 28, 2006.

141. Ibid.; Berger, *Outlaws of America*, 95.

142. In the early twentieth century, Amy Jacques Garvey maneuvered between black nationalism and feminism. See U. Taylor, "'Negro Women Are Great Thinkers as Well as Doers.'"

CHAPTER 6

1. Florynce Kennedy and Ti-Grace Atkinson to New Politics Women, September 1967, box 5, folder 3, NOW: NYC.

2. "Women and Black Power," flier, box 5, folder 13, NOW: NYC.

3. NOW New York City chapter meeting minutes (handwritten), November 11, 1967, and general meeting minutes (typed), November 21, 1967, box 5, folder 13, NOW: NYC.

4. "Women and Black Power" flier; NOW New York City chapter meeting minutes (handwritten), November 11, 1967, and general meeting minutes (typed), November 21, 1967. There was a temporary secretary at the time these notes were taken.

5. Atkinson interview with author, May 15, 2009.

6. Ibid.

7. Ibid.

8. Although women in factories had worn pants since World War I, policies against women wearing pants in many corporate workplaces existed until the 1970s. Hill, *As Seen in Vogue*, 108; Joselit, *Perfect Fit*, 195. Member of Congress and lawyer Yvonne Braithwaite-Burke describes how NOW member Shirley Chisholm wore very neat skirt suits and did not wear pants in her personal or professional life. Yvonne Braithwaite-Burke Oral History, Shirley Chisholm Project: Brooklyn Women's Activism from 1945 to the Present, Brooklyn College of the City University of New York, Brooklyn, New York, http://chisholmproject.com/scp/yvonne-brathwaite-burke; Atkinson interview with author, May 15, 2009.

9. Fahs, "Ti-Grace Atkinson and the Legacy of Radical Feminism," 569.

10. Dell'Olio interview with author; Fahs, "Ti-Grace Atkinson and the Legacy of Radical Feminism," 569.

11. Wyatt, "25G Bail Keeps Brown in Clink"; P. Levy, *Civil War on Race Street*, 139.

12. P. Levy, *Civil War on Race Street*, 139–41.

13. H. Rap Brown, "Speech," Cambridge, Maryland, July 24, 1967, quoted in ibid., 140.

For Brown's description of the events that transpired in Cambridge, see Al-Amin, *Die Nigger Die!*, 99–104.

14. Excerpts from the unpublished report "An Analysis of the Cambridge, Maryland Disturbance," box 7, folder "Cambridge Maryland Report," FKP.

15. Ibid.

16. Wyatt, "25G Bail Keeps Brown in Clink."

17. Investigative Report, New York, New York, August 29, 1967, FRK/FBI.

18. Lefcourt interview with author, July 5, 2011. Carol Lefcourt, Gerald's sister-in-law, was a friend of Kennedy's and introduced the two. At their first meeting he confided in Flo about the challenges he was facing at the New York Legal Aid Society. He had recently been fired by Legal Aid for attempting to unionize other lawyers and was profoundly discouraged with the profession. When he worked for Legal Aid as a law student and then as a first-year attorney, Gerald was appalled that lawyers had "no training" and an "incredible case load" and were tasked with the responsibility of defending poor people on serious charges. He hoped that unionizing the lawyers would improve their training, reduce their caseload, and ultimately improve the representation poor people received. Not long after the group began to meet, Lefcourt stated that the Legal Aid administrators learned of their plan and fired him. In 1968, Lefcourt explained to the *New York Times* that he was fired also because he allegedly said, "The way society treats its black criminal clients foments riots." During their talk, Kennedy pushed him to continue practicing law and organizing and congratulated him on attempting to change the accepted legal process: "You are going to be the best lawyer in the country" because "you refuse to consent to oppression." She promised to introduce him to H. Rap Brown's other defense attorney, Bill Kunstler. Kunstler filed a lawsuit against Legal Aid for firing Lefcourt. See also Sidney E. Zion, "Lawyer Sues Legal Aid Society over Loss of Job," *New York Times*, July 9, 1968.

19. Kennedy, unorganized notes, FKP.

20. Investigative Report, New York, New York, December 12, 1967, FRK/FBI.

21. "Officials Say They Lack Authority to Drop Charges," reprinted in Kennedy, *Color Me Flo*, 60.

22. Ibid.

23. Kennedy, *Color Me Flo*, 61.

24. Bob Fass is better known for giving airtime to new musicians, countercultural figures, and the Yippies.

25. "CORE Pair Arrested on Gun Charges," box 10, folder "Newspaper Clips," FKP.

26. Flo Kennedy, "Politics of Oppression," unpublished book manuscript, FKP.

27. Brennan interview with author; Atkinson interview with author, October 28, 2006.

28. Fahs, *Valerie Solanas*.

29. Valerie Solanas, "SCUM Manifesto," box 8, FKP.

30. "Ti-Grace Atkinson Press Conference Statement on Behalf of Valerie Solanas," June 13, 1968, box 8, FKP.

31. Echols, *Daring to be Bad*, 104–5.

32. "Warhol Suspect Loses 'Cool'"; "Suspect Says Warhol Tried to Block Play."

33. "Warhol Assailant Is Committed in N.Y."; "Ti-Grace Atkinson Press Conference Statement on Behalf of Valerie Solanas."

34. Fahs, *Valerie Solanas*.

35. "Suspect Says Warhol Tried to Block Play"; Solanas, *SCUM Manifesto*, 49.

36. Kennedy and Atkinson audiotaped interview with Kay Lindsey.

37. *The People of the State of New York v. Valerie Solanas*, box 8, FKP.

38. "Martyrization of Valerie Solanas."

39. "Suspect Says Warhol Tried to Block Play."

40. Ibid.

41. Ibid. Jean Genet was psychologically unstable and was convicted of minor crimes (including a homosexual act) in his youth, but he became a writer and supported oppressed peoples, especially the black liberation movement. Genet never shot anyone. Others thought of Solanas as more similar to Charlotte Corday, the French revolutionary who killed Jean-Paul Marat.

42. Ibid.; "Ti-Grace Atkinson Press Conference Statement on Behalf of Valerie Solanas."

43. Atkinson interview with author, October 28, 2006.

44. Ibid.

45. Kennedy, "Women Lawyers and the System of Oppression," 261.

46. Fahs, "Ti-Grace Atkinson and the Legacy of Radical Feminism," 577.

47. Bender, "Valeria Solanis [*sic*] a Heroine to Feminists."

48. Ibid.

49. "Martyrization of Valerie Solanas."

50. Ibid.

51. Fahs, "Ti-Grace Atkinson and the Legacy of Radical Feminism," 580.

52. Dunbar-Ortiz, *Outlaw Woman*, 119.

53. Ibid.

54. "Martyrization of Valerie Solanas," 20; Bender, "Valeria Solanis [*sic*] a Heroine to Feminists."

55. Dunbar-Ortiz, *Outlaw Woman*, 136–37, 156.

56. Fahs, "Ti-Grace Atkinson and the Legacy of Radical Feminism," 570.

57. Aileen C. Hernandez correspondence to feminists, December 26, 2000, in "Memories Flo Kennedy," FKP; Jacqui Ceballos correspondence to feminists, January 3, 2001, in ibid. Ceballos states that the people who passed through Kennedy's apartment were considered part of Kennedy's extended family.

58. Echols, *Daring to be Bad*, 158.

59. Baxandall and Gordon, *Dear Sisters*, 12.

60. Atkinson, *Amazon Odyssey*, 97; Baxandall and Gordon, *Dear Sisters*, 12.

61. Baxandall and Gordon, *Dear Sisters*, 12; Kelley, *Freedom Dreams*, 139.

62. Kennedy, Brooks, Smart-Grosvenor, and Norton, "Role of the Black Woman in America," audiotape. Also see R. Morgan, *Sisterhood Is Powerful*, 499. Kennedy continued to repeat her forecast that the feminist movement would "rival black and student struggles very soon." "Testimony of Miss Florynce R. Kennedy (to the Commission on Party Structure)," May 3, 1969, box 9, FKP.

63. Florynce Kennedy, Memorandum to the Officialdom of NOW: National and New York, November 18, 1968, box 7, folder 12, Dolores Alexander, Papers of NOW Officers,

Arthur and Elizabeth Schlesinger Library on the History of Women in America, Radcliffe Institute for Advanced Study, Harvard University, Cambridge, Mass.; Friedan, *It Changed My Life*, 109.

64. Betty Friedan telegram to Florynce Kennedy, date illegible, TGAP.

65. Friedan, *It Changed My Life*, 191.

66. Ibid., 108.

67. Ibid.

68. Atkinson reaffirmed this position in a 2011 interview with Breanne Fahs. See Fahs, "Ti-Grace Atkinson and the Legacy of Radical Feminism," 577.

69. "Martyrization of Valerie Solanas."

70. Ibid.

71. Atkinson and Kennedy audiotaped interview with Kay Lindsey.

72. Grant, *Confrontation on Campus*.

73. Investigative Report, New York, New York, March 20, 1968, April 28, 1968, FRK/FBI.

74. Bender, "Valeria Solanis [*sic*] a Heroine to Feminists."

75. Newton, Hilliard, and Weise, *Huey P. Newton Reader*, 129.

76. Kennedy referred to Black Power leaders who "inspire . . . confidence" and insisted that women would "gravitate toward groups dedicated to change 'by any means necessary.'" "Testimony of Miss Florynce R. Kennedy (to the Commission on Party Structure)."

77. Atkinson interview with author, October 28, 2006.

78. Ibid.

79. This argument also kept the door open for the later feminist defense of women who murdered an abusive husband or prison guard. See Thuma, "'Not a Wedge, But a Bridge.'"

CHAPTER 7

1. Kennedy interview with Marcia Cohen, 3.

2. Friedan, *It Changed My Life*, 109; Atkinson interview with author, May 15, 2009; Brennan interview with author.

3. Title VII of the Civil Rights Act of 1964 states: "It shall be an unlawful employment practice for an employer to fail or refuse to hire or to discharge any individual, or otherwise to discriminate against any individual with respect to his compensation, terms, conditions, or privileges of employment, because of such individual's race, color, religion, *sex*, or national origin"; quoted in Friedan, *It Changed My Life*, 104–5.

4. "Help Picket Colgate-Palmolive: Fight Sex Discrimination in Employment," flier, September 1968, box 4, folder 3, NOW: NYC.

5. Hammel, "Class of Fledgling Pickets Gets the Word"; "Don't Pay to Perpetuate Job Discrimination: Boycott Colgate-Palmolive Products," flier, box 6, FKP.

6. Kennedy, "Color Me Flo" original transcript, box 5, tape 21, p. 6, FKP.

7. Abby Karp, "Flo Kennedy," *Baltimore Sun*, February 14, 1988.

8. Kennedy interview with Jacqueline Ceballos.

9. "Old Black Flo," episode of *60 Minutes*.

10. Kennedy interview in *The First Time*, 144.

11. Karpel, "Not Much Cream in Their Coffee."

12. Dreifus, *Radical Lifestyles*, 104.

13. Arnold, *Fashion, Desire and Anxiety*, 122.

14. Hammel, "Class of Fledgling Pickets Gets the Word."

15. Ibid.

16. Kennedy, *Color Me Flo*, 54.

17. Ibid.; Betty Friedan speaking in "Old Black Flo," episode of *60 Minutes*.

18. Hammel, "Class of Fledgling Pickets Gets the Word."

19. Abrahams, "Will the Housewife Become a Picketer?"

20. Flo Kennedy, Songbook folder, box 4, FKP.

21. "Old Black Flo," episode of *60 Minutes*; Hanisch interview with author.

22. "Old Black Flo," episode of *60 Minutes*. Kennedy also cited Richard Nixon's frequent use of profanity. Nixon's vulgarity in response to anyone he considered an enemy was made public during the Watergate scandal. Robert Kennedy leaked accounts of Lyndon Johnson's use of profanity to *Newsweek* during Johnson's presidency. See Shesol, *Mutual Contempt*, 368; and Dean, *Nixon Defense*.

23. Kennedy, "Women Lawyers and the System of Oppression," 261.

24. Tai, "Miss America Pageant Chosen as the Latest Target of Protestors."

25. Hanisch interview with author; Kennedy interview with Marcia Cohen, 4.

26. Echols, *Daring to Be Bad*, 93.

27. Morgan, *Sisterhood Is Powerful*, 585.

28. Kennedy, *Color Me Flo*, 62; Hanisch, "Two Letters from the Women's Liberation Movement," 199.

29. Kennedy interview with Marcia Cohen.

30. Ibid.; Flo Kennedy, "Color Me Flo" original transcript, box 5, tape 21, p. 9, FKP.

31. Excerpt from New York Radical Women, "No More Miss America," 184.

32. Hanisch, "Two Letters from the Women's Liberation Movement," 199.

33. Kennedy interview with Barbara Cady.

34. Hanisch interview with author; Cellabos interview with author.

35. Hanisch interview with author.

36. Hanisch, "Two Letters from the Women's Liberation Movement," 199.

37. *Voice of the Women's Liberation Movement* newsletter for October 1968, p. 5, CWLU Herstory Archive, https://www.uic.edu/orgs/cwluherstory/CWLUArchive/voices/voices 4–5.html; Love, *Feminists Who Changed America*.

38. Millet, *Flying*, 60.

39. Cindy [Cisler] to Ti-Grace Atkinson, August 30, 1968, TGAP.

40. Black Power Conference press release, FKP. As a result, newspapers, magazines, and television networks were pushed to promote (usually white) women from the women's section or to hire black (typically male) journalists for the first time.

41. R. Morgan, *Saturday's Child*, 260.

42. Excerpt from New York Radical Women, "No More Miss America," 184.

43. Kennedy, "Color Me Flo" original transcript, box 5, tape 21, p. 8, FKP.

44. Hanisch interview with author; Kennedy, "Color Me Flo" original transcript, box 5, tape 21, p. 8, FKP.

45. Bradley, *Mass Media and the Shaping of American Feminism*, 72. For a newspaper article that mentions racist beauty standards of the pageant, see "Trash Can of Freedom."

46. Carlton, "Girl Next Door Turned Radical"; Tai, "Miss America Pageant Chosen as the Latest Target of Protestors"; Lear, "What Do These Women Want?"

47. Shirley Chisholm, a black feminist and member of NOW, was also at the meeting and gave a speech. Yet the media failed to mention her talk and her active participation in the gathering. "Women Rights Group Banned from Overseas Press Club," NOW New York chapter press release, box 12, FKP.

48. Bradley, *Mass Media and the Shaping of American Feminism*, 72.

49. Ibid., 61.

50. Friedan, *It Changed My Life*, 139.

51. Ibid., 108.

52. Atkinson, *Amazon Odyssey*, 10; "'Young, Black and Beautiful' Organize."

53. Friedan, *It Changed My Life*, 109.

54. Ransby, *Ella Baker and the Black Freedom Movement*, 309–10.

55. Atkinson interview with author, October 28, 2006.

56. Atkinson, *Amazon Odyssey*, 9.

57. Atkinson interview with author, October 28, 2006.

58. Ibid.; Kennedy, Memorandum to the Officialdom of NOW: National and New York.

59. Kennedy, Memorandum to the Officialdom of NOW: National and New York.

60. Cellabos interview with author.

61. Atkinson, *Amazon Odyssey*, 10.

62. Atkinson interview with author, October 28, 2006. At that time, Atkinson purposely misled reporters and described how she left with dissident members of NOW, stating that the new October 17th Movement had fifty members, "including Columbia students." Elizabeth Shelton, "Women's Group Split over the Meaning of Feminism: Feminist Leaders Divide," *Washington Post*, October 24, 1968, B1. By 1971, Atkinson admitted that she left NOW almost alone. See Ti-Grace Atkinson, "Self-Deception," August 6, 1971, in *Amazon Odyssey*, 213; and Echols, *Daring to be Bad*, 169–70.

63. Atkinson interview with author, October 28, 2006.

64. Kennedy, *Color Me Flo*, 62.

65. Ibid.

66. Kennedy, Memorandum to the Officialdom of NOW: National and New York.

67. Atkinson, *Amazon Odyssey*, 10; Shelton, "Women's Group Split over Meaning of Feminism"; Echols, *Daring to be Bad*, 168–69.

68. "October 17 Movement Bi-Weekly Meeting Schedule," box 7, FKP. For more information on the black feminist radio programs that Kay Lindsey produced, see Pacifica Radio Archives, North Hollywood, California.

69. "October 17 Movement Bi-Weekly Meeting Schedule."

70. "'Young, Black and Beautiful' Organize"; Shelton, "Women's Group Split over the Meaning of Feminism."

71. Echols, *Daring to Be Bad*, 169–70; "October 17 Movement Bi-Weekly Meeting Schedule"; Allyn, *Make Love, Not War*, 264.

72. Atkinson interview with author, May 15, 2009.

73. Pamela Kearon, "Man-hating" position paper in The Feminists vertical file, Tamiment Library, New York University, New York.

74. Atkinson's quote is from Atkinson, *Amazon Odyssey*, 90; Karenga's quote is from Woodard, *Nation within a Nation*, 86.

75. Atkinson and Kennedy audiotaped interview with Kay Lindsey.

76. Atkinson interview with author, May 15, 2009.

77. Kennedy interview with Marcia Cohen.

78. Atkinson interview with author, October 28, 2006.

79. "The Feminist Meeting Minutes," TGAP. Lindsey's name does not appear in meeting minutes of The Feminists. Echols, *Daring to be Bad*, 169.

80. Atkinson interview with author, May 15, 2009.

81. Rosen, *The World Split Open*; Echols, *Daring to Be Bad*, 167–70.

CHAPTER 8

1. Schulder and Kennedy, *Abortion Rap*, 4–5.

2. Ibid.

3. J. Nelson, *Women of Color*, 39.

4. Stearns interview with author.

5. Staggenborg, *Pro-Choice Movement*; Solinger, *Abortion Wars*; Ehrenreich, *Reproductive Rights Reader*; Breines, *The Trouble between Us*; Rosen, *The World Split Open*; Evans, *Tidal Wave*; Ruth Rosen, "Refugees of the Fifties," keynote address at the conference "A New Insurgency: The Port Huron Statement in Its Time and Ours," University of Michigan, Ann Arbor, October 31, 2012.

6. Bhattacharjee and Silliman, *Policing the National Body*; Nelson, *Women of Color*; Silliman, Fried, Ross, and Gutiérrez, *Undivided Rights*; Incite! Women of Color against Violence, *Color of Violence*; Knudsen, *Reproductive Rights in a Global Context*; Wheeler, *How Sex Became a Civil Liberty*; Kluchin, *Fit to be Tied*. Although Nelson, *Women of Color*, gives an account of Kennedy's involvement as a lawyer in the case, how Kennedy shaped the legal and political campaign is not central to Nelson's argument or analysis.

7. Gordon, *Woman's Body, Woman's Right*; Staggenborg, *The Pro-Choice Movement*; Solinger, *Abortion Wars*; Nelson, *Women of Color*; Ehrenreich, *The Reproductive Rights Reader*.

8. Nelson, *Women of Color*, 3.

9. Abrams interview with author.

10. See Mayeri, *Reasoning from Race*, for a study of ways the legal arguments of the civil rights movement informed those of the feminist movement.

11. Florynce Rae Kennedy, FBI File 0977697. For information on Kennedy's support of H. Rap Brown, see Investigative Report, New York, New York, March 20, 1967, August 20–August 22, 1967, August 29, 1969, FRK/FBI. See also "Don't Let H. Rap Brown Down" flier, box 13, folder "H. Rap Brown," FKP.

12. Wyatt, "25G Bail Keeps Brown in Clink"; "Officials Say They Lack Authority to Drop Charges," reprinted in Kennedy, *Color Me Flo*, 60; "CORE Pair Arrested on Gun Charges," box 10, folder "Newspaper Clips," FKP; Investigative Report, New York, New York, August 29, 1967, FRK/FBI.

13. Asbury, "Women Break up Abortion Hearing"; *From Danger to Dignity: The Fight for Safe Abortion*. Sutton's law would have merely codified a procedure hospitals were

already allowing. For example, women who threatened to kill themselves were often allowed abortions, even if the threats were pro forma.

14. Chisholm, *Unbought and Unbossed*, 113–15.

15. From 1967 to 1969, NOW focused primarily on reform and did not make legalized abortion its primary goal. Certain NOW members, however, were involved in the movement to decriminalize abortion and actively pushed NOW in a more expansive direction. Atkinson interview with author, October 28, 2006.

16. Asbury, "Women Break up Abortion Hearing."

17. Ibid.

18. Ibid.

19. Schulder and Kennedy, *Abortion Rap*, 92.

20. Solinger, *Abortion Wars*, 43; Bird, "Women and Doctors Sue to Upset Abortion Laws."

21. Schulder and Kennedy, *Abortion Rap*, 4.

22. Abrams interview with author.

23. Ibid.; Kennedy and Schulder, *Abortion Rap*, 95.

24. Stearns interview with author.

25. The lawyers' years of graduation were as follows: Ann Garfinkle, 1968; Nancy Stearns, 1967; Carol Lefcourt, 1967; Diane Schulder, 1965; Florynce Kennedy, 1951.

26. As one of the first steps in the case, the team contacted Gerald Lefcourt. In 1969, Lefcourt filed a suit on behalf of journalist Paul Krassner. Krassner was being forced by the district attorney to identify the unnamed abortionists mentioned in his article for the *Realist*. As a legal maneuver, Lefcourt brought a case against the state of New York challenging the constitutionality of New York abortion laws. Lefcourt admits to being unprepared to handle a large legal battle on the issue and was simply "trying to tie the hands of the court" so that his client would not have to go before the court. His legal maneuvering worked, and when the women's legal team approached him for his help with their case he was more than happy to hand over all of his work. Although most accounts of the *Abramowicz v. Lefkowitz* case fail to mention Lefcourt's early work, Kennedy frequently praised her mentee for "doing much of the original work on the suit." She believed that both male and female movement lawyers should be organizing on various fronts to dismantle oppression and wanted Lefcourt to be publicly recognized for "stepping aside gracefully . . . in deference to the feminist movement" and the all-women legal team that would continue to argue the case. Lefcourt interview with author, May 24, 2012; Bird, "Women and Doctors Sue to Upset Abortion Laws."

27. Abrams interview with author; Shakur interview with author, October 6, 2009.

28. Atkinson interview with author, October 28, 2006. Feminist Ti-Grace Atkinson was a plaintiff in the case.

29. Schulder and Kennedy, *Abortion Rap*, 100.

30. Stearns interview with author.

31. Schulder and Kennedy, *Abortion Rap*, 35.

32. The plaintiffs' names were changed in *Abortion Rap*.

33. Schulder and Kennedy, *Abortion Rap*, 32–35. Please note that I am taking excerpts from a passage that was already condensed from the original. The defense attorneys' names are listed in *Abortion Rap*.

34. Lefcourt, *Law against the People*; Langum, *William M. Kunstler*, 161, 175.

35. The Reminiscences of Bruce Bailey, November 17, 1987, in the Columbia University Center for Oral History, Butler Library, Columbia University, New York, New York; Lefcourt interview with author, July 5, 2011.

36. Florynce Kennedy, "Whorehouse Theory of Law"; Lefcourt interview with author, July 5, 2011. Kennedy's ideas predate similar theories advocated by the critical legal studies movement and the critical race theory movement. Kimberle Crenshaw, a critical race theory scholar and black feminist, was central in formulating the term "intersectionality."

37. Quoted in Lichtenstein, "Abortion Laws Opposed at Rally."

38. For a discussion of the Catholic Church's effort to translate Catholic doctrine on sexuality into law, see Miller, *Good Catholic*.

39. Kennedy, *Color Me Flo*, 65. African American organizations such as the Urban League had used consumer boycotts in campaigns against employment discrimination.

40. Kennedy, unorganized notes, FKP; Steinem, "Verbal Karate of Florynce R. Kennedy, Esq."; Hobbs, "If Men Could Get Pregnant, Abortion Would Be a Sacrament," 20.

41. Kennedy, *Color Me Flo*, 64.

42. Dreifus, *Seizing Our Bodies*, 321.

43. Abrams interview with author; J. Nelson, *Women of Color*, 45.

44. Schulder and Kennedy, *Abortion Rap*, xv.

45. The Feminist Party filed this lawsuit under Kennedy's direction. See "Complaint Re: Archdiocese of New York Terence Cardinal Cooke Birthright Knights of Columbus," box 10, FKP; "Stop Tax Exempt Status of Anti-Abortion Lobby Groups" petition, May 1971, box 10, FKP.

46. Flo Kennedy, "Color Me Flo" original transcript, box 5, tape 16, p. 12, FKP.

47. Black nationalists did not typically seek to engage the state in limiting birth control, so this was not a political campaign they waged in the same sense as the Catholic Church did.

48. Spencer and Wollman, *Nationalism*, 52.

49. Kennedy interview with Marcia Cohen.

50. Ross, "Abortion," 275.

51. Schulder and Kennedy, *Abortion Rap*, 97.

52. Kennedy, "Black Genocide," box 6, FKP.

53. Rice interview with author.

54. Baumgardner, *Abortion and Life*, 76–77.

55. Rice interview with author.

56. Schulder and Kennedy, *Abortion Rap*, 156. Several decades later, at the age of eighty-nine and after she had retired from domestic work, Rice publicly detailed her experience with illegal abortions in an interview published in Baumgardner, *Abortion and Life*. Rice also posed for a picture wearing a T-shirt that read "I had an abortion."

57. See Beale [*sic*], "Double Jeopardy"; Bambara, "The Pill"; Lindsey, "Poem"; and The Damned, *Lessons from the Damned*.

58. Chisholm, *Unbought and Unbossed*, 113–22; Florynce Kennedy interview with author.

59. Chisholm, *Unbought and Unbossed*, 114–15.

60. Schulder and Kennedy, *Abortion Rap*, xi.

61. "Young Lords Party Position Paper on Women"; Hernandez, "Denise Oliver and the Young Lords Party."

62. Lopez, *Matters of Choice*, 13–14.

63. Kennedy, Brooks, Smart-Grosvenor, and Norton, "Role of the Black Woman in America," audiotape.

64. Dietz, "Ultimate Question."

65. Kennedy worked with the Black Panther Party, leading fund-raisers and protests in defense of Angela Davis, the Panther 21, Fred Hampton, and Mark Clark. She also worked with broad-based alliances such as the Emergency Conference to Defend the Right of Black Panthers to Exist, the Westside Committee to Defend the Panthers, and the Emergency Fall Campaign for Angela Davis. Most of her participation was recorded by the FBI. See various Investigative Reports, FRK/FBI; and Shakur interview with author, December 29, 2009.

66. Hyson, "New York City Passed Abortion Law Effective July 1, 1970."

67. Ibid.

68. Schulder and Kennedy, *Abortion Rap*, 154; Wright, *Let's Work Together*; Wright, "Black Power vs. Black Genocide," 47.

69. Schulder and Kennedy, *Abortion Rap*, 161.

70. Rousseau, *Black Woman's Burden*, 110, 141; Schoen, *Choice and Coercion*.

71. Marjorie Spiegel Dammann's Final Report, Team 5, NCNWP.

72. Gardella, "Eugenic Sterilization in America and North Carolina," 108.

73. Schulder and Kennedy, *Abortion Rap*, 161.

74. Ibid., 160.

75. Ross, "Abortion," 156.

76. Chisholm, *Unbought and Unbossed*, 122; Beale [sic], "Double Jeopardy," 93–99.

77. Kennedy, *Color Me Flo*, 160.

78. U.S. Department of Labor Office of Policy Planning and Research, *The Negro Family*, chap. 4.

79. Ibid.

80. Kennedy, Brooks, Smart-Grosvenor, and Norton, "Role of the Black Woman in America," audiotape.

81. Ibid.

82. Ibid.

83. Ibid. For a recent historical assessment of this opinion about the impact of oral contraceptives, see May, *America and the Pill*.

84. Kennedy, Brooks, Smart-Grosvenor, and Norton, "Role of the Black Woman in America," audiotape.

85. Ibid.

86. Ibid. Quotation in Kennedy, "Women's Role in American Society," 88–89.

87. Kennedy, Brooks, Smart-Grosvenor, and Norton, "Role of the Black Woman in America," audiotape.

88. Ibid.

89. Kennedy, unorganized notes, FKP.

CHAPTER 9

1. "Black Expo Is a Smashing Success"; "Ms. Chisholm Says Support Is Growing."

2. *Chisholm '72: Unbought & Unbossed.*

3. "What Chisholm's Candidacy Means."

4. Florynce Kennedy interview with author, January 10, 1999.

5. McClory, "Shirley Chisholm."

6. Investigative Report, File 0977697, Pittsburgh, Pennsylvania, November 20, 1970, FRK/FBI; Boycott Holiday Buying flier, box 11, folder "Media Workshop: Boycott Holiday Buying until Beautiful Angela Davis . . . Is Free," FKP.

7. "Chisholm: Catalyst for Change."

8. "Other Voices, Other Views," *Encore* 24 (Spring 1972).

9. Swanteck, "Florynce Kennedy Says It Loud about Abortion, Church, Calley."

10. Irene Davall and Susan Margolis, Feminist Party organizers, collection of Flo quotes, box 7, FKP.

11. Rene Brown to Flo Kennedy, September 24, 1970, box 5, FKP.

12. Kennedy, unorganized notes, FKP.

13. After Chisholm officially announced her candidacy, many local and regional NOW chapters endorsed her. The National Welfare Rights Organization also endorsed her candidacy.

14. Kennedy interview with Marcia Cohen.

15. Ibid.

16. Steinem and Kennedy, "Steinem and Kennedy," audiotape of lecture.

17. Lowitt, *Fred Harris*, 140.

18. Quoted in ibid., 15.

19. Chisholm, *Good Fight*, 23.

20. Gittelson, "No Business Like Lecture Business."

21. Kennedy, unorganized notes, FKP.

22. Lefcourt interview with author, May 24, 2012.

23. Ibid.

24. The 1966 Black Panther Party Platform and Program, reprinted in Murch, *Living for the City*, 128–29.

25. Ibid., 131–36, 146–48.

26. Langum, *William M. Kunstler*, 79.

27. Investigative Report, Pittsburgh, Pennsylvania, November 20, 1970, FRK/FBI; Boycott Holiday Buying flier.

28. Investigative Report, New York, New York, July 15, 1969, FRK/FBI.

29. Bloom and Martin, *Black against Empire*, 214. While the Panther 21 were eventually acquitted, it took two years of trials for most of the Panthers to be released. This severely damaged the New York Panther Party chapter.

30. Investigative Report, New York, New York, February 26, 1970, FRK/FBI; Wu, *Radicals in the Road*, 126.

31. Shakur interview with author, October 6, 2009.

32. Ibid.

33. Investigative Report, Pittsburgh, Pennsylvania, November 20, 1970, FRK/FBI.

34. Boycott Holiday Buying flier.

35. Ibid.

36. Ibid.

37. Pickney, *Red, Black, and Green*, 104.

38. Ward, "Third World Women's Alliance," 141–42.

39. "Shirley Demands Bail for Angela Davis."

40. Investigative Report, unknown location, February 9, 1971, FRK/FBI. In 1967, Kennedy was also involved in a picket of the FBI office to "serve notice on the FBI and the government that we will not tolerate intimidation and suppression of legitimate dissent." Investigative Report, New York, New York, October 31, 1967, FRK/FBI.

41. Gloria Steinem to author, July 29, 2012, in author's possession.

42. Hughes interview with author.

43. Kennedy interview with Marcia Cohen.

44. Steinem, *Outrageous Acts and Everyday Rebellions*, 385.

45. "List of Flo Kennedy's Speaking Engagements," FKP; Kennedy interview with Marcia Cohen.

46. Steinem and Kennedy, "Steinem and Kennedy," audiotape of lecture.

47. Kennedy, "It's Damn Slick Out There," interview with Sohnya Sayres, 351.

48. "Florynce Kennedy Talks at Michigan State University," audiotape of lecture.

49. Ibid.

50. Attica flier, box 13, FKP. The Attica rebellion was precipitated by the killing of George Jackson by guards at the San Quentin prison. Those who served as mediators and wrote about the events afterward include Tom Wicker (*A Time to Die*) and Clarence B. Jones and Stuart Connelly (*Uprising: Understanding Attica, Revolution, and the Incarceration State* [New York: Amalgamated Publishers Inc., 2011]). See also Heather Ann Thompson lecture at the University of Michigan, Ann Arbor, May 10, 2013.

51. "Attica Amerika," essay in Flo Kennedy, "Politics of Oppression," unpublished manuscript, box 1, folder POO, FKP.

52. Kennedy, "Politics of Oppression," audiotape of lecture.

53. Don Burke to Kathy Kinsella Lordly and Dame, January 14, 1974, box 7, folder "Complaint Letters," FKP.

54. Steinem and Kennedy, "Steinem and Kennedy," audiotape of lecture; "Feminist Party News," March 1972, box 8, FKP.

55. Conversation with Anna Russo, Chicago, Illinois, August 28, 2007; *Feminist Party Newsletter*, 1973, box 8, FKP.

56. Steinem and Kennedy, "Steinem and Kennedy," audiotape of lecture.

57. Florynce Kennedy interview with author; *Feminist Party Newsletter*, March 1972, box 8, FKP.

58. *Making Policy, Not Coffee*.

59. Hochman interview with author, June 17, 2007.

60. Ibid.

61. Ibid.

62. Gallager, *Black Women and Politics*, 183.

63. Kennedy, National Organization for Women transcribed speech, box 7, FKP.

64. Ibid.

65. "Shirley Chisholm for President," Feminist Party flier, box 8, FKP.

66. Harvey, *Votes without Leverage*, 220; Young, *Feminists and Party Politics*, 90. See also Steinem, "Florynce of America."

67. Miroff, "Leadership and American Political Development," 43–44.

68. A. Levy, *Political Life of Bella Abzug*, 167–68.

69. Steinem, "Florynce of America"; Steinem to author, July 29, 2012. In 1952, the Mau Mau uprising was organized by the Kikuyu people in Kenya against British colonial rule. In October 1973, Kennedy and other women of color descended upon the first annual state/regional convention of the National Women's Political Caucus of California to make their voices heard. Many of them challenged the organization for not seeking out the opinions of black women in the early planning stages and for having the name of only one black woman on the original invitation list when distinguished women such as Ari Taylor, a legislator from Denver, should have been invited. Taylor was eventually placed on the list when another woman legislator could not attend the conference. Austin, "Black Women Upset Political Caucus."

70. *Feminist Party Newsletter*, February 1972, box 8, FKP.

71. "Shirley Chisholm for President," flier; *Feminist Party Newsletter*, date unknown, FKP.

72. *Feminist Party Newsletter*, March 1972, box 8, FKP; Theodore G. Miles, letter to the editor, *Life* magazine, June 30, 1972, 29. Miles asks why the article's writer only mentioned in passing Chisholm and her campaign.

73. Chisholm, *Good Fight*, 80.

74. *Chisholm '72: Unbought & Unbossed*.

75. Steinem, "Shirley Chisholm: Front-Runner."

76. Hochman interview with author, June 17, 2007.

77. Ibid.

78. Ibid.

79. Ibid.; *Year of the Woman*; Kennedy interview with Marcia Cohen.

80. *Year of the Woman*.

81. Ibid.

82. Ibid.

83. Hochman interview with author, June 17, 2007.

84. Kennedy, unorganized notes, FKP.

85. "Old Black Flo," episode of *60 Minutes*.

86. Chisholm never expected to win, but she did gain 152 votes (5 percent) on the first ballot after Humphrey threw his delegates to her instead of to McGovern. McGovern's platform did not support abortion rights. That the right-wing George Wallace got 12 percent of the first-ballot votes while the vice presidential nominee, Frances (Cissy) Farenthold, gained 405 ballot votes was a signal that race mattered in this election.

87. Guild, "To Make That Someday Come," 264.

88. Chisholm, *Good Fight*, 72.

89. Kennedy, *Color Me Flo*, 62. For examples of black male politicians ridiculing Chisholm and calling her a "matriarch" or "crazy," see *Chisholm '72: Unbought & Unbossed*; and Chisholm, *Good Fight*, 32.

90. *Chisholm '72: Unbought & Unbossed*.

91. Quoted in Steinem, "Ticket That Might Have Been . . . President Chisholm."

92. Chisholm, *Good Fight*, 77. While Kennedy fully supported Chisholm, she also supported McGovern as her "second choice." She sang songs with lyrics such as "It's Shirley Chisholm that we're lovin', but we'll settle for George McGovern." For more information see Feminist Party Song Book, box 1, FKP; and Kennedy, *Color Me Flo*, 135. Chisholm often criticized white feminists' equal support of both candidates, arguing that this type of "double-minded" support undermined her campaign.

93. S. Robinson, "Liberation Is Choice."

94. Kennedy interview with Marcia Cohen.

95. S. Robinson, "Liberation Is Choice."

96. Quoted in Hoffman, "Flo Kennedy and Irene Davall."

97. Quoted in B. Smith, "'Feisty Characters,'" 481.

98. Quoted in ibid.

99. "Kennedy Speaks on Black Rights."

100. Schulder and Kennedy, *Abortion Rap*, 161.

101. Kennedy, *Color Me Flo*, 95; "Flo in Black and White from Speech at Salem State," October 9, 1974, box 11, FKP.

102. Kennedy, *Color Me Flo*, 95, emphasis mine.

103. Ibid.

104. Voss, "Flo Kennedy and Her 'Pro Rata Share.'"

105. *United States v. Joanne Chesimard, Reddie* [sic] *Hilton and Avon White*, decided December 21, 1973. Kennedy worked to defend Assata Shakur (Joanne Chesimard) against alleged bank robbery charges after Shakur's aunt Evelyn Williams was jailed for contempt of court. In Shakur's autobiography, she briefly mentions Kennedy as one of her main legal advisers; she saw Kennedy as the type of political lawyer she needed in order to address the chaotic nature of the trial. Shakur wrote that Kennedy was "wild; she's flamboyant and eccentric; she might scare the jury," and for that reason she "fit the bill perfectly." Shakur, *Assata*, 97–98; Shakur interview with author, December 29, 2009.

106. Voss, "Flo Kennedy and Her 'Pro Rata Share.'"

107. Galvin-Lewis interview with author; Margaret Sloan, "What We Should Be Doing, Sister," *New York Times*, December 8, 1971.

108. Salisbury, "Feminist's Disturbing Vision."

109. Galvin-Lewis interview with author; Atkinson interview with author, May 15, 2009.

110. Galvin-Lewis interview with author.

111. Quoted in Roth, *Separate Roads to Feminism*, 107.

112. B. Campbell, "Black Feminists Form Group Here"; Eason, ". . . Black Refocus."

113. Galvin-Lewis interview with author.

114. Wallace, "On the National Black Feminist Organization," 174–75; B. Campbell, "Black Feminists Form Group Here"; Eason, ". . . Black Refocus."

115. See La Rue, "The Black Movement and Women's Liberation"; Lindsey, "Poem"; Beale [sic], "Double Jeopardy"; Bambara, "The Pill"; The Damned, *Lessons from the Damned*; Weathers, "Argument for Black Women's Liberation"; and Ware, *Woman Power*, 75–99.

116. Springer, *Living for the Revolution*, 93–102.

117. "Black Feminists Prepare Policies." Smith interview with author. Beverly Smith was a writer working at *Ms.* magazine and her sister Barbara Smith had a master's degree in literature from the University of Pittsburgh. Both had been active in CORE. With other black feminists, Demita Frazier formed the Boston chapter of NBFO.

118. Springer, *Living for the Revolution*, 29, 196.

119. Eason, "Black Feminists Form Battle Line."

120. Quoted in Williams, "Power Talk."

121. Ibid.

122. Ibid.

123. Brownmiller, "'Sisterhood Is Powerful.'"

124. "Old Black Flo," episode of *60 Minutes*.

125. Kimberly Springer demonstrates that the NBFO had a committee dedicated to connecting the concerns of black lesbians to the organization's agenda. However, there were contested definitions of the meaning of black feminism, and the homophobia of some of the heterosexual women in the group slowed the growth of a cohesive black feminist collective identity. Springer, *Living for the Revolution*, 137.

126. Williams, "Power Talk."

127. Verner, "Brenda Verner Examines 'Liberated' Sisters." Three years later, black feminist Michelle Wallace published a contentious article describing her critique of the early NBFO meetings and her opinion that the "NBFO was willed into existence by white feminists who get tired of being asked 'where are all the black women?'" Wallace, "On the National Black Feminist Organization," 174–75.

128. Verner, "Brenda Verner Examines 'Liberated' Sisters"; Wallace, "On the National Black Feminist Organization," 174–75; Cose, "Struggle of Black Feminists."

129. Galvin-Lewis interview with author.

130. Most of the founders of the NBFO had to repeatedly defend their reasons for creating a black feminist organization and explain that they were not dupes of white feminists.

131. Joyce Kennedy worked as a model in both the United States and abroad and published *The Neurotic Woman's Guide to Non-Fulfillment* in 1975. Faye Kennedy-Daly published *Good-Bye Diane* in 1976. In the mid-1970s, she moved from New York to Hawaii and become active in local Democratic Party politics.

132. Jefferson and Sloan, "Equal Time."

133. Galvin-Lewis interview with author.

134. Roth, *Separate Roads to Feminism*, 110.

135. "NBFO Sign in Sheet," box 6, folder "Black Women," FKP.

136. Roth, *Separate Roads to Feminism*, 109; Springer, *Living for the Revolution*, 93–102.

137. Baxandall and Gordon, *Dear Sisters*, 11; Atkinson interview with author, May 15, 2009.

138. Kennedy, "Color Me Flo" original transcript, box 5, tape 17, p. 9, FKP.

139. CARS press release, box 7, FKP.

140. *CARS Newsletter*, box 4, FKP.

141. CARS press release, box 6, folder "CARS press release," FKP.

142. Kennedy, "Color Me Flo" original transcript, box 5, tape 16, p. 12, FKP.

143. "Coalition Urges the Benign Neglect of Moynihan," press release, box 7, FKP.

144. Kennedy interview with Marcia Cohen; "Wiz Protest Continuing."

145. J. A. Gordon, *Why They Couldn't Wait*, 39; Mara, *Civil Unrest in the 1960s*, 50.

146. Other details of the BWUPA are hard to trace because the organization left very few written records and other unrelated organizations also used the same name. National Black Convention flier, box 6, folder "Black Women," FKP; "Education and Awareness of the Political System," BWUPA agenda, box 6, folder "Black Women," FKP.

147. Randolph interview with author.

148. Ibid.

149. Teresa McGriff to Flo Kennedy, November 11, 1980, box 6, folder "African American Women's Salon," FKP; Teresa McGriff to Flo Kennedy, September 1980, box 6, folder "African American Women's Salon," FKP; Black Women United in Boston flier, November 1980, box 6, folder "Black Women," FKP.

150. Kennedy interview with Marcia Cohen.

EPILOGUE

1. "Old Black Flo," episode of *60 Minutes*.

2. Flo Kennedy, "A Comparative Study: Accentuating the Similarities of the Societal Position of Women and Negroes," reprinted in Kennedy, *Color Me Flo*, 121.

3. Support Joanne Little flier, FKP; "Attica Amerika," essay in Flo Kennedy, "Politics of Oppression" unpublished manuscript, box 1, folder POO, FKP; *United States v. Joanne Chesimard, Reddie* [sic] *Hilton and Avon White*, decided December 21, 1973, FKP; *United States v. Joanne Chesimard and Freddie Hilton*, December 24, 1973, FKP.

4. The U.S. Supreme Court decision in *Regents of California v. Bakke* (1978) was the first ruling to limit affirmative action.

5. Kennedy, "Alliance of the Alienated," audiotape of lecture.

6. "Old Black Flo," episode of *60 Minutes*.

7. Kennedy, "It's Damn Slick Out There," interview with Sohnya Sayres, 355.

8. Abu-Jamal, *Live from Death Row*. In 1982, Mumia Abu-Jamal was convicted and sentenced to death for the murder of Philadelphia police officer Daniel Faulkner after a trial some viewed as prejudiced. Abu-Jamal was a prominent radio reporter and a member of the Black Panther Party. When Kennedy made fliers advocating for his freedom, Abu-Jamal was on death row. After national and international protests, the prosecution announced in 2001 that it would no longer seek the death penalty. He is now serving a life sentence in a Pennsylvania prison.

9. Judy Klemesrud, "International Women's Year World Conference Opening in Mexico City," *New York Times*, June 19, 1975, 56.

10. Papenek, "Work of Women."

11. Ibid., 216; Klemesrud, "International Women's Year World Conference Opening in Mexico City."

12. Bunch and Doughty, "IWY—Feminist Strategy for Mexico City"; Carol Kleiman, "On the Front Lines in the War against Sexism," *Chicago Tribune*, July 6, 1975, A1.

13. Most women at the conference were from similar class backgrounds; for less affluent women, the cost of travel was prohibitive.

14. Atkinson interview with author, May 15, 2009.; Kennedy, unorganized notes, FKP.

15. Kleiman, "On the Front Lines in the War against Sexism."

16. Song lyrics by Flo Kennedy, Feminist Party Song Book, box 1, FKP.

17. Papenek, "Work of Women," 217, 222; "Delegates Pour into Mexico City"; Kleiman,
"On the Front Lines in the War against Sexism."

18. Quoted in Hoffman, "Flo Kennedy and Irene Davall."

19. S. Martin, "Flo Kennedy Is Seen in Many Different Ways"; letter to the editor from
Germaine Blair Quigg, date unknown, FKP; Department of the Prime Minister and Cabinet, *Women in Politics Conference*.

20. Chesterman, *How Indigenous Australians Won Formal Equality*, 157–69. Kennedy's
relationships with aboriginal and island women continued for several years, and she was
invited back to Australia to attend the Land Rights and Future Race Relations Conference
in 1981. The meeting was developed by Meriam organizers to begin a case that would seek
recognition of their continuing native title rights to Murray Island.

21. Germaine Blair Quigg, "Feminist Ravings," letters to the editor, Porter Street, FKP.
Quigg did not use the term "antiracism"; she labeled Kennedy's words racist.

22. Department of the Prime Minister and Cabinet, *Women in Politics Conference*, 184.

23. Kennedy's full story quoted in Kaufman and Blakely, *Pulling Our Strings*, 88.

24. Kennedy, *Color Me Flo*, 39.

25. Department of the Prime Minister and Cabinet, *Women in Politics Conference*, 32.

26. "Flo Kennedy a Shocker," unidentified newspaper clipping, folder "Newspaper,"
FKP; Kennedy, "Color Me Flo" original transcript, box 5, tape 16, p. 3, FKP.

27. "Old Black Flo," episode of *60 Minutes*.

28. S. Martin, "Flo Kennedy Is Seen in Many Different Ways"; Kennedy, "Color Me Flo"
original transcript, box 5, tape 4, p. 2, FKP.

29. "Who Needs a 'License'?"

30. Ibid.

31. *Report of the World Conference of the International Women's Year*, 7, 31, 79.

32. Ibid., 79.

33. "Flo Kennedy a Shocker."

34. Kennedy, unorganized notes, FKP.

35. "Old Black Flo," episode of *60 Minutes*.

36. "New King Murder Hearings to Review 'Conspiracy' Theory."

37. For over a decade, Kennedy was friends with Mark Lane and William Pepper. She
organized with Pepper during the 1967 New Politics Conference, and with Lane she organized to bring attention to alleged government involvement in covering up the murder of
John F. Kennedy. In 1981, Pepper and Kennedy wrote a book together, *Sex Discrimination
in Employment*. As the FBI noted while tracking Kennedy's activism, Flo held debates at
her apartment where she would play tapes of Lane's speeches or discuss his ideas about
the assassination of John F. Kennedy. Throughout the 1960s, Flo accused the government
of being involved in the assassinations of both King and Kennedy. Lane no doubt contacted Kennedy to serve as Jerry Ray's attorney because he knew that Kennedy shared

many of his suspicions and because of her ability to turn a legal proceeding into a political stage. Investigative Report, New York, New York, February 5, 1965, and July 22, 1964, FRK/FBI; Kennedy, "Color Me Flo" original transcript, box 5, tape 10, pp. 4, 8, 11–12, FKP.

38. "Probers Link Ray's Brother to King Case."

39. Flo Kennedy, "The Politics of Oppression," excerpts from talk at Portland State University, date unknown, loose page, folder "Newspaper," FKP.

40. Testimony during the hearing suggested a bank robbery in James Earl Ray's home state of Illinois and his involvement in selling drugs as possible explanations for his income and connections. Connections with Cuba or the USSR were ruled out. Florynce Kennedy, handwritten notes on King assassination, FKP.

41. Kennedy, "The Politics of Oppression," excerpts from talk at Portland State University.

42. Kennedy, handwritten notes on King assassination, FKP; Lardner, "Jerry Ray Rejects Theory He Was 'Raoul.'"

43. Kennedy, handwritten notes on King assassination, FKP.

44. Ibid.

45. Lardner, "Jerry Ray Rejects Theory He Was 'Raoul.'"

46. Kennedy, "The Politics of Oppression," excerpts from talk at Portland State University; Kennedy, unorganized notes, FKP.

47. *Report of the Select Committee on Assassinations of the U.S. House of Representatives*, 372–74. In 1997, with the help of William Pepper, the King family argued that James Earl Ray was a "patsy" of a much larger cover-up. Chappell, "Question That Won't Go Away," 36, 42.

48. "Flo Kennedy: America Not Just Racist-Sexist, but Pathological."

49. Stanford, *Beyond the Boundaries*, 43, 52, 70.

50. Quoted in Edsall with Edsall, *Chain Reaction*, 207.

51. William Kunstler, interview on *The Flo Kennedy Show*, February 21, 1985, videotape; Queen Mother Moore, interview on *The Flo Kennedy Show*, December 10, 1985, videotape; Diane Schulder Abrams, interview on *The Flo Kennedy Show*, August 1, 1984, videotape, all in PFK.

52. "Flo Kennedy Sponsors Freedom, Justice Rally."

53. Frady, *Jesse*, 343. Jackson also used the anti-Semitic term "Hymietown" during an interview, at which point he lost what was left of his dwindling Jewish support. Kennedy supported Jackson's second bid for the presidency in 1988, still believing that his candidacy held the possibility for broad-based coalitions and change in Washington.

54. Kennedy, "It's Damn Slick Out There," interview with Sohnya Sayres, 358.

55. "Old Black Flo," episode of *60 Minutes*.

56. Atkinson, *Amazon Odyssey*, 97; Baxandall and Gordon, *Dear Sisters*, 12.

57. Freeman, "The Tyranny of Structurelessness."

58. "Being a Lawyer," unidentified newspaper clipping, folder "Newspaper," FKP.

59. "The Colored Lady," unidentified newspaper clipping, folder "Newspaper," FKP.

60. C. Cohen, "Punks, Bulldaggers, and Welfare Queens," 438.

Bibliography

NOTE ON PRIMARY SOURCES

The Florynce Kennedy papers were housed at her sister Joyce Kennedy Banks's home in East Orange, New Jersey, at the time of my research. I viewed *The Flo Kennedy Show* videos at her former producer's home in New York City with the permission of David Heeley. I organized and cataloged the papers and videos for citation purposes. Researchers can now find Kennedy's papers and *The Flo Kennedy Show* videos at the Schlesinger Library in Cambridge, Massachusetts. The library created its own catalog of Kennedy's papers and *The Flo Kennedy Show*, and while at times we share similar folder and document titles, folder and document titles and box numbers vary widely, and individuals should consult the Schlesinger catalog when attempting to conduct research in this collection. The Florence Rice Collection cited here is housed at the Schomburg Center for Research in Black Culture, which is part of the New York Public Library System, New York. I viewed a portion of this collection on the days that the Schomburg Center archivists were collecting the papers from Rice's private storage unit. The collection will eventually be organized and made available to the public, but at the time this book went to press the papers were unorganized and uncataloged. I viewed Ti-Grace Atkinson's papers at her home and storage unit in Cambridge, Massachusetts. Atkinson was in the process of cataloging her papers, and I followed her citation system when organizing and referencing documents from her private collection. Atkinson's papers are now also housed at the Schlesinger Library and are currently being formally organized and cataloged. Unfortunately, at the time of publication the library's catalog was not available.

Through the Freedom of Information Act, I petitioned the U.S. Department of Justice to obtain Florynce Kennedy's FBI file (0977697). This file has more than 150 pages that contain many factual errors. This source did, however, confirm Kennedy's attendance or participation in several organizing meetings, which I validated through interviews and other primary sources. Largely, the FBI files served as a resource for newspaper clippings on Kennedy, her numerous fliers and songs, and photographs of her changing clothing and hair throughout the 1960s.

ARCHIVAL COLLECTIONS

Atlanta, Georgia
    Manuscript, Archives, and Rare Book Library, Emory University
        Billie Holiday Collection
    National Archives
        Records of the Selective Service System (World War I), RG 163
    Spelman College Archives
        Toni Cade Bambara Collection

Cambridge, Massachusetts
    Arthur and Elizabeth Schlesinger Library on the History of Women in America,
            Radcliffe Institute for Advanced Study, Harvard University
        Dolores Alexander, Papers of NOW Officers, 1960–1973
        Marcia Cohen Papers, 1967–1985
        COYOTE Papers
        Papers of Betty Friedan, 1933–1985
        Diana Mara Henry Papers
        Papers of Florynce Kennedy
        Maren Carden Lockwood Papers
        Holly Near Papers
        Tully-Crenshaw Oral History Project
        Women's Encampment for a Future of Peace and Justice Papers
    Ti-Grace Atkinson Papers, in the possession of Ti-Grace Atkinson
East Orange, New Jersey
    Florynce Kennedy Papers, unprocessed manuscript collection in possession of
            Joyce Kennedy-Banks
New Haven, Connecticut
    New Haven Free Public Library
        New Haven Register and Courier Files, 1977–1982
New York, New York
    Brooklyn College Library Archives and Special Collection
        The Shirley Chisholm 72 Collection
        Emily Jane Goodman Papers
        Shola Lynch Collection
    Columbia University Archives Rare Books and Manuscript Library
        Commencement Files
        Office of Registrar: Annual Reports
    Columbia University Center for Oral History, Butler Library
        Florynce Kennedy
        Bruce Wright
    Columbia University School of Law Library
        School of Law Admission Card Collection, 1940–1950
        School of Law Yearbook Collections, 1948–1952
    The Flo Kennedy Show videotapes, in the possession of David Heeley
    Richard Avedon Foundation Archive
        The Sixties Collection
    Schomburg Center for Research in Black Culture
        Angela Davis Legal Defense Collection
        Organization of African American Unity Collection
        Florence Rice Collection
        Malcolm X Collection
    Tamiment Library, New York University
        The Feminists vertical file
        Fifth Avenue Peace Parade Committee vertical file

Peace and Freedom Party vertical file
National Conference for New Politics vertical file
National Organization for Women: New York Chapter Papers
Northampton, Massachusetts
Sophia Smith Collection, Smith College
Constance Baker Motley Collection
Gloria Steinem Collection
Palo Alto, California
Stanford University, Department of Special Collections and University Archives
Huey P. Newton Foundation Inc. Collection
Princeton, New Jersey
Princeton University, Seeley G. Mudd Manuscript Library
American Civil Liberties Union Records
Washington, D.C.
Federal Bureau of Investigation
Florynce Kennedy Files
Manuscript Division, Library of Congress
Kansas City, Missouri, Branch Records of the National Association for the Advancement of Colored People
National Association for the Advancement of Colored People Records
National Archives for Black Women's History, McLeod Bethune Council House National Historic Site
Wednesdays in Mississippi Papers

INTERVIEWS WITH THE AUTHOR

Abrams, Diane Schulder. New York, New York, May 15, 2010.
Atkinson, Ti-Grace. Cambridge, Massachusetts, October 28, 2006.
———. Cambridge, Massachusetts, May 15, 2009.
———. Telephone interview, October 21, 2013.
Brennan, Peg. San Francisco, California, March 7, 2008.
Cellabos, Jacqui. Telephone interview, December 11, 2014.
Dell'Olio, Anselma. Telephone interview, December 17, 2014.
Epstein, Cynthia. Telephone interview, October 18, 2013.
Galvin-Lewis, Jane. New York, New York, March 15, 2007.
Hanisch, Carol. Telephone interview, March 28, 2007.
Hochman, Sandra. New York, New York, June 16, 2007.
———. New York, New York, June 17, 2007.
Hughes, Dorothy Pitman. Telephone interview, March 7, 2007.
Kennedy, Florynce. Telephone interview, January 10, 1999.
Kennedy-Banks, Joyce. East Orange, New Jersey, October 16, 2004.
———. October 17, 2004.
Kennedy-Daly, Faye. Honolulu, Hawaii, December 7, 2003.
Lefcourt, Gerald B. New York, New York, July 5, 2011.
———. New York, New York, May 24, 2012.

Randolph, Linda. Telephone interview, January 15, 2012.
Rice, Florence. New York, New York, May 20, 2010.
Shakur, Assata. Telephone interview, October 6, 2009.
———. Telephone interview, December 29, 2009.
Smith, Barbara. Interview with author, Cambridge, Massachusetts, March 1, 1998.
Stearns, Nancy. Telephone interview, September 20, 2012.
Stollman, Bernard. New York, New York, June 5, 2012.

INTERVIEWS WITH OTHERS

Atkinson, Ti-Grace, and Florynce Kennedy. Audiotaped interview with Kay Lindsey
    for the WBAI radio program *Trial by Sex*, New York, August 7, 1968. Pacifica Radio
    Archives, San Francisco, California.
Kennedy, Florynce. Interview with Diane Schulder Abrams on the *Diane Abrams Show*,
    ca. 1985. In Diane Abrams's possession, New York, New York.
———. Interview with Diane Schulder Abrams as the guest host of *The Flo Kennedy
    Show*, February 21, 1985. https://vimeo.com/76460468, accessed October 30, 2014.
———. Interview with Doon Arbus, August 1, 1969, audiotape in the possession of the
    Avedon Foundation, New York, New York.
———. Interview with Barbara Cady titled "Florynce Kennedy on Watergate," KPFK
    radio, North Hollywood, California, August 1973.
———. Interview with Jacqueline Ceballos, February 18, 1991, Tully-Crenshaw Oral
    History Project, Arthur and Elizabeth Schlesinger Library on the History of Women
    in America, Radcliffe Institute for Advanced Study, Harvard University, Cambridge,
    Massachusetts.
———. Interview with Marcia Cohen, date unknown. Marcia Cohen Papers, Arthur
    and Elizabeth Schlesinger Library on the History of Women in America, Radcliffe
    Institute for Advanced Study, Harvard University, Cambridge, Massachusetts.
———. Interview in Claudia Dreifus, *Radical Lifestyles*. New York: Lancer Books, 1969.
———. Interview in *The First Time*, edited by Karl Fleming and Anne Taylor Fleming.
    New York: Simon and Schuster, 1975.
———. "It's Damn Slick Out There." Interview with Sohnya Sayres in *The 60s Without
    Apology*, edited by Sohnya Sayres, Anders Stephanson, Stanley Aronowitz, and
    Frederic Jameson. Minneapolis: University of Minnesota Press, 1984.

NEWSPAPER AND MAGAZINE ARTICLES

Abrahams, Arleen. "Will the Housewife Become a Picketer?" *Des Moines Register*,
    October 10, 1968.
Asbury, Edith Evans. "Women Break up Abortion Hearing." *New York Times*, February
    14, 1969.
"Atlanta Council of Negro Women Will Meet Thursday." *Atlanta Daily World*, March 23,
    1943, 3.
Austin, Edith. "Black Women Upset Political Caucus." *Sun Reporter* (San Francisco),
    October 6, 1973, 15.

"B&B Gets a Mickey Finn." *Advertising Age*, January 2, 1967.

"Barnard Girls Stronger, More Fertile—Dr. Alsop." *Columbia Daily Spectator*, November 25, 1942, 1.

Bender, Marylin. "Valeria Solanis [*sic*] a Heroine to Feminists." *New York Times*, June 14, 1968.

Bird, David. "Women and Doctors Sue to Upset Abortion Laws." *New York Times*, October 8, 1969.

"Black Expo Is a Smashing Success." *New York Amsterdam News*, October 9, 1971, A1.

"Black Feminists Prepare Policies." *New York Times*, December 3, 1973, 80.

"Black Power Concept Hit by Roy Wilkins." *Chicago Tribune*, July 5, 1966, B13.

"Black Power Insurgent Disturbing." *Chicago Daily Defender*, July 2, 1966, 11.

Broder, David S. "Negroes Push Left to 'Genocide' Black." *Washington Post*, September 3, 1967, A1.

Brownmiller, Susan. "'Sisterhood Is Powerful': A Member of the Women's Liberation Movement Explains What It's All About." *New York Times*, March 15, 1970, 230.

Bunch, Charlotte, and Frances Doughty. "IWY—Feminist Strategy for Mexico City." *off our backs* 5, no. 5 (May–June 1975).

Caldwell, Earl. "Two Police Inspectors from Here among the Newark Delegates." *New York Times*, July 22, 1967, 11.

Campbell, Barbara. "Black Feminists Form Group Here." *New York Times*, August 16, 1973

Carlton, Linda. "Girl Next Door Turned Radical." *New York Times*, December 1, 1969, 1.

Chappell, Kevin. "The Question That Won't Go Away: Who Killed King?" *Ebony*, May 1997, 36, 42.

"Chisholm: Catalyst for Change." *Sacramento Observer*, November 4, 1971, B1.

Cose, Ellis. "Struggle of Black Feminists." *Los Angeles Times*, December 9, 1974, F12.

"Court Orders School for Negro: Court Orders Negro School." *Washington Post*, January 18, 1948, M1.

Crosby, Alexander L. "For Vietnam Withdrawal." *New York Times*, May 1, 1965, 30.

"Delegates Pour into Mexico City: Clashes Expected over Women's Rights." *Globe and Mail*, July 19, 1975, F5.

Dietz, Jean. "The Ultimate Question: What Will Happen to the Men?" *Boston Globe*, April 4, 1971.

"Draft Women?" *Columbia Daily Spectator*, March 16, 1943.

Eason, Yla. "Black Feminists Form Battle Line against Racism, Sexism." *Chicago Tribune*, December 2, 1973, 32.

———. ". . . Black Refocus." *Chicago Tribune*, August 25, 1973.

"Educators Urge Women to Prepare as Homemakers." *Pittsburgh Courier*, October 2, 1943, 11.

"Entering Class of 205 Marks Return of School to Normalcy." *Columbia Law School News*, October 8, 1948.

Feehery, John. "Negro Has Precarious Foothold in Agency Field, 3 City Survey Shows." *Advertising Age*, October 17, 1966.

"The Fiery Cross Flames as in the Days of Old." *Kansas City Star*, May 13, 1921.

"Flo Kennedy: America Not Just Racist-Sexist, but Pathological." *Daily Iowan*, March 4, 1975.

"Flo Kennedy Sponsors Freedom, Justice Rally." *New York Amsterdam News*, July 21, 1984, 28.

Gittelson, Natalie. "No Business Like Lecture Business." *New York Times*, June 9, 1968.

Goodman, Walter. "Yessir, Boss, Said the White Radicals: When Blacks Run the New Left." *New York Times*, September 24, 1967, 257.

Graham, Alfredo. "Negro Artists Warned to Use Care in Contract with AGVA." *Pittsburgh Courier*, September 21, 1961, 25.

"Grumman, Columbia Plan Training for Women." *Columbia Daily Spectator*, March 23, 1943.

Hammel, Lisa. "A Class of Fledgling Pickets Gets the Word: Make It Exciting, Make It Swing!." *New York Times*, August 24, 1968, 33.

Handler, M. S. "Wilkins Says Black Power Leads Only to Black Death." *New York Times*, July 6, 1966, 1.

"Here Is List of Vigil Keepers: Walking around the Clock in Racial Harmony!" *New York Amsterdam News*, January 23, 1965, 1.

Hobbs, Chris. "If Men Could Get Pregnant, Abortion Would Be a Sacrament." *off our backs* 1, no. 23 (June 24, 1971).

Holstrom, David. "'Black Power' Parley in Newark." *Christian Science Monitor*, July 25, 1967, 3.

Hyson, Brenda. "New York City Passed Abortion Law Effective July 1, 1970." *Black Panther*, July 4, 1970.

Jefferson, Margo, and Margaret Sloan. "Equal Time: In Defense of Black Feminists." *Encore*, July 1974, 46.

"Job Outlook Excellent for June Graduates." *Columbia Law School News*, May 16, 1951.

Karpel, Craig. "Not Much Cream in Their Coffee." *New York Times*, August 24, 1969, D1.

"Kennedy Speaks on Black Rights." *New Pittsburgh Courier*, October 18, 1975, 9.

"Lady Lawyer Cries Police Brutality." *New York Amsterdam News*, August 14, 1965, 1.

Lardner, George, Jr. "Black Power Still Undefined after Meeting." *Washington Post*, September 4, 1966, A4.

———. "Jerry Ray Rejects Theory He Was 'Raoul.'" *Washington Post*, December 1, 1978, A2.

Lear, Martha Weinman. "What Do These Women Want? The Second Feminist Wave." *New York Times*, March 10, 1968, SM24.

Lichtenstein, Grace. "Abortion Laws Opposed at Rally." *New York Times*, March 29, 1970, 35.

Marable, Manning. "Time for Another Freedom Summer." *Free Press*, March 21, 2005. http://freepress.org/columns/display/4/2005/1094.

Martin, Seona. "Flo Kennedy Is Seen in Many Different Ways." *Fiji Times*, September 16, 1975.

"The Martyrization of Valerie Solonas." *East Village Other* 3, no. 3 (June 28, 1968): 20.

McClory, Robert. "Shirley Chisholm: I Am Not Kidding." *Chicago Daily Defender*, January 24, 1972.

Morris, John D. "Powell Confers on 'Black Power.'" *New York Times*, September 4, 1966, 5.

"Ms. Chisholm Says Support Is Growing." *New York Times*, October 4, 1971, 22.

"NBC, MCA Defendants in 100G Suit over Use of 'Suspicion' Title." *Variety*, April 19, 1961, 50.

"Negro Women Offered Big Opportunities in Nursing." *New York Amsterdam News*, April 24, 1943, 9.

"New King Murder Hearings to Review 'Conspiracy' Theory: Alleged FBI Link." *Jet*, November 16, 1978, 14.

"Oklahoma School Bars Negro Again: Mrs. Fisher Refuses to Enter Special Law Institution—U.S. Action Is Sought." *New York Times*, January 27, 1948, 29.

Pasternak, Judith, and Laura Sydell. "Flo Kennedy Still 'Kicking Ass' at 75." *Guardian* (New York, N.Y.), February 19, 1992.

"Powell Bars Heading Black Power Talks." *Washington Post*, November 16, 1966, A2.

"Powell Tells Howardites to Seek Audacious Power." *Chicago Defender*, June 11, 1966, 8.

"Probers Link Ray's Brother to King Case." *Christian Science Monitor*, December 1, 1978, 19.

"Revelry, Relaxation Keynote Kent Lounge." *Columbia Law School News*, May 16, 1951.

Robinson, S. "Liberation Is Choice." *Oregon Daily Emerald*, February 10, 1972.

Rogers, Ray. "Angry Black Power Militants Seize Control of Conference." *Los Angeles Times*, July 23, 1967, E12A.

Salisbury, Stephen. "A Feminist's Disturbing Vision." *Philadelphia Inquirer*, January 25, 1984.

"The Sexes: Blacks v. Feminists." *Time*, March 26, 1973.

"Shirley Demands Bail for Angela Davis." *New York Amsterdam News*, July 31, 1971, C1.

"6 Negroes Test Oklahoma Race Law." *New York Times*, January 28, 1948, 21.

"SNCC to Use March as a Vehicle for Power." *Afro American*, June 18, 1966, 3.

Steinem, Gloria. "Florynce of America." *Ms.*, April/May 2001, 93.

———. "Shirley Chisholm: Front-Runner." *New York Magazine*, January 17, 2005.

———. "The Ticket That Might Have Been . . . President Chisholm." *Ms.*, 1973.

———. "Verbal Karate of Florynce Kennedy, Esq." *Ms.*, March 1973, 54–55.

"Suspect Says Warhol Tried to Block Play." *Los Angeles Times*, June 5, 1968.

Swanteck, John. "Florynce Kennedy Says It Loud about Abortion, Church, Calley." *Troy (N.Y.) Record*, April 7, 1971.

Tai, Pauline. "Miss America Pageant Chosen as the Latest Target of Protestors." *Wall Street Journal*, September 6, 1968, 4.

"The Trash Can of Freedom." *Irish Times* (Dublin, Ireland), September 9, 1968, 7.

Verner, Brenda. "Brenda Verner Examines 'Liberated' Sisters." *Encore*, April 1974, 22–23.

"Veterans Boost Enrollment 67%." *Columbia Law School News*, April 22, 1947.

Voss, Melinda. "Flo Kennedy and Her 'Pro Rata Share.'" *Des Moines Sunday Register*, April 7, 1974.

"Warhol Assailant Is Committed in N.Y." *Washington Post*, June 6, 1968, A32.

"Warhol Suspect Loses 'Cool.'" *Hartford Courant*, June 5, 1968.

Washington, Betty. "Leaders to Build Up Black Power Concept." *Chicago Defender*, July 30, 1966, 1.

Wechsler, James A. "No Winners." *New York Post*, September 9, 1967.

"What Chisholm's Candidacy Means." *Chicago Daily Defender*, October 6, 1971, 2.

White, Cathy. "Integrated Teams of Women Report Fear of Progress in Mississippi." *New York Amsterdam News*, September 5, 1964, 21.

"Who Needs a 'License'? It's Women's Year, but Hooker's Night." *Chicago Tribune*, June 24, 1975, 3.

Williams, Anne. "Power Talk." *off our backs*, January 31, 1974.

"Wizard Says 'Let's Quit.'" *Kansas City Star*, September 25, 1924.

"Wiz Protest Continuing." *New York Amsterdam News*, October 8, 1977.

"Woman Attorney Requests $500,000 from New York." *Pittsburgh Courier*, November 14, 1965, 19.

"'Women in the War' Meeting Subject." *Columbia Daily Spectator*, February 19, 1943.

"Women's Law Society Founded, Dorothy Beck Elected Chairman." *Columbia Law School News*, April 24, 1950, 4.

"Women's Society Welcomes Frosh." *Columbia Law School News*, October 30, 1950.

Wyatt, Hugh. "25G Bail Keeps Brown in Clink." *Daily News* (New York, N.Y.), August 21, 1967.

"'Young, Black and Beautiful' Organize." *Los Angeles Times*, October 31, 1968, C4.

"Young Lords Party Position Paper on Women." *Rat* (New York, N.Y.), October 6, 1970.

"Young Women Warned of Wartime Marriage Hysteria." *Los Angeles Times*, January 12, 1942, 4.

GOVERNMENT DOCUMENTS

Commerce: Business, Patents, Trademarks and Foreign Trade. 36th ed. Washington, D.C.: Government Printing Office, 1960.

Department of the Prime Minister and Cabinet. *The Women in Politics Conference, 1975.* Vol. 2. Canberra: Australian Government Publishing Service, 1977.

Manuscript census returns, population, Tenth Census of the United States (1880), microfilm series T3, T9.

Manuscript census returns, population, Twelfth Census of the United States (1900), microfilm series T623.

Manuscript census returns, population, Thirteenth Census of the United States (1910), microfilm series T624.

Manuscript census returns, population, Fifteenth Census of the United States (1930), microfilm series M1930.

Report of the Select Committee on Assassinations of the U.S. House of Representatives. Washington, D.C.: Government Printing Office, 1979.

U.S. Department of Labor Office of Policy Planning and Research. *The Negro Family: The Case for National Action.* Washington, D.C.: Government Printing Office, 1965.

VISUAL AND AUDIO RESOURCES

Born in Flames. Directed by Lizzie Borden. Performances by Flo Kennedy and Hilary Hurst. Film, First Run Features, 1983.

Chisholm '72: Unbought & Unbossed. Directed and produced by Shola Lynch. New York:

Realside Production in association with Point of View/American Documentary, Inc., 2004.

Eyes on the Prize: America's Civil Rights Movement, 1964–1985. Episode "Power! 1966–68." Directed by Sheila Bernard and Sam Pollard. Boston: Blackside Films, 1990.

The Feminist Party. Film. Date unknown. In author's possession.

From Danger to Dignity: The Fight for Safe Abortion. Produced by Dorothy Fadiman, Daniel Meyers, and Beth Seltzer. New York: Women Make Movies, 1996.

Jeannette Rankin Brigade. Performances by Flo Kennedy, Jeanette Rankin, and Ella Baker. Film, Third World Newsreel, 1968.

Jones, Leroi. "Leroi Jones Press Conference." Audiotape of speech at the Black Power Conference in Newark, New Jersey, broadcast on KPFA, July 22, 1967.

Kennedy, Florence [*sic*]. "Politics of Oppression." Audiotape of lecture at the University of Colorado, April 30, 1973.

Kennedy, Florynce. "Alliance of the Alienated: Blacks, Women and Other Minorities." Audiotape of lecture given at Normandale Community College, date unknown.

——— (Flo). Audiotape of interview for *Speaking for America: Twelve Original Interviews with American Activists.* Berkeley: Visual Corporation, 1976.

———. "Feminist Activism and the Law." Audiotape of lecture at Cornell University, 1984.

———. "Florynce Kennedy Talks about Her New Book on Feminism, the Different Levels of Oppression of Women, and Racism vs. Sexism, on Women." Audiotape of lecture at unknown location, September 5, 1975.

———. "Florynce Kennedy Talks at Michigan State University about 'Pentagonorrhea, Sexual Freedom, Black Issues, Feminist Issues.'" Audiotape of lecture given at Michigan State University, February 16, 1978.

———. "People Organize." Audiotape of lecture, location and date unknown.

Kennedy, Florynce, et al. "International Struggle for Abortion Rights." Audiotape of speech at International Women's Day Solidarity Meeting, March 10, 1973.

———. "Martin Luther King Memorial in Central Park." Audiotape of speech at Central Park, New York City, April 5, 1968.

Kennedy, Flo, Peachie Brooks, Verta Mae Smart-Grosvenor, and Eleanor Holmes Norton. "The Role of the Black Woman in America." Audiotape, 1968, Pacifica Radio Archives, California.

Making Policy, Not Coffee. Produced and directed by Barbara Kaster. Boca Raton, Fla.: [Division of Continuing Education and Department of Communication, Florida Atlantic University], [1972].

"Old Black Flo." Episode of *60 Minutes*, CBS. Aired July 3, 1977.

Steinem, Gloria, and Flo Kennedy. "Steinem and Kennedy." Audiotape of lecture given at Texas A&M University, College Station, Texas, 1971.

Up Against the Wall Miss America. Performance by Flo Kennedy. Film, Thirdworld Newsreel, 1968.

The Year of the Woman. Written and directed by Sandra Hochman. Documentary, 1973.

SELECTED COURT CASES AND LEGAL DECISIONS

In the Matter of Donald E. Wilkes, an Attorney, and the Association of the Bar of the City of New York, 11 A.D.2d 35 (N.Y. App. Div. 1960).

Joseph Vallelunga v. Thurman Gardens Inc., 9 A.D.2d 696, 192 N.Y.S.2d 133 (N.Y. App. Div. 1959).

The People of the State of New York, Respondent, v. Florynce Kennedy, Appellant, 19 N.Y.2d 761 (1967).

United States v. Joanne Chesimard, Reddie [sic] Hilton and Avon White, 489 F.2d 271 (1973).

Willie M. Plummer et al. v. Christopher McHale et al., Supreme Court of New York, Trial Term, Queens County, 15Misc. 2d 35, 179 N.Y.S.2d 75 (1958 N.Y. Misc.).

BOOKS, DISSERTATIONS, AND JOURNAL ARTICLES

Abu-Jamal, Mumia. *Live from Death Row*. New York: Harper Perennial, 1996.

Acham, Christine. *Revolution Televised: Prime Time and the Struggle for Black Power*. Minneapolis: University of Minnesota Press, 2004.

Al-Amin, Jamil Abdullah. *Die Nigger Die! A Political Autobiography*. Chicago: Lawrence Hill Press, 2002.

Allen, Robert C. *Speaking of Soap Operas*. Chapel Hill: University of North Carolina Press, 1985.

Allen, Robert L. *Black Awakening in Capitalist America*. New York: Anchor Books, 1970.

Allyn, David. *Make Love, Not War: The Sexual Revolution, an Unfettered History*. New York: Little, Brown, 2000.

Amott, Teresa L., and Julie A. Mattaei. *Race, Gender, and Work: A Multi-Cultural Economic History*. Boston: South End Press, 1996.

Anderson, Karen Tucker. "Last Hired, First Fired: Black Women Workers during World War II." *Journal of American History* 69, no. 1 (1982): 82–97.

Anzaldua, Gloria, and Cherrie Moraga, eds. *This Bridge Called My Back: Writings by Radical Women of Color*. New York: Kitchen Table Press, 1983.

Arnold, Rebecca. *Fashion, Desire and Anxiety: Image and Morality in the Twentieth Century*. New Brunswick, N.J.: Rutgers University Press, 2001.

Atkinson, Ti-Grace. *Amazon Odyssey: The First Collection of Writings by the Political Pioneer of the Women's Movement*. New York: Links Books, 1974.

Bambara, Toni Cade, ed. *The Black Woman: An Anthology*. New York: Mentor Books, 1970.

———. "The Pill: Genocide or Liberation?" In *The Black Woman: An Anthology*, edited by Toni Cade Bambara, 162–69. New York: Mentor, 1970.

Banet-Welser, Sarah. "What's Your Flava? Race and Postfeminism in Media Culture." In *Interrogating Postfeminism: Gender and the Politics of Popular Culture*, edited by Yvonne Tasker, 201–26. Durham: Duke University Press, 2007.

Bates, Beth Tompkins. *Pullman Porters and the Rise of Protest Politics in Black America, 1925–1945*. Chapel Hill: University of North Carolina Press, 2001.

Baumgardner, Jennifer. *Abortion and Life*. New York: Akashic Books, 2008.

Baxandall, Rosalyn, and Linda Gordon, eds. *Dear Sisters: Dispatches from the Women's Liberation Movement; Broadsides, Cartoons, Manifestos and Other Documents from the Twentieth Century's Most Influential Movement*. New York: Basic Books, 2000.

Bay, Mia. *To Tell the Truth Freely: The Life of Ida B. Wells*. New York: Hill and Wang, 2009.

Beale [sic], Frances. "Double Jeopardy: To Be Black and Female." In *The Black Woman: An Anthology*, edited by Toni Cade Bambara, 90–100. New York: Mentor, 1970.

Beck, Jane. *Daisy Turner's Kin: An African American Family Saga*. Urbana: University of Illinois Press, 2015.

Bentley, Eric, ed. *Thirty Years of Treason: Excerpts from Hearings before the House Committee on Un-American Activities, 1938–1968*. New York: Thunder Mouth Press, 2002.

Berger, Dan. *Captive Nation: Black Prison Organizing in the Civil Rights Era*. Chapel Hill: University of North Carolina Press, 2014.

———. *Outlaws of America: The Weather Underground and the Politics of Solidarity*. Oakland: AK Press, 2006.

Berrett, Joshua. *Louis Armstrong and Paul Whiteman: Two Kings of Jazz*. New Haven, Conn.: Yale University Press, 2004.

Best, Wallace D. *Passionately Human, No Less Divine: Religion and Culture in Black Chicago, 1915–1952*. Princeton, N.J.: Princeton University Press, 2005.

Dhattacharjee, Anannya, and Jael Silliman. *Policing the National Body: Race, Gender, and Criminalization in the United States*. Boston: South End Press, 2002.

Biondi, Martha. *To Stand and Fight: The Struggle for Civil Rights in Postwar New York City*. Cambridge, Mass.: Harvard University Press, 2003.

Blackburn, Julia. *With Billie: A New Look at the Unforgettable Lady Day*. New York: Knopf, 2005.

Bloom, Joshua, and Waldo E. Martin Jr. *Black against Empire: The History and Politics of the Black Panther Party*. Berkeley: University of California Press, 2013.

Bolton, Henry Carrington. *The Counting-Out Rhymes of Children: Their Antiquity, Origin, and Wide Distribution*. New York: D. Appleton, 1888.

Bradley, Patricia. *Mass Media and the Shaping of American Feminism, 1963–1975*. Jackson: University Press of Mississippi, 2003.

Breines, Wini. "Sixties Stories' Silences: White Feminism, Black Feminism, Black Power." *National Women's Studies Association Journal* 8, no. 3 (1996): 101–21.

———. *The Trouble between Us: An Uneasy History of White and Black Women in the Feminist Movement*. New York: Oxford University Press, 2006.

Brewer, Rose. "Black Radical Theory and Practice: Gender, Race and Class." *Socialism and Democracy* (Winter–Spring 2003): 109–22.

Brimmer, Brandi C. "'Her Claim for Pension Is Lawful and Just': Representing Black Union Widows in Late-Nineteenth Century North Carolina." *Journal of the Civil War Era* 1, no. 2 (2011): 207–36.

Brown, Scot. *Fighting for US: Mualana Karenga, the US Organization and Black Cultural Nationalism*. New York: New York University Press, 2003.

Brown-Nagin, Tomiko. *Courage to Dissent: Atlanta and the Long History of the Civil Rights Movement*. New York: Oxford University Press, 2011.

Burrell, John Angus. *A History of Adult Education at Columbia University: University*

Extension and the School of General Studies. New York: Columbia University Press, 1954.

Campbell, D'Ann. "The War and Beyond: Women's Place in American Life." In *World War II: Crucible of the Contemporary World; Commentary and Readings,* edited by Loyd E. Lee, 276–99. New York: M. E. Sharpe, 1991.

Carden, Maren Lockwood. *The New Feminist Movement.* New York: Russell Sage Foundation, 1974.

Caron, Simone M. "Birth Control and the Black Community in the 1960s: Genocide or Power Politics?" *Journal of Social History* 31 (Spring 1998): 545–69.

Carson, Clayborne. *In Struggle: SNCC and the Black Awakening of the 1960s.* 1981; repr., Cambridge, Mass.: Harvard University Press, 1996.

Cassel, Joan. *A Group Called Women: Sisterhood & Symbolism in the Feminist Movement.* New York: David McKay, 1977.

Castledine, Jacqueline. *Cold War Progressives: Women's Interracial Organizing for Peace and Freedom.* Urbana: University of Illinois Press, 2012.

Chalmers, David. *The Crooked Places Made Straight: The Struggle for Social Change in 1960.* Baltimore: Johns Hopkins University Press, 1991.

Charron, Katherine Mellon. *Freedom's Teacher: The Life of Septima Clark.* Chapel Hill: University of North Carolina Press, 2009.

Chesterman, John. *How Indigenous Australians Won Formal Equality.* St. Lucia, Queensland: University of Queensland Press, 2005.

Chevigny, Paul. *Gigs: Jazz and the Cabaret Laws in New York City.* New York: Routledge, 1991.

Chisholm, Shirley. *The Good Fight.* New York: Harper and Row, 1973.

———. *Unbought and Unbossed: An Autobiography.* New York: Houghton and Mifflin, 1970.

Cohen, Cathy J. "Punks, Bulldaggers, and Welfare Queens: The Radical Potential of Queer Politics?" *GLQ: A Journal of Lesbian and Gay Studies* 3, no. 4 (1977): 437–65.

Cohen, Marcia. *The Sisterhood: The True Story of the Women Who Changed the World.* New York: Simon and Schuster, 1988.

Collier-Thomas, Bettye, and V. P. Franklin, eds. *Sisters in Struggle: African American Women in the Civil Rights–Black Power Movement.* New York: New York University Press, 2001.

Collins, Patricia Hill. *Black Feminist Thought: Knowledge, Consciousness, and the Politics of Empowerment.* Boston: Unwin Hyman, 1990.

———. *Fighting Words: Black Women and the Search for Justice.* Minneapolis: University of Minnesota Press, 1998.

Columbia University Bulletin of Information: Announcement of the School of Law for the Summer, Winter, and Spring Sessions, 1947–1948. New York: Columbia University Press, 1947–48.

Columbia University Bulletin of Information: Announcement of the School of Law for the Winter and Spring Sessions, 1950–1951. New York: Columbia University, 1950–51.

Columbia University in the City of New York: Report of the Registrar. New York: Columbia University, 1936–48.

Columbia University, Report of the Registrar for the Academic Year Ending June 30, 1951 and for the Summer Session of 1951. New York: Columbia University, 1951.

Coontz, Stephanie. *Marriage, a History: From Obedience to Intimacy*. New York: Viking, 2005.

————. *The Way We Never Were: American Families and the Nostalgia Trap*. New York: Basic Books, 1992.

Coulter, Charles Edward. *Take Up the Black Man's Burden: Kansas City's African American Communities, 1865–1939*. Columbia: University of Missouri Press, 2006.

Countryman, Matthew. *Up South: Civil Rights and Black Power in Philadelphia*. Philadelphia: University of Pennsylvania Press, 2006.

Craig, Maxine Leeds. *Ain't I a Beauty Queen? Black Women, Beauty, and the Politics of Race*. New York: Oxford University, 2002.

Crawford Vicki L., Jacqueline L. Rouse, and Barbara Woods, eds., *Women in the Civil Rights Movement: Trailblazers and Torchbearers, 1941–1965*. Bloomington: Indiana University Press, 1993.

Crenshaw, Kimberle. "Mapping the Margins: Intersectionality, Identity Politics, and Violence against Women of Color." *Stanford Law Review* 43, no. 6 (1991): 1241–99.

Curwood, Anastasia C. *Stormy Weather: Middle-Class African American Marriages between the Two World Wars*. Chapel Hill: University of North Carolina Press, 2003.

Davis, Amanda J. "Black Nationalism: The Sixties and the Nineties." In *The Angela Y. Davis Reader*, edited by Joy James, 289–93. Malden, Mass.: Blackwell, 1998.

————. "To Build a Nation: Black Women Writers, Black Nationalism, and the Reduction of Wholeness." *Frontiers* 25, no. 3 (2005): 25–53.

Davis, Angela. *Blues Legacies and Black Feminism: Gertrude "Ma" Rainey, Bessie Smith, and Billie Holiday*. New York: Vintage Books, 1999.

Davis, Flora. *Moving the Mountain: The Women's Movement in America since 1960*. Urbana: University of Illinois Press, 1999.

Dean, John W. *The Nixon Defense: What He Knew and When He Knew It*. New York: Viking Press, 2014.

D'Emilio, John. *Lost Prophet: The Life and Times of Bayard Rustin*. Chicago: University of Chicago Press, 2004.

Devine, Thomas. *Henry Wallace's 1948 Presidential Campaign and the Future of Postwar Liberalism*. Chapel Hill: University of North Carolina Press, 2013.

Directory of U.S. Negro Newspapers and Magazines and Periodicals and African Trade Travel and Industry. New York: World Mutual Exchange, 1966.

Dreifus, Claudia, ed. *Radical Lifestyles*. New York: Lancer Books, 1969.

————. *Seizing Our Bodies: The Politics of Women's Health*. New York: Knopf, 1977.

Dunbar-Ortiz, Roxanne. *Outlaw Woman: A Memoir of the War Years, 1960–1975*. San Francisco: City Lights Books, 2002.

DuPlessis, Rachel Blau, and Ann Snitow, eds. *The Feminist Memoir Project: Voices from Women's Liberation*. New York: Three Rivers Press, 1998.

Echols, Alice. *Daring to Be Bad: Radical Feminism in America, 1967–1975*. Minneapolis: University of Minnesota, 1989.

Edsall, Thomas Byrne, with Mary D. Edsall. *Chain Reaction: The Impact of Race Rights and Taxes on American Politics*. New York: W. W. Norton, 1992.

Ehrenreich, Barbara, ed. *The Reproductive Rights Reader: Law, Medicine, and the Construction of Motherhood*. New York: New York University Press, 2008.

Elbaum, Max. *Revolution in the Air: Sixties Radicals Turn to Lenin, Mao, and Che*. New York: Verso, 2002.

Engelman, Peter C. *A History of the Birth Control Movement in America*. Santa Barbara, Calif.: Greenwood, 2011.

Evans, Sara. *Personal Politics: The Roots of Women's Liberation in the Civil Rights Movement and the New Left*. New York: Vintage, 1980.

———. *Tidal Wave: How Women Changed America at Century's End*. New York: Free Press, 2004.

Ezekiel, Judith. *Feminism in the Heartland*. Columbus: Ohio State University Press, 2002.

Fahs, Breanne. "Ti-Grace Atkinson and the Legacy of Radical Feminism." *Feminist Studies* 37 (Fall 2011): 561–90.

———. *Valerie Solanas: The Defiant Life of the Woman Who Wrote SCUM (and Shot Andy Warhol)*. New York: Feminist Press, 2014.

Farber, David. *The Sixties: From Memory to History*. Chapel Hill: University of North Carolina Press, 1994.

Farmer, Melanie H. "College Marks 25 Years of Coeducation." *The Record: News and Ideas for the Columbia Community*, n.d. http://www.columbia.edu/cu/news/record/coeducation.html. Accessed October 28, 2014.

Ferguson, Jeffrey B. *The Sage of Sugar Hill: George S. Schuyler and the Harlem Renaissance*. New Haven, Conn.: Yale University Press, 2005.

Fernández, Johanna. "Denise Oliver and the Young Lords Party: Stretching the Political Boundaries of Struggle." In *Want to Start a Revolution? Radical Women in the Black Freedom Struggle*, edited by Dayo F. Gore, Jeanne Theoharis, and Komozi Woodard, 271–93. New York: New York University Press, 2009.

Ferree, Myra Marx, and Beth B. Hess. *Controversy and Coalitions: The New Feminist Movement across Three Decades of Change*. New York: Twayne, 1994.

Flamming, Douglas. *Bound for Freedom: Black Los Angeles in Jim Crow America*. Berkeley: University of California Press, 2005.

Flynt, Wayne. *Alabama in the Twentieth Century*. Tuscaloosa: University of Alabama Press, 2004.

Ford, Tanisha. "Soul Generation: Radical Fashion, Beauty, and the Transnational Black Liberation Movement, 1954–1980." Ph.D. diss., Indiana University, 2011.

Forman, James. *The Making of Black Revolutionaries*. Seattle: University of Washington Press, 1985.

Frady, Marshall. *Jesse: The Life and Pilgrimage of Jesse Jackson*. New York: Simon and Schuster, 2006.

Freeman, Jo. *The Politics of Women's Liberation: A Case Study of an Emerging Social Movement and Its Relation to the Policy Process*. New York: McKay, 1975.

———. "The Tyranny of Structurelessness." *Berkeley Journal of Sociology* 14 (1972–1973): 151–64.

Friedan, Betty. *It Changed My Life: Writings on the Women's Movement*. New York: Random House, 1976.

Frost, Jennifer. *An Interracial Movement of the Poor: Community Organizing and the New Left in the 1960s*. New York: New York University Press, 2005.

Gallager, Julie A. *Black Women and Politics in New York City*. Urbana: University of Illinois Press, 2012.

Gardella, John E. "Eugenic Sterilization in America and North Carolina." *North Carolina Medical Journal* 56, no. 2 (1995): 106–10.

Garrow, David J. *Bearing the Cross: Martin Luther King and the Southern Christian Leadership Conference*. New York: William Morrow, 1986.

Giddings, Paula. *Ida: A Sword*. New York: Harper Collins, 2009.

———. *When and Where I Enter: The Impact of Black Women on Race and Sex in America*. New York: Bantam Books, 1984.

Gilmore, Stephanie. *Feminist Coalitions: Historical Perspective on Second-Wave Feminism in the United States*. Urbana: University of Illinois Press, 2008.

———. *Groundswell: Grassroots Feminist Activism in Postwar America*. New York: Routledge, 2013.

Gilens, Martin. "How the Poor Became Black: The Racialization of American Poverty in the Mass Media." In *Race and the Politics of Welfare Reform*, edited by Sanford F. Schram, Joe Soss, and Richard C. Fording, 101–30. Ann Arbor: University of Michigan Press, 2003.

Golland, David. *Constructing Affirmative Action: The Struggle for Equal Employment Opportunity*. Lexington: University Press of Kentucky, 2011.

Gordon, Jacob. *Black Leadership for Social Change*. Westport, Conn.: Greenwood Press, 2000.

Gordon, Jane Anne. *Why They Couldn't Wait: A Critique of the Black-Jewish Conflict over Community Control in Ocean Hill–Browsnville, 1967–1971*. New York: Routledge, 2001.

Gordon, Linda. *The Moral Property of Women: A History of Birth Control Politics in America*. Urbana: University of Illinois Press, 2002.

———. *Woman's Body, Woman's Right: Birth Control in America*. New York: Penguin, 1990.

Gore, Dayo F. *Radicalism at the Crossroads: African American Women Activists in the Cold War*. New York: New York University Press, 2011.

Grant, Joanne. *Confrontation on Campus: The Columbia Pattern for the New Protest*. New York: Signet Books, 1969.

Green, Richard, and Monique Guillory, eds. *Soul: Black Power, Politics, and Pleasure*. New York: New York University Press, 1998.

Greenberg, Cheryl Lynn. *To Ask for an Equal Chance: African Americans in the Great Depression*. Lanham, Md.: Rowman and Littlefield, 2009, 27.

Greene, Christina. *Our Separate Ways: Women and the Black Freedom Movement in Durham, North Carolina*. Chapel Hill: University of North Carolina Press, 2005.

Greene, Lorenzo, Gary R. Kremer, and Antonio F. Holland. *Missouri's Black Heritage*. Columbia: University of Missouri Press, 1993.

Gregory, Steven. *Black Corona: Race and the Politics of Place in an American Urban Community*. Princeton, N.J.: Princeton University Press, 1998.

Griffin, Farah Jasmine. *If You Can't Be Free, Be a Mystery: In Search of Billie Holiday*. New York: Free Press, 2001.

Grothaus, Larry. "'The Inevitable Mr. Gaines': The Long Struggle to Desegregate the University of Missouri, 1936–1950." *Arizona and the West* 26 (Spring 1984): 21–42.

Guild, Joshua. "To Make That Someday Come: Shirley Chisholm's Radical Politics of Possibility." In *Want to Start a Revolution? Radical Women in the Black Freedom Struggle*, edited by Dayo F. Gore, Jeanne Theoharis, and Komozi Woodard, 248–70. New York: New York University Press, 2009.

Guy-Sheftall, Beverly, ed. *Words of Fire: An Anthology of African American Feminist Thought*. New York: New Press, 1995.

Hall, Simon. "'On the Tail of the Panther': Black Power and the 1967 Convention of the National Conference for New Politics." *Journal of American Studies* 37, no. 1 (2003): 59–78.

Hall, Thomas, and J. David Ferguson. *The Great Depression: An International Disaster of Perverse Economic Policies*. Ann Arbor: University of Michigan Press, 1998.

Hamer, Fannie Lou. "Federal Trial Testimony, Oxford Mississippi, December 2, 1963." In *The Speeches of Fannie Lou Hamer: To Tell It Like It Is*, edited by Megan Parker Brooks and Davis W. Houck, 7–35. Jackson: University Press of Mississippi, 2011.

Hamilton, Charles V. *Adam Clayton Powell Jr.: The Political Biography of an American Dilemma*. Lanham, Md.: Rowman and Littlefield, 2001.

Hanisch, Carol. "Two Letters from the Women's Liberation Movement." In *The Feminist Memoir Project: Voices from the Women's Liberation Movement*, edited by Rachel Blau DuPlessis and Ann Snitow, 197–207. New York: Three Rivers Press, 1998.

Hanlon, Gail, ed. *Voicing Power: Conversations with Visionary Women*. Boulder, Colo.: Westview Press, 1997.

Hansen, Moya B. "'Try Being a Black Woman! Jobs in Denver, 1900–1970." In *African American Women Confront the West, 1600–2000*, edited by Quintard Taylor and Shirley Ann Wilson Moore, 207–27. Oklahoma: University of Oklahoma Press, 2003.

Hanson, Joyce. *Mary McLeod Bethune and Black Women's Political Activism*. Columbia: University of Missouri Press, 2003.

Harris, Duchess. *Black Feminist Politics: From Kennedy to Obama*. New York: Palgrave Macmillan, 2011.

Hartmann, Susan. *The Home Front and Beyond: American Women in the 1940s*. Boston: Twayne, 1982.

Harvey, Anna L. *Votes without Leverage: Women in American Electoral Politics*. Cambridge: Cambridge University Press, 1998.

Harwell, Debbie. *Wednesdays in Mississippi: Proper Ladies Working for Radical Change*. Jackson: University Press of Mississippi, 2014.

———. "Wednesdays in Mississippi: Uniting Women across Regional and Racial Lines." *Journal of Southern History* 76 (August 2010): 617–54.

Hayden, Tom. *Rebellion in Newark: Official Violence and Ghetto Resistance*. New York: Vintage, 1967.

Haygood, Wil. *King of the Cats: The Life and Times of Adam Clayton Powell Jr.* New York: Houghton Mifflin, 1993.

Height, Dorothy. *Open Wide the Freedom Gates: A Memoir*. New York: Public Affairs, 2003.

———. *Step by Step with Interracial Groups*. New York: Publication Services, National Board of the YWCA, 1955.

Heitner, Devorah. *Black Power TV*. Durham, N.C.: Duke University Press, 2013.

Hewitt, Nancy, ed. *No Permanent Waves: Recasting Histories of U.S. Feminism*. New Brunswick, N.J.: Rutgers University Press, 2010.

Hicks, Cheryl D. *Talk with You Like a Woman: African American Women, Justice, and Reform in New York, 1890–1935*. Chapel Hill: University of North Carolina Press, 2010.

Higashida, Cheryl. *Black Internationalist Feminism: Women Writers of the Black Left, 1945–1995*. Urbana: University of Illinois Press, 2011.

Higginbotham, Evelyn Brooks. "African American Women's History and the Metalanguage of Race." *Signs* 17 (Winter 1992): 251–74.

Hill, Daniel Delis. *As Seen in Vogue: A Century of American Fashion*. Lubbock: Texas Tech University Press, 2004.

Hill, Lance. *The Deacons for Defense: Armed Resistance and the Civil Rights Movement*. Chapel Hill: University of North Carolina Press, 2004.

Hill, Rebecca N. *Men, Mobs, and Law: Anti-Lynching and Labor Defense in U.S. Radical History*. Durham, N.C.: Duke University Press, 2008.

Hoffman, Merle. "Flo Kennedy and Irene Davall: Forever Activists." *On the Issues: The Progressive Women's Quarterly* 5 (1985), http://www.ontheissuesmagazine.com /1985vo15/mh_vo15_1985.php, accessed October 30, 2014.

Honey, Maureen. *Creating Rosie the Riveter: Class, Gender, and Propaganda during World War II*. Amherst: University of Massachusetts Press, 1984.

Horowitz, Daniel. *Betty Friedan and the Making of "The Feminine Mystique": The American Left, the Cold War, and Modern Feminism*. Amherst: University of Massachusetts Press, 1998.

Hughes-Peterson, Lyn. *An Anthology of Respect: The Pullman Porters National Historic Registry of African American Railroad Employees*. Chicago: Outskirts Press, 2007.

Hull, Geoffrey. *The Music Business and the Recording Industry*. Boston: Allyn and Bacon, 1998.

Hull, N. E. H. *Roscoe Pound and Karl Llewellyn: Searching for an American Jurisprudence*. Chicago: University of Chicago Press, 1998.

Hunter, Tera W. *To 'Joy My Freedom: Southern Black Women's Lives and Labors after the Civil War*. Cambridge, Mass.: Harvard University Press, 1997.

Imber-Black, Ivan. *The Secret Life of Families: Making Decisions about Families, Making Decisions about Secrets*. New York: Random House, 2009.

Incite! Women of Color against Violence, ed. *The Color of Violence*. Boston: South End Press, 2006.

Isaacson, Darlene, and Elizabeth Wallace. *Kansas City in Vintage Postcards*. Chicago: Arcadia Publishing, 2003.

James, Joy, ed. *The Angela Y. Davis Reader*. Malden, Mass.: Blackwell Publishers, 1998.

———. *Shadowboxing: Representations of Black Feminist Politics*. New York: St. Martin's Press, 1999.

James, Stanlie, and Abena Busia, eds. *Theorizing Black Feminism: The Visionary Pragmatism of Black Women*. New York: Routledge, 1993.

Johnson, David Miles. "Beyond Freedom: The Black North, 1863–1883." Ph.D. diss., University of California, Berkeley, 2007.

Jones, Jacqueline. *Labor of Love, Labor of Sorrow: Black Women, Work, and the Family from Slavery to the Present*. New York: Basic Books, 1985.

Jones, Richard. "The Politics of the Ku Klux Klan in Kansas during the 1920s." M.A. thesis, Emporia State University, 2007.

Joselit, Jenna Weissman. *A Perfect Fit: Clothes, Character, and the Promise of America*. New York: Macmillan, 2001.

Joseph, Gloria I., and Jill Lewis. *Common Difference: Conflicts in Black and White Perspectives*. Boston: South End Press, 1981.

Joseph, Peniel E. *Waiting 'til the Midnight Hour: A Narrative History of Black Power in America*. New York: Henry Holt, 2006.

Kasinitz, Philip. *Caribbean New York: Black Immigrants and the Politics of Race*. Ithaca, N.Y.: Cornell University Press, 1992.

Kaufman, Gloria J., and Mary K. Blakely, eds. *Pulling Our Strings: Feminist Humor and Satire*. Bloomington: Indiana University Press, 1980.

Kelley, Robin D. G. *Freedom Dreams: The Radical Black Imagination*. Boston: Beacon Press, 2002.

———. *Race Rebels: Culture Politics and the Black Working Class*. New York: Free Press, 1994.

———. *Thelonious Monk: The Life and Times of an American Original*. New York: Simon and Schuster, 2009.

———. *Your Mama's Dysfunctional! Fighting the Culture Wars in Urban America*. Boston: Beacon Press, 1997.

———. " 'We Are Not What We Seem': Rethinking Black Working-Class Oppression in the Jim Crow South." *Journal of American History* 80 (June 1993): 75–112.

Kelley, Robin D. G., and Earl Lewis, eds. *To Make the World Anew: A History of African Americans from 1880*. New York: Oxford University Press, 2000.

Kennedy, Flo. *Color Me Flo: My Hard Life and Good Times*. Englewood Cliffs, N.J.: Prentice-Hall, 1976.

———. "A Comparative Study: Accentuating the Similarities of the Societal Position of Women and Negroes." Reprinted in Flo Kennedy, *Color Me Flo: My Hard Life and Good Times*. Englewood Cliffs, N.J.: Prentice-Hall, 1976.

———. "Institutionalized Oppression vs. the Female." In *Sisterhood Is Powerful: An Anthology of Writings from the Women's Liberation Movement*, edited by Robin Morgan, 492–501. New York: Vintage Books, 1970.

———. "The Whorehouse Theory of Law." In *Law against the People: Essays to Demystify Law, Order, and the Courts*, edited by Robert Lefcourt, 81–89. New York: Random House, 1971.

———. "Women Lawyers and the System of Oppression." In *Radical Lawyers: Their Role in the Movement and the Courts*, edited by Jonathan Black, 261–64. New York: Avon, 1971.

———. "Women's Role in American Society: Retrospect and Prospect: To Be Black and a Woman." In *Women's Role in Contemporary Society: The Report of the New York*

City Commission on Human Rights, September 21–25, 1970, 82–85. New York: Avon Books, 1972.

Kirkendall, Richard. *A History of Missouri, 1919–1953*. Columbia: University of Missouri Press, 1986.

Kirkman, Paul. *Forgotten Tales of Kansas City*. Charleston, S.C.: History Press, 2012.

Kluchin, Rebecca M. *Fit to Be Tied: Sterilization and Reproductive Rights in America*. New Brunswick, N.J.: Rutgers University Press, 2009.

Knudsen, Lara M. *Reproductive Rights in a Global Context*. Nashville, Tenn.: Vanderbilt University Press, 2006.

Kornbluh, Faith. "Black Buying Power: Welfare Rights, Consumerism, and Northern Protest." In *Freedom North: Black Freedom Struggles outside the South, 1940–1980*, edited by Jeanne F. Theoharis and Komozi Woodard, 198–222. New York: Palgrave, 2003.

Ladd-Taylor, Molly. *Mother-Work: Women, Child Welfare, and the State, 1890–1930*. Urbana: University of Illinois Press, 1995.

Langum, David J. *William M. Kunstler: The Most Hated Lawyer in America*. New York: New York University Press, 1999.

La Rue, Linda. "The Black Movement and Women's Liberation." *The Black Scholar* 1 (May 1970): 36–42.

Lee, Chana Kai. *For Freedom's Sake: The Life of Fannie Lou Hamer*. Urbana: University of Illinois Press, 2000.

Lefcourt, Robert, ed. *Law against the People: Essays to Demystify Law, Order, and the Courts*. New York: Random House, 1971.

Lentz, Kirsten Marthe. "Quality versus Relevance: Feminism, Race, and the Politics of the Sign in 1970s Television." *Camera Obscura* 15, no. 1 (2000): 45–93.

Levy, Alan H. *The Political Life of Bella Abzug, 1920–1976: Political Passions, Women's Rights and Congressional Battles*. Lanham, Md.: Lexington Books, 2013.

Levy, Peter B. *Civil War on Race Street: The Civil Rights Movement in Cambridge, Maryland*. Gainesville: University Press of Florida, 2003.

Lindsey, Kay. "Poem." In *The Black Woman: An Anthology*, edited by Toni Cade Bambara, 92. New York: Mentor, 1970.

Lipsitz, George. *A Life in the Struggle: Ivory Perry and the Culture of Opposition*. Philadelphia: Temple University Press, 1988.

Lopez, Iris. *Matters of Choice: Puerto Rican Women's Struggle for Reproductive Freedom*. New Brunswick, N.J.: Rutgers University Press, 2008.

Love, Barbara, ed. *Feminists Who Changed America, 1963–1975*. Urbana: University of Illinois Press, 2006.

Lowitt, Richard. *Fred Harris: His Journey from Liberalism to Populism*. Lanham, Md.: Rowman and Littlefield, 2002.

MacDonald, Fred J. *Blacks and White TV: Blacks and Whites in Television since 1948*. New York: Wadsworth, 1992.

Mack, Kenneth W. *Representing the Race: The Creation of the Civil Rights Lawyer*. Cambridge, Mass.: Harvard University Press, 2012.

Maier, Thomas. *Dr. Spock: An American Life*. New York: Basic Books, 2003.

Mallory, Noreen. *Harlem in the Twentieth Century*. Charleston, S.C.: History Press, 2011.

Mann, Susan Archer, and Douglas J. Huffman, "The Decentering of Second Wave Feminism and the Rise of the Third Wave." *Science and Society* 69 (January 2005): 56–91.

Mara, Wil. *Civil Unrest in the 1960s: Riots and Their Aftermath*. New York: Marshall Cavendish Benchmark, 2009.

Marable, Manning. *Malcolm X: A Life of Reinvention*. New York: Viking Press, 2011.

Margolick, David. *Elizabeth and Hazel: Two Women of Little Rock*. New Haven, Conn.: Yale University Press, 2012.

———. *Strange Fruit: Billie Holiday, Cafe Society, and an Early Cry for Civil Rights*. Philadelphia: Running Press, 2000.

———. *Strange Fruit: The Biography of a Song*. New York: Harper Perennial, 2001.

Maris, Isabel, ed. *Essays on Duty and Discipline: A Series of Papers on the Training of Children in Relation to Social and National Welfare*. New York: Cassel, 1913.

The Martindale-Hubbell Law Directory. New York: Martindale-Hubbell, 1945–1965.

Maurrasse, David. *Listening to Harlem: Gentrification, Community and Business*. New York: Routledge, 2006.

May, Elaine Tyler. *America and the Pill: A History of Promise, Peril, and Liberation*. New York: Basic Books, 2010.

Mayeri, Serena. *Reasoning from Race: Feminism, Law, and the Civil Rights Revolution*. Cambridge, Mass.: Harvard University Press, 2011.

McCann, Joseph T. *Terrorism on American Soil: A Concise History of Plots and Perpetrators from the Famous to the Forgotten*. Boulder, Colo.: Sentient Publications, 2006.

McCaughey, Robert A. *Stand, Columbia: A History of Columbia University in the City of New York, 1754–2004*. New York: Columbia University Press, 2003.

McDuffie, Erik. *Sojourning for Freedom: Black Women, American Communism, and Black Left Feminism*. Durham, N.C.: Duke University Press, 2011.

McGuire, Danielle. *At the Dark End of the Street: Black Women, Rape and Resistance— A New History of the Civil Rights Movement from Rosa Parks to the Rise of Black Power*. New York: Knopf, 2010.

McLeod, Jacqueline A. *The Life of Judge Jane Bolin: Daughter of the Empire State*. Urbana: University of Illinois Press, 2011.

McNeil, Genna Rea. *Groundwork: Charles Hamilton Houston and the Struggle for Civil Rights*. Philadelphia: University of Pennsylvania Press, 2011.

McVeigh, Rory. *The Rise of the Ku Klux Klan: Right-Wing Movements and National Politics*. Minneapolis: University of Minnesota Press, 2009.

Meier, August, and Elliott Rudwick. "The Origins of Nonviolent Direct Action in Afro-American Protest: A Note on Historical Discontinuities." In *Along the Color Line: Explorations in the Black Experience*, edited by August Meier and Elliott Rudwick, 307–404. Urbana: University of Illinois Press, 1976.

Merril, Judith, and Emily Pohl Weary, *Better to Have Loved: The Life of Judith Merril*. Toronto, Canada: Between the Lines Publisher, 2002.

Meyerowitz, Joanne, ed. *Not June Cleaver: Women and Gender in Postwar America, 1945–1960*. Philadelphia: Temple University Press, 1994.

Millen, Rochelle L. "Blanche Goldman Etra, 1915–1995." Jewish Women's Archive Encyclopedia. http://jwa.org/encyclopedia/article/etra-blanche-goldman, accessed October 28, 2014.

Miller, Patricia. *Good Catholic: The Battle over Abortion in the Catholic Church*. Berkeley: University of California Press, 2014.

Millet, Kate. *Flying*. New York: Knopf, 2000.

———. *Sexual Politics: The Classic Analysis of the Interplay between Men, Women, and Culture*. New York: Doubleday, 1970.

Mills, Kay. *This Little Light of Mine: The Life of Fannie Lou Hamer*. New York: Plume, 1993.

Miroff, Bruce. "Leadership and American Political Development." In *Formative Acts: American Politics in the Making*, edited by Stephen Skowronek and Matthew Glasson, 32–51. Philadelphia: University of Pennsylvania Press, 2007.

Mohanty, Chandra Talpade, Anna Russo, and Lourdes Torres, eds. *Third World Women and the Politics of Feminism*. Indianapolis: Indiana University Press, 1991.

Moore, Jacqueline M. *Leading the Race: The Transformation of the Black Elite in the Nation's Capital, 1880–1920*. Charlottesville: University Press of Virginia, 1999.

Morello, Karen Berger. *The Invisible Bar: The Woman Lawyer in America, 1638–1986*. New York: Random House, 1986.

Morgan, Robin. *Saturday's Child: A Memoir*. New York: W. W. Norton, 2001.

———, ed. *Sisterhood Is Powerful: An Anthology of Writings from the Women's Liberation Movement*. New York: Vintage Books, 1970.

Morgan, Ted. *Reds: McCarthyism in Twentieth-Century America*. New York: Random House, 2004.

Morris, Tiyi. "Local Women and the Civil Rights Movement in Mississippi: Re-visioning Women Power Unlimited." In *Groundwork: Local Black Freedom Movements in America*, edited by Jeanne Theoharis and Komozi Woodard, 193–214. New York: New York University Press, 2005.

Motley, Constance Baker. *Equal Justice under Law: An Autobiography of Constance Baker Motley*. New York: Farrar, Straus and Giroux, 1998.

Motz, Ann. *Toxic Couples: The Psychology of Domestic Violence*. New York: Routledge, 2014.

Mumford, Kevin. *Newark: A History of Race, Rights and Riots in America*. New York: New York University Press, 2007.

Murch, Donna. *Living for the City: Migration, Education, and the Rise of the Black Panther Party in Oakland, California*. Chapel Hill: University of North Carolina Press, 2010.

Murray, Pauli. *The Autobiography of a Black Activist, Feminist, Lawyer, Priest, and Poet*. Knoxville: University of Tennessee Press, 1989.

Musgrove, Derek George. *Rumors, Repression, and Racial Politics: How the Harassment of Black Elected Officials Shaped Post–Civil Rights America*. Athens: University of Georgia Press, 2012.

Nadasen, Premilla. "Expanding the Boundaries of the Women's Movement: Black Feminism and the Struggle for Welfare Rights." *Feminist Studies* 28, no. 2 (Summer 2002): 271–96.

———. *Welfare Warriors: The Welfare Rights Movement in the United States*. New York: Routledge, 2005.

Nelson, Alondra. *Body and Soul: The Black Panther Party and the Fight against Medical Discrimination*. Minneapolis: University of Minnesota Press, 2011.

Nelson, Jennifer. *Women of Color and the Reproductive Rights Movement*. New York: New York University Press, 2003.

Neubeck, Kenneth J., and Noel A. Cazenave. *Welfare Racism: Playing the Race Card against America's Poor*. New York: Routledge, 2011.

Newton, Huey P., David Hilliard, and Donald Weise, eds. *The Huey P. Newton Reader*. New York: Seven Stories Press, 2002.

New York Radical Women. "No More Miss America." In *Dear Sisters: Dispatches from the Women's Liberation Movement: Broadsides, Cartoons, Manifestos and Other Documents from the Twentieth Century's Most Influential Movement*, edited by Rosalyn Baxadall and Linda Gordon, 184–85. New York: Basic Books, 2000.

Nicholson, Stuart. *Billie Holiday*. London: Victor Gollancz, 1997.

O'Brien, David. *Constitutional Law and Politics*. Vol. 2, *Civil Rights and Civil Liberties*. New York: W. W. Norton, 2008.

O'Brien, Gail Williams. *The Color of the Law: Race, Violence, and Justice in the Post–World War II South*. Chapel Hill: University of North Carolina Press, 1999.

Ogbar, Jeffrey O. G. "Rainbow Radicalism: The Rise of the Radical Ethnic Nationalism." In *The Black Power Movement: Rethinking the Civil Rights–Black Power Era*, edited by Peniel E. Joseph, 193–228. New York: Routledge, 2006.

O'Meally, Robert G. *Lady Day: The Many Faces of Billie Holiday*. Cambridge, Mass.: Da Capo Press, 2000.

Orleck, Annelise. *Storming Caesars Palace: How Black Mothers Fought Their Own War on Poverty*. Boston: Beacon Press, 2005.

Painter, Nell Irvin. *Exodusters: Black Migration to Kansas after Reconstruction*. New York: W. W. Norton, 1992.

———. *Sojourner Truth: A Life, a Symbol*. New York: W. W. Norton, 1996.

Papenek, Hanna. "The Work of Women: Postscript from Mexico City." *Signs* 1, no. 1 (1975): 215–17.

Parker, Chan. *My Life in E-Flat*. Columbia: University of South Carolina Press, 1998.

Peiss, Kathy. *Cheap Amusements: Working Women and Leisure in Turn-of-the-Century New York*. Philadelphia: Temple University Press, 1986.

Pepper, William F., and Florynce Kennedy. *Sex Discrimination in Employment: An Analysis and Guide for Practitioners and Students*. Charlottesville, N.C.: Michie, 1981.

Perucci, Toni. *Paul Robeson and the Cold War Performance Complex: Race, Madness, Activism*. Ann Arbor: University of Michigan Press, 2012.

Pickney, Alphonso. *Red, Black, and Green: Black Nationalism in the United States*. New York: Cambridge University Press, 1978.

Powell, Adam Clayton. *Adam by Adam: The Autobiography of Adam Clayton Powell*. New York: Kensington Books, 1971.

Price, David H. *Threatening Anthropology: McCarthyism and the FBI's Surveillance of Activist Anthropologists*. Durham, N.C.: Duke University Press, 2004.

Prince, Sabiyha. *Constructing Belonging: Class, Race, and Harlem's Professional Workers*. New York: Routledge, 2004.

Purnell, Brian. *Fighting Jim Crow in the County of Kings: The Congress of Racial Equality in Brooklyn*. Lexington: University of Kentucky Press, 2013.

Quick, Paddy. "Rosie the Riveter: Myths and Realities." *Radical America* 9 (July–August 1975): 115–32.

Rainwater, Lee, and William L. Yancey, eds. *The Moynihan Report and the Politics of Controversy*. Cambridge, Mass.: MIT Press, 1967.

Feldstein, Ruth. *How It Feels to Be Free: Black Women Entertainers and the Civil Rights Movement*. Oxford: Oxford University Press, 2013.

Ransby, Barbara. *Ella Baker and the Black Freedom Movement: A Democratic Vision*. Chapel Hill: University of North Carolina Press, 2003.

———. *Eslanda: The Large and Unconventional Life of Mrs. Paul Robeson*. New Haven, Conn.: Yale University Press, 2013.

Rattenbury, Ken. *Duke Ellington, Jazz Composer*. New Haven, Conn.: Yale University Press, 1993.

Reagan, Leslie J. *When Abortion Was a Crime: Women, Medicine, and Law in the United States, 1867–1973*. Berkeley: University of California Press, 1997.

Reid, Mark A. *Redefining Black Film*. Berkeley: University of California Press, 1993.

Report of the World Conference of the International Women's Year, Mexico City, 19 June–2 July 1975. New York: United Nations, 1976.

Rich, Mark. *C. M. Kornbluth: The Life and Works of a Science Fiction Visionary*. Jefferson, N.C.: McFarland, 2010.

Riley, Glenda. *Divorce: An American Tradition*. New York: Oxford University Press, 1991.

R. L. Polk and Co.'s Kansas City, Missouri, Directory. Kansas City, Mo.: Gate City Directory Co., 1910–1942.

Roberts, Randy. *Joe Louis: Hard Times Man*. New Haven, Conn.: Yale University Press, 2012.

Robnett, Belinda. *How Long? How Long? African American Women in the Struggle for Civil Rights*. New York: Oxford University Press, 1997.

Rosen, Hannah. *Terror in the Heart of Freedom: Citizenship, Sexual Violence and the Meaning of Race in the Postemancipation South*. Chapel Hill: University of North Carolina Press, 2009.

Rosen, Ruth. *The World Split Open: How the Modern Women's Movement Changed America*. New York: Viking, 2000.

Rosenberg, Rosalind. *Changing the Subject: How the Women of Columbia Shaped the Way We Think about Sex and Politics*. New York: Columbia University Press, 2004.

Ross, Loretta. "African American Women and Abortion, 1800–1970." In *Theorizing Black Feminisms: The Visionary Pragmatism of Black Women*, edited by Stanlie James and Abena Busia, 141–59. New York: Routledge, 1993.

Roth, Benita. "The Making of the Vanguard Center: Black Feminist Emergence in the 1960s and 1970s." In *Still Lifting, Still Climbing: African American Women's Contemporary Activism*, edited by Kimberly Springer, 70–90. New York: New York University Press, 1999.

———. *Separate Roads to Feminism: Black, Chicana, and White Feminist Movements in America's Second Wave*. Cambridge: Cambridge University Press, 2004.

Rothman, Ellen K. *Hands and Hearts: A History of Courtship in America*. New York: Basic Books, 1987.

Rousseau, Nicole. *Black Woman's Burden: Commodifying Black Reproduction*. New York: Macmillan, 2009.

Runstedtler, Theresa. *Jack Johnson, Rebel Sojourner: Boxing in the Shadow of the Global Color Line*. Berkeley: University of California Press, 2012.

Ryan, Barbara. *Feminism and the Women's Movement: Dynamics of Change in Social Movement Ideology and Activism*. New York: Routledge, 1992.

Sargent, Frederic O. *Civil Rights Revolution: Events and Leaders, 1955-1968*. Jefferson, N.C.: McFarland, 2004.

Schecter, Patricia Ann. *Ida B. Wells Barnett and American Reform, 1880-1930*. Chapel Hill: University of North Carolina Press, 2001.

Schirmer, Sherry Lamb. *A City Divided: The Racial Landscape of Kansas City, 1900-1960*. Columbia: University of Missouri Press, 2002.

Schoen, Johanna. *Choice and Coercion: Birth Control, Sterilization and Abortion in Public Health Welfare*. Chapel Hill: University of North Carolina Press, 2005.

Schulder, Diane, and Florynce Kennedy. *Abortion Rap: Testimony by Women Who Have Suffered the Consequences of Restrictive Abortion Laws*. New York: McGraw-Hill, 1971.

Schultz, Debra L. *Going South: Jewish Women in the Civil Rights Movement*. New York: New York University Press, 2001.

Schweninger, Loren. *Black Property Owners in the South, 1790-1915*. Urbana: University of Illinois Press, 1997.

Sewell, Stacy Kinklock. "The 'Not-Buying Power' of the Black Community: Urban Boycotts and Equal Employment Opportunity, 1960-1964." *Journal of African American History* 89, no. 2 (2004): 132-51.

Shakur, Assata. *Assata: An Autobiography*. Chicago: Lawrence Hill, 1987.

Shaw, Stephanie J. *What a Woman Ought to Be and Do: Professional Black Women Workers during the Jim Crow Era*. Chicago: University of Chicago Press, 1995.

Shesol, Jeff. *Mutual Contempt: Lyndon Johnson, Robert Kennedy, and the Feud That Defined a Decade*. New York: W. W. Norton, 1997.

Sides, Josh. *L.A. City Limits: African American Los Angeles from the Great Depression to the Present*. Berkeley: University of California Press, 2006.

Silliman, Jael, Marlene Gerber Fried, Loretta Ross, and Elena Gutiérrez. *Undivided Rights: Women of Color Organize for Reproductive Justice*. Boston: South End Press, 2004.

Singh, Nikhil Pal. *Black Is a Country: Race and the Unfinished Struggle for Democracy*. Cambridge, Mass.: Harvard University Press, 2004.

Smith, Barbara. "'Feisty Characters' and 'Other People's Causes': Memories of White Racism and U.S. Feminism." In *The Feminist Memoir Project: Voices from the Women's Liberation Movement*, edited by Rachel Blau DuPlessis and Ann Snitow, 477-81. New York: Three Rivers Press, 1998.

Smith, John Clay, ed. *Rebels in Law: Voices in History of Black Women Lawyers*. Ann Arbor: University of Michigan Press, 1998.

Smith, Valerie. *Not Just Race, Not Just Gender*. New York: Taylor and Francis, 1998.

Solanas, Valerie. *SCUM Manifesto*. San Francisco: AK Press, 1996.

Solinger, Rickie, ed. *Abortion Wars: A Half Century of Struggle, 1950–2000*. Berkeley: University of California Press, 1998.

Spencer, Philip, and Howard Wollman. *Nationalism: A Critical Introduction*. Thousand Oaks, Calif.: Sage, 2003.

Springer, Kimberly. *Living for the Revolution: Black Feminist Organizations, 1968–1980*. Durham, N.C.: Duke University Press, 2005.

————, ed. *Still Lifting, Still Climbing: African American Women's Contemporary Activism*. New York: New York University Press, 1999.

Staff of the Foundation for Research in Legal History. *A History of the School of Law: Columbia University*. New York: Columbia University Press, 1955.

Staggenborg, Suzanne. *The Pro-Choice Movement: Organization and Activism in the Abortion Conflict*. New York: Oxford University Press, 1994.

Stanford, Karin L. *Beyond the Boundaries: Reverend Jesse Jackson in International Affairs*. Albany: State University of New York Press, 1997.

Stansell, Christine. *American Moderns: Bohemian New York and the Creation of a New Century*. New York: Macmillan, 2000.

Statler, Kathryn. *Replacing France: The Origins of American Intervention in Vietnam*. Lexington: University of Kentucky Press, 2007.

Steinem, Gloria. *Outrageous Acts and Everyday Rebellions*. 2nd ed. New York: Henry Holt, 1995.

Stern, Bernhard. *Understanding the Russians: A Study of Soviet Life and Culture*. New York: Barnes and Noble, 1947.

Stern, Bernhard, and Alain Locke, eds. *When Peoples Meet: A Study in Race and Culture Contact*. New York: Committee on Workshops, Progressive Education Association, 1942.

Stolzfus, Emilie. *Citizen, Mother, Worker: Debating Public Responsibility for Child Care after the Second World War*. Chapel Hill: University of North Carolina Press, 2003.

Stone, Chuck. "The National Conference on Black Power." In *The Black Power Revolt: A Collection of Essays*, edited by Floyd B. Barbour, 189–98. Boston: Porter Sargent, 1968.

Swan, Quito. *Black Power in Bermuda: The Struggle for Decolonization*. New York: Palgrave Macmillan, 2009.

Taylor, Jon E. *Freedom to Serve: Truman, Civil Rights, and Executive Order 9981*. New York: Routledge, 2013.

Taylor, Ula Y. "'Negro Women Are Great Thinkers as Well as Doers': Amy Jacques-Garvey and Community Feminism in the United States, 1924–1927." *Journal of Women's History* 12, no. 2 (2000): 104–26.

————. "'Read[ing] Men and Nations': Women in the Black Radical Tradition." *Souls* 1 (Fall 1999): 72–80.

————. *The Veiled Garvey: The Life and Times of Amy Jacques Garvey*. Chapel Hill: University of North Carolina Press, 2002.

The Damned. *Lessons from the Damned: Class Struggle in the Black Community*. New York: Times Change Press, 1973.

Theoharis, Jeanne. *The Rebellious Life of Mrs. Rosa Parks*. New York: Beacon Press, 2014.

Theoharis, Jeanne F., and Komozi Woodard, eds. *Freedom North: Black Freedom Struggles outside the South, 1940–1980*. New York: Palgrave, 2003.

———, eds. *Groundwork: Local Black Freedom Movement*. New York: New York University Press, 2005.

Thompson, Becky. "Multiracial Feminism: Recasting the Chronology of Second Wave Feminism." *Feminist Studies* 8, no. 2 (2002): 333–55.

———. *A Promise and a Way of Life: White Antiracist Activism*. Minneapolis: University of Minnesota Press, 2001.

Thuma, Emily. "'Not a Wedge, But a Bridge': Prison, Feminist Activism, and the Politics of Gendered Violence." Ph.D. diss., New York University, 2011.

Tobias, Sheila. *Faces of Feminism: An Activist's Reflections on the Movement*. Boulder, Colo.: Westview Press, 1997.

Tuttle, William M., Jr. *Daddy's Gone to War: The Second World War in the Lives of America's Children*. New York: Oxford University Press, 1993.

Tyson, Timothy. *Radio Free Dixie: Robert F. Williams and the Roots of Black Power*. Chapel Hill: University of North Carolina Press, 1999.

Umansky, Lauri. "'The Sisters Reply': Black Nationalist, Pronatalism and the Quest for a Multiracial Women's Movement." *Critical Matrix* 8 (December 1994): 19–50.

Umoja, Akinyele. *We Will Shoot Back: Armed Resistance in the Mississippi Freedom Movement*. New York: New York University Press, 2013.

Underdown, Emanuel Maguire. *The Law of Art Copyright: The Engraving, Sculpture and Design Acts*. London: J. Crookford, 1863.

Vail, Ken. *Lady Day's Diary: The Life of Billie Holiday*. Chessington, Surrey: Sanctuary Publishing, 1998.

Valentine, David. *Imagining Transgender: An Ethnography of a Category*. Durham, N.C.: Duke University Press, 2007.

Valk, Anne M. *Radical Sisters: Second-Wave Feminism and Black Liberation in Washington, D.C.* Urbana: University of Illinois Press, 2008.

Van Deburg, William L., ed. *Modern Black Nationalism: From Marcus Garvey to Louis Farrakhan*. New York: New York University Press, 1997.

———. *New Day in Babylon: The Black Power Movement and American Culture, 1965–1975*. Chicago: University of Chicago Press, 1992.

Wallace, Michelle. "On the National Black Feminist Organization." In *Feminist Revolution*, edited by Kathie Sarachild, 174–75. New York: Random House, 1978.

Ward, Stephen. "Ours Too Was a Struggle for a Better World: Activist Intellectuals and the Radical Promise of the Black Power Movement, 1962–1972." Ph.D. diss., University of Texas, 2002.

———. "The Third World Women's Alliance: Black Feminist Radicalism and Black Power Politics." In *The Black Power Movement: Rethinking the Civil Rights–Black Power Era*, edited by Peniel E. Joseph, 119–44. New York: Routledge, 2006.

Ware, Cellestine. *Woman Power: The Movement for Women's Liberation*. New York: Tower Publications, 1970.

Washington, Margaret. *Sojourner Truth's America*. Urbana: University of Illinois Press, 2009.

Watkins, James Lawrence. *King Cotton: A Historical Statistical Review, 1790–1908*. 1908; repr., Whitefish, Mont.: Literary Licensing, 2011.

Weathers, Mary Ann. "An Argument for Black Women's Liberation as a Revolutionary Force." *No More Fun and Games: A Journal of Female Liberation* 1, no. 2 (February 1969): 66–70.

Weber, Shirley N. "Black Power in the 1960s: A Study of Its Impact on Women's Liberation." *Journal of Black Studies* 11 (June 1981): 483–97.

Weems, Robert E., Jr. "African-American Consumer Boycotts during the Civil Rights Era." *Western Journal of Black Studies* 19 (Spring 1995): 72–79.

Weiner, Harold M. "Negro Picketing for Employment Equality." *Howard Law Journal* 13 (Spring 1967): 270–302.

Weiss, Jason. *Always in Trouble: An Oral History of ESP-Disk', The Most Outrageous Record Label in America*. Middleton, Conn.: Wesleyan University Press, 2012.

Wheeler, Leigh Ann. *How Sex Became a Civil Liberty*. New York: Oxford University Press, 2013.

White, Deborah Gray. *Too Heavy a Load: Black Women in Defense of Themselves, 1894–1994*. New York: W. W. Norton, 1999.

White, E. Frances. *Dark Continent of Our Bodies: Black Feminism and the Politics of Respectability*. Philadelphia: Temple University Press, 2001.

Wicker, Tom. *A Time to Die*. New York: Quadrangle Books, 1975.

Wilkerson, Isabel. *The Warmth of Other Suns: The Epic Story of America's Great Migration*. New York: Random House, 2010.

Williams, Chad. *Torchbearers of Democracy: African American Soldiers and the Era of the First World War*. Chapel Hill: University of North Carolina Press, 2010.

Williams, Rhonda. "Black Women, Urban Politics, and Engendering Black Power." In *The Black Power Movement: Rethinking the Civil Rights–Black Power Era*, edited by Peniel E. Joseph, 79–104. New York: Routledge, 2013.

———. *Concrete Demands: The Search for Black Power in the 20th Century*. New York: Routledge, 2014.

———. *The Politics of Public Housing: Black Women's Struggles against Urban Inequality*. New York: Oxford University Press, 2004.

Woodard, Komozi. *A Nation within a Nation: Amiri Baraka (Leroi Jones) & Black Power Politics*. Chapel Hill: University of North Carolina Press, 1999.

Wright, Nathan. "Black Power vs. Black Genocide." *Black Scholar* 1, no. 2 (December 1960): 45–72.

Wright, Nathan, Jr. *Let's Work Together*. New York: Hawthorn Books, 1968.

Wu, Judy Tzu-Chun. *Radicals in the Road: Internationalism, Orientalism, and Feminism during the Vietnam War*. Ithaca, N.Y.: Cornell University Press, 2013.

Wynn, Neil. *The African American Experience during World War II*. Lanham, Md.: Rowman and Littlefield, 2010.

Young, Lisa. *Feminists and Party Politics*. Vancouver: University of British Columbia Press, 2000.

Zak, Albin. *I Don't Sound Like Nobody: Remaking Music in 1950s America*. Ann Arbor: University of Michigan Press, 2010.

Index

Italicized page numbers refer to illustrations and illustration captions.

lyzes formation of new organizations, 204–7, 211–14; and reproductive rights, 169, 177–82, 185; and street theater, 224. *See also* Black Power movement and feminism

Black feminists: hostility toward, 209; and Kennedy's radio programs, 163–64; at Miss America Pageant protest, 158; support Chisholm's campaign for presidency, 202; views on birth control, 182–83; withdraw from The Feminists, 166

"Black genocide," 177–78, 180

Black nationalists: and abortion, 170, 177–82, 185, 263 (n. 47); Kennedy on; promote unlimited childbearing, 183; promote revolution rather than reform, 165

Black Panther Party (BPP), 191–95, 197, 249 (n. 131), 264 (n. 65). *See also* Abu-Jamal, Mumia

Black Panthers: and abortion, 180; and Angela Davis arrest, 187; interracial groups support, 194; Kennedy defends members of, 191–93; killing of members of by Chicago Police, 2. *See also* Davis, Angela; Clark, Mark; Emergency Conference to Defend the Right of the Black Panthers to Exist; Emergency Fall Campaign for Angela Davis; Hampton, Fred; Panther 21; Westside Committee to Defend the Panthers

Black Power movement: advocates self-defense, 13, 99, 115, 142, 192; campaigns to defend, 194; civil rights leaders denounce, 99; coalitions and, 110–11, 115–19, 125, 194; harassment and repression of, 2, 191, 204, 216; Kennedy as organizer and fund-raiser for, 8, 191, 193; and Kennedy's legal strategies, 170; and the media, 102–7, 111, 159, 187, 259 (n. 40); and National Conference for New Politics, 121–22; origins of in March Against Fear, 98–99; self-determination and, 116; sexism

within, 177, 180, 183–84, 216; Workers World Party supports, 249 (n. 131). *See also* Ahmed, Omar Abu; Baird, Bill; Baraka, Amiri; Black Caucus of the National Conference for New Politics; Brown, H. Rap; Carmichael, Stokely; Gregory, Dick; Hill, Adelaide Cromwell; Karenga, Maulana; Lynch, Lincoln; McKissick, Floyd; National Black Power Conference; Powell, Adam Clayton, Jr.; Wright, Nathan

Black Power movement and feminism, 258 (n. 76); Betty Friedan disapproves of links between, 149, 160–61, 163; and white feminists' failure to embrace, 203; failure to address issues of pay and child care, 206; errors in historiography of, 2, 5, 101–2, 225, 228 (n. 5); Kennedy as bridge between, 2–8, 101; Kennedy includes white feminists at National Black Power Conference, 116–18; Kennedy works to convince white feminists to embrace, 113–15, 120; Kennedy's feminism shaped by, 2, 97, 101, 125, 169; at National Conference for New Politics, 122–25, 137; NOW and, 113–15, 138–40, 148; October 17th Movement/The Feminists and, 164–66; and Valerie Solanas case, 150

Black Women United for Political Action (BWUPA), 213, 270 (n. 146

Blumenthal, Albert, 171

Boas, Franz, 47

Bolin, Jane, 56, 241 (n. 68)

Bombings: in Kansas City, 17–18; in Mississippi, 94; at 16th Street Baptist Church in Birmingham, 82

Bottini, Ivy, 114

Brennan, Peg, 116–17, 244 (n. 159), 254 (n. 102)

Brooklyn CORE chapter, 82, 142–43, 247 (n. 74)

Brotherhood of Sleeping Car Porters, 15

Brown, H. Rap, 2–3, *129*, *130*, 256 (n. 18): on black self-determination in cross-racial alliances, 122; joins Black Panther Party, 146; Kennedy defends, 3, 140–43, 146, 151, 170; and National Black Power Conference, 115; speech in Cambridge, Maryland, 140–41, 256 (n. 13)

Brown, Peter Megargee, 78, 80

Brown v. Board of Education, 35

Canberra conference, 217–20, 271 (n. 20)

Cardozo, Benjamin, 53

Carmichael, Stokely, 155; and Media Workshop, 107; and National Black Power Conference, 98–99, *128*, 249 (n. 12)

Carroll, Diahann, 250 (n. 24)

Ceballos, Jacqui, 153

Cell 16, 147–48, 161

Center for Constitutional Rights, 171

Chaney, James, 87

Child care, 41, 169, 195, 198, 206–7, 214

Chisholm, Shirley, 3, 7; and abortion, 114, 171, 181; builds broad coalition of support, 186–87; campaign for president, *132*, 186–87, 199, 202, 267 (n. 86), 268 (n. 92); cofounds National Women's Political Caucus, 199; fashion style of, 139, 255 (n. 8); and Kennedy, 8; and National Black Feminist Organization, 207; and NOW, 114, 199; media ignores presidential campaign of, 200–201; pushes for release of Angela Davis, 194–95; sees limitations of white feminists, 199–200, 202–3, 268 (n. 92); young feminists support, 188–90, 198

CIA (Central Intelligence Agency), 81–82, 184, 221–22

Civil rights organizations. *See* Congress of Racial Equality; NAACP (Kansas City); National Association for the Advancement of Colored People; National Council of Negro Women; Southern Christian Leadership Conference; Student Nonviolent Coordinating Committee; Wednesdays in Mississippi

Clark, Mark, 2, 264 (n. 65)

Clyne, Ronald, 61, 242 (n. 98)

Coalition Against Racism and Sexism (CARS), 211–12

Coalition for the Benign Neglect of Moynihan, 212

Colgate-Palmolive protest, 152–53, 155–56, 160

Color Me Flo: My Hard Life and Good Times, 3–4, 6, 15, 24, 27–28, 47, 63

Columbia Law School, 6, 31, 48–52, 239 (n. 16), 239 (n. 22), 239 (n. 28), 249 (n. 2)

Columbia University, 6, 31, 35–37, 43, 150, 236 (n. 34), 236 (n. 35), 236 (n. 39)

Combahee River Collective, 210

Committee of Concerned Mothers, 95

Communist Party (USA), 47, 66, 101, 116, 195, 212

Congress of Racial Equality (CORE), 190, 205, 249 (n. 8), 250 (n. 24), 269 (n. 117); sit-ins in 1940s, 28; and consumer boycotts, 251 (n. 32); and March Against Fear, 98; picket Benton and Bowles, 106; question effectiveness of nonviolence, 111; and National Black Power Conference, 100. *See also* Brooklyn CORE chapter; Harlem–East River CORE chapter

Coca-Cola Bottling Company, 27

Consciousness-raising, 161, 213–14. *See also* African American Women's Salon

Consumer boycotts: of Barq's beverage company in Mississippi, 88; "Don't buy where you can't work" campaigns, 251 (n. 32); of Florida citrus products, 109; Free Angela Davis campaign and, 193; Kennedy and, 7, 27–28; of the media, 110, 212; of phone companies, 106; as a source of power for black community, 175, 188. *See also* Benton and Bowles; Colgate-Palmolive protest; Harlem Consumer Education Council; Rice, Florence; Urban League

Copyright law, 71, 77–78, 80, 246 (n. 61)

cizes U.S. government, 184, 192, 197; death of, 217; dissatisfaction with legal system, 7, 44, 53–54, 56–57, 65, 71–72, 74, 76–78, 80, 111, 175–76, 191–92, 204, 223–24, 263 (n. 36); fashion style of, 1, 94, 139, 145, 154, 188, 215; FBI's surveillance of, 95, 117, 141–42, 195; and international feminism, 217–19, marriage to Charlie Dye, 60–64, 69–70, 242 (n. 113)

—on abortion: collects depositions about women's experiences with abortion, 172–73; opposes abortion laws, 84–85; and work on *Abramowicz* case, 168–70, 173–76, 261 (n. 6)

—as black feminist theorizer: advises younger generation of feminists about strategy, 188; advocates decriminalization of sex work, 219; argues that lack of access to abortion constituted genocide, 177–81; believes that white feminists can learn from Black Power activists, 116–17, 123; develops ideas about similar employment position of black people and white women, 43–44, 51; disappointment with white feminists, 203–4; emphasizes interlocking forms of oppression, 166, 189–90, 214, 216; feminism of shaped by Black Power movement, 101; helps shape strategies of reproductive rights movement, 169; response to separatism, 164–65; views of marriage, 38–41, 62, 70, 176, 219–20. *See also* Black Power movement and feminism

—and Black Power movement: at National Black Power Conference, 2, 7, 99–100, 110–11, 115–18, 125, 180; on Black Power as movement theory, 111–12; and Media Workshop, 102–10; on oppression against Black Power movement members, 216. *See also* Black Power movement and feminism

—childhood/young adulthood, 10–29; as domestic worker in Kansas City, 24–25;

in Los Angeles, 22–23; positive sexual development of, 25–28, 234 (n. 128)

—as coalition builder: advocates black movements as the vanguard, 121–22; at Colgate-Palmolive protest, 155; handling of disagreements with Black Power leaders, 180, 185; at Miss America Pageant protest, 158; at National Conference for New Politics, 123, 125; mentors black feminists in coalition building, 205, 208–9; mentors younger people in coalition building, 187–88; pushes white feminists to join interracial coalitions, 198; and rejection of feminist separatism, 164–65; supports interracial political alliances, 194; use of apartment as social movement center, 103, 147–48, 164, 172, 178, 193, 205–6, 210, 257 (n. 57)

—income-earning activity of: as a domestic worker in Kansas City, 24–25; lectures, *133*, 191, 205; speaking on college campuses, 188, 195–96; at U.S. Treasury Department in New York, 34, 45–46; at Veterans Benefits Administration in New York, 34. *See also* Kennedy, Florynce—legal career of

—injury and illness: back injury, 28; benefits for injured back from New York State, 47, 54; surgery for diverticulitis, 59

—legal career of: assists other women attorneys, 244 (n. 158); at Columbia Law School, 48–56, *127*, 239 (n. 14), 240 (n. 51), 241 (n. 64), 262 (n. 25); creates professional network, 58; critiques legal profession, 53–54; defends H. Rap Brown, *129*, 140–43, 146, 151, 170; defends James Earl Ray, 221; defends Assata Shakur, 3, 193, 204, 268 (n. 105); early employment as attorney, 57; on intellectual property rights, 77–80, 246 (n. 61); law firm of, 58–60; politicizes court cases, 149–50, 174–75; pro

13, 91, 100, 112, 240 (n. 48); and consumer boycotts, 251 (n. 32); develops
Legal and Education Defense Fund,
54; and Constance Baker Motley, 56;
and federal funding, 109; fights segregation, 35, 51; and James Meredith,
98, 249 (n. 2); Kennedy disagrees with
strategy of, 111; refuses to help musicians charged with drug violations, 64.
See also NAACP (Kansas City)
National Black Feminist Organization
(NBFO), 9, 205–11, 228 (n. 11), 269
(n. 117), 269 (n. 125), 269 (n. 127), 269
(n. 130). *See also* Wallace, Michele
National Black Political Assembly (Gary
Convention), 202
National Black Power Conference, 120,
138, 164, 250 (n. 12); and the press, *129*,
159, 259 (n. 40); and H. Rap Brown,
140; emphasis on coalitions, 100,
115–16; and feminism, 115–16, 125–26;
Kennedy and, 2, 7, 99–100, 102–3, 110–
11, 115–18; and National Conference for
New Politics, 121, 124, 143; networking
at, 205; NOW and, 143; Adam Clayton Powell Jr. and, 98–99, 108–10, *128*;
racial tension at, 116–17; resolution on
birth control, 180; Stokely Carmichael
and, 98–99, *128*, 249 (n. 12). *See also*
Ahmed, Omar Abu; Atkinson, Ti-
Grace; Baraka, Amiri; Brennan, Peg;
Davis, Ossie; Green, Carol; Hill, Adelaide Cromwell; Karenga, Maulana;
Lynch, Lincoln; McKissick, Floyd;
Queen Mother Moore; Richardson,
Gloria; Tayari, Jim; Wright, Nathan
National Conference for New Politics:
Black Caucus of, 121–22, 182; Kennedy
helps organize, 271 (n. 37); network-
ing at, 205, 271 (n. 37); and NOW, 137,
143; objectives of, 120; racial tensions
at, 116–18, 121; Women's Workshop of,
122–25, 255 (n. 132)
National Council of Negro Women
(NCNW), 85–86

National Mobilization Committee to End
War in Vietnam, 141
National New Politics Conference
National Organization for Women
(NOW). *See* NOW
National Welfare Rights Organization, 213,
265 (n. 13)
National Women's Political Caucus, 199,
267 (n. 69)
Nation of Islam, 165, 180, 223
*Negro Family, The: The Case for National
Action* (Moynihan), 182–83, 212
New Left, 2, 3, 6, 7, 118, 122, 125, 163. *See
also* National Conference for New
Politics
Newton, Huey, 191
New York Citizens Committee for Chil-
dren, 247 (n. 91)
New York Eight, 203
New York Legal Aid Society, 56, 241
(n. 64), 256 (n. 18)
New York Radical Women, 156–58, 160–61,
198
New York State legislature and abortion,
8, 170–71, 176
Nixon, Richard, 197, 208, 217, 222, 259
(n. 22)
Norton, Eleanor Holmes, 164, 182–83,
206–7
NOW (New York City chapter), 2, 137, 254
(n. 102); on abortion laws, 171; divided
by Solanas case, 148–49; endorses
Chisholm, 199; founding and goals of,
112–13, 253 (n. 75); Kennedy pushes to
adopt a more expansive agenda, 7, 101,
137, 139–40; and lessons from black liberation movement, 143, 147, 152; and
Miss America Pageant protest, 157; rejects black politics, 138–40; supports
efforts to free H. Rap Brown, 143; tensions within, 160–63
NOW Legal Defense Fund, 153

October 17th Movement, 163–64, 166, 260
(n. 62). *See also* Feminists, The

Index **309**

Oliver, Denise, 179
Open Mind (television program), 84–85
Operation PUSH, 222
Opinions (radio program), 94, 107, 102

Pacifica Radio, 163–64
Panther 21, 192–93, 204, 264 (n. 65), 265 (n. 29)
Parker, Chan, 75, 245 (n. 34)
Parker, Charlie, 66, 71, 73–75, 76, 245 (n. 34)
Parker, Doris, 73–75, 77, 245 (n. 34)
Participatory democracy, 161–64
Peace and Freedom Party, 190, 194
People to Abolish Abortion Laws, 175
Pepper, William, 123, 221–22, 271 (n. 37), 272 (n. 47)
Plessy v. Ferguson, 35, 240 (n. 48)
Poitier, Sidney, 250 (n. 24)
Police harassment/brutality, 177; of Brooklyn CORE members, 142–43; in Cambridge, Md., 140; of H. Rap Brown, 140–41; of Kennedy, 95–97, 216; in the South, 90; after World War II, 42. *See also* Racist violence
Powell, Adam Clayton, Jr., *128*; and Black Power, 98–100, 110, 115, *128*, 250 (n. 12); plan to remove from Committee on Education and Labor, 107–9; Kennedy asks for help with music industry case, 74; leadership roles of in Harlem, 32–33; use of humor; 155; on federal programs linking funding to nondiscrimination, 109
Progressive Party, 48–49
Putting the state on trial, 146, 169, 173–74, 192, 221

Queen Mother Moore, 116, 155, 194, 223
Queens Voice (newspaper), 80–84, 103

Racism and sexism, 8, 9, 31, 42, 45, 49, 51, 56, 119, 166, 189, 203, 205, 207, 211–12, 214–15, 216, 219. *See also* Imperialism; Interlocking forms of oppression; Sexism and racism

Racism in the media: and Black Power movement, 13, 84, 97, 100, 187, 192–94; coverage of Democratic National Convention, 200; coverage of lynching, 81; in *Daily News* reporting, 83; and black women, 124, 159–60, 260 (n. 47); and Jackson campaign, 223; Kennedy targets, 8, 81–83, 103–6, 110, 113, 116, 196–97, 204, 208–9, 211–12, 224; and myth of reverse discrimination, 216; and Chisholm campaign, 200–205; after World War II, 215. *See also* Benton and Bowles; Media Workshop
Racist violence, 54; in Birmingham, 82; against Black Panther members, 3; bombings, 16–18, 82, 94; in Cambridge, Md., 140; and Black Power movement, 99; against Freedom Summer volunteers, 86–87; against James Meredith, 98; in Kansas City, 10–14, 16–17; Ku Klux Klan and, 17–18, 221, 249 (n. 4); lynching, 14, 17, 65, 81, 215; media and, 192; rape/sexual violence, 12, 41, 64, 168, 196, 215–16, 228 (n. 4), 229 (n. 10); Chisholm speaks about, 186–87; and socialization of Kennedy sisters, 19–20; southern women disbelieve reports of, 87; state-sanctioned, 64, 81, 111, 177, 187, 215; WIMS members learn about, 90; after World War I, 17. *See also* Police harassment/brutality
Radical black queer politics, 225
Radical feminism: and Black Power movement, 101–2, 166–67, 225; development of in New York City, 153, 165; and Kennedy's focus on institutions, 165; and Miss America Pageant protest, 157, 160; and National Black Power Conference, 122–24; and need to work outside courts, 224; NOW and, 161–63; and use of humor, 155; and use of profanity, 156, 259 (n. 22); and Valerie Solanas case, 144, 147–50; and white feminists' failure to incorporate critique of interlocking systems of oppression, 166–67,

MIX
Paper from
responsible sources
FSC® C013483